LUFTWAFFE EFFICIENCY & PROMOTION REPORTS

Also by the Author
The Camp Men: The SS Officers Who Ran the Nazi Concentration Camp System
The Cruel Hunters: SS-Sonderkommando Dirlewanger, Hitler's Most Notorious Anti-partisan Unit
The Field Men: The SS Officers Who Led the Einsatzkommandos - the Nazi Mobile Killing Units
The Ghetto Men: The SS Destruction of the Jewish Warsaw Ghetto, April-May 1943
Quiet Flows the Rhine: German General Officer Casualties of World War II

LUFTWAFFE EFFICIENCY & PROMOTION REPORTS
for the Knight's Cross Winners

Volume One

French L. MacLean

Schiffer Military History
Atglen, PA

Acknowledgements

As with my previous works, I could not have written this book without significant help, both actual pen to paper and moral support. These unsung heroes, over the years, included the following family, friends, colleagues and acquaintances: my wife Olga; my father Mac; my mother Julie; my brother Dave; my grandmothers Marie and Grace; Aunt Carroll and Uncle Dave; Hank Adams; Bob Biondi; Marv Decker; Lou DiMarco; Marianne Driscoll; Mike Dykes; John Fede; Georgia Garrett; Andre Huesken; Bruno Kahl; Sir John Keegan; Hans-Georg Lemm; Mike Mahan; Steve McAuliffe; Montgomery C. Meigs; Detlev Niemann; Jack Pattison; Terry Patton; George Peterson; Scott Pritchett; Jakob Schmitt; Dave Shutt; Tim Smith; Manfred Sommer; Martin Steglich; Tom Veve; Jodie White; Alan Windsor; Hans Winzer; John Womack; Brook and Paymon of Advanced Photo Inc.; the hundreds of Soldiers, Non-Commissioned Officers and Officers, who put up with a lieutenant/captain/major/lieutenant colonel/colonel, whom they knew obviously marched to the beat of a different drummer; countless document collectors, who graciously donated exhibits in this book; our dogs Max and Benji.

Badge photography and book design by Robert Biondi.

Copyright © 2007 by French L. MacLean.
Library of Congress Catalog Number: 2007921527.

All rights reserved. No part of this work may be reproduced or used in any forms or by any means – graphic, electronic or mechanical, including photocopying or information storage and retrieval systems – without written permission from the publisher.

The scanning, uploading and distribution of this book or any part thereof via the Internet or via any other means without the permission of the publisher is illegal and punishable by law. Please purchase only authorized editions and do not participate in or encourage the electronic piracy of copyrighted materials.

"Schiffer," "Schiffer Publishing Ltd. & Design," and the "Design of pen and ink well" are registered trademarks of Schiffer Publishing, Ltd.

Printed in China.
ISBN: 978-0-7643-2657-8

We are always looking for people to write books on new and related subjects. If you have an idea for a book, please contact us at the address below.

Published by Schiffer Publishing Ltd.	In Europe, Schiffer books are distributed by:
4880 Lower Valley Road	Bushwood Books
Atglen, PA 19310	6 Marksbury Ave.
Phone: (610) 593-1777	Kew Gardens, Surrey TW9 4JF
FAX: (610) 593-2002	England
E-mail: Info@schifferbooks.com.	Phone: 44 (0)20 8392-8585
Visit our web site at: www.schifferbooks.com	FAX: 44 (0)20 8392-9876
Please write for a free catalog.	E-mail: info@bushwoodbooks.co.uk
This book may be purchased from the publisher.	www.bushwoodbooks.co.uk
Please include $3.95 postage.	Free postage in the UK. Europe: air mail at cost.
Try your bookstore first.	Try your bookstore first.

FOREWORD

This is my sixth book on World War II. After beginning a decade ago with a look at German general officer casualties, I subsequently gravitated to the "dark side" of the war – although in war, there are very few truly "light sides" – and wrote four books that dealt primarily with the Nazi SS, the Nazi concentration camps, the *Einsatzkommandos* (the Nazi mobile killing units, primarily on the Eastern Front), and the SS destruction of the Warsaw Jewish Ghetto in 1943. Throw in a true story about Germany's "Dirty Dozen," an SS unit composed of convicts and most likely led by a serial sex offender, and clearly I was spending the best years of my life dwelling on the worst deeds of mankind. It was an interesting, yet punishing tour of duty, and despite some very well-appreciated comments by notable and respected people on my work, the books were a drain on my psyche, and I wanted to write something more combat-related and hopefully more uplifting.

Fifteen years ago, while a U.S. Army lieutenant colonel stationed in Germany, I had an opportunity to meet and extensively talk with some of Germany's greatest heroes of World War II. To my surprise, they were not superhuman fighting machines – although they all had a faint look in their eye indicating that they had been fairly hard men, when the chips were down – but seemed like typical grandfathers everywhere. They were gray, not blond, had a *bierbauch*, not six-pack abs, and spoke slowly and softly, not screaming out guttural commands to attack. Knight's Cross of the Iron Cross with Oak Leaves and Swords winner Hans-Georg Lemm, for example, proved to be a distinguished-looking gentleman, who my wife has insisted to this day was an identical twin of Sir Lawrence Olivier. Martin Steglich, an Oak Leaves winner who survived the hell of the Demjansk encirclement, walked with a limp, named his house after his wife and doted over his long-haired dachshund. Bruno Kahl, an Oak Leaves winner who had lost a mouthful of teeth at the tank battle at Kursk in 1943, proved he could be a sweet-talker as he "maneuvered" me out of a parking ticket in Cologne. And Jakob Schmitt, an Army non-commissioned officer, graciously hosted a quiet Sunday lunch for my wife and me, and one would have never known that sixty years earlier he had destroyed two T-34 tanks, all by himself, in close combat on the Eastern Front.

So who were they? Were they mass-murderers that I once wrote were "formed under an evil ideology, led by a social outcast and composed of vicious criminals [that would] sink to its lowest common denominator – hate?"[1] Or were they prim and proper Prussians, depicted in the movies with gleaming boots, iron wills, and mathematical minds, who saw the world only in terms of tactical key terrain? My father, an American infantry private first class, who fought in the Hürtgen Forest and the Battle of the Bulge with the 9th Infantry Division, simply called them "tough bastards," when my brother and I asked him about what the Germans were like in the war. And like so many others of his "Greatest Generation," he did not elaborate much more than that.

Post-war memoirs and histories reveal some of the thoughts the German leadership had for many of these men in general. Thus, Werner Baumbach, *Luftwaffe* Colonel and Commodore of the 30th Bomber Wing (*Kampfgeschwader 30*), winner of the Knight's Cross of the Iron Cross with Oak Leaves and Swords, and later the Commodore, 200th Bomber Wing (*Kampfgeschwader 200*), said the following about *Luftwaffe* fighter and bomber pilots:[2]

Thus the front line [fighter] units were led exclusively by 'aces' whose ambition was, and must be, to keep ahead of everyone else in their personnel kills and keep their squadron ahead of any other. They were not yet tactical leaders of large formations, though the position changed later-on with the growth of the enemy fighter and bomber arm.

A good fighter type was seldom a good bomber type and vice-versa.

Adolf Galland, *Luftwaffe* Lieutenant General, Commodore of the 26th Fighter Wing "Schlageter" (*Jagdgeschwader 26 "Schlageter"*), Inspector-General of Fighters, and winner of the Knight's Cross of the Iron Cross with Oak Leaves, Swords and Diamonds, said of fighter pilots in his excellent post-war work:[3]

It is true to say that the first kill can influence the whole future career of a fighter pilot. Many to whom the first victory over the opponent has been long denied either by unfortunate circumstances or by bad luck can suffer from frustration or develop complexes he may never rid himself of again.

But these generalized comments were too much "one size fits all." People aren't like that, not even in a regimented military system. We will have to look elsewhere. Other former *Luftwaffe* leaders made comments about specific officers. Günther Rall, *Luftwaffe* Major and Commander 3rd Group, 52nd Fighter Wing (*Jagdgeschwader 52*), Commander, 2nd Group, 11th Fighter Wing (*Jagdgeschwader 11*), and Commodore, 300th Fighter Wing (*Jagdgeschwader 300*), winner Knight's Cross with Oak Leaves and Swords, and Chief of the Air Staff of the post-war *Luftwaffe*, said the following many years after the conflict:[4]

• on himself: "I really had no system of shooting; I just had a feeling for the right place to aim and the right amount of lead to use."

• on *Luftwaffe* ace Heinz Bär: "He was honest through and through. Whatever he told you was the truth. He never tried to cover things up as some pilots did."

• on *Luftwaffe ace* Walter Krupinski: "He was a good friend of mine. He was not an easy guy to know on a personal level but I respected him. He was brilliant, simply brilliant and was swiftly promoted. I had the greatest admiration for his combat skills."

• on *Luftwaffe* ace Joachim Marseille: "He only needed a fraction of the ammunition all the rest of us fired and flew unbelievable missions, chasing aircraft all over the sky."

• on *Luftwaffe* ace Werner Mölders: "He was a marvelous tactician. My admiration for him was boundless. He had a great wit and a great personality. He was the most highly-principled man I ever met."

But was this ex-post-facto look fair, or did years of time soften the edges of the magnifying glass, to the point where those writing the memoirs, and giving the interviews, presented their evaluations not as they actually were, but as they wished they would be viewed in the light of history?

A truer look of these men could only be gained by examining what leaders said and wrote in the "heat of battle," and fortunately, the German military provided this mechanism through their extensive officer efficiency reporting system. Within this necessary piece of bureaucracy that has been cursed by countless generations of commanders, in countless militaries, in countless nations – when reports are due to be submitted – lay the genesis of this book. This efficiency report system, exacerbated by mounting casualties among the junior, mid-level and even senior leaders, forced the commanders at all levels to honestly evaluate who should go on to command greater numbers of men in life and death situations and who should not. Like everything else in life, the air warriors of Germany ranked on a bell curve – with some more proficient with more potential than others – and to not implement a system of honest evaluation and promotion would only result in the bell tolling sooner for the *Luftwaffe*, and more importantly, for the Fatherland.

I hope this work does them, and history, justice.

DISCLAIMER

A team of a native-German speakers, active duty military officers, and retired officers helped translate the documents herein. Where differences of opinion (and thus word choice) occurred, I bear responsibility for making the final decision on how the contents would appear in English.

The vast majority of the efficiency reports in these volumes originally came from Germany, from which I made color copies, which the editor incorporated in the book. Due to concerns of potential harassment, these collectors did not wish to receive written credit for their contributions in the book, and so they will remain anonymous. In fact, I kept no record of which report came from which source, which hopefully will help them sleep better after they see "their" document within these pages. I purchased most of the photos from military antique dealers here and abroad.

The face of war: from seconds of glory, moments of happiness, hours of fear, days of boredom, weeks of unease, months of pain, years of disfigurement, and lifetimes of sorrow.

Hermann Göring – in all his official glory.

Happier times – the wedding of *Luftwaffe* ace and Olympic champion, Gotthard Handrick.

Anxious moments – an injured *Luftwaffe* prisoner of war.

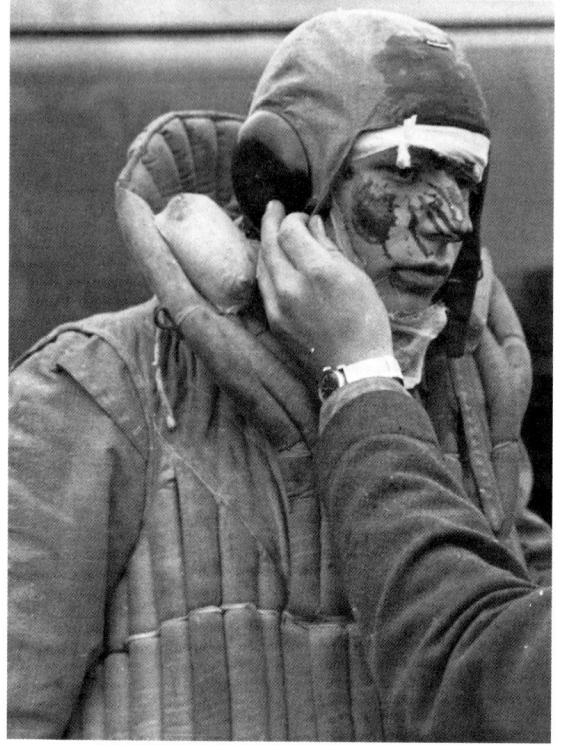

Wounded bomber crewman returns from a mission.

Permanently scarred by war – disfigured *Luftwaffe* trooper.

One, who would not come back from the frozen north – death notice for 23-year old technical sergeant and pilot Josef Herb, killed in an aircraft crash, April 5, 1942 in Norway, while serving in a bomber wing.

One, who would not come back from the sunny south – grave of a fighter pilot of the Condor Legion, who was killed in aerial combat over Spain on May 4, 1938.

Last resting place – grave of sergeant and pilot Willi Strube. Killed January 25, 1940. Headstones such as this one featuring the image of a *Luftwaffe* pilot's badge, remaining today in Germany, have the swastika chipped away.

INTRODUCTION

"The quality of an army depends on the quality of its officers."[1]

Introduction

Of all the awards produced during World War II in Nazi Germany, none hold the mystique as much as the Knight's Cross of the Iron Cross. Many of these Knight's Cross "Knight's of the Air," be they fighter pilots, Stuka pilots or German airborne troops (*Fallschirmjäger*), were not only excellent individual warriors, but later became elite unit commanders. To select the "best of the best" for these prestigious posts, the German military developed an efficiency report and promotion system whereby experienced commanders – often heroes in their own right – submitted confidential personnel reports on these men to the *Luftwaffe* High Command in Berlin. These reports, brutally honest in their content – remarkably not every Knight's Cross winner received the highest overall rating of "above average" (*über Durchschnitt*) – have lain dormant for years, unexposed to the light of history … until now.

While many post-war authors have ventured their own opinions concerning the *Luftwaffe's* best, this work is the first of its kind to present what the *Luftwaffe* chain of command actually thought and wrote at that time, in a system that required truthfulness, about the best the *Luftwaffe* had to offer – the men who shot down hundreds of enemy aircraft, destroyed dozens of trains and tanks on the ground or soared from the skies under parachutes or in gliders to seize Eben Emael and Crete.

Organization

It is hoped that this work provides something for a wide variety of readers. First, it is a window into the world of *Luftwaffe* efficiency reports and recommendations during World War II. Second, it is a collection of biographies of some of the most significant *Luftwaffe* leaders, pilots and paratroopers during the war. Last, it hopefully sheds some light – as well as some illustrations – on many of the numerous awards and decorations won by *Luftwaffe* soldiers during the conflict. That came with a price, however; the author and editor painfully found that to accommodate the massive number of illustrations for the efficiency reports in this work – while retaining a detailed historical narrative – it became imperative to produce a two-volume set. Part 1 of Volume 1 presents an overview of the German awards system and the efficiency report system. It describes when the reports were due, who was required to submit them, how the promotion/selection system used the reports and what was required in them. This section also describes the *Luftwaffe* rank system and a brief overview of *Luftwaffe* organizational structure of flying and airborne units. Part 2 of Volume 1 presents – in alphabetical order – some 53 *Luftwaffe* Knight's Cross winners, whose efficiency reports and promotion recommendations appear in the book whose last names began with A through L. Each description contains a biography, as well as the most important piece – a translation of key pieces of the narrative of the report. Most of the biographies also show a photograph of the report and often a photograph of the individual. Part 3 of Volume 1 presents a shortened biography – also in alphabetical order – of each of the men who signed the reports, so the reader can put this information into context and assist autograph collectors in identification. Part 4 of Volume 1 is a glossary of German words and definitions associated with efficiency reports to assist historians and collectors, as well as a bibliography. Volume 2 begins with a continuation of the awards system, describing additional awards. Part 2 of Volume 2 contains

60 *Luftwaffe* Knight's Cross winners, the contents of which parallel those in Volume 1. Part 3 of Volume 2 presents a shortened biography – also in alphabetical order – of each of the men who signed the reports contained in this volume, while Part 4 of Volume 2 again presents a glossary of German words and definitions associated with efficiency reports and a bibliography, so the reader will not have to consult the first volume when looking for a definition.

The Knight's Cross, German Efficiency Reporting System and Luftwaffe Organization

The Knight's Cross

As every officer and enlisted man described by efficiency reports in this book was a recipient of some grade of the Knight's Cross, it would be prudent to quickly review the award at this point. The Knight's Cross of the Iron Cross sprang from the mind of Adolf Hitler. In former times, Germany's Kaisers did not envision the common enlisted man worthy of obtaining any decoration that would put him on a true par with that portion of the officer corps that was also part of the nobility. But Hitler, who had won the Iron Cross 1st Class in the Great War, desired that the Knight's Cross achieve two objectives. First, because the award could be won by even junior enlisted men, it would prove to the masses that the common man – the symbolized "Nazi man" – was the true hero and future of Germany, not the outdated noble elites of the past. Like the reinstituted Iron Cross 2nd and 1st Class, this new medal would not have at its center the royal crown symbolizing the nobility of the past, but rather the symbol of the new "Nazi man" and state – the swastika. Second, the award also crystallized the Nazi ideological crusade theory, which did incorporate past concepts. Hundreds of years before, it had been the Teutonic Knights "crusaders from the mystical…forests of medieval Germany," who had ridden east to conquer new lands. Now, the new knights of Germany would conquer all of Europe, defeat bolshevism and secure living space for greater Germany – and the leaders of these modern knights would be wearing the Knight's Cross.[2]

On September 1, 1939 – the first day of the war in Europe – Adolf Hitler instituted this new decoration, the Knight's Cross of the Iron Cross (*Ritterkreuz des Eisernen Kreuzes*) for continuous actions of exceptional bravery, or in the cases of higher ranking officers, for successful execution of battle-

Knight's Cross of the Iron Cross this example was won by an infantry captain, and battalion commander in 1942. It was produced by the firm of C.E. Juncker in Berlin. The ribbon is actually that from an Iron Cross 2nd Class, used in a "field modification."

plans or general high-level success. The recommendation for the award required the endorsement of the chain of command through army commander (air fleet) level, with the final decision resting with Hitler. Prerequisites for the award included the previous award of both classes of the Iron Cross.[3] Of the 7,318 Knight's Crosses awarded during the war, some 1,785 went to soldiers in the *Luftwaffe*. Of these, 578 went to fighter and destroyer pilots, 640 to bomber personnel and 155 to paratroopers.[4]

On June 3, 1940 – with the war now raging in France – Hitler instituted the next higher grade of the Knight's Cross, the Knight's Cross of the Iron Cross with Oak Leaves (*Ritterkreuz des Eisernen Kreuzes mit Eichenlaub*). The award recognized previous winners of the Knight's Cross for continued significant acts of bravery and initiative. As with the Knight's Cross, the Oak Leaves could be won by both officer and enlisted personnel.[5] Some 882 officers and enlisted men in the *Wehrmacht* went on to win the Oak Leaves; 244 of them were in the *Luftwaffe*.[6]

One year later – with Germany beginning its titanic struggle with the Soviet Union – Hitler again introduced another higher grade of the award, the Knight's Cross with Oak Leaves and Swords (*Ritterkreuz des Eisernen Kreuzes mit Eichenlaub und Schwerten*), for winners of the Oak Leaves who continued to perform significant accomplishments and brave acts. Although all German military personnel, officer and enlisted, theoretically were eligible to receive this award, all recipients ended up being officers.[7] The "Swords" went to 159 German military personnel – 54 to the *Luftwaffe*.[8]

On July 15, 1941, Hitler introduced what he believed would be the final upgrade of the Knight's Cross – the Knight's Cross with Oak Leaves, Swords and Diamonds (*Ritterkreuz des Eisernen Kreuzes mit Eichenlaub, Schwerten und Brillianten*). Again, it was designed to award recipients of the previous award (in this case the Swords), who continued to excel.[9] Some 27 officers in the *Wehrmacht* won this grade; 12 of them belonged to the *Luftwaffe*.[10]

But the war continued, and although many of the previous winners of these prestigious awards were killed in action, on December 29, 1944, Hitler and the German High Command decided that one ultimate award be created for an intended dozen of Germany's bravest men – the Knight's Cross of the Iron Cross with Golden Oak Leaves, Swords and Diamonds (*Ritterkreuz des Eisernen Kreuz mit Goldenem Eichenlaub, Schwerten und Brillanten*). The sole winner of the award was *Luftwaffe* Stuka pilot and leader Hans-Ulrich Rudel.[11]

Within the fighter arm of the *Luftwaffe*, 578 fighter and destroyer pilots won the award, and 99 went on to win the Knight's Cross with Oak Leaves, 25 were awarded the Knight's Cross with Oak Leaves and Swords, and 9 received the Knight's Cross with Oak Leaves, Swords and Diamonds.[12] That so many fighter pilots won the award is not surprising; *Luftwaffe* day and night fighters claimed the destruction on all fronts of some 70,000 enemy aircraft. Two pilots scored over 300 victories apiece; 13 scored over 200 kills, and 103 chalked up 100 or more aerial victories.[13] However, the award came with a high price tag. Of these 578 aces, 301 were killed in action, missing in action, or died in accidental aircraft crashes.[14] Fighter pilots received their Knights Crosses based on a points system that gave one point for shooting down a single-engine aircraft, two points for twin-engine aircraft, three points for a four-engine aircraft (usually a heavy bomber) and doubled points for night fighter kills. At the beginning of the war, a fighter-pilot needed 40 points to be considered for the Knight's Cross; by 1943, he needed 50 for the Knight's Cross, 120 for the Oak Leaves, 200 for the Swords and 250 for the Diamonds.

In practical terms, this meant that to win the Oak Leaves in 1940 or 1941, a fighter pilot needed to shoot down 40 enemy aircraft. By 1944, a fighter pilot on the Eastern Front (in part because of the relatively few enemy four-engine aircraft in Russia, (unlike the vast fleets of Royal Air Force and 8th Air Force "heavies" over Germany) probably needed about 125 to 150 aerial victories. In the West, a potential Oak Leaves candidate needed to record 60 to 70 kills. Concerning the Swords, we can see an additional factor creep into the analytical framework for bestowing the awards – the perception that western allied fighter pilots and their aircraft were qualitatively superior to the enemy encountered over the Eastern Front. Clearly, there was some basis in fact for this belief, considering the qualitative performance of such aircraft as the British Spitfire and De Haviland Mosquito, and the American P-51 Mustang and P-47 Thunderbolt – not to mention the withering .50-caliber defensive fire of an intact combat box formation of B-17 Flying Fortresses.[15] Thus, in 1944, a *Luftwaffe* fighter pilot, who flew exclusively on the Eastern Front needed to have been credited with 200 to 220 aerial victories to reach the Swords. A second fighter pilot, whose combat experiences mixed operations over both the Eastern and Western Fronts, might qualify for serious consideration with 150 victories. And a third pilot, who flew exclusively in the West, might need "only" about 100 victories.[16]

Night fighter pilots had their own parameters to receive the award due to the uniqueness of this type of aerial combat. In 1942, a *Luftwaffe* night fighter might need 15 to 20 nighttime victories for award of the Knight's Cross. This requirement did not succumb to inflation and by the end of the war, 25 victories would still qualify.[17]

Bomber, Stuka, destroyer and ground-attack pilots generally received their awards based on two factors: number of combat missions flown and specific accomplishments. From just a missions' perspective, in 1941 a Stuka pilot needed to accumulate between 100 and 300 combat missions. By 1942, flying on the Eastern Front, a Stuka pilot would need from 250 to 500 combat missions, and in 1943-1944, this rough cut for consideration would be 400 to 600 combat missions. Significant accomplishments could include sinking individual enemy warships, sinking an aggregate tonnage of enemy supply ships, destroying significant bridges and knocking out a significant number of enemy tanks, artillery pieces or planes on the ground.[18]

It was sometimes more difficult to measure specific achievements for level-flight bombers, as an entire formation bombed a target, and individual hits could not be determined with much accuracy. In March 1943, the following numbers of combat missions were necessary for awarding these individual awards:[19]

Combat Missions	Award
15	Iron Cross 2nd Class
20	Operational Flying Clasp for Bomber Pilots in Bronze
25-40	Iron Cross 1st Class
60	Operational Flying Clasp for Bomber Pilots in Silver
80	*Luftwaffe* Honor Goblet
110	Operational Flying Clasp for Bomber Pilots in Gold
140	German Cross in Gold
200-400	Knight's Cross of the Iron Cross

These numbers changed upwards as the war progressed.

Paratroopers won the various grades of the Knight's Cross in a manner similar to their Army brethren – bravery, independent action (doing something significant and dangerous without being ordered) and achievement.

Im Namen des Führers und Obersten Befehlshabers der Wehrmacht

verleihe ich

dem

Gefreiten

Kurt Rometsch

II./F.J.R. 1

das

Eiserne Kreuz 2. Klasse.

Twede Tol, den 23. Mai 1940

(Dienstsiegel)

Oberst u. Rgts.-Kdr.
(Dienstgrad und Dienststellung)

Award document for Iron Cross 2nd Class to a *Luftwaffe* paratrooper in the 1st Paratroop Regiment during the 1940 campaign in Holland, signed by Colonel Bruno Bräuer.

Im Namen des Führers und Obersten Befehlshabers der Wehrmacht

verleihe ich

dem

Leutnant d.R.

Ludwig Gärtner

das

Eiserne Kreuz 1. Klasse.

Hauptquartier d.Ob.d.L., den 28. Mai 1940

Der Reichsminister der Luftfahrt
und Oberbefehlshaber der Luftwaffe

Generalfeldmarschall
(Dienstgrad und Dienststellung)

(Dienstsiegel)

Award document for Iron Cross 1st Class to a second lieutenant reconnaissance pilot during the 1940 campaign in France, signed by Hermann Göring.

Officer Promotions

Most of the men featured in this book were commissioned officers, although many had spent several years as non-commissioned officers. The *Luftwaffe* officer promotion system traced its roots to the old post-World War I Germany Army, the *Reichswehr*. This was quite natural as the Treaty of Versailles, which went into force on January 10, 1920, prevented Germany from adding air formations to its existing land and sea defense forces. In addition, the victorious allies successfully demanded disbanding all existing air squadrons and air stations – thus, Germany had no air force.[20]

Although the *Reichswehr* found a way to retain 120 former pilots in non-flying positions, the future in the air for the German military looked bleak until April 16, 1922, when Germany and the Soviet Union signed the Treaty of Rapallo. Among other things, the treaty laid the foundation for future cooperation between the *Reichswehr* and the Red Army. Shortly thereafter, the *Reichswehr* established a "Moscow Detachment" – a coordinating staff in the Soviet capital – far away from prying western power eyes. This liaison unit soon coordinated clandestine production and delivery of 50 Fokker Type D XIII fighters for the Soviet military flying school established at Lipezk, north of Voronezh. In return, German military aviators would train at Lipezk from 1925 to 1933.[21]

At 11:00 a.m., on January 30, 1933, Adolf Hitler was sworn in as the chancellor of Germany. Shortly thereafter, he named Hermann Göring as the *Reichs* Minister for Aviation. Göring subsequently announced the impending build-up of a German Air Force (*Luftwaffe*).[22] Some months later Hitler and Göring selected the chief executive officer of *Lufthansa*

Hermann Göring in the early 1930s.

Secretary of State for Aviation Erhard Milch.

– the German national airline – Erhard Milch, to be the first Secretary of State for Aviation. Milch soon divided the young *Reichs* Aviation Ministry (*Reichsluftfahrtministerium* [RLM]) into six departments, to include the *Luftwaffe* Personnel Office.[23] Every organization needs competent people, so Göring and Milch subsequently went to Army Lieutenant General Werner von Blomberg, then Minister of Defense. Von Blomberg, who recognized the future importance of the air force, graciously transferred 550 quality officers from the Army to the RLM in 1933 and would follow that up by sending a further 4,000 junior officers and non-commissioned officer (NCO) volunteers to the junior service. One of these officers was Lieutenant Colonel Hans-Jürgen Stumpff, who would head up the personnel office.[24]

The chiefs of the *Luftwaffe* Personnel Office established the details of how the officer promotion – and supporting efficiency report – system would operate. These powerful officers included:[25]

Brigadier General Hans-Jürgen Stumpff	September 1, 1933-May 31, 1937
Brigadier General Robert von Greim	June 1, 1937-January 31, 1939
Lieutenant General Gustav Kastner-Kirdorf	February 1, 1939-February 23, 1943
Colonel General Bruno Loerzer	February 24, 1943-December 20, 1944
Lieutenant General Rudolf Meister	December 22, 1944-May 8, 1945

Other officers within the personnel office, who assisted these men in formulating personnel policy, selecting officers for promotion, and reviewing efficiency reports (and whose last initials are sometimes found on those reports) included: Major General Karl Barlen, Brigadier General Fritz Koehler, Brigadier General Werner von Rudloff, Brigadier General Franz Nowak, Colonel Walter Boenicke, Colonel Günther Börner, Colonel Anselm Brasser, Colonel Richard Heuser, Colonel Hans von Ploetz and Colonel Karl-Eduard Wilke.[26]

As almost all senior *Luftwaffe* officers had previously served in the Germany Army in World War I and the post-war *Reichswehr*, much of the *Luftwaffe* promotion system had as its antecedents the promotion system used in the German Army.[27] As such, these men developed an officer promotion system to recognize personal achievement and future potential. They wanted officer progression to be rapid, steady and based on uniformly applied criteria. These criteria were based on two principles: some officers would be promoted based on the principle of seniority and some officers would receive preferential – or early – promotion. By using both principles, the *Luftwaffe* could ensure it met a variety of personnel goals.[28] Promotion by seniority ensured that officers spent a reasonable amount of time in each grade – time spent so an officer could thoroughly learn his craft. It also limited the turnover of officers within units, because a high officer turnover rate would adversely affect unit training and cohesion. Promotion by seniority was a fairly simple process. Every officer in every grade had a date of rank, the designation by the personnel office of a specific effective date an officer began his service within that grade. Every year, the personnel department issued lists, by grade, of those officers, who according to their date of rank (known as *Patent*, in German), were eligible for consideration for promotion to the next higher grade.[29]

"Consideration" was key, as seniority alone was not sufficient for promotion. In addition, the *Luftwaffe* High Command wanted to be confident that each officer thus selected had demonstrated – as described in various efficiency reports – the potential for command levels required of officers at the next higher grade. For example, a first lieutenant in command of a fighter squadron would need to demonstrate that he could most likely successfully command a fighter group after promotion to captain. In addition, personal character was extremely important.[30] This is best seen in the 1921 *Reichswehr* regulation on officer efficiency reports, which read, in part:[31]

> First and foremost there belongs in the report a statement of the character and personal qualities of the person reported on, then his military and mental ability … and his physical efficiency and vigor.

The manual went on to state that the main consideration in rating an officer was to be the officer's personality and his human and military qualifications (character traits, which presumably would remain the same over time), rather than actual performance.[32] These character qualities included: subordination of personal interests to higher goals, devotion to duty, willingness to make decisions and accept responsibility, concern for the welfare of subordinates and comradeship with his fellow officers.[33]

The *Luftwaffe* Personnel Office would determine if an officer fell into the zone of consideration based on his date of rank, review efficiency reports on file, and read any letters of recommendation from the higher levels of an officer's chain of command (some included later as examples) that might accompany recent efficiency reports, and make a determination. If the decision was to promote the officer, Berlin would issue a new date of rank for the officer's next grade and notify the individual's unit so it could organize the promotion.

However, the *Luftwaffe* leaders understood that some highly-competent, particularly-gifted officers were better suited to advance through the ranks at a much faster pace, and thus also instituted a preferential, or early, promotion opportunity.[34] Preferential promotions were bottom-up driven. An officer's chain of command, after viewing a particular officer's demonstrated performance of duty and analyzing his potential, would submit a special efficiency report that clearly requested preferential promotion to the next higher grade. This report was often accompanied by a cover letter signed by a general officer, higher in the chain of command, reiterating support for this early promotion. Requests for preferential promotion appear to be less stylized than regular efficiency reports, and often were simply long narratives listing the rationale for such a request. While we do not know the overall success rate for these requests for the entire *Luftwaffe* officer corps, by examining the ones requested for these Knight's Cross winners, we can say that they were frequently successful in the case of officers who had won, or were near to winning, this award.

Officer Efficiency Reports

In addition to observations on character, German efficiency reports addressed the effect an officer had on his subordinates, and how he interfaced with his peers and superiors. For example, some degree of ambition and zeal for a common cause was considered laudable, but if perceived to be selfish in nature, this was considered a weakness. Therefore, if an officer drove his men too hard to reach a performance goal – but in the process lowered their morale – he was considered lacking in character. Officers were to be well-rounded; officers who sacrificed themselves in their devotion to duty and became spiritually exhausted might lack the time to explore general fields of culture. Personal reputation was considered important, as was the ability to inspire confidence of superiors and subordinates. As former Lieutenant General Rudolf Hofmann, who rose to become the chief of staff of an army group, wrote, "The entire purpose of the rating was to recognize officers who had **undesirable** traits in their make-up and to prevent their admission to positions of high responsibility." (Author emphasis)[35]

The personnel system considered personal impressions as the best basis for preparing each efficiency report, and rating officers were urged to take every opportunity to know their subordinates personally, so they could constantly revise their opinions based on changing conditions. When this was not possible, senior raters often annotated that they did not personally know the rated officer. Raters were also cautioned not to include personal prejudices and that the quality of ratings given to subordinates was also often a valuable guide for reports that would be rendered on the rating officers themselves![36]

Rated officers, in theory, were not to be rated unless they had been under the supervision of the rating officer for at least six months. Due to wartime requirements, this was not always possible, so many of the pre-printed rating forms had a line on them to indicate how long the rated officer had been under the rating officer, and for how long the rater knew the rated officer. This was normally given in the form "since December 1941," etc. In addition, these forms had categories that dealt with character, personal values, National Socialist attitude, military proficiency, mental and physical attributes, accomplishments before the enemy, service accomplishments, strong traits, weak traits, suitability for promotion, and suitability for future assignments. In addition, the rater took into consideration off-duty behavior, social adjustment and financial and family circumstances; it is often interesting to see comments about an officer's manners mentioned in the same section as the number of enemy planes he shot down.[37]

Although there was to be no omission of any facts, the samples examined for this work reveal that the section devoted to "weak traits" was often not completed.[38] In other instances, because the boundary between a healthy and selfish ambition could often be obscure, a rating officer might word his report to shade the description so it would not harm the career of a selfishly ambitious officer – especially as many of these officers fulfilled their positions very well.[39] While most efficiency reports appear to have been typed – at least this was true in the samples found in this work – some were hand-written on pre-printed forms. Some reports featured one rating officer, most had two raters, and a few had three and even four senior rating officials.

While much of the report depended on the ability of the rating officers to provide a succinct, well-composed discussion of the rated officer, in two areas comments were limited to certain categories. On most of the reports, the rater had to answer the following question: How is the current position being fulfilled? For this question, the rater could only use one of four responses: ***very well fulfilled***, ***well fulfilled***, ***fulfilled***, or ***not fulfilled***. Toward the end of the report, the rating officer was required to provide a summarized evaluation. For this section, the rating officer could only use the terms: ***above average***, ***average***, or ***below average***. There were no numbers used to rank-order officers, nor were there rating quotas for how many officers a rater could give a ***very well fulfilled***, or ***above average***, etc.[40]

During the war, the *Luftwaffe* Personnel system introduced an abbreviated style of rating, the "Efficiency Notes" (*Beurteilungnotiz*). It was somewhat shorter than the pre-war type of report and included a listing of decorations awarded or recommended during the war. It appears that these wartime reports were prepared in triplicate, with one copy sent to the *Luftwaffe* Personnel Office in Berlin, and two copies sent to higher tactical headquarters. The rating officer retained a draft of the report (presumably to assist him in completion of the next report.) Procedures dictated that the rating officer was to store these drafts in a special locked file, and when the rater transferred, he was to turn these reports over to his successor to help the new commander prepare the next reports. If the rated officer was transferred, the losing command would forward the draft reports through normal channels to the officer's new post or unit.[41]

There is some ambiguity concerning whether or not the rated officer ever saw the actual reports completed on him. Rudolf Hofmann states that the reports were not available for wide dissemination and that only the preparers of the reports and the personnel responsible for processing them in the *Luftwaffe* Personnel Office actually saw them.[42] We can assume that the adjutants at higher headquarters that would pass the reports to Berlin also had access to the reports. Hofmann also states that the rating officer had the duty "to keep his subordinates informed on their progress in respect to personal behavior and performance in the service." Hofmann, however, then shades the issue at this point by stating, "In general, though, he [the rating officer] had ample opportunity to do so [keep the rated officers informed] in the daily routine, and it was rarely necessary for an honorable and capable commander to so inform his officers after he had rated them since each of them knew just where he stood."[43] This would suggest that the rated officers did not see the reports prepared on them, although they may have been given a verbal summary. Hofmann supports that view applied in selective cases, stating, "If an officer's performance had neither improved nor grown worse, and the previous rating had been unfavorable, or if the quality of performance had decreased, the rating officer was required to so inform the officer being rated. Depending upon the nature of the case and the personality of the officer involved, the information given was usually restricted to the derogatory points and the good points." He also states that at the rating officer's discretion, he could inform the rated officers of the rating he had awarded them (he probably means the ***above average***, ***average***, or ***below average*** ratings.)[44]

Therefore, we can conclude that the rated officers almost never saw the actual report in its totality. After all, Hofmann concludes that "there were limits to the degree of knowledge which officers could be allowed to have [about] the ratings awarded them."[45]

In paratroop units, the lowest level at which a commander was required to submit efficiency reports was the battalion. In flying units, some reports appear to have been generated at the wing (*Geschwader*) level, while others seem to have originated at the group (*Gruppe*).

Although there was no system of reliability checks for the reports as a whole, sudden marked changes in ratings were often regarded with suspicion; in those cases where there were no apparent causes for these sudden changes, intermediate raters would check the reliability. When favorable changes included a recommendation that the officer be employed elsewhere besides his current assignment, the report was examined to see if it was an attempt to "kick the officer upstairs."[46]

The efficiency report was the same for fighter pilots, Stuka pilots, bomber pilots and paratroopers, although the organization and rank structure of senior commanders – and thus the ranks of raters and senior raters – differed by *Luftwaffe* branch organization.

Other Significant Awards

All of the fliers and paratroopers within this work received significant military awards in addition to the Knight's Cross.

The German Cross in Gold

On September 28, 1941, Adolf Hitler instituted the German Cross in Gold to recognize a degree of bravery or service – combat related – above that commensurate for the Iron Cross 1st Class, but not sufficient to be awarded a Knight's Cross. A recipient had to first have received an Iron Cross 1st Class; a soldier could only receive one award of the German Cross in Gold. The German Cross in Gold was not in the line of succession with the Iron Cross-Knight's Cross series. Most, but not all, Knight's Cross winners – who were also German Cross winners – won the German Cross in Gold before they won the Knight's Cross. The *Wehrmacht* issued some 30,000 German Crosses in Gold during the war; about 7,600 went to *Luftwaffe* personnel.[47]

German Cross in Gold – this example was won by an infantry captain and battalion commander, who was also a Knight's Cross winner. It was produced by the firm of C.F. Zimmermann in Pforzheim.

The Luftwaffe Honor Goblet

On February 27, 1940, *Reichs* Marshal Hermann Göring instituted the *Luftwaffe* Honor Goblet for special recognition of aerial achievements. The concept was not new; the Imperial German air arm had done a similar award in World War I. Göring, however, considered the award his personal creation, although the award obviously could not be worn, nor was it recognized throughout the *Wehrmacht* as an official award. Having said that, presentation of this award was mentioned in official *Luftwaffe* personnel documents; some 58,000 were awarded before July 5, 1944, when the creation of the *Luftwaffe* Honor Roll Clasp replaced the goblet. Göring awarded the Honor Goblet to air crewmen who had already received the Iron Cross 1st Class, but whose accomplishments did not yet merit the award of the German Cross in Gold or the Knight's Cross of the Iron Cross.[48]

Operational Flying Clasp to Fighter Pilots in Bronze – awarded to fighter pilots after completion of 20 operational missions. This example is an early-war model of heavy silver and nickel alloy.

Operational Flying Clasp to Fighter Pilots in Silver – awarded to fighter pilots after completion of 60 operational missions. This example is an early-war model of heavy silver and nickel alloy.

Operational Flying Clasps

On January 30, 1941, *Reichs* Marshal Hermann Göring instituted a series of operational flying clasps intended to award pilots, observers, radio-operators, bombardiers, flight mechanics, air gunners and selected others for the cumulative number of operational flights. Initially, the clasps were awarded in bronze (for 20 operational flights), silver (for 60 operational flights) and gold (for 110 operational flights). Operational flights were defined as those in which the enemy was engaged or if enemy airspace was penetrated by a given distance. Originally, the clasps came in three distinctions: fighter – to include long-range day fighters and air-to-ground squadrons; bomber – to include horizontal bombers, dive-bombers, transport and glider squadrons; and reconnaissance – which included air/sea rescue and meteorological squadrons.[49]

Ich verleihe
dem

Feldwebel
Leonhard Burr
in Anerkennung seiner hervorragenden Tapferkeit
und der besonderen Erfolge als Sturzkampfflieger

den Ehrenpokal
für besondere Leistung
im Luftkrieg

Hauptquartier des Ob. d. L., den 20. Juni 1942

Der Reichsminister der Luftfahrt
und Oberbefehlshaber der Luftwaffe

Göring

Reichsmarschall

Die erfolgte Verleihung wird beglaubigt:
Der Chef des Luftwaffenpersonalamts

General der Flieger

Award document for the *Luftwaffe* Honor Goblet to Stuka pilot and Knight's Cross winner, Leonhard Burr. Document has a stamped signature of Göring and an actual signature of the chief of the *Luftwaffe* Personnel Office, Lieutenant General Gustav Kastner-Kirdorf.

Verleihungsurkunde

Im Namen des Oberbefehlshabers der Luftwaffe

verleihe ich dem
Leutnant

Heinz Reiche

5./J.G. 26

die

Frontflug-Spange für Jäger
– in Bronze

Gefechtsstand, den 15. August 1941

Oberstleutnant und Geschwaderkommodore.

Award document for the Operational Flying Clasp to Fighter Pilots in Bronze to fighter pilot and second lieutenant, signed by the commander of the 26th Fighter Wing, Lieutenant Colonel Adolf Galland. The recipient was killed in action over the English Channel in 1942.

Verleihungsurkunde

Im Namen des
Oberbefehlshabers der Luftwaffe

verleihe ich dem

Unteroffizier

Georg Amon

die

Frontflug-Spange für Jäger

in Silber

Gefechtstand den 31. Jan 1943

Müller

Hauptmann u. stv. Geschwaderkommodore

Award document for the Operational Flying Clasp to Fighter Pilots in Silver to fighter pilot and sergeant, signed by the acting commander of the 53rd Fighter Wing, Captain Friedrich Karl Müller.

Operational Flying Clasp to Fighter Pilots in Gold – awarded to fighter pilots after completion of 110 operational missions. This example is an early-war model of heavy silver and nickel alloy.

Operational Flying Clasp to Reconnaissance Pilots in Bronze – awarded to reconnaissance pilots (and their crewmen) after completion of 20 operational missions. This example is an early-war model of heavy silver and nickel alloy.

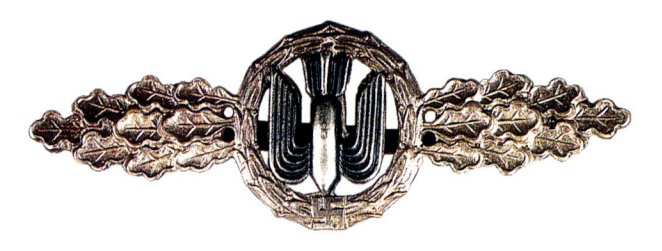

Operational Flying Clasp to Bomber Pilots in Bronze – awarded to bomber pilots (and their crewmen) after completion of 20 operational missions. This example is an early-war model of heavy silver and nickel alloy.

Operational Flying Clasp to Reconnaissance Pilots in Silver – awarded to reconnaissance pilots (and their crewmen) after completion of 60 operational missions. This example is an early-war model of heavy silver and nickel alloy, produced by the firm of Imme & Sohn in Berlin.

Operational Flying Clasp to Bomber Pilots in Silver – awarded to bomber pilots (and their crewmen) after completion of 60 operational missions. This example is an early-war model of heavy silver and nickel alloy.

Operational Flying Clasp to Reconnaissance Pilots in Gold – awarded to reconnaissance pilots (and their crewmen) after completion of 110 operational missions. This example is an early-war model of heavy silver and nickel alloy, produced by the firm of Imme & Sohn in Berlin.

Operational Flying Clasp to Bomber Pilots in Gold – awarded to bomber pilots (and their crewmen) after completion of 110 operational missions. This example is an early-war model of heavy silver and nickel alloy.

Verleihungsurkunde

Im Namen des Oberbefehlshabers der Luftwaffe

verleihe ich dem

Unteroffizier

Georg Amon

die

Frontflug=Spange für Jäger in Gold

Gefechtstand, den 16.3. 1943

Oberstleutnant und Geschwaderkommodore

Award document for the Operational Flying Clasp to Fighter Pilots in Gold to fighter pilot and sergeant, signed by the acting commander of the 53rd Fighter Wing, Lieutenant Colonel Günther von Maltzahn.

Verleihungsurkunde

Im Namen des Oberbefehlshabers der Luftwaffe

verleihe ich dem

Feldwebel Eberhard Voß

I./Sturzkampfgeschwader 3.

die

Frontflug-Spange für Kampfflieger

in Bronze

Gefechtsstand, den 1. Mai 1941

Oberstleutnant u. Geschwaderkommodore.

Award document for the Operational Flying Clasp to Bomber Pilots in Bronze to Stuka pilot and technical sergeant, signed by the Commodore of the 3rd Stuka Wing, Lieutenant Colonel Oskar Dinort.

Verleihungsurkunde

Im Namen des
Oberbefehlshabers der Luftwaffe

verleihe ich dem

Leutnant

Peter Dolberg

die

Frontflug-Spange für Aufklärer

in Silber

Gefechtsstand, den 20. Nov. 1941

Kommandeur III. Seenotgruppe

Barkhen
Oberstleutnant

Award document for the Operational Flying Clasp to Reconnaissance Pilots in Silver to a lieutenant in the 3rd Sea Rescue Group.

Operational Flying Clasp to Transport Pilots in Bronze – awarded to transport pilots (and their crewmen) after completion of 20 operational missions. This example is an early-war model of heavy silver and nickel alloy.

Operational Flying Clasp to Transport Pilots in Silver – awarded to transport pilots (and their crewmen) after completion of 60 operational missions. This example is an early-war model of heavy silver and nickel alloy.

Operational Flying Clasp to Transport Pilots in Gold – awarded to transport pilots (and their crewmen) after completion of 110 operational missions. This example is an early-war model of heavy silver and nickel alloy.

Operational Flying Clasp to Bomber Pilots in Gold with Pendant – awarded to bomber pilots (and their crewmen) after completion of 300 operational missions for level-bombers or 400 operational missions for dive-bombers. This example is an early-war model of heavy silver and nickel alloy.

Over the next several years, the emergence of additional specialized units caused an expansion in the types of clasps from fighters, bombers and reconnaissance to: day fighters, heavy/medium/dive-bombers, reconnaissance, transport/glider, long-range day fighters, long-range night fighters, short-range night fighters and ground-attack squadrons. As the war continued, the *Luftwaffe* High Command realized that some form of recognition must be instituted to aircrew, who exceeded 110 operational flights. On June 26, 1942, the *Luftwaffe* added a pendant device to be suspended beneath the operational flying clasp in gold for the following operational missions: fighters and transport crew – 500; dive-bomber, long-range day fighter and ground-attack squadrons – 400; heavy/medium bomber, air/sea rescue and meteorological squadrons – 300; and reconnaissance and night fighter squadrons – 200.[50]

Many German flying personnel soon exceeded even these high standards. On April 29, 1944, the *Luftwaffe* modified the gold pendant and replaced the device with a gold box bearing a number of operational flights – in black – beginning with 100 and increasing in increments of 100 to a known high of 2,000 (awarded to Stuka pilot and commander Hans Rudel).[51]

Operational Flying Clasp to Fighter Pilots in Gold with Pendant – awarded to fighter pilots after completion of 500 operational missions. This example is an early-war model of heavy silver and nickel alloy, and was worn by *Luftwaffe* ace and Knight's Cross with Oak Leaves winner, Erwin Clausen.

Operational Flying Clasp to Reconnaissance Pilots in Gold with 500 Mission Pendant – awarded to reconnaissance pilots (and their crewmen) after completion of 500 operational missions. This example is made of zinc and was awarded to Knight's Cross winner Helmut Pless.

Verleihungsurkunde

Im Namen des
Oberbefehlshabers der Luftwaffe

verleihe ich dem

Gefreiten

Max Lau

die

Frontflug-Spange für Transportflieger

in Bronze

Gefechtsstand, den 25. Mai 1943

Transportfliegergeschwader 5

Oberstleutnant u. Geschwaderkommodore.

Award document for the Operational Flying Clasp to Transport Pilots in Bronze to a private first class in the 5th Transport Wing. Signed by Lieutenant Colonel Gustav Damm. The unit flew the Messerschmitt Me 323 "Gigant" 6-engine transport during this period.

Verleihungsurkunde

Im Namen des
Oberbefehlshabers der Luftwaffe

verleihe ich dem

Obergefreiten

Max Lau

die

Frontflug-Spange für Transportflieger

in Silber

Gefechtsstand, den 11.7. 1943.

Transportfliegergeschwader 5

Oberstleutnant u. Geschwaderkommodore

Award document for the Operational Flying Clasp to Transport Pilots in Silver to a private first class in the 5th Transport Wing. Signed by Lieutenant Colonel Gustav Damm.

Luftwaffe Organization

Concerning flying formations, and more specifically fighter units, the basic fighting element was a two-aircraft formation known as a *Rotte* (or gang). The leader of this element was known as the *Rottenführer*, while his wingman was the *Rottenflieger*. There were no particular ranks associated with a *Rotte*; in some situations it could consist of two non-commissioned officers, while in others it might even be a wing commander and his adjutant. Two *Rotten* paired together made up a flight of four aircraft, or *Schwarm*, the leader of which was known as the *Schwarmführer*. Bomber units often had a different basic element, the *Kette* or three-aircraft formation. In both the *Rotte* and the *Schwarm*, the leader was almost exclusively concerned with aerial combat and had few ground duties. Not so in the next higher element, the squadron (*Staffel*). A squadron, at least on paper, had three *Schwärme*, a nominal strength of 12 aircraft (which increased to 16 in 1943) and was normally commanded by a lieutenant or captain. A captain in command of a squadron, with all official regulatory requirements fulfilled, was known as the squadron commander (*Staffelkapitän*), while a more junior officer, in temporary command, would be referred to as the squadron leader (*Staffelführer*). The *Luftwaffe* used several gradations of acting and temporary commander, which had to do more with what they were authorized to undertake on the ground, rather than giving orders in the air. Generally, the *Rotte*, *Schwarm* and *Staffel* all flew the same type of aircraft; when a unit was scheduled to receive a new aircraft, at least in the early phases of the war, these elements were temporarily withdrawn from combat to draw new equipment and familiarize themselves on the new aircraft. Squadron commanders and acting squadron commanders had administrative duties on the ground, such as completing efficiency reports on junior personnel. Squadrons were numbered 1, 2, 3, etc.

The *Luftwaffe* considered the group (*Gruppe*) the basic fighting unit. Each group generally consisted of 3 squadrons plus a staff (which manned 3-4 aircraft). Captains, majors and lieutenant colonels usually commanded groups (*Gruppenkommandeur*). Like squadrons, officers could be placed in acting or temporary command of a group; these individuals often appeared designated on efficiency reports as *"mit der Führung beauftragt"* (m.d.F.b.) – in temporary command, or *Gruppenführer*, acting group commander. A group could operate as part of a wing in a general geographic area, or it could operate independently – even in different theaters of operation (Russia, Mediterranean, Channel Front, etc.). Groups were designated by Roman numerals, I, II, III and IV. The first group (I) consisted of the 1st, 2nd and 3rd Squadrons; the second group (II) was made up of the 4th, 5th and 6th Squadrons; the third group (III) would have the 7th, 8th and 9th Squadrons assigned, while the fourth group (IV) would control the 10th, 11th and 12th Squadrons. This would give a group 30-40 aircraft, although combat and maintenance effects would often limit what could actually be put in the air on any given day. Sometimes a group would have no parent wing, especially in reconnaissance and transport units. The largest group known fielded 67 aircraft.[52]

The wing (*Geschwader*) was the largest tactical air formation in the *Luftwaffe*. Each wing consisted of three or four (and on rare occasions five, towards the end of the war) groups and a staff flight with four aircraft – bringing the total strength of a wing from 90 to 120 aircraft. A major, lieutenant colonel or colonel normally commanded a wing and received the honorary title of commodore (*Kommodore*). In some instances in bomber units, a brigadier general could be in command. For those individuals in an acting, temporary or probationary command, they would not be termed the *Kommodore*.

Later in the war, the *Luftwaffe* employed air divisions and fighter divisions (and even air corps and fighter corps); the major air fighting formation throughout the conflict, however, was the air fleet (*Luftflotte*). Each air fleet contained a combination of combat flying units and their supporting services and operated within a defined geographical area. Wings could easily transfer between air fleets depending on requirements. In practical terms, an air fleet could have several hundred to over 1,250 aircraft.

German paratroop units (*Fallschirmjäger*) were, of course, organized as ground combat elements. The lowest tactical element for which an officer would be in charge was the platoon (*Zug*) – although many platoons were, in fact, led by non-commissioned officers. Depending on the type of platoon and its actual present-for-duty-strength, a platoon normally had between 25 and 40 men – a typical paratroop rifle platoon in 1940 had 38. When an officer was in charge of a platoon, he was a second lieutenant. A paratroop company (*Kompanie*) usually had three platoons, a small company headquarters and a mortar section, about 144 personnel in total. A company was normally commanded by a first lieutenant; prior to the war, captains commanded companies as well. Companies were designated by Arabic numbers, 1st Company, 2nd Company, etc. In combat emergencies, a company was often led by a non-commissioned officer until a lieutenant could be brought in.

A battalion (*Bataillon*), which was designated by Roman numerals, (I, II, III and IV), generally had three or four line companies. The first battalion (I) would have the 1st, 2nd, 3rd and 4th Companies as well as a battalion headquarters. The second battalion (II) would have the 5th, 6th, 7th and 8th Companies, while the third battalion (III) would be organized with the 9th, 10th, 11 and 12th Companies. At some points in the war, a battalion might have three line companies and a machine-gun company. It would also have a battalion headquarters and a signal platoon. Battalion commanders could be captains, majors or even a lieutenant colonel. Putting three battalions together, adding a 13th and 14th Company containing light infantry guns and anti-tank guns, and a headquarters, would create a regiment. Regiments were normally commanded by majors, lieutenant colonels and colonels.

A paratroop, or airborne, division could have 2 or 3 regiments, along with an anti-tank detachment (battalion), an engineer battalion, an artillery battalion, a machine-gun anti-aircraft battalion, a medical battalion and a division staff – some 11,000 men altogether. Normally, a brigadier general or a major general would be in command of a paratroop division; sometimes a colonel would serve for a short time as an acting commander.

While platoons, companies, battalions and regiments generally fought together, a division might have one regiment fighting in a different sector of the line under the temporary command of a different division. Thus, when the 7th Air Division (*7. Flieger-Division*) deployed to Russia in 1941, the division generally fought together in the Leningrad area, but one regiment was deployed hundreds of miles to the south.

CONTENTS

Biographies in Volume 1

Rudolf Abrahamczik, *"Exemplary willingness for combat and risk-taking."* 35
Herbert Bachnick, *"Temperamental character, sometimes a little flippant."* 38
Josef Barmetler, *"With a good talent for comprehension and a talent for clear judgment."* 41
Viktor Bauer, *"The squadron under his command did not lose a single pilot through enemy action."* 45
Ludwig Becker, *"His lack of talent for improvisation and quick decision-making are disturbing."* 49
Friedrich Beckh, *"He is never satisfied with his own accomplishments."* 54
Hans Beisswenger, *"He enjoys the full confidence of the other pilots."* 60
Hans-Wilhelm Bertram, *"Demonstrates courage paired with calculation and logical thinking."* 64
Heinrich Boecker, *"Goal-oriented."* 67
Rudolf Boehlein, *"He has endurance and is tough."* 69
Rudolf Böhmler, *"He is firm during a crisis and prevails with an iron tranquility."* 72
Hans-Joachim Brand, *"The proof of descent from German or related blood of Hans-Joachim Brand
    and his spouse has been obtained."* 76
Werner Breese, *"Passionate pilot."* 77
Gerhard Brenner, *"Demonstrated superhuman accomplishments."* 80
Max Buchholz, *"Toward the men under his command strict, but always correct."* 84
Kurt Bühligen, *"He possesses élan."* 89
Horst Carganico, *"Personal courage and daring in combat."* 93
Wilhelm Crinius, *"He is tough, but he fights with calculation and deliberation."* 96
Adolf Dickfeld, *"He sometimes tends towards high-handedness."* 101
Erwin Diekwisch, *"One can always trust him."* 105
Anton Döbele, *"He can be harsh and one-sided in judging the people around him."* 108
Alfred Druschel, *"Distinct talent for improvisation."* 112
Hans Ehlers, *"Of particular note is that on October 8, 1943, after he had completely depleted his ammunition,
    he rammed a four-engine bomber."* 116
Siegfried Engfer, *"His appearance is modest and reserved."* 120
Waldemar Felgenhauer, *"Not totally free of personal ambition."* 122
Leopold Fellerer, *"Untiring willingness for action, coupled with an iron will for victory."* 126
Karl Fitzner, *"Mentally very alert with the best ability to comprehend."* 128
Erwin Fleig, *"As an acting squadron commander, he is an exemplary officer on the ground and in the air."* ... 130

Ernst Frömming, *"Over Crete, he conducted his first jump into enemy territory, without prior training."* 132
Wilhelm Fulda, *"While with the 3rd Squadron, Air-Landing Wing, he received the Knight's Cross of the Iron Cross from the Führer due to his courage in combat."* 137
Robert Gast, *"Alert and open to new ideas."* 141
Walter Gericke, *"Major Gericke has fully proven himself as a battalion commander."* 145
Siegfried Gerstner, *"A healthy degree of self-confidence and ambition."* 148
Franz Grassmel, *"Sometimes a little stubborn."* 152
Alfred Gross, *"Keeps rather to himself."* 155
Hans Grünberg, *"In his nature are hidden leadership qualities."* 158
Andreas Hagl, *"He is no longer able to withstand the hardships of war."* 162
Reino Hamer, *"He sweeps the men under his command along with him."* 166
Friedrich-August von der Heydte, *"Distinguished himself through prudent leadership of his battalion and ruthless personal action."* 170
Herbert von Hoffer, *"He is very sensitive, easily becomes nervous."* 173
Franz Hrdlicka, *"He has read the Führer's Mein Kampf."* 177
Eberhard Jacob, *"Man of character."* 182
Karl Janke, *"He lacks the talent to sweep the soldiers along with him and to create enthusiasm for something."* 186
Peter Jenne, *"Unwavering spirit for battle."* 189
Karl Kennel, *"He is well liked due to his calm, but also humorous and very friendly manner."* 193
Alfred Kindler, *"He is an example for his squadron."* 198
August Lambert, *"He was mentioned several times in official Wehrmacht dispatches."* 201
Emil Lang, *"Demands of himself first."* 203
Karl-Heinz Langer, *"After the encirclement of Stalingrad, showed unusual courage on numerous combat missions out of the fortress."* 207
Erich Leie, *"Has excelled in his current assignment."* 210
Ludwig Leingärtner, *"Has fully distinguished himself as an officer with great willingness for combat against the enemy."* 213
Lothar Linke, *"Possesses good social manners."* 215
Helmut Lipfert, *"He is a shining example for his squadron."* 218

Rudolf Abrahamczik
Bomber Pilot

"Exemplary willingness for combat and risk-taking."

Captain Rudolf Abrahamczik was born April 17, 1920 in Kurzendorf, Silesia. He volunteered for the *Luftwaffe* in 1939, and after training reported to the 2nd Bomber Wing "Wooden Hammer" (*Kampfgeschwader 2 "Holzhammer"*). In April 1941, he was promoted to second lieutenant. By the fall of 1941, he had flown 69 combat missions in Russia – as part of the 8th Air Corps (1st Air Fleet) offensive against Leningrad and the Moscow-Leningrad railroad – before his unit was transferred to the Western Front. Abrahamczik won the Iron Cross 2nd Class on October 12, 1941 and the Iron Cross 1st Class on April 8, 1942. On July 29, 1942, he won the Operational Flying Clasp for Bombers in Gold, and followed this by winning the *Luftwaffe* Honor Goblet on September 30, 1942. On January 1, 1943, Abrahamczik received the German Cross in Gold, while serving with the 6th Squadron, 40th Bomber Wing (*Kampfgeschwader 40*), which had recently become part of the 2nd Bomber Wing; he became the acting commander of the 14th Squadron, 2nd Bomber Wing on October 25, 1943, and the actual commander in February 1944. He had been promoted to first lieutenant on April 1, 1943. During 1943, his unit served under the 3rd Air Fleet in missions against England, flying out of the Netherlands. In June 1943, Abrahamczik's group became the 5th Group, 2nd Bomber Wing. On February 29, 1944, Rudolf Abrahamczik won the Knight's Cross of the Iron Cross as a first lieutenant and squadron commander of the 14th Squadron, which was flying the Messerschmitt Me 410A. The squadron was designated the 4th Squadron, 51st Bomber Wing "Edelweiss" (*Kampfgeschwader 51 "Edelweiss"*) on February 6, 1944.

On April 4, 1944, the acting commander of the 2nd Group, 51st Bomber Wing, Captain Karl-Egon von Dalwigk zu Lichtenfels, submitted an efficiency report on the recent Knight's Cross winner, which reads in part:[1]

Short Evaluation (Personal values, National Socialist attitude, accomplishments before the enemy, service accomplishments, mental and physical attributes and suitability, infantry experience, when and how obtained): Open, natural personality of most decent character, goal oriented and ambitious. National Socialist attitude. During 164 combat flights, he has at all times distinguished himself through his exemplary willingness for combat and risk-taking. Good military knowledge and capabilities. Immaculate military attitude. As a pilot, far above the average. Skillful and conscientious instructor for new pilots. Mentally very flexible with diverse interests. Aptitude for clear thinking. Full of ideas and capable to improvise, particularly in technical and tactical areas. Due to his fresh, natural ways, he is very well liked in the circle of his comrades. Towards superiors correct and polite. Vis-à-vis his subordinates, he is assertive and understands how to sweep them along, due to his exemplary willingness for combat and his battle spirit.

Strong Traits: Good capabilities as a pilot, rich experience and great know-how in combat. Good technical knowledge.

Summarized evaluation: Above average
(Above Average, Average, Below Average)

How is the current position being fulfilled? Well fulfilled.
(Use only: Very well fulfilled, well fulfilled, fulfilled, not fulfilled)

Suitable for promotion to next higher service grade? Fully suitable for promotion to captain.

Suitable for which next-higher position: continue as Squadron Commander.

Known to the person submitting this review: since September 1, 1943.

Subordinated to the person submitting this review: since January 22, 1944.

Abrahamczik continued to perform well and was promoted to captain on May 1, 1944. His unit began training on the Messerschmitt Me 262 jet aircraft in late 1944; he survived the war. Rudolf Abrahamczik died December 4, 1996 in Ibbenbueren in North Rhine-Westphalia.[2]

Luftwaffe Efficiency & Promotion Reports

II./Kampfgeschwader 51 Gef.-Stand den 4. April 1944. Anlage 1
(Dienststelle, nicht Feldpostnummer)   zu Nr. 610

Kriegs-Beurteilung zum 4. April 1944

für Offz. ausschl. San.-, Vet.-Offz.

über den

Oberleutnant (Tr.O.)   1.4.43   Rudolf, Franz, Joseph   Abrahamczik
Dienstgrad 1)   R.D.A. (Ord.-Nr.) und   Vorname   Name
                 Dienstaltersliste

17.4.1920 .... verheiratet, ledig, verwitwet, geschieden .... kv.
geboren am   (Zutreffendes unterstreichen)   Wehrdiensttauglichkeit 2)
                                                        (kv, gv Feld, gv H, tropenuntgl., tropenuntgl.)

                                    Zivilberuf (falls vorhanden)

Staffelführer seit: 25.10.43   Flg. Ausb.Rgt. 61, Oschatz
Staffelkapitän "   26. 2.44   W.B.K. Breslau I
   jetzige Verwendung seit   Friedensdienststelle und W. B. K. 3)

                    Versetzung zur IV.K.G.51
                         Anlass der Vorlage 4)

Deutsche Auszeichnungen des jetzigen Krieges mit Verleihungsdaten und Angabe, ob und
zu welchen Auszeichnungen vorgeschlagen: EK.II.Kl. am 12.10.41, EK I.Kl. am
8.4.42, Frontflg.Sp.i.Gold am 29.7.42, Ehrenpokal am 30.9.42,
Deutsches Kreuz i. Gold am 12.1.43, Ritterkreuz z.E.K. am 29.2.44.

1) Genaue Angabe, ob. Tr.-Offz., Erg.-Offz., Offz. z. D., Res.-Offz., Kr.-Offz., z. V.-Offz. — 2) In zweifelhaften Fällen neu festzustellen.
— 3) Dienststelle, welche Friedensgebührnisse zahlt und zuständiges Wehrbezirkskommando. — 4) z. B.: Versetzung zum ....,
terminmäßige Vorlage zum 1.5.43.

Kurze Beurteilung (Persönlichkeitswert, nationalsozialistische Haltung, Bewährung vor dem Feinde,
 dienstliche Leistungen, geistige und körperliche Anlagen und Eignung, infanteristische Erfahrungen, wann und wo erworben): Aufgeschlossene, natürliche Persönlichkeit
von grundanständigem Charakter, zielbewußt u. strebsam. - Nationalsozialistisch ausgerichtet. - Hat sich bei 164 Feindflügen durch vorbildliche Einsatzfreudigkeit u. Draufgängertum zu jeder Zeit bewährt.-
Gute milit. Kenntnisse u. Fähigkeiten. Einwandfreie soldatische Haltung. Fliegerisch weit über Durchschnitt. Geschickter u. gewissenhafter Lehrer für Nachwuchsbesatzungen. - Geistig sehr beweglich u. vielseitig interessiert. Klares Denkvermögen. Besonders auf technischem u.
              taktischem Gebiet ideenreich u. improvisationsfähig.- Durch
              sein frisches, natürliches Wesen im Kameradenkreis sehr beliebt. Vorgesetzten gegenüber korrekt u. taktvoll. Bei Untergebenen
setzt er sich durch u. versteht diese durch seine vorbildliche Einsatzbereitschaft u. seinen Kampfgeist mitzureißen.

Schwache Seiten:
Starke Seiten : Gute fliegerische Fähigkeiten, reiche Erfahrung und
               großes Können im Einsatz. Gute technische Kenntnisse.

Zusammenfassendes Urteil :
   (über Durchschnitt, Durchschnitt, unter Durchschnitt) :   Über Durchschnitt

Wie wird jetzige Stelle ausgefüllt? (Es sind nur die Ausdrücke „sehr gut ausgefüllt", „gut ausgefüllt", „ausgefüllt", „nicht ausgefüllt" zu verwenden.)   gut ausgefüllt.

Geeignet zur Beförderung zum nächsthöheren Dienstgrad?   zum Hauptmann voll geeignet.

Efficiency Report for First Lieutenant Rudolf Abrahamczik (front side) – dated April 4, 1944, on pre-printed form, from the Hess firm in Brussels, with typed comments.

Eignung für welche nächsthöhere Verwendung⁵)?
für welche besondere oder anderweitige Verwendung⁶)?   } weiterhin Staffelkapitän
Vorschlag für Verwendung in nächster Zeit⁷)?

Sprachkenntnisse (keine Schulkenntnisse)
  a) abgelegte Prüfungen
      (z. B.: Dolmetscherprüfung 1. 10. 42)   **keine**
  b) Beherrschung der Sprache :
      (z. B.: durch Aufenthalt im Ausland)   **keine**

Eröffnung zu welchen Punkten, wann, wie   **keine**
  (mündlich oder schriftlich) und durch wen?

Strafen sind mit vollem Straftenor sowie Vermerk über Vollstreckung abschriftlich als Anlage der
  Kriegsbeurteilung beizuheften.   **keine**

Dem Beurteilenden bekannt seit   1.9.43
                    unterstellt seit   22.1.44

Ausbildung
  a) erworbene Scheine :
      (L.F., E.L.F., L.B. usw.)   **ELF, Bli. II.**
  b) Sonderausbildung :
      (z. B. Bild-Offz., Techn. Offz., Mess-Offz.,
      Funk-D/Lultnachr. Offz (W. K. S.)

_____   **Hauptmann und Gruppenkommandeur**
Unterschrift   Dienstgrad und Dienststellung
                                                                 m.d.W.d.G.b.

Beitrag des Chefs des Generalstabes der vorgesetzten Kommandobehörde (nur bei Genst.-Offz. in
Stabsstellungen und zur Dienstleistung zum Generalstab kommandierten Offizieren) :

Zusätze vorgesetzter Dienststellen :

⁵) Gilt für alle Offz., für Truppen-Offz. hinsichtlich Eignung zur Führung des nächsthöheren Verbandes für Genst.-Offz. hinsichtlich Eignung zum Chef oder Ia, Ic der Luftfl., Flieger-Korps, Flak-Korps, Fl.-Div., Flak-Div., zur Versetzung in den Genst., zur Kommandierung in den Genst.
⁶) z. B.: Höherer Adjutant, Erzieher, Lehrer auf Spezialgebieten, auf Grund von Sprachkenntnissen im Attachédienst, für Genst.-Offz. hinsichtlich Eignung für Verwendung im Quartiermeisterdienst, im Ic-Dienst, im Transportwesen, als Lehrer für Genst. Lehrgang (Taktik bzw. Qu.-Dienst), besondere Anlagen für Kriegsgeschichte, Wehrwirtschaft.
⁷) r. R. « noch halbjährige Belassung in bisheriger Stelle » oder « alsbaldige Verwendung als Geschw.-Kommodore ».

Efficiency Report for First Lieutenant Rudolf Abrahamczik (back side) – signed by acting group commander Captain Karl-Egon von Dalwigk zu Lichtenfels.

Herbert Bachnick
Fighter Pilot

"Temperamental character, sometimes a little flippant."

Second Lieutenant Herbert Bachnick was born in Mannheim, Baden, on February 9, 1920. He entered the *Luftwaffe* in 1938 and became a pilot, reporting to the 9th Squadron, 52nd Fighter Wing (*Jagdgeschwader 52*), on December 5, 1942, as a corporal. He recorded his first two aerial victories on July 5, 1943; by the end of the year, flying in southern Russia as part of the 4th Air Fleet, Bachnick had been promoted to sergeant and had reached 50 kills; he received the *Luftwaffe* Honor Goblet on December 13 (at the 40-kill mark). During this stretch, he had previously received the Operational Flying Clasp for Fighters in Gold on July 31, the Iron Cross 2nd Class on August 8 (after he had achieved his 6th aerial victory), and the Iron Cross 1st Class on September 7 (by which time he had achieved 17 kills).

On December 12, 1943, Major Günther Rall submitted a special report on Bachnick, who was then an officer candidate:[3]

> Mentally sharp, open and self-reliant. Speaks well and shows interest. General knowledge is sufficient. Physically of short stature and slender, good stamina, good athlete, fully able to serve. Open, decent, temperamental character, sometimes a little flippant, willing and decisive, hard, self-reliant and ambitious, liked by his comrades. His military knowledge and accomplishments are very good. Good Non-Commissioned Officer with strapping and secure appearance. Very good fighter pilot with courage and dash. With respect to character, mental and physical attributes, as well as his service knowledge and accomplishments, he lives up to the requirements which are demanded from an officer candidate.

By March 22, 1944, Herbert Bachnick had achieved 76 victories; during this victory spurt, he received the German Cross in Gold on February 5, 1944, as a technical sergeant. For the next three months, he served as a flight instructor with the 2nd Squadron, Supplemental Training Group "East"; he was promoted in this unit to second lieutenant on May 1, 1944. On July 7, 1944 he was wounded in action in aerial combat with American B-17s. On July 27, 1944 Bachnick received the Knight's Cross of the Iron Cross; his score stood at 79 kills by this point. Bachnick returned to *Jagdgeschwader 52*, just in time to engage a B-17 Flying Fortress of the 3rd Bomb Division, 8th Air Force, on August 8, 1944 over Myslowitz, Silesia.[4] Just after shooting down one of the escorting P-51 Mustangs, his own Messerschmitt Me 109G-6 was damaged, and he attempted to land the stricken aircraft. Herbert Bachnick could not control the plane and it crashed into a railway embankment, killing him.

Second Lieutenant Bachnick flew 373 combat missions and shot down 80 enemy aircraft, 79 on the Eastern Front, a sortie-to-victory ratio of 4.66 to 1. He scored three kills on five different dates: July 5, 1943, August 21, 1943, September 14, 1943, September 18, 1943 and March 21, 1944. Bachnick achieved four aerial victories on the following three dates: November 27, 1943, November 28, 1943, and March 12, 1944. And he reached five aerial victories on three other dates: January 7, 1944, March 13, 1944 and March 19, 1944. Bachnick was a master of the low-level kill; he scored 15 kills at an altitude of 500 to 1,000 feet, and a further 12 under 500 feet – 4 of these latter victories occurred at an altitude of less than 200 feet, where the margin for error indeed required the pilot to be "mentally sharp."[5]

Formblatt 1 für den zukünftigen K.O.A.

7.11.

Luftflotte: Lfl.Kdo. 4	Heimat-Luftgau: Lg.Kdo. VII München
Waffengattung*): Fliegertruppe Flugzeugführer	W.B.K.: Mannheim
Truppenteil: III./Jagdgeschwader 52 (9./Staffel)	(wird von L.P. ausgefüllt) 2

Name: Bachnick
Vorname: Herbert
Dienstgrad: Feldwebel

Geburtstag: 9.2.1920
Geburtsort: Mannheim
Beruf: kfm. Angestellter
Abiturient: ja — nein**)
Heimatanschrift: Mannheim, Traitteurstr. 38

Militärischer Werdegang:

Aktive Dienstzeit in der neuen Wehrmacht: von 1.10.38 ~~10.11.1939~~ bis 10.11.1940

(bzw. Kurzausbildung)

Weitere Dienstverpflichtung auf 3 = 4½ = 12 u. mehr Jahre   auf 12 Jahre

Bei ehem. Soldaten, Dienstgrad bei Eintritt in die neue Wehrmacht:

Friedensübungen:

Dienstzeit während des mobilen Verhältnisses: seit 26.8.1939

Beförderungen: 1.10.39 Gefreiter / 1.7.40 Uffz.Anw. / 1.10.40 Uffz./ 1.8.43 Feldwebel

Tag der Auswahl zum K.O.A.Anwärter Fhj.-(Kr.) 1.12.1943

Hat — nicht — mit Erfolg — ohne Erfolg —**) am _____ Vorauswahllehrgang

vom _____ bis _____ teilgenommen.

Ist zur Wiederholung eines Vorauswahllehrganges — nicht — vorgesehen.**)

---

*) Unter Waffengattung ist die Spezialausbildung mit anzugeben (Fliegertruppe: Flugzeugführer, Beobachter, Fallschirmtruppe: springendes Personal, Bodenpersonal. Flakartillerie: schwere Flak, leichte Flak, Scheinwerfer. Luftnachrichtentruppe: Funker, Fernsprecher).
**) Nichtzutreffendes ist zu streichen.

1917 Din A 4 Heidelberger Gutenberg-Druckerei GmbH. XII. 42.

Special Report for Technical Sergeant Herbert Bachnick (front side) – dated December 7, 1943, on pre-printed form from the Heidelberger-Gutenberg firm, with typed comments.

Zur Beförderung zum Offizier vorgeschlagen am: _____

Bewährung vor dem Feinde: Bis 7.12.43 : 38 bezeugte Luftsiege als Jagdflieger an der Ostfront

Feindflüge: 286

Auszeichnungen: 6.8.43: E.K.2.Kl. / 7.9.43: E.K.1.Kl. / 31.7.43: Frontflugspange f.Jäger in Gold / 14.11.43: Ehrenpokal / am 12.11.43 zum Deutschen Kreuz in Gold eingereicht

Bestrafungen: keine

Kurze Beurteilung: Geistig frisch, aufgeschlossen und selbständig. Redegewandt und interessiert. Allgemeinwissen ausreichend. Körperlich klein und schlank, sehr ausdauernd, guter Sportler, voll einsatzfähig. Offener, ehrlicher, temperamentvoller Charakter, manchmal etwas vorlaut, willig und entschlossen, hart, selbstbewußt und ehrgeizig, bei Kameraden beliebt.
Seine milit. Kenntnisse und Leistungen sind sehr gut. Guter Unteroffizier mit strammen und sicherem Auftreten. Sehr guter Jagdflieger mit Mut und Schneid. Hat sich im Einsatz sehr gut bewährt. Entspricht in charakterlicher, geistiger und körperlicher Hinsicht, sowie in seinen dienstlichen Kenntnissen und Leistungen den Anforderungen, die an einen Offz.-Anwärter zu stellen sind.

Uk.-Stellung während des Krieges:

von _____ bis _____

Kurze Angabe des Grundes: _____

Im Felde, den 7.12.1943
(Ort und Datum)

(Unterschrift)
Major und Gruppenkommandeur

Special Report for Technical Sergeant Herbert Bachnick (front side) – signed by Major Günther Rall, Commander, 3rd Group, 52nd Fighter Wing.

Josef Barmetler
Fallschirmjäger

"With a good talent for comprehension and a talent for clear judgment."

Major Josef Barmetler was born in Kempten, Bavaria on March 11, 1904. He entered the *Reichswehr's* 19th Infantry Regiment on April 2, 1924 and served for ten years as an enlisted man in the infantry. Barmetler then joined the reserves; on August 26, 1939 he was mobilized as a second lieutenant and assigned as a heavy machinegun platoon leader in the 316th Infantry Regiment. On December 1, 1939, Barmetler assumed acting command of the 2nd Company, 316th Infantry Regiment and remained in this organization until June 1940 when he completed airborne school. Now a first lieutenant, he formally transferred to the *Luftwaffe* on August 1, 1940, and one month later became the Commander, 7th Company, 1st Paratroop Air Landing Regiment (*Luftlande-Sturm-Regiment 1*). On May 20, 1941, his unit jumped into Crete as part of the German airborne invasion of the island. Shortly after landing, Barmetler led his company across the Tavronitis River in an attack on Hill 107 and secured the heights – which commanded the Máleme Airfield – the following morning. On May 25, in another action, he maneuvered his unit behind the enemy at Red Hill near Galatas and linked up with German mountain troops, a decisive action of the entire campaign. He was wounded in action during this attack. Barmetler received the Iron Cross 1st Class on June 18, 1941 for these actions (he had won the Iron Cross 2nd Class on June 22, 1940). On July 9, 1941, First Lieutenant (Reserve) Josef Barmetler received the Knight's Cross of the Iron Cross for his actions on Crete. He was promoted to captain (Reserve) on July 25, 1941.

On October 15, 1941, his unit deployed to Russia, with Barmetler serving as the acting commander of the 2nd Battalion, 1st Paratroop Air Landing Regiment. He was wounded in action on November 29, 1941 and transported out of the theater. His wounds both on Crete and in Russia were serious and Barmetler was reassigned to the 1st Paratroop Supplemental Regiment (*Fallschirmjäger Ergänzungs-Regiment 1*) at Stendal, Germany in February 1942. In September, he was assigned to the Paratroop Replacement Battalion at Stendal (*Fallschirmjäger-Ersatz-Bataillon Stendal*), where he took command of the 5th Company.

On March 16, 1943, the battalion commander of the Paratroop Replacement Battalion Stendal submitted a request for the transfer of Captain (Reserve) Josef Barmetler, to the regular, active *Luftwaffe* officer corps. The major wrote:[6]

Evaluation:
Personality: Self-reliant colleague, dutiful and reliable.

Suitability as to character: Without criticism, mature character with clear goal-setting.

Mental disposition: Mentally well-gifted, with a good talent for comprehension and a talent for clear judgment, as well as talented organizer.

Military disposition: Very polite and correct vis-à-vis superiors, enjoys great popularity among his comrades due to his open nature and is respected and liked by his subordinates because of his caring and just attitude.

Physical properties: Stocky built, physically capable, tough and resistant.

Other details (particularly regarding actions against the enemy, in the current service position and qualification for promotion to next higher service grade): Captain Barmetler is an officer who is above average; due to his rich experiences and service knowledge, he fulfills all demands which are posed to an active officer. Because of outstanding courage and circumspect leadership during the fighting on Crete, he was awarded the Knight's Cross of the Iron Cross. Captain Barmetler is suited for promotion to the next higher service grade.

On April 20, 1943, Lieutenant General Kurt Student added: "Without reservation, Captain of Reserves Barmetler (a Knight's Cross winner) is suited for transfer to the active officer corps."

Josef Barmetler requested that he be allowed to return to frontline service in spite of his wounds; he joined the staff of the 2nd Battalion, 6th Paratroop Regiment (*Fallschirmjäger-Regiment 6*) on December 10, 1943. Now again in Russia, he took acting command of the 2nd Battalion on March 1, 1944; the battalion left Russia on March 31, 1944, but Barmetler was experiencing even more physical difficulty. He was promoted to major (Reserve) on June 1, 1944. After returning to his hometown at the beginning of 1945, he died of his wounds on February 20, 1945.[7]

Fallschirmjäger-Ersatz-Batl. Stendal, den 16. März 1943.
    S t e n d a l

<u>Waffengattung:</u> Fallschirmtruppe

<u>W.B.K.:</u> Kempten / Allgäu

<u>V o r s c h l a g</u>
zur Überführung des Hauptmann d.R. ~~(Kriegsoffizier,Offiz.~~
~~d.xx~~⁺)
zu den aktiven Friedensoffizieren.

<u>Familienname, Vorname:</u> B a r m e t l e r , Josef

<u>geb. am:</u> 11. 3. 04   <u>zu:</u> Kempten   <u>Konfession:</u> kath.

<u>Verheiratet,</u> ~~ledig, verwitwet, geschieden~~:⁺)

<u>Dienstgrad:</u> Hauptmann ~~d.R.~~ <u>Rangdienstalter:</u> 1. 7. 1941

<u>Diensteintritt:</u> 2. 4. 1924

<u>Militärische Dienstzeiten (bei Unterbrechungen) und Werdegang:</u>

      s.Anlage

<u>Jetzige Verwendung:</u> Kompanie-Chef   5./Fallsch.Jg.Ers.Btl.

<u>Für welche weiteren Verwendungen geeignet:</u> Batls.-Führer

<u>Bestrafungen vor Diensteintritt:</u> k e i n e

<u>Bestrafungen während der milit. Dienstzeiten:</u>   k e i n e

<u>Bildungsgang (Schulabschluss):</u> Schlusszeugnis - Volkshauptschule der
                               Stadt Kempten   8.Klasse

<u>Zivilberuf:</u> Verwaltungsinspektor

<u>Beruf des Vaters:</u> Gärtnermeister

<u>Erworbene Lw.-Scheine:</u> Fallschirmschützenschein

                                              Major und Batl.-Kommandeur.

⁺) Nichtzutreffendes ist zu streichen.

Request for Transfer for Captain Josef Barmetler from Wartime Officer to Career Status (first page) – dated March 16, 1943, on blank paper with typed comments. Signed by a major and battalion commander.

Stendal, den 29. März 1943

— 2 —

Beurteilung:

1. **Persönlichkeit :**

   Selbständiger Mitarbeiter pflichtbewusst und zuverlässig.

2. **Charakterliche Eignung:**

   Einwandfreier, abgeschlossener Charakter mit klarer Zielsetzung.

3. **Geistige Veranlagung:**

   Geistig gut veranlagt mit guter Auffassungsgabe und klarem Urteilsvermögen sowie organisatorischer Begabung.

4. **Militärische Veranlagung:**

   Vorgesetzten gegenüber sehr taktvoll und korrekt, erfreut sich im Kameradenkreis durch sein aufgeschlossenes Wesen grosser Beliebtheit und ist trotz Strenge bei seinen Untergebenen wegen seiner Fürsorge und gerechten Einstellung angesehen und beliebt.

5. **Körperliche Veranlagung:**

   Untersetzte Erscheinung, körperlich gut veranlagt, zäh und widerstandsfähig.

6. **Sonstiges (Insbesondere über Bewährung vor dem Feinde, in der jetzigen Dienststellung und über Eignung zur Beförderung zum nächsthöheren Dienstgrad):**

   Hauptmann Barmetler ist ein über dem Durchschnitt stehender Offizier, auf Grund seiner reichen Erfahrungen und dienstlichen Kenntnisse erfüllt er alle Voraussetzungen, die an einen aktiven Offizier gestellt werden. Wegen hervorragender Tapferkeit und umsichtiger Führung beim Einsatz Kreta mit dem Ritterkreuz des Eisernen Kreuzes ausgezeichnet. Hauptmann B. ist zur Beförderung zum nächsthöheren Dienstgrad geeignet.

   Major u. Batl.-Kommandeur

   b.w.

Request for Transfer for Captain Josef Barmetler from Wartime Officer to Career Status (second page)
– signed by a major and battalion commander.

Gen.Kdo.XI.Fliegerkorps
Der Kommandierende General

den 20.4.1943

Hptm. d. Rf. Barmetler (Ritterkreuzträger) ist zur Überführung zu den Truppenoffizieren uneingeschränkt geeignet.

Student
General der Flieger

Request for Transfer for Captain Josef Barmetler from Wartime Officer to Career Status (third page)
– signed by Lieutenant General Kurt Student, Commander, 11th Air Corps.

Viktor Bauer

Fighter Pilot

"The squadron under his command did not lose a single pilot through enemy action."

Major Viktor Bauer was born on September 19, 1915 in Löcknitz, Pomerania. He initially served as a private in the Army's 1st Infantry Regiment. He joined the *Luftwaffe* on April 1, 1936 as an officer candidate, attended flight training and then joined the 1st Squadron, 77th Fighter Wing (*Jagdgeschwader 77*). He was promoted to second lieutenant on January 1, 1938. Bauer received the Iron Cross 2nd Class on November 1, 1939. On May 15, 1940, as a pilot in the 2nd Squadron, 77th Fighter Wing, he shot down his first enemy aircraft – a Hurricane – west of Brügge, Belgium. Bauer scored his second kill – another Hurricane – east of Cambrai, France on May 18, 1940, flying a Messerschmitt Me 109E-1. He then joined the 9th Squadron of the 3rd Fighter Wing (*Jagdgeschwader 3*). He shot down a third aircraft – a Spitfire – twelve miles south of Southend, England on November 1, 1940, and reached his fourth kill – a Hurricane – over the English Channel on February 5, 1941 – a fairly slow start for a later ace, who would shoot down 106 aircraft. He received the Iron Cross 1st Class on November 18, 1940. Promoted to first lieutenant on April 1, 1940, he became the commander of the 9th Squadron in June 1941, shortly before the invasion of the Soviet Union, and his pace accelerated. Bauer shot down 15 enemy aircraft that June – including 5 on June 26 – and a further 17 in July – again tallying five in a single day. He received the Knight's Cross of the Iron Cross on July 30, 1941, when his score had reached 36 aerial victories. However, he received the award in the hospital because he had been seriously wounded in his Messerschmitt Me 109F-2 on July 23, 1941 by friendly anti-aircraft fire and was forced to make an emergency landing at Belaja-Zerkow, all but totaling his aircraft. Bauer would spend several months convalescing, not returning to action until February 1942.

During this convalescence, on January 16, 1942, Bauer's chain of command submitted him for an early promotion to captain. Major Werner Andres, the 3rd Group Commander, wrote this strong recommendation:[8]

> The 3rd Group, Fighter Wing *Generaloberst Udet* requests from the Wing through the Air Ministry the preferential promotion of First Lieutenant Bauer to Captain. Due to his personality traits and his outstanding accomplishments against the enemy, First Lieutenant Bauer is far superior to the average of his peers. First Lieutenant Bauer was born on September 19, 1915, and as to his age, he is older than the average of his comrades. On April 1, 1936 he entered the *Luftwaffe* as officer candidate, was promoted to second lieutenant on January 1, 1938 and to first lieutenant on April 1, 1940. Before entering the *Luftwaffe*, he served as a private in the 1st Infantry Regiment from April 1, 1935 to December 31, 1935, after that he was in the Labor Service to March 31, 1936. From March 1934, First Lieutenant Bauer was a student in secret courses of the *Reichswehr*; among them he participated in a six-week long exercise in East Prussia. The period of service in the 1st Infantry Regiment has not been taken into consideration in determining his rank service age.
>
> Since October 1939, First Lieutenant Bauer has been a squadron leader, and up to now he has shot down 37 enemy airplanes, 5 of which occurred in the battle against England. At the same time it has to be considered that he participated in the Russian Campaign only up to July 23, 1941. On July 23, 1941, a hit that his airplane suffered in air battle caused his plane to be shot down. During this occurrence, First Lieutenant Bauer was injured so severely that he was only released from the field hospital in December 1941. Therefore, during the first month of the Russian Campaign, he shot down 32 Russian planes.
>
> His outstanding accomplishments as squadron leader are demonstrated in his successful results of the 9th Squadron, Fighter Wing "Colonel General Udet," the leadership of which he took over in September of 1940. At that time, the squadron had 33, but by now has 203 aerial victories. From among the pilots of the squadron, Master Sergeant Stechmann and Technical Sergeant Schentke succeeded in 31 aerial victories each, First Lieutenant Mertens and Master Sergeant von Boremski 27 aerial victories each. These successes are of particular note because the squadron under his command did not lose a single pilot through enemy action. First Lieutenant Bauer is not only a particularly courageous fighter plot who is leading his unit very well, but he is a particularly good troop leader at the same time, who has educated his squadron with a very good military spirit. First Lieutenant Bauer is an exemplary officer, who undoubtedly will become a good group commander due to his outstanding

accomplishments and his mature personality. According to the opinion by the group, he is already at present suited for it.

Bauer reached the 40-kill plateau on February 18, 1942 (an I-61 fighter near Staraja Russa), the 50-kill mark on April 4, 1942 and the 60-victory level on May 22, 1942. Bauer received the *Luftwaffe* Honor Goblet on June 22, 1942, but July would prove even more significant. Five times in the month he shot down 4 aircraft in a single day, while twice he shot down 5 aircraft in a 24-hour period, bringing his July total to 33 kills and his overall score to 101. On July 26, 1942, Bauer received the Oak Leaves to the Knight's Cross, the 107th *Wehrmacht* soldier to win the award. On August 10, 1942, he shot down his 106th enemy aircraft, but was also shot down in the encounter, making a belly-landing at Novy-Kalatsch, severely wounded. After recovering, Bauer assumed duties as a squadron commander in Supplementary Group East (*Ergänzungsgruppe Ost*) – an operational training formation – and later became the group commander on July 1, 1943. He held this position until he became the commodore of the 1st Supplementary Wing – another operational training formation – (*Ergänzungsgeschwader 1*) on October 1, 1944 and ended the war as a colonel.

The 92nd highest scoring *Luftwaffe* ace in World War II, Viktor Bauer died on December 13, 1969 in Bad Homburg. During his career he flew about 400 combat missions. Of his 106 aerial victories, 102 occurred on the Eastern Front and included 31 bombers and 23 Il-2 Sturmovik ground-attack aircraft, a sortie-to-victory ratio of about 3.77 to 1.[9]

Geheim!

III./Jagdgeschwader
Gen.Oberst- U d e t

Gefechtsstand, 16.1.1942.

Bezug: F.S.J.G. Gen.Ob.Udet Br.B.Nr. 1992/41 geh.
Betr.: Beförderung Oblt. Bauer.

Br. B. Nr. 39/42 geh.

An

Jagdgeschwader Gen.Oberst Udet.
=====================================

[Stamp: Jagdgeschwader "Generaloberst Udet"
Eing.: 11. FEB. 1942
Az.: ....
Br.B.Nr. 34/42 geh.]

    Die III./J.G. Gen.Ob.Udet bittet das Geschwader beim R.L.M. die vorzeitige Beförderung des Oblt. Bauer zum Hauptmann zu erwirken.

    Oblt. Bauer ist nach seinem Persönlichkeitswert und auf Grund seiner hervorragenden Leistungen vor dem Feind dem Durchschnitt seines Jahrganges weit überlegen.

    Oblt. Bauer ist am 19.9.1915 geboren u. ist an Lebensjahren älter als der Durchschnitt seines Jahrganges. Am 1.4.1936 ist er als Offizieranwärter in die Luftwaffe eingetreten, wurde am 1.1.1938 zum Leutnant u. am 1.4.1940 zum Oblt. befördert. Vor seinem Eintritt in die Luftwaffe hat er vom 1.4.1935-31.12.1935 als Schütze im Inf.Regt. 1 gedient, anschließend war er bis zum 31. 3. 1936 im Arbeitsdienst. Seit März 1934 hat Oblt. Bauer als Schüler an geheimen Kursen der Reichswehr darunter an einer 6-wöchentlichen Übung in Ostpreußen teilgenommen. Die Dienstzeit beim I.R. 1 ist ihm bei der Festsetzung seines Rangdienstalters nicht angerechnet worden.

    Oblt. Bauer ist seit Oktober 1939 Staffelkapitän u. hat bisher 37 feindliche Flugzeuge, davon 5 im Kampf gegen England abgeschossen. Dabei ist zu berücksichtigen, daß er den Rußlandfeldzug nur bis zum 23.7.1941 mitgemacht hat. Am 23.7.1941 führten einige Treffer, die sein Flugzeug im Luftkampf erhielt, zum Absturz seines Flugzeuges. Oblt. Bauer erlitt dabei so schwere Verletzungen, daß er erst im Dezember 1941 aus dem Lazarett entlassen werden konnte. Er hat also in dem ersten Monat des Rußlandfeldzuges 32 russ. Flugzeuge abgeschossen.

    Seine außergewöhnlichen Leistungen als Staffelkapitän gehen aus den Erfolgen der 9./J.G. Gen.Ob. Udet hervor, deren Führung er im September 1940 übernommen hat. Die Staffel hatte damals 33 und hat jetzt 203 Abschüsse. Von den Flugzeugführern der Staffel konnten Oberfeldwebel Stechmann u. Feldwebel Schentke je 31, Oblt. Mertens u. Oberfeldwebel v. Boremski je 27 Abschüsse erzielen. Diese Erfolge sind besonders hoch zu werten, weil die Staffel unter seiner Führung keinen einzigen Flugzeugführer durch Feind-

-2-

Request for Promotion for First Lieutenant Viktor Bauer (front side) – dated January 16, 1942, on blank paper with typed comments. Upper right hand corner rectangular stamp shows the request was received at the wing headquarters on February 11, 1942.

-2-

Feindeinwirkung verloren hat.

Oblt. Bauer ist aber nicht nur ein besonders schneidiger Jagdflieger, der seine Einheit in der Luft sehr gut führt, sondern er ist gleichzeitig ein besonders guter Truppenführer, der seine Staffel in einem sehr guten soldatischen Geist erzogen hat.

Oblt. Bauer ist ein vorbildlicher Offizier, der auf Grund seiner hervorragenden Leistungen und auf Grund seiner gereiften Persönlichkeit zweifellos ein guter Gruppenkommandeur wird, wozu er nach Ansicht der Gruppe bereits jetzt geeignet ist.

Major u. Gruppenkommandeur.

2 Anlagen:
Kriegsstammrollenauszug
Beurteilungsnotiz

Request for Promotion for First Lieutenant Viktor Bauer (back side) – signed by the Commander, 3rd Group, 3rd Fighter Wing, Major Werner Andres.

Ludwig Becker
Night Fighter Pilot

"His lack of talent for improvisation and quick decision-making are disturbing."

Night fighter pilot Captain Ludwig Becker was born in Dortmund-Aplerbeck, North Rhine-Westphalia, on August 22, 1911. As a student, he was an avid glider pilot; he joined the *Luftwaffe* and initially became a destroyer pilot, joining the 3rd Squadron, 1st Destroyer Wing (*Zerstörergeschwader 1*) at the beginning of 1940. In June 1940, he transferred to the night fighters; he received the Iron Cross 2nd Class on July 3, 1940. As a lieutenant in the 4th Squadron, 1st Night Fighter Wing (*Nachtjagdgeschwader 1*), he scored his first kill during the night of October 16/17, 1940 – a Wellington; he won the Iron Cross 1st Class on December 23, 1940.

Becker was a very innovative pilot, pioneering the use of radar-directed aerial attacks. On his first kill, a ground-based radar operator vectored Becker to the vicinity of the target until he could gain visual contact. On the night of August 9/10, 1941, Becker also carried out the first German fighter interception using onboard radar. Flying in a Dornier Do 215, he gained his own radar contact at a distance of 6,500 feet from the target, moved in and shot the bomber down. On November 11, 1941, he assumed command of 6th Squadron, 2nd Night Fighter Wing; he had 7 aerial victories by this date. During the night of January 20/21, 1942, Becker shot down three British Wellington Bombers, part of a RAF Bomber Command raid against Emden. Becker won the *Luftwaffe* Honor Goblet on March 2, 1942 and the German Cross in Gold on May 4, 1942, as a first lieutenant.[10] Ludwig Becker achieved his 22nd kill on June 7, 1942 (during an RAF Bomber Command 233-aircraft attack on Emden) and received the Knight's Cross of the Iron Cross on July 1, 1942 after his 25th kill. On September 5, 1942, he shot down another three Wellington bombers (participating in an RAF Bomber Command 251-aircraft attack on Bremen) and reached his final total of 44 victories (all at night) by January 31, 1943.

On October 28, 1942, Becker's chain of command recommended him for promotion to captain. Captain and Group Commander Helmut Lent began the report:[11]

> First Lieutenant Becker is of medium height, tough, but due to his age no longer totally flexible and agile; however, he attempts to train his body by sports activities. As to his character, he is a friendly, well-meaning and sincere being. Particular attributes are his toughness, endurance and great thoroughness. Against that, his lack of talent for improvisation and quick decision-making are disturbing. He is more the type of a detailed planner. At times, his insecurity cannot be overlooked. He has a rather lively temperament, which borders on nervousness. His insecurity may be explained because for a long time he was looking for a suitable occupation, and only during the war, particularly due to his successes, did he decide to become a soldier. His mental capabilities can be called very good. Due to his studies in law and economics, he has a rich font of knowledge, which is an attribute in his capacity of squadron leader. However, he is also very much interested in technical problems and in the developmental possibilities for night fighting.

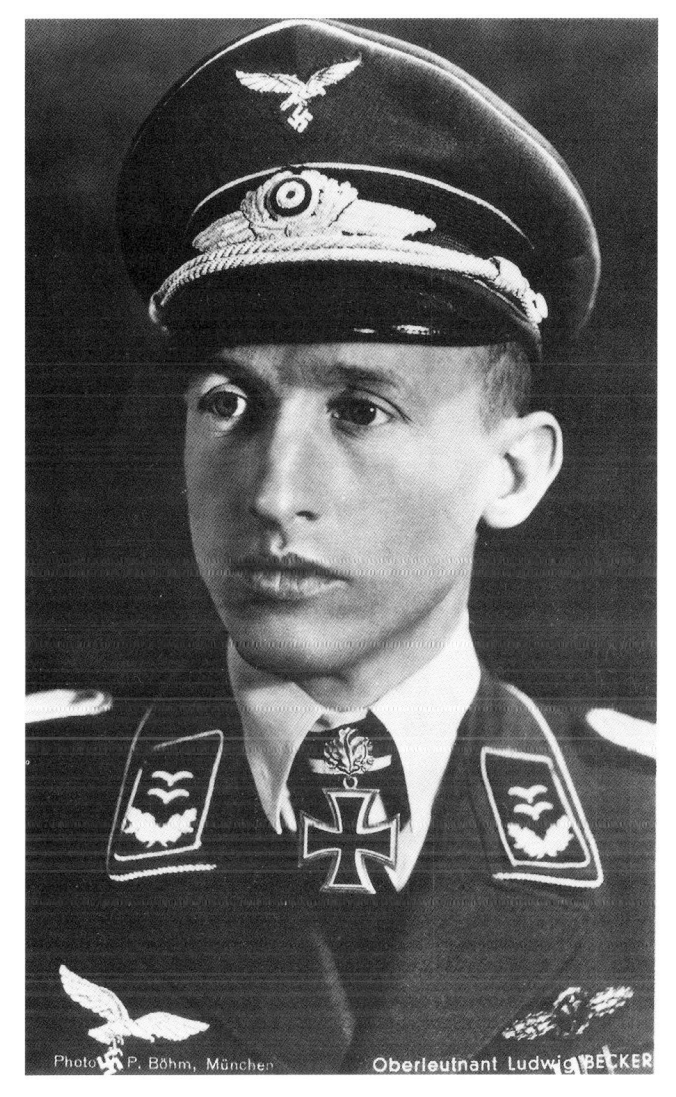

He is untiring in his aggressiveness and his passion for flying. He has proven his perseverance and toughness as well as knowledge of flying in 45 day and 116 night missions. With 39 night victories, he has proven himself to the best degree before the enemy and was awarded the Knight's Cross on July 1, 1942. Of particular note is his involvement in the development of special night fighter equipment, which advanced night fighting to a great degree. For this apparatus developed to become useful at the front was to a great degree thanks to the endeavors of First Lieutenant Becker. Since December 1, 1941, he has led a night fighter squadron. The young squadron, which had little experience, was brought, slowly but surely, to a high level, due to his thorough training regimen. Wherever there appears to be a lack in military capability, it is balanced by his extraordinary maturity, which provides him counsel to let him find advice and action in many situations. In this manner, he has fulfilled his duty as squadron commander to the fullest satisfaction. First Lieutenant Becker is strongly rooted in National Socialist philosophy. From the aspect of the Group, there are no concerns regarding a promotion.

Lieutenant Colonel Wilhelm von Friedberg, filling in for the wing commodore, added his own comments, appearing to soften some of the remarks made by the group commander:

First Lieutenant Becker, who has been active in night fighting since its inception, has quickly developed into one of the best night fighters due to his outstanding flying capabilities. First Lieutenant Becker is very much interested in technology, whereby his behavior is often misinterpreted. Despite his temperament, which borders on nervousness, First Lieutenant Becker is secure in his decisions and has proven this with his successes in night fighting. As a squadron commander, he quickly adapted to his duty by reason of his age and very comprehensive knowledge and has satisfactorily led his squadron. First Lieutenant Becker was awarded the Knight's Cross of the Iron Cross on July 1, 1942. With his enthusiasm for combat, he is an example to all the men under his command and he possesses very good teaching capabilities. Completely suitable for promotion to Captain.

Finally, the commander of the 1st Fighter Division (*1. Jagddivision*), Kurt von Döring, writing on November 2, added his own brief observations:

First Lieutenant Becker has made 39 night victories and as squadron commander attained overwhelming successes for himself as well as his squadron, through remarkable thoroughness, great energy and strong endurance. He is suitable for promotion to Captain in every respect.

Becker had less than four months to live after the report. On February 26, 1943, Becker's unit, 12th Squadron, 4th Group, 1st Night Fighter Wing, was pressed into a daytime action against U.S. bombers of the 1st and 2nd Bomb Wings, 8th Air Force – on a mission to bomb Wilhelmshaven – north of Schiermonnkoog, in the North Sea. Ominously, the daylight mission was unusual for the night fighters, and one that even with "improvisation and quick decision-making" would be extremely hazardous. Flying with his radioman, Sergeant Josef Straub, in a Messerschmitt Me 110G-4 twin-engine destroyer, Captain Ludwig Becker did not return to base and was posted missing in action. His body was never recovered. He posthumously received the Oak Leaves to the Knight's Cross, the 198th *Wehrmacht* soldier to do so.[12]

1.) Gen.Kdo. XII. Flg. Korps   Gefechtsstand, den 28.10.42
2.) Nachtjagdgeschwader 1   Wehrmachtteil : Luftwaffe
3.) W.B.K. Dortmund I
4.) Vorgeschlagen gem.: R.d.L.u.Ob.d.L. -L.P.- Az.21
                    Nr. 71489/42 (2ID) v.16.10.42.
5.) Waffengattung : Fliegertruppe (Flugzeugfhr.)

V o r s c h l a g
======================

zur Beförderung eines Offiziers (d.B.)
zum nächsthöheren Dienstgrad .

Vor- und Zuname :   Ludwig B e c k e r
Geburtsdatum :   22.8.1911
Jetziger Dienstgrad :   Oberleutnant d.Res.
Rangdienstalter :   1.11.40
6.) Eingesetzt als :   Staffelkapitän
7.) Geeignet zum :   Hauptmann d.Res.
Aktiver Wehrdienst seit : 1.8.39 : 28.8.39 - heute
Verwendung uns seit wann : 28.8.39 - 31.1.42 Staffeloffizier
                                          und Flugzeugführer
                          1.2.42 - jetzt   Staffelkapitän
Teilnahme an welchen Kämpfen : v. 28.8.39 - 23.4.40 Einsatz in der
                                  Luftverteidigung
                          v. 26.4.40 - 9.5.40 Einsatz im Opera-
                          tionsgebiet "West" (V.(Z) L.G. 1)
                          v. 10.5.40 - 3.7.40 Einsatz im West-
                          feldzug
                          v. 4.7.40 - heute Einsatz in der
                          Nahnachtjagd im besetzten Gebiet.

Wird vorgeschlagen zur Beförderung zum : Hauptmann d. Res.
Kurze Beurteilung durch den Regimentskommandeur (selbst.Btl.-usw.Kdr.
    Oblt. Becker ist von mittelgroßer, zäher, nicht mehr wegen sei-
nes Alters ganz wendiger und elastischer Statur, jedoch versucht er
durch Betätigung auf sportlichem Gebiet seinen Körper zu trainieren.
Charakterlich ist er von freundlichem, gutmütigem und ehrlichem Wesen.
Insbesondere zeichnen ihn Zähigkeit, Ausdauer und große Gründlichkeit
aus. Dagegen macht sich ein Mangel an Improvisationsvermögen und
schneller Entschlußkraft störend bemerkbar. Er ist mehr der Typ des
Schematikers. Teilweise ist eine Unsicherheit nicht zu verkennen.
Er besitzt ein ziemlich lebhaftes Temperament, das an Nervosität grenz
Seine Unsicherheit läßt sich vielleicht dadurch erklären, dass er sehr
lange nach einen für ihn geeigneten Beruf suchte und erst jetzt im Kri
ge, besonders durch seine Erfolge bedingt, sich für den Soldatenberuf
entschieden hat. Seine geistigen Anlagen sind als sehr gut zu bezeichnen. Er besitzt infolge seines Studiums in der Jura und Volkswirt-
schaft ein reiches Wissen, das ihm in seiner Tätigkeit als Staffelkapitän zustatten kommt. Jedoch besitzt er auch großes Interesse für
technische Probleme und für Entwickelungsmöglichkeiten innerhalb der
Nachtjagd.
                                                                                     wenden

Request for Promotion for First Lieutenant (Reserve) Ludwig Becker (first page) – dated October 28, 1942, on blank paper with typed comments. Three sets of initials in upper right are from reviewing officers at the *Luftwaffe* Personnel Headquarters, as are numerous red and purple pencil underlines.

In seiner Einsatzbereitschaft und seiner fliegerischen Passion ist er unermüdlich. Ausdauer und Zähigkeit sowie großes fliegerisches Können bewies er in 45 Tag- und 116 Nachteinsätzen. Mit 39 Nachtabschüssen hat er sich vor dem Feinde bestens bewährt und wurde am 1.7.42 mit dem Ritterkreuz ausgezeichnet. Besondere Verdienste erwarb er sich bei der Entwicklung eines Nachtjagdsondergerätes, dessen erfolgreiche Verwendung die Nachtjagd ein gewaltiges Stück vorwärts brachte. Daß dieses Gerät frontreif wurde, ist zum großen Teil ein Verdienst des Oblt. Becker. Seit dem 1.12.41 führt er eine Nachtjagdstaffel. Die junge mit wenig Erfahrungen ausgestattete Staffel hat er langsam aber sicher, infolge seiner gründlich durchgeführten Ausbildungstätigkeit, auf einen guten Stand gebracht. Wo Mängel an militärischen Fähigkeiten auftraten, wurden sie aufgewogen durch seine außerordentlich Lebensreife, die ihn in vielen Lagen Rat und Tat finden läßt. So hat er seine Aufgabe als Staffelkapitän zur vollen Zufriedenheit gelöst. Oblt. Becker steht fest auf dem Boden der nationalsozialistischen Weltanschauung. Von Seiten der Gruppe stehen einer Beförderung keine Bedenken entgegen.

[signature]

Hauptmann und Gruppenkommandeur.

Stellungnahme des Geschwaders:

Oblt. B e c k e r, seit Aufstellung der Nachtjagd in derselben tätig, hat sich auf Grund seiner hervorragenden fliegerischen Leistungen bald zu einem der besten Nachtjäger entwickelt. Oblt. B. ist technisch sehr stark interessiert, wodurch sein Verhalten oft falsch ausgelegt wird. Trotz seines an Nervösität grenzenden Temperaments ist Oblt. B. in seinen Entschlüssen sicher und hat dies durch seinen Erfolg in der Nachtjagd unter Beweis gestellt. Als Staffelkapitän hat er sich auf Grund seines Alters und seines sehr umfangreichen Wissens sehr schnell eingelebt und seine Staffel zur Zufriedenheit geführt. Oblt. B. wurde am 1.7.1942 mit dem Ritterkreuz d Eisernen Kreuzes ausgezeichnet. Er ist durch seine Einsatzfreude e Vorbild aller Untergebenen und verfügt über eine sehr gute Lehrfähigkeit. Zur Beförderung zum Hauptmann voll geeignet.

I. V.

[signature]

Oberstleutnant

Request for Promotion for First Lieutenant (Reserve) Ludwig Becker (second page) – signed by the group commander, Captain Helmut Lent and by Lieutenant Colonel Wilhelm von Friedberg, for the wing commodore, sometime after January 1, 1943.

1. J a g d d i v i s i o n   Divisionsgefechtsstand, den 2.11.1942
    Der Kommandeur

Oberleutnant B e c k e r hat 39 Nachtabschüsse und hat als Staffelkapitän mit bemerkenswerter Gründlichkeit, großer Energie und starker Beharrlichkeit, sowohl sich wie seine Staffel zu überragenden Erfolgen geführt.

Er ist zur Beförderung zum Hauptmann in jeder Hinsicht geeignet.

Request for Promotion for First Lieutenant (Reserve) Ludwig Becker (third page) – signed by the Commander, 1st Fighter Division, Kurt von Döring.

Friedrich Beckh
Fighter Pilot

"He is never satisfied with his own accomplishments."

Lieutenant Colonel Friedrich Beckh was born January 17, 1908 in Nürnberg, Bavaria. He entered the Army in 1926, serving initially as an officer candidate in communications in a cavalry unit and transferred to the *Luftwaffe* as a first lieutenant on April 1, 1935. In 1937 he was assigned to the 134th Fighter Wing "Horst Wessel" (*Jagdgeschwader 134 "Horst Wessel"*) as a captain.[13] Beckh's chain of command submitted an officer efficiency report on August 8, 1937. Lieutenant Colonel Theo Osterkamp, the group commander, wrote:[14]

> Captain Beckh is a vigorous personality with a definite concept of how to be an officer. His character is beyond criticism; despite his relatively young age, he has completed his growth and is mature. In appearance he is always correct and at times close to being shy; he is often of the opinion that his accomplishments are not yet sufficient. Has a high-level awareness of duty and responsibility, result-oriented, self-reliant and puts his whole personality into the matter at hand and is lively. As a captain in the staff, he is called on to voice his opinion in all important decisions and there he demonstrates an understanding and a concept which is far above the framework of his rank and age. As a subordinate, he is a very valuable colleague, absolutely reliable as a comrade, an example in his role as superior. Immaculate social behavior and tact.
>
> Excellent military ways, knowledge and attributes. Very good instructor. Despite the very high demands he places on his troops, he is very well liked due to his personal alertness and tough, but straight-forward and objective leadership, and he is able to sweep his men along. Beckh has definite natural leadership. As a pilot, immensely passionate, his demands are exceedingly high and he tackles his training as a fighter pilot with immense energy. In a short time, he has bridged his lack of education through intensive training on theoretical and practical subjects. Due to this – he is never satisfied with his own accomplishments – and despite otherwise severe service requirements (captain on the staff, motor vehicle officer, technical officer, mess hall supervisor), he has attained a level, which even today can be called far above the average. Relentless in his action, aware of his responsibility and with his whole personality entwined with the task, he is one of the few suitable to be the leader of a squadron, and if necessary, a group.
>
> It is recommended that Captain Beckh be retained in his position as captain on the staff and, within the group, he be introduced during the winter, by way of exchange with an older squadron leader, to the command of a fighter squadron. Then, by-passing a longer period as squadron leader, he will be considered fully suitable for employment as leader of a fighter group. Captain Beckh fills his position very well and is fully suited for promotion to the next higher service position and for attending the Air War Academy.

Lieutenant Colonel Kurt-Bertram von Döring, the wing commodore, added:

> I am in agreement with the evaluation in all points. Captain Beckh is a capable officer, far above the average.

Colonel Kurt Student, the higher air commander, could add little except: "Not yet better known to me." Major Friedrich Vollbracht, a later group commander for Beckh and the last officer to comment on the report, wrote, "Nothing to be added."

Friedrich Beckh attended the *Luftwaffe* War Academy and General Staff training and renewed a friendship with Werner Mölders, who arranged for him to serve on the staff of the 51st Fighter Wing (*Jagdgeschwader 51*) in 1940. Promoted to major, he assumed command on March 1, 1941 of the 4th Group, *Jagdgeschwader 51*, where, on March 5, he shot down his first enemy aircraft – a British Spitfire – west of Boulogne, France. He shot down a Spitfire twelve miles west of Le Tréport, France on March 10, 1941 for his second victory. He scored his third kill, a Spitfire, twelve miles north of Cap Blanc Nez, France on May 6, 1941. On May 21, 1941, Beckh achieved his fourth aerial victory, a Hurricane, six miles north of Calais, France.

Beckh took command of *Jagdgeschwader 51* on July 19, 1941 and got right to work. He shot down one enemy aircraft on July 23, two on August 8, two on August 10, one on August 12, one on August 15, one on August 16, one on August 25, three on August 27, two on September 6, two on September 8 (the 2000th victory for *Jagdgeschwader 51*) and one on September 10. On a mission on September 16, he was seriously wounded in the air by an incendiary round. The tracer went through his left foot; Beckh emergency-landed his aircraft successfully, but once on the ground did not go to a hospital for treatment. By October 3, his wound was thoroughly infected, and he entered a field hospital, where he remained until December 21, 1941. Beckh was awarded the Knight's Cross of the Iron Cross on September 18, 1941; by this date he had shot down 26 enemy aircraft and destroyed an additional 20 on the ground. The first few months of 1942 were equally successful and included 5 enemy aircraft downed on March 31, and 6 – including 3 in four minutes – on April 5. He left command of the 51st Fighter Wing "Mölders" on April 11, 1942, and briefly served on the *Luftwaffe* Air Ministry in Berlin, during which time he received the *Luftwaffe* Honor Goblet on May 11, 1942. On June 3, 1942, Lieutenant Colonel Friedrich Beckh took

Funeral for Werner Mölders – after his death, the 51st Fighter Wing (*Jagdgeschwader 51*) received the honorary title of "Mölders". Hermann Göring, in long, light coat, walking behind the caisson. Honorary pallbearers (all Knight's Cross winners, carrying swords) on each side included (in the foreground) Johann Schalk, Günther Lützow, Walter Oesau and Joachim Müncheburg. On the opposite side marched Adolf Galland, Wolfgang Falck, Herbert Kaminski and Karl-Gottfried Nordmann.

command of the 52nd Fighter Wing (*Jagdgeschwader 52*), but his tenure was brief. On June 21, 1942 his Messerschmitt Me 109F-4 took another anti-aircraft round hit during a ground-attack mission, and Beckh made an emergency landing near Waloizkij, east of Kharkov. There were some reports that he was captured alive by the Russians, but he was never seen again. At the time of his disappearance he had shot down 48 enemy aircraft, 44 on the Eastern Front.[15]

One history of *Jagdgeschwader 51 "Mölders"* opines that Beckh was not well-loved by his men during his stint as the unit commander; possibly he was viewed as a General Staff Officer from Berlin, who had come to the unit to advance his career.[16] Another source claims he was near-sighted and had a difficult time flying. But it must be remembered that Beckh was in a no-win situation, assuming command of the 51st Fighter Wing from the immensely popular, charismatic Werner Mölders, when the latter was promoted in July 1941. Mölders was less critical of Beckh and once said that Beckh flew so low in conducting ground-attack missions that he could read the house numbers on the streets of Dover.

JAGDGESCHWADER HORST WESSEL NR! 134

II. Gruppe

Nr. 1

Beurteilung

anl. der Kommandierung zum 5. Lehrgang der Höheren Luftwaffenschule, Berlin-Gatow vom 1.11. – 8.2.1938.

über den Hauptmann Friedrich B e c k h

Dienststellung: Hauptmann beim Stabe, Chef der Stabskompanie

I. Geboren am: 17.1.1908   Religion: ev.

in: Nürnberg

Verheiratet: –   Kinder: –   Söhne: –   Töchter: –

Diensteintritt: 1.4.26 Funker (Offizieranwärter)

Laufbahn: aktiv 1.4.26 bis 31.3.35 Heer
ab 1.4.35 Luftwaffe

Rangdienstalter: 1.11.35 (14)

Zeitpunkt der Übernahme der oben angegebenen Stellung: 1.3.37

Besoldungsdienstalter: 1.11.35 (C 7-I)

II. Körperliche Eignung: große, kräftige gute militärische Erscheinung

Wirtschaftliche Verhältnisse: geordnet, ohne Barvermögen, auf Gehalt angewiesen

Bestrafungen:
    keine

Stammwaffe: Artillerie

Fliegerische Verwendung:
  a) vor dem Weltkriege:
  b) im Weltkriege:
  c) im Reichsheer (Reichsmarine):
  d) in der Luftwaffe:
    Flugzeugführer: ja (Mil. Flgzf. Schein)
    Beobachter:

Sonderausbildung:
  a) vor dem Kriege oder Reichswehr: M.K.S., Fahrlehrer
  b) in der Luftwaffe:

III.

Efficiency Report for Captain Friedrich Beckh (first page) – dated August 27, 1937, on pre-printed form from the 6th Military District, with both typed and handwritten comments.

III. **Allgemeines Urteil:** Der Hauptmann B e c k h ist eine markige Persönlichkeit mit ausgeprägter Offiziersauffassung. Von untadeligem Charakter, trotz seiner verhältnismäßig jungen Jahre in sich abgeschlossen und gereift. im Auftreten stets korrekt und gelegentlich beinahe zu bescheiden, ist er oft der Meinung, noch immer nicht genügendes geleistet zu haben. Hohes Pflicht- und Verantwortungsbewustsein, zielbewußt, selbstschöpferisch und mit der ganzen Persönlichkeit in der Sache stehend und lebend. Als Hauptmann beim Stabe wird er zu allen wichtigen Entscheidungen gehört und zeigt dabei ein Verständnis und eine Auffassung, die weit über den Rahmen seiner Dienststellung und seines Alters hinausgeht. Als Untergebener ein sehr wertvoller Mitarbeiter, als Kamerad absolut verlässlich als Vorgesetzter vorbildlich. Tadellose gesellschaftliche Formen und Takt.

Ausgezeichnete militärische Formen, Kenntnisse und Eigenschaften. Sehr guter Ausbilder. Ist trotz sehr hoher Anforderungen, die er an die Truppe stellt, infolge persönlicher Frische und harter aber streng sachlicher und objektiver Frische Führung sehr beliebt und reisst mit. B e c k h ist ausgesprochene Führernatur.

Fliegerisch riesig passioniert, er verlangt ausserordentlich viel von sich und geht mit ungeheuerrer Energie an seine jagdfliegerische Ausbildung heran. Er hat in kürzester Zeit durch intensive Schulung auf theoretischer und praktischer Grundlage die mangelnde Ausbildung überbrückt. Er hat dabei - nie zufrieden mit seiner eigenen Leistung - trotz seiner sonstigen starken dienstlichen Belastung (Hauptmann beim Stabe, Kraftfahroffizier, T. Kasinovorstand) einen Stand als Jagdflieger erreicht, der heute schon als über dem Durchschnitt stehend bezeichnet werden kann. Rücksichtsloser Einsatz, jedoch verantwortungsbewusst und mit seiner ganzen Persönlichkeit mit der Sache verwachsen, ist er wie wenige zum Führer einer Staffel , gegebenenfalls einer Gruppe, geeignet.

Es wird vorgeschlagen, Hauptmann B e c k h zunächst noch in seiner Stellung als Hauptmann beim Stabe zu belassen und ihn intern innerhalb der Gruppe im Winterhalbjahr durch Austausch mit einem älteren Staffelführer, als Führer einer Jagdstaffel sich einarbeiten zu lassen. B e c k h wird dann, unter Überspringung einer längeren Staffelführerzeit, für voll geeignet gehalten, als Führer einer Jagdgruppe Verwendung zu finden.

Hauptmann B e c k h füllt seine Stellung sehr gut aus und ist zur nächsthöheren Dienststellung und zur Einberufung zur Luftkriegsakademie voll geeignet.

W e r l , den 27. 8. 37

Osterkamp
Oberstleutnant und Gruppenkommandeur

Efficiency Report for Captain Friedrich Beckh (second page) – signed by Lieutenant Colonel Theo Osterkamp, 2nd Group Commander, 134th Fighter Wing, on pre-printed form, with typed comments.

Efficiency Report for Captain Friedrich Beckh (third page) – signed by Lieutenant Colonel Kurt-Bertram von Döring, the 134th Fighter Wing commodore, by Colonel Kurt Student, the higher air commander, and by Major Friedrich Vollbracht, a later group commander for Beckh, all comments handwritten.

Hans Beisswenger
Fighter Pilot

"He enjoys the full confidence of the other pilots."

First Lieutenant Hans Beisswenger was born in the village of Mittelfischbach in the district of Schwäbisch-Hall in Württemberg on November 8, 1916. He originally entered the Army in 1937 in the *flak* artillery, but quickly began flight training. In the fall of 1940, he was assigned to the 6th Squadron of the 54th Fighter Wing "Green Heart" (*Jagdgeschwader 54 "Grünherz"*) as a second lieutenant.[17] During the Yugoslavian campaign, he registered his first aerial victory – a Yugoslav Air Force Hurricane – on April 7, 1941, and he received the Iron Cross 2nd Class on May 6, 1941.[18] On August 24, 1941 he scored his 20th victory (an I-18 fighter) – and had won the *Luftwaffe* Honor Goblet on August 9, the Iron Cross 1st Class on August 16, and the Operational Flying Clasp for Fighters in Gold on August 20 – although he had also been shot down and made a belly-landing on July 16 and had to make his way back to German lines. Beisswenger won the German Cross in Gold on October 17, 1941. By April 6, 1942 – almost one year after his first kill – he had reached 40 victories (his 40th a MiG-3); he reached 50 kills on May 8, 1942 and received the Knight's Cross of the Iron Cross from Lieutenant General Helmuth Förster at Ryelbitzi the following day, as a second lieutenant. On August 11, 1942, Beisswenger became the squadron commander of the 6th Squadron, 54th Fighter Wing; four days later he reached 75 victories. On August 23, 1942 he had his greatest day in the air up to that time, shooting down five enemy aircraft.

On September 4, 1942, Beisswenger's chain of command submitted an officer efficiency report. Captain Dietrich Hrabak, the group commander, summarized his qualifications and performance as follows:[19]

> Tall, slender appearance. Very good attributes as an athlete. Open, sincere character. Decisive and mature. Good general knowledge. Officer without criticism with well-rooted, clear opinions and appropriate demeanor. Very good military personality, self-assured. Very talented as a flyer, <u>he has excelled in action as a fighter pilot</u>.[20] During <u>449</u> combat flights, he has <u>97 kills</u> because of his audacity. As a flight and squadron leader in the air, he demonstrated discretion and good leadership talent. He enjoys the full confidence of the other pilots.

> Well-liked as a comrade and superior, and correct towards superiors. Positive as a National Socialist. Second Lieutenant Beisswenger has applied for transfer to active duty, regular peace-time officers' list. His activation would definitely be a plus for the officer corps of the *Luftwaffe*.

> As a squadron leader, he fulfilled his task <u>very well</u> and he is <u>fully eligible</u> for promotion to First Lieutenant.

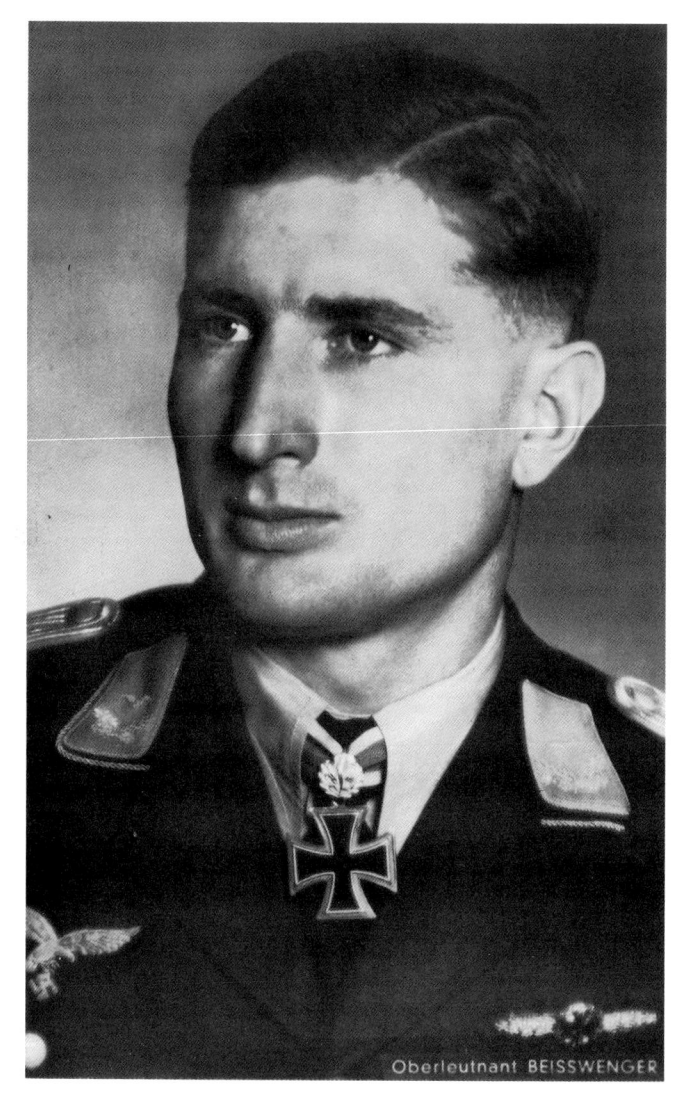

On September 26, 1942, he reached 100 aerial victories; he received the Oak Leaves to the Knight's Cross three days later, the 130th *Wehrmacht* soldier to be so honored. By the end of the year, Beisswenger had reached 119 victories; by January 23, 1943, this total had increased to 125, and by February 11th he had reached 135. Five kills on March 5, 1943 brought his total to 150. The following day, March 6, he shot down two Lavochkin LaGG-3 fighters, but during the

60

fight, his Messerschmitt Me 109G-2 took return fire in a melee with ten other enemy aircraft. Another German pilot observed Beisswenger's aircraft at low level with engine problems, attempting to return to friendly territory. Hans Beisswenger's plane crashed south of Lake Ilmen near Staraja Russa behind enemy lines, and he was posted as missing in action. His body was apparently never recovered.

First Lieutenant Hans Beisswenger, nicknamed "Biter" (*Beisser*), flew over 500 combat missions by the time of his death, achieving 152 aerial victories, of which 151 were on the Eastern Front (a sortie-to-victory ratio of about 3.29 to 1), making him the 34th highest-scoring *Luftwaffe* fighter pilot of World War II.[21]

II./Jagdgeschwader 54   Im Felde, den 4. 9. 1942
(Dienststelle, Truppenteil)

Feldpostnummer: L 37 824, Lg.Pa.Königsberg

Lichtbild

Beurteilungsnotiz

über den Leutnant (d.R.) und Staffelführer
                        Dienstgrad, Dienststellung

Vor- und Zuname: Hans Beisswenger   geb. 8.11.1916

Rangdienstalter: 1.11.1940   Dienstalterliste: B

Verheiratet, ledig, verwitwet, geschieden (Zutreffendes unterstreichen)

Jetzige Verwendung: (z. B. Staffelkapitän seit   ) Staffelführer seit 12.8.1942

Eignungsbeurteilung: siehe Rückseite

Wie wird jetzige Stelle ausgefüllt?

Geeignet zur Beförderung zum nächsthöheren Dienstgrad zum Oberleutnant

Erworbene Lw.-Scheine?   Lw.Fl.Schein

Strafen: keine

Verwendungsvorschläge: (besondere Eignung, weitere Verwendung)   Staffelkapitän einer Jagdstaffel

Unterschrift

Hauptmann und Gruppenkommandeur.
Dienstgrad und Dienststellung

876a Maximilian-Verlag, Berlin SW 68, Ritterstr. 33   Wenden!

Efficiency Report for Second Lieutenant Hans Beisswenger (front side) – dated September 4, 1942, on pre-printed form from Maximilian Publishing in Berlin, with typed comments, and one handwritten remark. Marks in pencil probably made at the *Luftwaffe* Personnel Office. Form has a place for a photo, but one was never affixed. Signed by Captain Dietrich Hrabak, Commander, 2nd Group, 54th Fighter Wing.

Zusätze zur Beurteilungsnotiz:
(Nur bei Vorlage an höhere Dienststellen)

Große, schlanke Erscheinung. Sportlich sehr gut veranlagt.

Offener, gerader Charakter. Bestimmt und ausgereift. Gutes Allgemeinwissen. Tadelloser Offizier mit gefestigten, klaren Anschauungen und entsprechendem Auftreten.

Sehr gute militärische Erscheinung, sicher in seinem Auftreten. Fliegerisch sehr gut veranlagt hat er sich im Einsatz als Jagdflieger hervorragend bewährt. In 449 Feindflügen konnte er durch sein schneidiges Draufgängertum bisher 97 Abschüsse erzielen. Als Schwarm- und Staffelführer zeigte er in der Luft Umsicht und gute Führungseigenschaften. Er genießt volles Vertrauen sämtlicher Flugzeugführer.

Als Kamerad und Vorgesetzter beliebt, gegen Vorgesetzte korrekt. Überzeugter Nationalsozialist.

Lt. Beisswenger hat einen Antrag auf Überführung zu den aktiven Friedensoffizieren gestellt. Seine Aktivierung würde unbedingt einen Gewinn für das Offz.-Korps der Luftwaffe bedeuten.

Er füllt seine Dienststellung als Staffelführer – sehr gut – aus und ist zur Beförderung zum Oberleutnant voll geeignet.

Verliehene Auszeichnungen:

E.K. 2	verliehen am 6. 5.1941
E.K. 1	verliehen am 16. 8.1941
Ehrenpokal für bes.Leist.im Luftkrieg	verliehen am 9. 8.1941
Frontflugspange in Gold	verliehen am 20. 8.1941
Deutsche Kreuz in Gold	verliehen am 27.10.1941
Ritterkreuz z.Eis.Kreuz	verliehen am 9. 5.1942

Hauptmann und Gruppenkommandeur.

Efficiency Report for Second Lieutenant Hans Beisswenger (back side) – signed by Captain Dietrich Hrabak. Includes list of awards that Beisswenger received.

Hans-Wilhelm Bertram
Bomber Pilot

"Demonstrates courage paired with calculation and logical thinking."

Captain Hans-Wilhelm Bertram was born on May 17, 1918 in Breitenhof, Saxony. Bertram joined the *Luftwaffe* on August 1, 1939. He joined several air-sea units before being assigned to the 106th Bomber Group (*Kampfgruppe 106*). On July 1, 1940, Bertram, flying in a Junkers Ju 88, won the Iron Cross 2nd Class for operations against England as part of the 9th Air Division, flying out of the Netherlands. He received the Iron Cross 1st Class on April 6, 1941 and the Operational Flying Clasp for Bombers in Gold on May 24, 1941.

On February 20, 1942, his chain of command in *Kampfgruppe 106* submitted him for promotion to first lieutenant. By this time, Bertram had flown 122 combat missions, including long-range reconnaissance. The acting commander of the group, Captain Sämischen, wrote, in part:[22]

> **Short evaluation by the group commander:** Open, decent character. Very talented with diverse interests. Possesses healthy ambition, good service knowledge. Immaculate appearance within and outside of the service. Modest officer with expressed feeling for duty and eagerness for service. Second Lieutenant Bertram is in possession of expressed sense for flying and has a talent for adaptation. Against the enemy, Second Lieutenant Bertram demonstrates courage paired with calculation and logical thinking. For his eagerness for combat, he was awarded the Iron Cross 2nd Class on July 1, 1940, the Iron Cross 1st Class on April 6, 1941 and the Operational Flying Clasp for Bombers in Gold on May 24, 1941. Second Lieutenant Bertram possesses immaculate military and social style. Well-liked comrade. Second Lieutenant Bertram is fully eligible for promotion to First Lieutenant (Reserve).

Five days later, Major General Ullrich Kessler, the Air Commander Atlantic (*Fliegerführer Atlantik*), added his own short comment: "In agreement."

In August 1942, the 106th Bomber Group became part of the 6th Bomber Wing (*Kampfgeschwader 6*), and Bertram served as the Commander of the 3rd Squadron, 6th Bomber Wing, as part of the 3rd Air Fleet. He won the *Luftwaffe* Honor Goblet on September 13, 1942 and the German Cross in Gold on May 25, 1944, which listed him in the 5th Squadron, 6th Bomber Wing. After conducting 169 combat missions over England and on the Invasion Front in France, Captain Hans-Wilhelm Bertram received the Knight's Cross of the Iron Cross on January 14, 1945, as the Commander, 3rd Squadron, 6th Bomber Wing.[23]

Geheim!

1. Luftflottenkommando 3   Gefechtsstand, den 20.2.42.
2. Kampfgruppe 106   Wehrmachtteil: Luftwaffe
3. WBK S a g a n
4. Vorgeschlagen gem.: R.d.L.u.Ob.d.L.-LP- Az.21.p.12.12.Nr.7612/42
                     vom 29.Januar 1942
5. Waffengattung: Fliegertruppe

V o r s c h l a g
zur Beförderung eines Offiziers(d.B.)zum nächsthöheren Dienstgrad

Auf dem Dienstwege
         an
                 R.d.L.u.Ob.d.L.-LP-
                                 B e r l i n.

Zur Beförderung zum Oberleutnant (d.R.) wird in Vorschlag gebracht:

Vor u. Zuname: Wilhelm B e r t r a m
Geburtsdatum: 17.Mai 1918
Jetziger Dienstgrad: Leutnant d.Res.
Rangdienstalter: 1.Dezember 1939
6. Eingesetzt als: Flugzeugführer und T.O.
7. Geeignet zum: Staffel-T.O.
Aktiver Wehrdienst seit 1.8.39: von 1.7.39 bis 30.9.39 Flg.W.Sch.See
                                       Parow,
                                 vom 1.10.39 bis 21.10.39 3./Fl.E.Batl.26
                                 Cammin,
                                 vom 22.10.39 bis17.12.39 K.A.St.2/406
                                 Hörnum/Sylt,
                                 vom 19.12.39 bis 10.1.40 3./Flg.Erg.Batl
                                 26 Ost-Dievenow,
                                 vom 11.1.40 bis 30.6.40 Flg.Erg.Gr.See
                                 1.Staffel Kamp,
                                 ab 1.7.40 K.St. 1/106

Teilnahme an welchen Kämpfen: ab 1.7.40 Fernaufklärung in der Nordsee
                                 und im Atlantik,Bekämpfung engl.Ein=
                                 fuhrhäfen u.Industriezentren,Schiffs=
                                 zielbekämpfung (insgesamt 122 Feindfl.)

Wird vorgeschlagen zur Beförderung zum: Oberleutnant d.R.

Kurze Beurteilung durch den Regimentskommandeur,selbst.Batl.-usw.Kdr. hinsichtlich dienstlicher Leistung,Führerpersönlichkeit und Stellung im Kameradenkreise.

                                                       b.wenden !

Request for Promotion for Second Lieutenant (Reserve) Wilhelm Bertram (front side) – dated February 20, 1942, typed on blank paper. Markings in various colors of pencil were probably made later at the *Luftwaffe* Personnel Office.

Kurze Beurteilung durch den Gruppenkommandeur:

Offener, ehrlicher Charakter. Sehr gut begabt und vielseitig interessiert. Besitzt gesunden Ehrgeiz, gute dienstl. Kenntnisse. Tadelloses Auftreten in u. außer Dienst. Bescheidener Offizier mit ausgeprägtem Pflichtgefühl und Diensteifer.

Ltn. B. besitzt ausgesprochenes flieg. Gefühl und Einfühlungsvermögen.

Vor dem Feind zeigte Ltn. B. Schneid gepaart mit Besonnenheit u. logischer Überlegung. Seine Einsatzfreudigkeit wurde mit dem EK II am 1.7.40, mit dem EK I am 6.4.41 und der Frontflugspange in Gold am 24.5.41 anerkannt.

Ltn. B. besitzt einwandfreie militärische und gesellschaftliche Formen. Beliebter Kamerad.

Ltn. B. ist voll zur Beförderung zum Obltn. d. R. geeignet.

Sämischen

Durch Offizier geschrieben!   Hauptmann und Gruppenkommandeur

Fliegerführer Atlantik   Gefechtsstand, den 25. Februar 1942.

Einverstanden,

Generalleutnant u. Fliegerführer Atlantik

Request for Promotion for Second Lieutenant (Reserve) Wilhelm Bertram (back side) – signed by Captain Sämischen as the rater and Major General Ulrich Kessler as the senior rater.

Heinrich Boecker
Bomber Pilot

"Goal-oriented."

Captain Heinrich "Pelle" Boecker was born April 14, 1912 near Herford in North Rhine-Westphalia. His father was killed in action in World War I on January 4, 1915. Very early in his career, on December 28, 1940, Boecker was evaluated in an efficiency report submitted by his squadron commander, First Lieutenant Horst Beeger, who wrote, in part:[24]

Mental and physical attributes: intelligent, mentally flexible, many interests. Strong, slim appearance.

Character attributes: As to character without criticism; immaculate appearance, energetic, goal-oriented, very good understanding of service, military demeanor.

Service use: pilot

Service knowledge and accomplishments: Boecker is a very good pilot with great experience in the air. He has proven his talent on 50 combat missions, which he conducted with skill and deliberation and has shown courage, dash and prudence. He possesses a correct, military appearance, has a good general education, and due to his modesty and spirit of camaraderie, he is well regarded and liked.

Leadership: very good

Suitability: For nomination as a candidate for wartime officer

Assigned to the 3rd Squadron, 1st Demonstration Wing (*Lehrgeschwader 1*), on May 20, 1941, Master Sergeant Boecker's Junkers Ju 88A-5 sank a 6,000-ton transport ship off Crete. Two days later, on May 22, his aircraft was shot down off Monemvasia, Greece by British naval anti-aircraft fire, but he and his crew were rescued. Flying out of Rhodes in the 3rd Squadron on August 6, 1941, First Lieutenant Heinrich Boecker – in his Junkers Ju 88A-5 – conducted a bombing mission against the Port of Suez, Egypt. The electric fuel pump on his aircraft malfunctioned and Boecker was forced to make an emergency landing on the Turkish coast. He was interned (Turkey was a neutral power) from August 7 to December 31, 1941. Boecker later assumed command of the 12th Squadron on March 20, 1942 and held this position until July 9, 1944. Initially, the squadron was directly subordinated to the Air Commander Africa (*Fliegerführer Afrika*), flying escort missions for supply ships crossing the Mediterranean.

The squadron's missions soon broadened. On June 8, 1942, Boecker and his 12th Squadron – in concert with Stukas from the 3rd Stuka Wing (*Sturzkampfgeschwader 3*) – bombed the fortifications at Bir Hacheim, the southernmost pillar of the British Gazala defensive line, 55 miles southwest of Tobruk. Some 4,000 Free French troops, augmented by British Commonwealth soldiers, held the strongpoint, which included concrete emplacements and deep dugouts. The Africa Corps launched numerous attacks on the position – spearheaded by the 90th Light Africa Division – but these final air attacks finally expedited its collapse on June 11, 1942. Tobruk fell to Field Marshal Rommel ten days later. Boecker won the German Cross in Gold on June 9, 1942 for these attacks. In another bombing mission, Boecker attacked a British tank column at Alam el Halfa. Captain Heinrich Boecker won the Knight's Cross of the Iron Cross as the Commander, 12th Squadron, *Lehrgeschwader 1* on February 29, 1944, just after the unit's operations against the Allied amphibious landings at Anzio, Italy. Heinrich "Pelle" Boecker died on February 2, 1987 in Bielefeld.[25] He is buried there at the *Sennefriedhof* (Section N, Grave 2395).

Luftwaffe Efficiency & Promotion Reports

3./L G 1   Orleans-Bricy 28.12.40
(Dienststelle)   (Ort und Tag)

Beurteilung*)

des *Ofw. Heinrich Boecker*
(Dienstgrad, Vor- und Familienname)

a) Geistige und körperliche Anlagen: *Intelligent, geistig beweglich, militärisch interessiert. Kräftige, schlanke Erscheinung.*

b) Charaktereigenschaften: *[handwritten entry]*

c) Dienstliche Verwendung: *Rottenführer*
(z. B. Flugzeugführer, Hilfsbeobachter, Bordfunker, Flugmotorenschlosser, Horchfunker, Meßmann, Geräteverwalter, Krankenträger usw.)

d) Besondere Ausbildung: *ELF Blindflug 2 (Bricy)*
(z. B. abgelegte Prüfung, Militärführerschein, Blindflugausbildung usw.)

e) Dienstliche Kenntnisse und Leistungen: *Er ist ein sehr guter Rottenflieger mit großer fliegerischer Erfahrung, hat mit 50 mit Geschick u. Erfolgen auch gegen Feindflieger ... besitzt ein korrektes, militärisches Auftreten ...*

f) Führung: *sehr gut*

g) Eignung: 1. Zur Beförderung zum nächsthöheren Dienstgrad: _____

2. Zur Ernennung: *Einsatz-Offz.-Anwärter*
(z. B. Uffz. Anw. d. B., Res. Offz. Anw.)

3. Für welche Verwendung: _____
(z. B. Bordmechaniker, Bekl. Verw., Oberfeldw.)

Beeger
(Unterschrift des Disziplinarvorgesetzten)
Oberleutnant u. Staffelkapitän

*) Zum Vervollständigen und zum Abschließen der Beurteilung kann auch die Rückseite benutzt werden.

Nr. 132 c. WL. Nordmann & Paersche, Erfurt.

Efficiency Report for Heinrich Boecker (one side only) – dated December 12, 1940 and signed by First Lieutenant Horst Beeger. Form is pre-printed from the Nordmann firm in Erfurt, and completed in ink by the rater.

Rudolf Böhlein

Fallschirmjäger

"He has endurance and is tough."

Captain Rudolf Böhlein was born on January 4, 1917 in Schwabach near Nürnberg, Bavaria. He entered the Army in 1936, and after two years at the Army Non-commissioned Officer School, was assigned to several mountain infantry units. He fought in Poland in 1939, winning the Iron Cross 2nd Class on October 1. In 1941, Böhlein transferred to the *Luftwaffe* and attended airborne school in Stendal. He was also promoted to second lieutenant on June 17, 1941. He was named a platoon leader in the 9th Company, 4th Paratroop Regiment (*Fallschirmjäger Regiment 4*) on March 1, 1942. Three months later, he took command of the regiment's engineer platoon. Fighting in Russia, he won the Iron Cross 1st Class on January 4, 1943.

The unit then deployed to Sicily, south of Catania. Defending at the Bottaceto Ditch, south of the city, they held out until August when they withdrew to the Italian mainland. Böhlein made first lieutenant on December 10, 1943 and became the acting commander of the 2nd Company on January 15, 1944. Now fighting on the Italian mainland, the regiment then moved into the Cassino defensive positions. Böhlein received the German Cross in Gold on February 24, 1944. On March 19, the Germans conducted a fierce night attack against Castle Hill, overlooking Cassino, with the 1st Battalion, 4th Paratroop Regiment. The 2nd Company, led by the engineer platoon, proved especially noteworthy in the attack, with some of the paratroopers reaching the medieval keep held by the 5th Indian Brigade and entering the courtyard of the fort. He took command of the 2nd Company on June 15, 1944, but was wounded in action on June 26.

On November 11, 1944, the chain of command recommended Rudolf Böhlein for accelerated promotion to captain. Rudolf Böhmler, his commander, wrote the following:[26]

> First Lieutenant Boehlein is above average in his general education and military knowledge. Physically, he is trained in many sport disciplines; he has endurance and is tough. Boehlein possesses a great amount of energy.

> As to his character, First Lieutenant Boehlein is an open, true and uncomplicated person, who loves truth and has an expressed feeling for justice. His outer appearance presents a hard, good soldierly image. First Lieutenant Boehlein has the nature of a leader, whom the soldiers willingly follow; he is able to create enthusiasm and is uplifting. First Lieutenant Boehlein is the typical paratrooper officer. His attitude towards National Socialism is well-rooted and convincing. Due to his many operational experiences, he is well-versed in service knowledge and accomplishments. Talented as instructor.

> He has excelled as a company leader. His alertness and his awareness of his responsibility as well as his readiness for combat, have matured him into a good troop leader. In addition, as company leader, he again and again excelled in his care for and personal engagement with his soldiers. He is a passionate soldier and is exemplary in his readiness for combat. First Lieutenant Boehlein is fully qualified for preferential promotion to captain.

Brigadier General Richard Heidrich, 1st Paratroop Division Commander, added the following comment.

> In agreement and seconding. First Lieutenant Böhlein [Boehlein], 4th Paratroop Regiment is, without reservation, qualified for preferential promotion to Major.

On November 30, 1944, First Lieutenant Rudolf Böhlein received his long-overdue Knight's Cross of the Iron Cross for his actions at Cassino. He was promoted to Captain on January 1, 1945, and on March 13, 1945 assumed command of the 2nd Battalion, 4th Paratroop Regiment. There is considerable doubt concerning his fate at the end of the war. Franz Thomas and Günter Wegmann in *Die Ritterkreuzträger der Deutschen Wehrmacht 1939-1945, Teil II: Fallschirmjäger*, state that he survived the war and spent through 1946 as a prisoner of war. The official on-line website concerning the Knight's Cross also shows that he survived. However, the German War Graves Commission states that Böhlein was killed in action on April 19, 1945 south of Buotto, Italy and is buried in the Germany Military Cemetery at Futa Pass (Block 45, Grave 130).[27]

Fallschirm-Jaeger-Regiment 4   O.U., d. 8.11.44.
Abt. IIa

V o r s c h l a g
zur
b e v o r z u g t e n   B e f o e r d e r u n g

gem.R.d.L.u.Ob.d.L. LP.Nr.71 489(2,ID)
II.Angel.vom 22.12.42.,Abschn.A.

zum	:	Hauptmann (Tr.O.)
fuer	:	Oblt.(Tr.O.) B o e h l e i n , Rudolf
Dienststellung	:	Komp.-Fuehrer seit 15.1.44. (2.Komp.) ab 8.11.Fuehrer 11./Fsch.Jg.Rgt.4
Rangdienstalter	:	1.12.41. (483)
Befoerderungsdaten	:	1.4.41. Leutnant, 1.1.44. Oberleutnant
Geburtsdatum	:	4.1.17.
Auszeichnungen	:	E.K.II.Kl. am 1.10.39., E.K.I.Kl. am 4.1.43., Deutsche Kreuz in Gold am 24.2.44.z Ritterkreuz des Eisernen Kreuzes vorgeschlagen 2.11.1944

B e u r t e i l u n g :

    Oblt. Boehlein steht in seiner Allgemeinbildung und militaerischem Wissen ueber dem Durchschnitt. Koerperlich ist er sportlich vielseitig durchgebildet, ausdauernd und zaeh. Oblt.Boehlein verfuegt ueber grosse Energie.
    Charakterlich ist Oblt.Boehlein ein offener, ehrlicher und unkomplizierter Mensch, sehr wahrheitsliebend und mit einem ausgepraegten Gerechtigkeitsgefuehl. Aeusserlich straffes Auftreten, gute soldatische Erscheinung.
    Oblt.Boehlein ist eine Fuehrernatur, dem die Soldaten gern und willig folgen, er kann begeistern und mitreissen. Oblt.Boehlein ist der typische Fallschirmjaegeroffizier.
    Seine Einstellung zum Nationalsozialismus ist gefestigt und ueberzeugt.
    In dienstlichen Kenntnissen und Leistungen ist er auf Grund seiner vielen Einsaetze erfahren. Gute Ausbilderbegabung.
    Als Kompanie-Fuehrer hat er sich hervorragend bewaehrt. Seine Umsicht und sein Verantwortungsbewusstsein, sowie seine Einsatzbereitschaft haben ihn zu einem guten Truppenfuehrer heranreifen lassen. Ferner hat er sich als Kompanie-Fuehrer immer wieder durch seine Fuersorge und seinen persoenlichen Einsatz fuer seine Soldaten ausgezeichnet.
    Er ist mit Passion Soldat und in seiner Einsatzbereitschaft mustergueltig.
    Oblt.Boehlein ist zur bevorzugten Befoerderung zum Hauptmann voll geeignet.

                                                 Böhmler
                                      Oberstleutnant und Rgt.-Fuehrer.

Request for Preferred Promotion for First Lieutenant Rudolf Böhlein (front side) – dated November 8, 1944, on blank paper with typed comments, signed on this side by Lieutenant Colonel Rudolf Böhmler. Report mentions that Böhlein has been submitted for the Knight's Cross of the Iron Cross; marks in pencil probably made at the *Luftwaffe* Personnel Office.

Stellungnahme des Divisionskommandeurs:

Einverstanden und befürwortet. Oberleutnant (Tr.O.) Böhlein (Rudolf), Fsch.Jg.Regiment 4 ist zur Beförderung zum Hauptmann uneingeschränkt geeignet.

Div.Gef.Stand, den 5.11.1944.

Generalleutnant und Divisionskommandeur.

Request for Preferred Promotion for First Lieutenant Rudolf Böhlein (back side) – signed by Major General Richard Heidrich, Commander, 1st Paratroop Division.

Rudolf Böhmler
Fallschirmjäger

"He is firm during a crisis and prevails with an iron tranquility."

Colonel Rudolf Böhmler was born on June 12, 1914 in Weilimdorf/Stuttgart in Baden-Württemberg. He joined the German Army as an officer candidate on April 5, 1934 and initially served with the 13th Infantry Regiment. Böhmler then attended the War School at Dresden and the Infantry School at Döberitz, before becoming second lieutenant and a platoon leader in the 55th Infantry Regiment on April 1, 1936. In 1938, Böhmler was assigned to the Paratroop Infantry Company at Stendal, still in the Army. On August 1, 1938, the unit became a battalion, and Böhmler – along with the other soldiers – transferred to the *Luftwaffe* on December 31, 1938. Promoted to first lieutenant on April 1, 1939, Böhmler fought in Poland at the battle of Wola-Gulowska – against a Polish artillery regiment (winning the Iron Cross 2nd Class on October 13, 1939 for his actions) before becoming the acting commander of the 8th Company, 1st Paratroop Regiment (*Fallschirmjäger-Regiment 1*) on May 1, 1940. He jumped into Moerdijk, Holland with this unit (part of the 2nd Battalion) to seize a key railroad bridge over the Maas River leading to Rotterdam, holding it for seven days of continuous fighting until relieved by the advancing 9th *Panzer* Division and won the Iron Cross 1st Class on May 23, 1940.[28]

Böhmler and his unit jumped into Crete at Herákleion on the afternoon of May 20, 1941 as part of the German airborne invasion of the island.[29] On June 1, he became the acting commander of the 2nd Battalion, 3rd Paratroop Regiment (*Fallschirmjäger-Regiment 3*), a position he held until January 15, 1942. From October 1, 1941 to November 20, 1941, the unit fought along the Newa River east of Leningrad, Russia under his leadership. He was promoted to captain on February 1, 1942. On February 20, 1942, Böhmler assumed acting command of the 4th Battalion, 3rd Paratroop Regiment (and becoming commander on October 23, 1942.) He received the German Cross in Gold on April 3, 1942. On October 25, 1942, the unit deployed again to Russia and remained in the fight until March 25, 1943. During this time, Böhmler was wounded in action and received the Black Wound Badge on January 5, 1943.

On May 4, 1943, Böhmler's chain of command submitted him for an accelerated promotion to major. The regimental commander, Lieutenant Colonel Ludwig Heilmann, wrote the following:[30]

> Captain Böhmler is an energetic personality with firm character and good leadership qualities. Physically he is fit and has endurance; mentally he is inquisitive, and he possesses a good general education. His military capabilities and knowledge are very good. In training as well as the education of the soldiers in his unit as company commander and as battalion commander, he has demonstrated excellent accomplishments. He was the acting commander of the 2nd Battalion, 3rd Paratroop Regiment from June 1, 1941 to January 15, 1942 and has been the acting commander of the 4th Battalion, 3rd Paratroop Regiment since February 20, 1942. He was an exemplary leader in all the operations at the front, and he has mastered many difficult situations. He is firm during a crisis and prevails with an iron tranquility. He is also able to improvise and quickly adapts himself to every situation.
>
> In an untiring way, he cares for the men under his command, and he represents each one in a personal way. Through this, he possesses the definite confidence of his soldiers and he is valued everywhere as a just leader. He is a pleasant comrade whom you can trust anytime. The complete picture shows Böhmler as a passionate, young battalion commander, who has his unit firmly in his hands and who understands how to be its leader and who, as a National Socialist officer, lends spirit and drive to his unit.
>
> During the most recent operations on the Eastern Front, from October 25, 1942 to March 25, 1943, he once again excelled as a battalion commander. Due to the value of his personality and his accomplishments, I consider him qualified for preferential promotion.

Brigadier General Richard Heidrich added the following comment the next day:

> In agreement and seconding. Captain Böhmler, 3rd Paratroop Regiment is, without reservation, qualified for preferential promotion to Major.

On June 15, 1943, the unit was re-designated the 1st Battalion, 3rd Paratroop Regiment, and Böhmler remained in command. His unit took part in the defense at Cassino, where the battalion repelled a determined attack by the 4th Indian Division on March 17, 1944 and seized Hill 435 of Hangman's Hill. He received the Knight's Cross of the Iron Cross for this action on March 26, 1944. He took part in several more combat actions at Cassino, including a defense on May 12, 1944 against the 5th Polish Division, during which he was again wounded in action. He was subsequently promoted to lieutenant colonel on June 1, 1944. On August 20, 1944, Böhmler assumed acting command of the 4th Paratroop Regiment (*Fallschirmjäger-Regiment 4*). He was made permanent commander of the unit on January 10, 1945 and promoted to colonel on January 30, 1945. At the end of the war, Böhmler commanded several ad hoc battle groups. Rudolf Böhmler died November 11, 1968 in Stuttgart.[31]

```
Fallschirm-Jäger-Regiment 3                O.U., den 4. 5. 1943
IIa         /        21
```

<u>V o r s c h l a g</u>

zur

<u>b e v o r z u g t e n   B e f ö r d e r u n g .</u>

Gemäss R.d.L.u.Ob.d.L. LP Nr. 71 489/42 (2, ID)
II.Ang.v.22.12.42 Abschnitt A

für   Hauptmann   B ö h m l e r   Rudolf
         (Tr.O.)

<u>Dienststellung:</u>   Btl.-Kdr IV./F.J.R. 3
<u>Rangdienstalter:</u>   1. 2. 1942   (136)
Beförderungsdaten zu den beiden   1. 4. 39 zum Oberleutnant
letzten Offz.-Dienstgraden: 1. 2. 42 zum Hauptmann
<u>Geburtsdatum:</u>   12. 6. 1914
<u>Auszeichnungen:</u>   Dienstauszeichnung IV. Klasse,
                       Erinnerungsmedaille Österreich u. Sudetenland,
                       E.K. II. und I. Klasse,
                       Verwundetenabzeichen in schwarz,
                       Deutsches Kreuz in Gold.

B e g r ü n d u n g :

A) <u>Allgemeine Leistungen:</u>

Hauptmann Böhmler ist eine energische Persönlichkeit mit
festem Charakter und guten Führereigenschaften.
Er ist körperlich gewandt und ausdauernd, geistig regsam
und verfügt über eine gute Allgemeinbildung.
Sein militärisches Können und Wissen ist sehr gut. Sowohl
in der Ausbildung als auch in der Erziehung der Soldaten
hat er als Kp.-Chef und auch als Btl.-Kdr. hervorragende
Leistungen gezeigt. Er führte das II./F.J.R. 3 vom 1.6.41 -
15.1.42 und jetzt das IV./F.J.R. 3 seit dem 20.2.42. Vorbildlich als Führer war er auch bei allen Einsätzen an der
Front und hat viele schwierige Lagen gemeistert. Er ist
krisenfest und setzt sich mit eiserner Ruhe durch.
Auch improvisieren kann er und paßt sich jeder Lage rasch
an.
Für seine Untergebenen sorgt er unermüdlich und tritt für
jeden persönlich ein. Dadurch besitzt er das unbedingte
Vertrauen seiner Soldaten und ist überall als gerechter
Vorgesetzter geschätzt. Er ist ein liebenswürdiger Kamerad, auf den man sich jederzeit verlassen kann.
Im Gesamtbild zeigt Böhmler den jungen passionierten Btl.-
Kdr., der seinen Verband fest in der Hand hat und ihn zu
führen versteht und der als nationalsozialistischer Offizier der Truppe Geist und Auftrieb gibt.

<u>Wenden!</u>

Request for Preferred Promotion for Captain Rudolf Böhmler (front side) – dated May 4, 1943, on blank paper with typed comments.

20ª

B) Einzelangaben:

Böhmler hat teigenommen an folgenden Gefechten:

    am 24.9.1939   Gefecht bei Wola-Gulowska als Zug- und Stoßtruppführer,

    vom 10. - 31.5.1940 Einsatz Holland

    10. - 16.5.1940 Gefecht um die Moerdijk-Brücken (nach Fallschirmabsprung), als Führer der 8./F.J.R. 1,

    vom 20.5. - 11.7.41 Luftlandeoperation Kreta, (nach Fallschirmabsprung)

    am 21.5.1941   Seegefecht der leichten Schiffstaffel vor Kreta, als Führer einer Sondereinheit.(Einheit Böhmler),

    28.5.1941   Unterstützung der Kampfgruppe Bräuer bei Iraklion, als Führer der gleichen Einheit,

    vom 1.10.-20.11.41 Einsatz im Operationsgebiet der Ostfront, Abwehrkämpfe vor Leningrad, als Btl.-Führer.

Beim letzten Einsatz an der Ostfront vom 25.10.1942 - 25.3.194 hat er sich wiederum als Btl.-Kdr. hervorragend bewährt.

Auf Grund seines Persönlichkeitswertes und seiner Leistungen halte ich ihn zur bevorzugten Beförderung für würdig.

                                                Heilmann
                                                Oberstleutnant.

                                                Div.Gef.Std., den 5.5.1943

Stellungnahme des Divisionskommandeurs:

E i n v e r s t a n d e n und b e f ü r w o r t e t.
Hptm.(a) B ö h m l e r (Rudolf), Fallschirm-Jäger-Rgt. 3, ist zur bevorzugten Beförderung zum Major uneingeschränkt geeignet.

                                                Heidrich
                                        Generalmajor und Divisionskommandeur.

Request for Preferred Promotion for Captain Rudolf Böhmler (back side) – signed by Lieutenant Colonel Ludwig Heilmann and Brigadier General Richard Heidrich, Commander, 1st Paratroop Division.

Hans-Joachim Brand
Stuka Pilot

"The proof of descent from German or related blood of Hans-Joachim Brand and his spouse has been obtained."

Captain Hans-Joachim Brand was born May 16, 1916 at Lüneburg. He entered the *Luftwaffe* on April 1, 1936. Nicknamed "Cherry," he flew combat missions with the 77th Stuka Wing (*Sturzkampfgeschwader 77*) during the Polish campaign against targets at Hela, Modlin and Warsaw – winning the Iron Cross 2nd Class on November 1, 1939. In May 1940, during the French campaign, Brand flew with the 4th Squadron, 2nd Stuka Wing "Immelmann" (*Sturzkampfgeschwader 2 "Immelmann"*) against enemy targets at Eben Emael, Liege, the Maas River, Flanders and Dunkirk.[32] He won the Iron Cross 1st Class on July 7, 1940 and was promoted to technical sergeant on August 1.

Brand was on track to be commissioned, but one of the requirements to be an officer was for his chain of command to certify his background and fitness. On June 22, 1941, First Lieutenant Helmut Leicht, the commander of the Supplemental Squadron – a training formation for new unit pilots – of the 77th Stuka Wing submitted the following evaluation:[33]

> The final results concerning suitability outside of the service of Brand, Hans-Joachim, born on May 16, 1916, to become wartime officer was presented by the respective troop commander according to regulations as follows:
> According to the Office of the State Police, Lüneburg, Brand is charged neither with matters of political nor of an espionage nature.
> According to the State Judicial Offices, Lüneburg, Brand has no convictions of any kind against him.
> An immaculate certificate of conduct by the police has been submitted. A personal hand-written curriculum vitae stating the date of its execution has been presented. An explanation for preliminary proof of suitability outside of the service according to "Summary regulations regarding future wartime officer" has been submitted. Immaculate character information by 3 citizens of good reputation has been submitted. The proof of descent from German or related blood of Hans-Joachim Brand and his wife has been obtained.[34]

Brand was promoted to second lieutenant near the start of the 1941 campaign against Russia, achieving his 200th combat mission in January 1942, now with the 8th Squadron, *Sturzkampfgeschwader 77* (with the 4th Air Fleet), against Russian shipping off Feodosia in the Crimea. Brand received the German Cross in Gold for these achievements on January 13, 1942. He was promoted to first lieutenant on April 1, 1943 and to captain on November 1, 1943. He flew his 500th combat mission on August 3, 1943. Hans-Joachim Brand was awarded the Knight's Cross of the Iron Cross on December 12, 1943 as a captain and Squadron Commander, 1st Squadron, 77th Ground-Attack Wing (*Schlachtgeschwader 77*, which had been formed in October 1943 from *Sturzkampfgeschwader 77*). By May 16, 1944, Brand had totaled 800 combat missions, now as the Commander, 2nd Squadron. In November 1944, he assumed command of the 1st Group, *Schlachtgeschwader 77*.

On April 18, 1945, while flying a ground-attack mission, Hans-Joachim Brand's Focke-Wulf Fw 190F was struck by Russian anti-aircraft fire at a height of 1600 feet, and he fatally crashed near Alteno/Luckau, between Cottbus and Jüterbog, in the Spreewald. His body was never recovered. He had flown 964 combat missions and was recommended for the award of the Oak Leaves to his Knight's Cross, but it was never approved.[35]

Werner Breese
Reconnaissance Pilot

"Passionate pilot."

Captain Werner Breese was born April 6, 1913. Flying out of Cologne-Wahn, during the French campaign, he won the Iron Cross 2nd Class on May 27, 1940 and the Iron Cross 1st Class on August 10, 1940, in support of the 2nd Air Fleet. Breese won the *Luftwaffe* Honor Goblet on August 20, 1941 and the German Cross in Gold on November 21, 1941 as a second lieutenant in the 5th Squadron, 122nd Reconnaissance Group (*Aufklärungsgruppe 122*). Flying Junker Ju 88s, the squadron – initially based at Pleskau and subsequently at Grosskino – flew long-range reconnaissance missions for the 1st Air Corps in the northern sector of operations on the Eastern Front from 1941 to 1944. On March 30, 1943, Breese earned the Operational Flying Clasp for Reconnaissance in Gold with Pendant. He was awarded the Knight's Cross of the Iron Cross on February 29, 1944 as a pilot in the 5th Squadron. On April 1, 1944, he became a flight instructor at the 101st Long-Range Reconnaissance Wing (*Fernaufklärungsgeschwader 101*), a school unit.

On July 10, 1944, the chain of command in the 101st Long-Range Reconnaissance Wing submitted an officer efficiency report on Werner Breese. Captain Hünsdorff, the acting group commander, wrote the following:[36]

Short Assessment (Personal values, National Socialist attitude, accomplishments before the enemy, service accomplishments, mental and physical attributes and suitability, infantry experience, when and how obtained)**:** Open and self-confident character, he is a mature person, definitely reliable and conscientious. His understanding of the service is exemplary. Well-liked among his comrades. Respected by his superiors due to his eagerness to serve and his sense of duty. Convinced National Socialist, able to pass on this philosophy to others. He has fully stood the test in front of the enemy. Was awarded the Knight's Cross. Has very well mastered his position as flight instructor. He understands how to correctly employ pilots. His eagerness in service is untiring. Mentally very well gifted. Good talent for understanding and reaction. Physically tough and able to bear any burden. Initiative and improvisational talents are present to a high degree. Based on his military attitude and his personal values, he is promising for becoming a very good squadron commander. No infantry experience.

Strong Traits: Passionate pilot. Strong sense of duty and untiring work ethic.

Weak Traits: None are shown.

Summary Assessment: Above Average.
(Above Average, Average, Below Average)

How well is the current position being fulfilled: Very well fulfilled.
(Use only: Very well fulfilled, well fulfilled, fulfilled, not fulfilled)

Suitable for promotion to the next higher service grade: Yes, without reservations.

Suitable as: Squadron Commander

Subordinated to the person submitting this review: since April 29, 1944.

Colonel Roman Schneider, the *Geschwader* commander – and who had been Breese's commander earlier in *Aufklärungsgruppe 122* – wrote the following at Perleberg on July 18: "I am in agreement with the evaluation. Captain Breese has proven himself in his position as flight instructor."

Werner Breese survived the war and died on February 17, 1995 at Hohenwestedt/Rendsburg in Schleswig-Holstein.[37]

I./Fernaufkl.Geschwader 101
(Dienststelle, nicht Feldpost-Nr.) Großenhain, den 10. Juli 19 44

Kriegsbeurteilung zum 1. August 19 44   56

für Offiziere, ausschl. San.-, Vet.-Offz.

über den

Hptm.(Tr.)   1.1.43 (-) A1   Werner   Breese
Dienstgrad¹) R.D.A.(Ord.Nr.)u. Dienstaltersliste   Vorname   Name

6.4.1913   kv. - tdf.
geboren am   verheiratet, ledig, verwitwet, geschieden   Wehrdienstauglichkeit²)
              (Zutreffendes unterstreichen)   (kv., gv. Feld, gv. H., tropentauglich, tropenuntauglich)

Drogist
Zivilberuf (falls vorhanden)

Fl.Horstkdtr. A (o) 39/III, Großenhain   W.B.K. Stargard/Pomm.
jetzige Verwendung seit 1.4.44 Flugausb.Ltr. Friedensdienststelle und W.B.K.³)

terminmäßige Vorlage zum 1.8.1944.
Anlaß der Vorlage⁴)

Deutsche Auszeichnungen des jetzigen Krieges mit Verleihungsdaten und Angabe, ob und zu welchen Auszeichnungen vorgeschlagen: Ostmed. 7.7.42, EK.II 27.5.40, EK.I 10.8.40, Ehrenpokal 20.8.41, Dt.Kr.i.Gold 21.11.41, Fr.Fl.Sp.i.Gold m.Anhäng. 30.3.43, Ritterkreuz d. Eisernen Kreuzes 29.2.1944.

¹) Genaue Angabe, ob Tr.-Offz., Erg.-Offz, Offz. z. D., Res.-Offz., Kr.-Offz., z. V. Offz.
²) In zweifelhaften Fällen neu festzustellen.
³) Dienststelle, welche Friedensgebührn. zahlt, und zuständiges Wehrbezirkskommando.
⁴) Z. B. Versetzung zur III./K. G. 2, terminmäßige Vorlage zum 1. 5. 1943.

Kurze Beurteilung (Persönlichkeitswert, nationalsozialistische Haltung, Bewährung vor dem Feinde, dienstliche Leistungen, geistige und körperliche Anlagen und Eignung, infanteristische Erfahrungen, wann und wo erworben):
Offener und selbstbewußter Charakter, gereifter Mensch, unbedingt zuverlässig und gewissenhaft. Seine Dienstauffassung ist vorbildlich. Im Kameradenkreise beliebt. Bei Vorgesetzten infolge seiner Einsatzfreude und seines Pflichtbewußtseins geachtet. Überzeugter Nationalsozialist, der dieses Gedankengut anderen vermitteln kann. Vor dem Feinde hat er sich voll bewährt. Wurde mit dem Ritterkreuz ausgezeichnet. Hat sich als Flugausbildungsleiter sehr gut eingearbeitet. Er versteht es, die Flugzeugführer richtig anzusetzen. Sein Diensteifer ist unermüdlich. Geistig gut veranlagt. Gutes Auffassungs- und Reaktionsvermögen. Körperlich zäh und belastungsfähig. Eigeninitiative und Improvisationsgabe in reichem Maße vorhanden. Auf Grund seiner soldatischen Einstellung und seiner Persönlichkeitswerte verspricht er ein guter Staffelkapitän zu werden. Infanteristische Erfahrungen wurden nicht erworben.

Starke Seiten: Passionierter Flugzeugführer. Starkes Pflichtbewußtsein und unermüdliche Arbeitsnatur.

Schwache Seiten: Treten nicht hervor.

Zusammenfassendes Urteil: Über Durchschnitt
(über Durchschnitt, Durchschnitt, unter Durchschnitt):

Wie wird jetzige Stelle ausgefüllt? Sehr gut ausgefüllt
(Es sind nur die Ausdrücke „sehr gut ausgefüllt", „gut ausgefüllt", „ausgefüllt", „nicht ausgefüllt" zu verwenden).

Geeignet zur Beförderung zum nächsthöheren Dienstgrad? Zur Beförderung zum nächsthöheren Dienstgrad uneingeschränkt geeignet.

2409. Druck: Alfred Hermanns, Klotzsche 9.'43 — Din A 4

Efficiency Report for Captain Werner Breese (front side) – dated July 10, 1944, on pre-printed form, from the Alfred Hermanns firm, with typed comments.

Eignung für welche nächsthöhere Verwendung?⁵)	Staffelkapitän
für welche besondere oder anderweitige Verwendung?⁶)	Staffelkapitän
Vorschlag für Verwendung in nächster Zeit?⁷)	Vorerst noch Belassung an bisheriger Stelle
Sprachkenntnisse (keine Schulkenntnisse) a) abgelegte Prüfungen: (z. B. Dolmetscherprüfung 1. 10. 42) b) Beherrschung der Sprache: z. B. durch Aufenthalt im Ausland)	Keine Keine
Eröffnung zu welchen Punkten, wann, wie (mündlich oder schriftlich) und durch wen?	Keine
Strafen sind mit vollem Straftenor sowie Vermerk über Vollstreckung abschriftlich als Anlage der Kriegsbeurteilung beizuheften.	Keine
Dem Beurteilenden bekannt seit / unterstellt seit	29.4.1944
Ausbildung a) erworbene Scheine: (L.F., E.L.F., L.B. usw.) b) Sonderausbildung: (z. B. Bild-Offz., Techn. Offz., Meß-Offz., Funk-Drahtnachr.-Offz., W.K.S.)	ELF. II, LB. Keine

Unterschrift   Hauptmann, m.d.W.d.G.d.Kdrs.b.
Dienstgrad und Dienststellung

Beitrag des Chefs des Generalstabes der vorgesetzten Kdo.-Behörde (nur bei Genst.-Offz. in Stabsstellungen und zur Dienstleistung zum Generalstab kommandierten Offizieren):

Zusätze vorgesetzter Dienststellen:
Fernaufklärungsgeschwader 101   Perleberg, 18. 7. 44
K o m m o d o r e

Mit der Beurteilung einverstanden. Hptm. Breese hat sich in seiner Stellung als Flugausbildungsleiter bewährt.

---

⁵) Gilt für alle Offz., für Truppenoffz. hinsichtlich Eignung zur Führung des nächsthöheren Verbandes, für Genst.-Offz. hinsichtlich Eignung zum Chef oder Ia, Ic der Luftfl., Flieger-Korps, Flak-Korps, Flieger-Div., Flak-Div. zur Versetzung in den Genst., zur Kommandierung in den Genst.

⁶) Z. B. höherer Adjutant, Erzieher, Lehrer, auf Spezialgebieten, auf Grund von Sprachkenntnissen, im Attachédienst; für Genst.-Offz. hinsichtlich Eignung für Verwendung im Quartiermeisterdienst, im Ic-Dienst, im Transportwesen, als Lehrer für Genst.-Lehrgang (Taktik bzw. Qu.-Dienst); besondere Anlagen für Kriegsgeschichte, Wehrwirtschaft.

⁷) Z. B. „noch halbjährige Belassung in bisheriger Stelle" oder „alsbaldige Verwendung als Geschwaderkommodore".

Efficiency Report for Captain Werner Breese (back side) – signed by Captain and acting group commander Hünsdortt as the rater and Colonel Roman Schneider as the senior rater.

Gerhard Brenner
Bomber Pilot

"Demonstrated superhuman accomplishments."

First Lieutenant Gerhard Brenner was born August 29, 1918 in Ludwigsburg, Baden-Württemberg. He entered the *Luftwaffe* on November 11, 1942 and subsequently attended flight training at Herzogenaurach and Darmstadt. Upon completion of training, he joined the 1st Demonstration Wing (*Lehrgeschwader 1*). During the German campaign in Norway, Brenner flew one combat mission; during the first ten days of the French campaign, he flew an additional seven combat missions with the 2nd Squadron. At the end of May, he flew thirteen combat sorties against British forces in Flanders and at Dunkirk. On June 4, he flew a combat mission against French airfields near Paris. He flew two combat missions during the first two weeks of the Battle of Britain and followed that on August 27, 1940 with an attack on the docks at Southampton.[38] Between August 29, 1940 and January 1, 1941, Brenner flew fifty-two combat missions over England, to include the attack on Coventry on November 14/15, as part of the 4th Air Corps (3rd Air Fleet).[39] He assumed command of the 1st Squadron, 1st Group (Bombers), 1st Demonstration Wing on December 12, 1941. Between April 4, 1941 and May 9, 1941, he flew additional combat flights against Yugoslavian and Greek targets. From May 10, 1941, he was in continuous combat in the Mediterranean, North Africa and against Malta. Gerhard Brenner received the Knight's Cross of the Iron Cross as a second lieutenant on July 5, 1941.

On April 4, 1942, his group commander, Captain Joachim Helbig, submitted a special efficiency report on Gerhard Brenner. It read in part:[40]

> With an exceedingly valuable combination of outstanding mental and physical attributes, combined with excellent, exemplary character attributes, Brenner has real leadership qualities far beyond the average which, despite his young age, have demonstrated excellent military knowledge (accomplishments) and a particular excellent conduct in the face of the enemy during the war.
>
> After his transfer on November 1, 1939, as officer candidate to a frontline unit, in a short period of time he gained the highest respect and recognition, and developed a mature understanding and attitude towards the profession of an officer. First as a pilot, later as squadron technical officer and representative of his squadron, he proved through his untiring work and by perfecting his military knowledge, his high personality values and his accomplishments against the enemy. His unselfish work attained, and will continue to attain in the future, the highest results, by exemplary heroic leadership of his personality against the enemy. On 259 combat flights against the enemy, Brenner demonstrated superhuman accomplishments and attained the greatest results, which assured that he was the most successful bomber pilot in the group.
>
> Due to his military accomplishments in general and his successes in the face of the enemy, on March 1, 1942 he was made acting commander of his squadron, ahead of four active-duty first lieutenants and in a short time will take over the position of squadron commander.
>
> Awards to date: Iron Cross 2nd Class, Iron Cross 1st Class, Knight's Cross of the Iron Cross, after 202 combat missions against the enemy.
>
> Special successes after the awarding of the Knights Cross: A further 57 combat missions, damaged a heavy cruiser through a direct hit, 14,000 to 16,000 tons of commercial shipping, approximately 25 vehicles, two enemy barracks, about 6 enemy planes on the ground and key war installations on Malta (airfields of Luka and Gudia). In just three of the heaviest air battles, his aircraft was damaged to such an extent that he had to conduct the return flights on a single engine and land on a damaged landing gear. One confirmed downing of a Gloster and one severely damaged Wellington through shots to the engines.
>
> Indisputable military leadership and immaculate behavior. Brenner is well-grounded in National Socialist ideology.

On May 11, 1942, Brenner took part in an attack, led by Captain Jochen Helbig, on a force of British destroyers south of Crete. During the fight, Brenner's crew reported achieving a direct hit on one of the enemy ships; the *HMS Lively*, *HMS Kipling* and *HMS Jackal* were all sunk in the encounter.

Gerhard Brenner's Junkers Ju 88A-4 was shot down south of Crete during an attack on a British convoy. Brenner and his crew survived ditching at sea and deployed a rubber dinghy, floating for several days. Bad weather and high seas, however, doomed the crew and they could not be rescued. His body was never found.[41]

I./Lehrgeschwader 1 Gefechtsstand, den 14.4.1942
    Abt. II

S o n d e r b e u r t e i l u n g

des Oberleutnant Gerhard B r e n n e r.

Vor - u. Zuname:	Gerhard B r e n n e r
Geburtsdatum:	29. August 1918
Rangdienstalter:	1. 4. 1942
Jetziger Dienstgrad:	Oberleutnant (akt.)
Eingesetzt als :	Staffelführer
Geeignet zum:	Staffelkapitän
Aktiver Wehrdienst seit:	3. 11. 1937

Teilnahme an welchen Kämpfen:

    26.8.39 bis 12.9.39 Feldzug gegen Polen.
    13.9.39 bis 27.11.39 Verwendung im Heimatkriegsgebiet.
    1.5.40 bis 9.5.40 Luftkrieg gegen Norwegen (1 Feindflug bei 2./L.G.1)
    10.5.40 bis 20.5.40 Luftkrieg gegen Frankreich. Planmäßige Bekämpfung der französischen Luftwaffe und ihrer Bodenorganisation und der franz. Verkehrsanlagen (7 Feindflüge bei 2./L.G.1)
    21.5.40 bis 2.6.40 Einschließung der Feindkräfte in Flandern und Schlacht bei Dünkirchen(13 Feindflüge bei 2./L.G.1)
    3.u.4.6.40 Großangriff auf Flughäfen im Raume Groß-Paris. (1 Feindflug bei 2./L.G.1)
    13.8.40 bis 26.8.40 Luftkrieg gegen England und auf offener See. Großangriff gegen die englischen Flughäfen (2 Feindflüge bei 2./L.G.1)
    27.u.28.8.40 Großangriff auf Southampton (1 Feindflug bei 2./L.G.1)
    29.8.40 bis 20.1.41 Vergeltungsangriffe auf London und die engl. Großstädte Liverpool, Birkenhaed, Coventry, Manchester unter Fortsetzung der planmäßigen Bekämpfung der engl. Luftwaffe und ihrer Bodenorganisation, der Luftwaffenindustrie, der Einfuhrhäfen und Einfuhrtransporte (52 Feindflüge bei 2./L.G.1),14. u.15.11.40 Großangriff auf Coventry(1 Feindflug).
    12.2.41 bis 4.4.41 Bereitstellung der Gruppe innerhalb des VIII. Fl.-Korps im Raume Südost (Rumänien, Bulgarien).

Efficiency Report for First Lieutenant Gerhard Brenner (first page) – dated April 14, 1942. Small stamp in upper right corner indicates that this copy was received at the military district center at Ludwigsburg on July 11, 1942.

5.4.41 bis 9.5.41 Feldzug gegen Jugoslavien und Griechenland.
Ab 10.5.41 Einsatz im Mittelmeerraum, Nordafrika und gegen Malta.
Gesamtanzahl der Feindflüge: 259

Bei einer überaus wertvollen Vereinigung von hervorragenden geistigen und körperlichen Anlagen mit einwandfreien, vorbildlichen Charaktereigenschaften ist B. eine ausgesprochene, weit über dem Durchschnitt stehende Führerpersönlichkeit, die trotz des jugendlichen Alters sehr gute militärische Kenntnisse, (Leistungen) und eine besonders hervorragende Bewährung vor dem Feind während des Krieges gezeigt hat.

Nach seiner Versetzung am 1.11.1939, als Fähnrich zum Frontverband, hat er sich in Kürze höchste Achtung und Anerkennung verschafft, eine ausgereifte Auffassung und Einstellung zum Offizierberuf erarbeitet. Zunächst als Flugzeugführer, später zusätzlich als Staffel-T.O. und z.b.V. einer Staffel, stellte er in unermüdlicher Selbstarbeit und Vervollkommnung seine militärischen Kenntnisse, seinen hohen Persönlichkeitswert und seine Bewährung vor dem Feinde unter Beweis. Seine selbstlose Arbeit erreichte und wird auch weiterhin erreichen, ihre höchste Krönung, im beispielhaften soldatisch heldischen Einsatz seiner Person vor dem Feinde. Auf 259 Feindflügen zeigte B. übermenschliche Leistungen und erzielte größte Erfolge die ihn zum erfolgreichsten, an erster Stelle stehenden Flugzeugführer und Kommandanten einer Kampfmaschine der Gruppe stempeln.

Am 1.3.1942 wurde er auf Grund seiner allgemeinen militärischen Leistungen und seiner Erfolge vor dem Feinde außer der Reihe vor 4 aktiven Oberleutnanten mit der Führung einer Kampfstaffel beauftragt, die er in Kürze als Staffelkapitän übernehmen wird.

Bisherige Auszeichnungen: E.K.II, E.K.I, nach 202 Feindflügen Ritterkreuz zum Eisernen Kreuz.

Besondere Erfolge nach der Verleihung des Ritterkreuzes:

Auf 57 Feindflügen: Beschädigung durch Volltreffer eines schweren Kreuzer, 14 000 to

Efficiency Report for First Lieutenant Gerhard Brenner (second page)

14 000 to Handelsschiffsraum, etwa 25 Kraftfahrzeuge, mehrere Unterkünfte von zwei Barackenlagern, etwa 6 feindliche Flugzeuge am Boden und kriegswichtige Anlagen auf Malta (Flugplätze Luka und Gudia). In allein drei schwersten Luftkämpfen wurde sein Flugzeug so beschädigt, dass er die Rückflüge im Einmotorenflug mit anschließend glatten Landungen mit ausgefahrenem Fahrwerk durchführen mußte. 1 anerkannter Abschuß vom Muster Gloster und 1 schwere Beschädigung durch Motorbeschuss eines Flugzeuges vom Muster Wellington.

Einwandfreie militärische Führung und makelloser Lebenswandel. B. steht auf dem Boden der nationalsozialistischen Weltanschauung.

Helbig
Hauptmann und Gruppenkommandeur

Max Buchholz
Fighter Pilot

"Toward the men under his command strict, but always correct."

Major Max Buchholz was born on November 3, 1912 in Zerbst in Anhalt. He entered the Army on April 1, 1931 and transferred to the *Luftwaffe* on May 16, 1939. Buchholz began the war as a master sergeant with the 1st Squadron, 3rd Fighter Wing (*Jagdgeschwader 3*). On May 17, 1940, Buchholz shot down four British Blenheim bombers west of St. Quentin, France. Later that day, south of St. Quentin, he shot down a French Curtiss fighter, and that evening he shot down another Curtiss north of Cambrai. Buchholz received the Iron Cross 2nd Class on May 26, 1940 and the Iron Cross 1st Class on May 30, 1940. During the Battle of Britain, with the wing subordinated to the 2nd Air Fleet, he shot down a British Hurricane over Maidstone, England on September 2, 1940 and two French Morane-Saulnier MS 406 fighters over Rochester, England on September 7. On September 15, 1940, Buchholz was shot down in aerial combat and crashed into the sea. He was later awarded the Black Wound Badge; Buchholz finished the year receiving the *Luftwaffe* Honor Goblet.[42]

On January 1, 1941, Captain Hans von Hahn, First Lieutenant (Reserve) Buchholz's group commander, submitted an efficiency report which read in part:[43]

> **Appearance during service:** Straight and deliberate. Immaculate concept of service.
>
> **Demeanor outside of service:** Without criticism or failings. Good social manners.
>
> **Behavior vis-à-vis superiors, men under his command and position within his circle of comrades** (does the person in question possess leadership qualities)**:** Behavior vis-à-vis superiors always straight and official, very modest. Toward the men under his command strict, but always correct. A very good comrade. Good leadership qualities.
>
> **Particular outstanding character attributes:** Strongly disciplined, with an expressed sense of justice, great willingness for service and a very good comrade.
>
> **Particular military capabilities and recommendations for possible use:** Very good pilot. After training, can become squadron leader.
>
> **Summarized evaluation:** (When strong standards are applied, is the person in question "above average," "average" or "below average.") Buchholz is talented above average, a very diligent and eager officer. He shows great interest for all aspects of the service. Buchholz is a very good pilot with outstanding eye and risk taking. His talents and accomplishments are above average.

Six days later, Major Günther Lützow, Commodore, 3rd Fighter Wing, wrote: "Nothing to add. Agree with the evaluation of the Group Commander."

Shortly after this report, Buchholz was assigned to the 3rd Squadron and then the group staff in Russia. He continued to prove his skills in the air, scoring 4 kills on June 29 and another 5 on July 13, while flying in southern Russia as part of the 4th Air Fleet. He assumed command of the 2nd Squadron, 3rd Fighter Wing on July 15, 1941. On August 12, 1941, First Lieutenant Max Buchholz received the Knight's Cross of the Iron Cross with 27 aerial victories in 160 combat missions. Shortly thereafter, the 1st Group transferred to the West and became the 2nd Group, 1st Fighter Wing (*Jagdgeschwader 1*). Buchholz scored his 28th – and final – victory, a British Blenheim bomber west of Terschelling Island on February 12, 1942, while flying combat air patrol over the "Channel Dash" of the *Scharnhorst* and *Gneisenau* battlecruisers from France to Germany; he remained in command of the 5th Squadron to 1943.[44] Buchholz spent the remainder of the war as a flight instructor with the 1st Group, 106th Fighter Wing, and the 102nd Fighter Wing – both training units. Max Buchholz died on July 19, 1996 at Warnemünde, Mecklenburg-Vorpommern.[45]

Luftflotte: 2   W.B.K.: Zerbst (Anh.)

Waffengattung: Fliegertruppe

Truppenteil: I./Jagdgeschwader 3
             - Stab -

Beurteilung.

Name: Buchholz

Vorname: Max

Dienstgrad: Oberleutnant d.R.   R.D.A.: ohne

Geburtsdatum und -ort: 12.5.1912 zu Zerbst/Anh.

Beruf: Schlosser, Maschinenbauer.

Abiturient: ja / nein

Aktive Dienstzeit: seit 1.4.1931   Berufssoldat.

bei: 2./S.S.O. Stralsund eingetreten.

am 16.5.39 in die Luftwaffe (D.V.S. Warnemünde) übernommen.

Bisherige dienstliche Verwendung als Offizier:

von 3.11.1940 bis .... als Nachrichtenoffizier

von .... bis .... als u. Flugzeugführer.

von .... bis .... als

von .... bis .... als

Sonderausbildung:

Flugzeugführer B 2, K I, erw. C II Land und See,

Jagdausbildung.

Sprachkenntnisse:

Schulkenntnisse: ./.

Wort und Schrift: ./.

B 691. 11. 40

Efficiency Report for First Lieutenant (Reserve) Max Buchholz (first page) – dated January 2, 1941, on preprinted form with both typed and handwritten comments.

— 2 —

Dienstliches Auftreten:
Straff und überlegt, sehr eifrig und selbständig. Tadellose Dienstauffassung.

Außerdienstliches Verhalten:
Tadellos und einwandfrei. Gute gesellschaftliche Formen.

Auszeichnungen:
26.5.40 E.K.II, 30.5.40 E.K.I, 26.11.40 Verw.-Abzeichen 3.St.
11.10.40: Ehrenbecher der Luftwaffe.

Bestrafungen:
keine

Verhalten gegenüber Vorgesetzten, Untergebenen und Stellung im Kameradenkreis (besitzt der Beurteilte Führereigenschaften):
Verhalten gegen Vorgesetzte immer straff und dienstlich, sehr bescheiden. Gegen Untergebene scharf aber immer gerecht. Sehr guter Kamerad. Gute Führereigenschaften.

Wesentlich hervortretende Charaktereigenschaften:
Straff diszipliniert, Gerechtigkeitsgefühl, diensteifrig und sehr guter Kamerad.

Efficiency Report for First Lieutenant (Reserve) Max Buchholz (second page)

— 3 —

Besondere militärische Fähigkeiten und Vorschläge für Verwendungsmöglichkeiten:

Sehr guter Flugzeugführer. Kann nach Einarbeitung Staffelkapitän werden.

Zusammenfassendes Urteil:
(Steht der Beurteilte bei Anlegung eines strengen Maßstabes „über dem Durchschnitt", „im Durchschnitt" oder „unter dem Durchschnitt")

B. ist ein überdurchschnittlich begabter, sehr arbeitsamer und diensteifriger Offizier. Er zeigt für alle Dienstzweige starkes Interesse. B. ist ein sehr guter Flugzeugführer mit hervorragendem Auge und Draufgängertum.

Anlagen und Leistungen stehen über dem Durchschnitt.

Gefechtsstand, 2.1.1941.
(Ort und Datum)

(Unterschrift)
(Name und Dienstgrad)
Hauptmann u. Gruppenkommandeur

Efficiency Report for First Lieutenant (Reserve) Max Buchholz (third page) signed by Captain, and 1st Group, 3rd Fighter Wing Commander, Hans von Hahn.

JAGDGESCHWADER 3   Gefechtsstand, 8.1.41

                    S t e l l u n g n a h m e.
                    Nichts hinzuzufügen. Mit der Beurteilung des Grup-
                    penkommandeurs einverstanden.

                                        [signature]
                                        M a j o r und
                                        Geschwader - Kommodore.

Efficiency Report for First Lieutenant (Reserve) Max Buchholz (fourth page) – typed comments on reverse of page three; signed by Major and 3rd Fighter Wing Commodore, Günther Lützow.

Kurt Bühligen
Fighter Pilot

"He possesses élan."

Lieutenant Colonel Kurt Bühligen, later nicknamed "Bogeyman" ("*Bühlmann*"), was born December 13, 1917 in Granschütz near Weissenfels, Thuringia. He entered the *Luftwaffe* on October 13, 1936 – at age 18 – as an aircraft mechanic and was initially assigned to the 153rd Bomber Wing (*Kampfgeschwader 153*). Bühligen joined the 2nd and subsequently the 4th Squadron, 2nd Fighter Wing "Richthofen" (*Jagdgeschwader 2 "Richthofen"*) as an acting corporal, flying five missions out of Beaumont-le-Roger, France between August 13 and 18, 1940 against Royal Air Force airfields as the Battle of Britain commenced.[46]

Between August 19 and September 6, 1940, Bühligen flew an additional fourteen missions against the enemy (with the wing subordinated to the 3rd Air Fleet), protecting bombers attacking industrial targets. Promoted to sergeant, he shot down his first enemy aircraft – a Hurricane over Kent – on September 4, 1940, while flying a Messerschmitt Me 109E; he received the Iron Cross 2nd Class on September 10, 1940. From September 7, 1940 to June 21, 1941, Bühligen and *Jagdgeschwader 2* supported the *Luftwaffe's* reprisal attacks against London, as well as continued attacks against industrial and transportation targets. During this time, Bühligen flew 41 missions against the Royal Air Force and shot down 5 Hurricanes and 5 Spitfires (two of the Spitfires were destroyed in one minute on June 21). He was rewarded for this effort on October 29, 1940 with the Iron Cross 1st Class, on July 7, 1941 with a *Luftwaffe* Honor Goblet and on July 31 with the Operational Flying Clasp for Fighters in Gold.

Bühligen received a Knight's Cross of the Iron Cross on September 4, 1941 as a master sergeant and was promoted to second lieutenant two days later. Between June 21, 1941 and November 20, 1942 he flew 66 missions against the RAF in the skies over Belgium and northern France, scoring 15 additional kills, as he transitioned to an Messerschmitt Me 109F. On August 1, 1942 he became the squadron commander of the 4th Squadron. Eighteen days later, during the abortive Allied attack at Dieppe, Bühligen claimed the destruction of four Spitfires.[47] In November 1942, now with 29 aerial victories, Bühligen and the 2nd Group of the 2nd Fighter Wing transferred to Tunisia. On the first day that the 2nd Group commenced operations out of Kairouan, Tunisia, he chalked up the unit's first kill – a Spitfire Mark V fighter. He would add two P-38 Lightnings on December 26. Now flying a Focke-Wulf Fw 190A-4, he would shoot down 40 British and American aircraft by mid-March 1943. This included shooting down five aircraft of February 2, 1943 (including two Curtiss P-40 Tomahawk fighters and a B-25 Marauder bomber) and four the following day (two Bell P-39 Airacobra fighters and two P-40 Tomahawk fighters), which gave him his 50th overall.

The following recommendation for promotion, dated December 5, 1942, requests promotion for Kurt Bühligen to the grade of first lieutenant. It listed him as a squadron commander and said he was qualified for promotion to first lieutenant. The bulk of the report was written by First Lieutenant Adolf Dickfeld, the acting group commander. Because the report occurred while Bühligen and his unit were in Africa, it was endorsed by the commander of the 2nd Air Corps (*II. Fliegerkorps*), Lieutenant General Bruno Loerzer, headquartered in Taormina, Sicily. The senior reviewer of the report was Field Marshal Albert Kesselring, Commander-in-Chief South (*Oberbefehlshaber Süd*), the German theater headquarters in Italy that oversaw operations in Africa. In the report Adolf Dickfeld stated:[48]

> Lieutenant Bühligen's intellectual and physical attributes are above average. He is tough and persevering; a decent, open-minded character, very reliable, well liked by superiors, the men under him and within his circle of comrades. He has good technical capabilities and for weeks substituted for the Technical Officer of the group.
>
> Since July 3, 1942, he has been the action commander of the 4th Squadron and (from November 5, 1942 on) as Squadron Commander and has proven himself very well in flying as well as troop duty. He possesses élan, pulls the men in his command along with him and knows how to differentiate between the essential and unessential. Bühligen is generous.
>
> Lieutenant Bühligen has proven himself in more than 100 combat missions. On September 6, 1941, he received the Knight's Cross of the Iron Cross. To date, he has shot down 27 enemy planes. Bühligen has initiative and knows how to respond in every situation. He is a National Socialist.

Bruno Loerzer added his own comment: "I am in agreement with this good evaluation and second the preferential promotion to First Lieutenant." Finally, Albert Kesselring summed up his own feelings in a single word: "Agree."

Kurt Bühligen was promoted to captain on April 1, 1943. At that time, Bühligen, now the acting group commander, and the unit returned to the Channel Front in France, where they took on the B-17s of the 8th U.S. Air Force. He scored his 75th kill on July 17, 1943 and received the German Cross in Gold on August 2, 1943 for these exploits. On September 1, 1943 he assumed command of the 2nd Group and continued to dominate in the air, reaching his 85th kill on October 3, 1943. On March 2, 1944, Kurt Bühligen – now a major – received the Oak Leaves to the Knight's Cross, the 413th member of the *Wehrmacht* to be so honored. On the first day of May he assumed command of *Jagdgeschwader 2 "Richthofen,"* a position he would hold through the end of the war, four days after the previous commander Major Kurt Ubben was shot down by P-47 fighters west of Rheims, France and his parachute failed to open. During the invasion of Normandy, Bühligen – now flying a Focke-Wulf Fw 190A-8 – shot down three P-47s, his 99th (just before noon on June 6th over the Orne Estuary,) 100th and 101st (both late afternoon of June 7th) aerial victories, thus edging his friend "Pips" Priller to this total in the West. After achieving his 104th kill, he became the 88th *Wehrmacht* soldier to win the Swords to his Knight's Cross and Oak Leaves on August 14, 1944. He would finish the war with over 700 combat missions against the enemy, 112 kills – all against western Allied pilots – a sortie-to-victory ratio of 6.25 to 1 – with at least 47 Spitfires. His total kills included 24 four-engine bombers and 12 two-engine aircraft.

In April 1945, *Jagdgeschwader 2 "Richthofen"* transferred to Eger, Bohemia, where they became part of *Luftwaffenkommando 8*, with a mission of protecting Messerschmitt Me 262 jets during landings and takeoffs. On April 17, 1945, Bühligen led the unit back to Bavaria, where they surrendered to General George Patton's 3rd U.S. Army after formally inactivating east of Munich on May 7, 1945. Never shot down in combat, although technical problems led to three emergency landings, his luck ran out in May when he was apprehended by the Russians. It remains unclear whether he had decided to return to his home town in the Soviet Occupation Zone but was quickly recognized as notable official, or whether his aircraft suffered engine failure at the end of the war and crash-landed behind enemy lines. In any case, he remained in a Soviet prisoner of war camp until December 1949, when he returned to West Germany. Kurt Bühligen, who once returned unharmed from a mission with 35 bullet holes in his aircraft, died on August 11, 1985 – at age 67 – in Nidda, Hesse.[49] He is buried at the *Stadtfriedhof* in Nidda (Section D, Grave 42).[50]

1.) Oberbefehlshaber Süd   Gefechtsstand, den 5.12.1942
2.) II./Jagdgeschwader Richthofen Nr.2   Wehrmachtteil: Luftwaffe
3.) W.B.K.: Naumburg/Saale
4.) Vorgeschlagen gem.: R.d.L.u.Ob.d.L. (Luftwaffenpersonalamt)Az.21
                        Nr. 71 489/42 (2,I B) vom 16.10.1942.
5.) Waffengattung: Fliegertruppe.

                            V o r s c h l a g

               zur Beförderung eines Offiziers (Kr.O.) zum
                        nächsthöheren Dienstgrad.

Vor- und Zuname: Kurt B ü h l i g e n
Geburtsdatum: 13.12.1917
Jetziger Dienstgrad: Lt. (Kr.O.)
Rangdienstalter: 1. 1. 1942
6.) Eingesetzt als: Staffelkapitän
7.) Geeignet zum: Oberleutnant (Kr.O.) und Staffelkapitän
Aktiver Wehrdienst: vom 13.10.1936 - heute
Teilnahme an welchen Kämpfen: 2.7.40-12.8.40 Planmäßige Bekämpfung
der engl.Luftwaffe und ihrer Bodenorganisation, der Lw.Industrieziele,
der Einfuhrhäfen und Einfuhrtransporte.
13.8.40-18.8.40 Großangriff gegen die engl.Flughäfen (5 Feindflüge)
19.8.40-6.9.40 Planmäßige Bekämpfung der engl. Luftwaffe und ihrer
Bodenorganisation, der Lw.Industrieziele, der Einfuhrhäfen und Einfuhrtransporte.(14 Feindflüge, 1 Abschuß)
7.9.40-20.6.41 Vergeltungsangriffe auf London und die engl.Großstädte
unter Fortsetzung der planmäßigen Bekämpfung der engl. Luftwaffe und
ihrer Bodenorganisation, der Luftwaffenindustrieziele, der Einfuhrhäfen
und der Einfuhrtransport. (41 Feindflüge, 10 Abschüsse)
21.6.41-20.11.42 Luftverteidigung im besetzten Gebiet Belgien /Nord-
frankreich. (66 Feindflüge, 15 Abschüsse)
21.11.42-heute Einsatz als Jagdflieger im Mittelmeerraum und Luftkrieg
gegen England in Nordafrika. (4 Feindflüge) (1 Abschuß)
Wird vorgeschlagen zur Beförderung zum: Oberleutnant (Kr.O.)
Kurze Beurteilung durch den Regimentskommandeur, selbst.Batl.usw.
Kdr.hinsichtlich dienstlicher Leistungen, Führerpersönlichkeit
und Stellung im Kameradenkreise.
Lt. Bühligen besitzt geistige und körperliche Anlagen über Durchschnitt. Er ist zäh und ausdauernd; ein anständiger, offener Charakter, sehr zuverlässig, bei Vorgesetzten, Untergebenen und im Kameradenkreise in gleicher Weise beliebt. Er hat eine gute technische Veranlagung und hat den T.O. der Gruppe wochenlang vertreten.
Er führt seit 3.7.42 die 4. Staffel und hat sich als Staffelführer und
(seit 5.11.42) Staffelkapitän in fliegerischer wie truppendienstlicher
Hinsicht sehr gut bewährt. Er besitzt Schwung, reisst seine Untergebenen mit und versteht, das Wesentliche vom Unwesentlichen zu unter-
scheiden. B. ist grosszügig.
Lt.B. hat sich in weit über 100 Feindflügen bewährt. Am 6.9.41 erhielt
er das Ritterkreuz des Eisernen Kreuzes. Er hat bis heute 27 Feindab-
schüsse. - B. besitzt eigene Initiative und weiss sich in jeder Lage zu

Request for Promotion for Second Lieutenant Kurt Bühligen (front side) – dated December 5, 1942, on blank paper, with typed and handwritten comments. Initial in the top right corner shows an official at the *Luftwaffe* Personnel Department reviewed the report on receipt and underlined several key items.

helfen. Er ist Nationalsozialist.

Oberleutnant und stellv. Gruppenkommandeur

Zusatz:
  Ich bin mit der guten Beurteilung einverstanden und
befürworte die bevorzugte Beförderung zum Oberleutnant(Kr.O.)

Gefechtsstand, den 19.12.1942
Der Kommandierende General
des II.Fliegerkorps

General der Flieger

Der Oberbefehlshaber Süd   H.Qu., den

Generalfeldmarschall

Request for Promotion for Second Lieutenant Kurt Bühligen (back side) – signed by First Lieutenant Adolf Dickfeld, the acting 2nd Group, 2nd Fighter Wing. Because the report occurred while Bühligen and his unit were in Africa, it was endorsed by the commander of the 2nd Air Corps, Lieutenant General Bruno Loerzer. The senior reviewer of the report was Field Marshal Albert Kesselring, Commander-in-Chief South.

Horst Carganico
Fighter Pilot

"Personal courage and daring in combat."

Major Horst Carganico was born on September 27, 1917 at Breslau, Silesia. He joined the *Luftwaffe* in 1937 as an officer candidate. The outbreak of World War II found him serving as Technical Officer on the staff of the 1st Fighter Wing (*Jagdgeschwader 1*). In the spring 1940, he became the Adjutant of the 2nd Group, 77th Fighter Wing "Ace of Hearts" (*Jagdgeschwader 77 "Herzas"*), serving in Norway with this unit beginning April 11, 1940. On June 21, 1940, he scored his first victory, downing a British RAF Hampden west of Hardanger Fjord, Norway, protecting the battleship *Scharnhorst*. He followed that up on July 9, 1940 by downing two Blenheim bombers northwest of Stavanger, Norway. On October 14, he shot down a Hudson bomber, while on November 30, 1940 he claimed his fifth victory when he shot down an RAF Blenheim bomber over the English Channel.

Carganico was appointed Commander of the 1st Squadron, *Jagdgeschwader 77* on January 1, 1941, operating from Sola, Norway. He transferred with the unit to Kirkenes, Norway in May 1941. On July 25, 1941, he shot down a Russian flying boat. With his score at 27, Carganico was awarded the Knight's Cross of the Iron Cross on September 25, 1941. The 1st Squadron was redesignated the 1st Squadron, 5th Fighter Wing "Polar Sea" (*Jagdgeschwader 5 "Eismeer"*) on January 20, 1942. With his unit redesignated for a third time – the 6th Squadron, 5th Fighter Wing – on March 16, 1942, he shot down 23 enemy aircraft in a six-week period ending in June 1942. He received the German Cross in Gold on May 25, 1942. On May 18, 1942, Captain Carganico assumed acting command of the 2nd Group, 5th Fighter Wing. On a mission on July 22, 1942, his Messerschmitt Me 109F-4 suffered an engine failure, forcing him to land at Murovskij, but he returned to his unit the following day.

On July 26, 1942, Colonel General Jürgen Stumpff, the commander of the 5th Air Fleet (*Luftflotte 5*) wrote the *Luftwaffe* Personnel Department with an enclosure on a recommendation for preferential promotion to captain (and requesting Carganico be made the permanent commander of the 2nd Group, 5th Fighter Wing), in which he stated:[51]

First Lieutenant Horst Carganico – official date of rank of September 1, 1940 – is being recommended for preferential promotion to captain. Engaged at the battle front of Northern Finland, with short interruption, from the beginning of the Eastern Campaign, he proved his heartfelt preparedness for engagement full of unbridled courage in 50 aerial victories. This officer, who was awarded the Knight's Cross of the Iron Cross for fighter engagement on the Murmansk Front, has demonstrated excellent skills in the operations of the fighter squadron under his command, in addition to his personal courage and daring in combat. His fighter group has accomplished a total of 604 kills. First Lieutenant Carganico has been tasked with the acting leadership of the 2nd Group, 5th Fighter Wing since May 18, 1942. During this time until now, in his capacity as acting group commander, he has personally scored six aerial victories, and the group under his command has 164 kills. In view of his demonstrated accomplishments as a group leader, his appointment to command the 2nd Group, 5th Fighter Wing is also being requested.

On August 12, 1942, Carganico was part of an escort for a reconnaissance flight over the front near Murmansk. The formation was intercepted by Russian fighters and in the ensuing aerial combat his aircraft received hits, forcing a second emergency landing in three weeks. Once again, Carganico evaded capture and returned safely to his unit the next day. On March 26, 1944, Captain Carganico assumed command of the 1st Group, 5th Fighter Wing "Eismeer", which was engaged in the defense of Germany-proper. On May 27, 1944, following aerial combat with USAAF B-17 Flying Fortresses, Major Horst Carganico was killed when his Messerschmitt Me 109G-5 crashed after hitting high tension cables, while attempting to make a forced landing near Chevry, France. During his career, he flew 600 combat missions and shot down 60 enemy aircraft, a sortie-to-victory ratio of about 10 to 1. He was the son of *Luftwaffe* Lieutenant General, Viktor Carganico.[52] Horst Carganico is buried in the military section of the *Waldfriedhof* in Berlin-Zehlendorf.

Luftflottenkommando 5   Gefechtsstand, den 26.7.1942
   Gefechtsstab
Brb.Nr. 1233 /42 IIa

Betr.: Antrag auf bevorzugte Beförderung des Oblt. (Tr.O.) Carganico
und Ernennung zum Kommandeur II./J.G. 5

An

Reichsminister der Luftfahrt
und Oberbefehlshaber der Luftwaffe
- Luftwaffenpersonalamt -
B e r l i n.

      Oblt. (Tr.O.) Horst C a r g a n i c o - R.D.A.: 1.9.40 wird zur bevorzugten Beförderung zum Hauptmann vorgeschlagen. Seit Beginn des Ostfeldzuges mit kurzer Unterbrechung an der nordfinnischen Kampffront als Jagdflieger eingesetzt, bewies er in 50 Luftsiegen seine von unbändigem Draufgängertum beseelte Einsatzbereitschaft. Der mit dem Ritterkreuz zum Eisernen Kreuz ausgezeichnete Offizier ist an der Murmanfront zum Träger des Jagdeinsatzes geworden und hat neben persönlicher Tapferkeit und Schneid hervorragendes Geschick im Einsatz der ihm unterstellten Jagdstaffeln in der Luft gezeigt. Die von ihm geführte Jagdgruppe hat insgesamt 604 Abschüsse erzielt.
      Oblt. Carganico ist seit 18.5.42 mit Führung der II./J.G. 5 beauftragt. Seit dieser Zeit hat er bis heute in seiner Eigenschaft als Gruppenkommandeur 6 Abschüsse, die von ihm geführte Gruppe 164 Luftsiege, erzielt. Im Hinblick auf die erfolgte Bewährung auch als Gruppenkommandeur wird seine Ernennung zum Gruppenkommandeur der II./J.G. 5 beantragt.

                                                  Generaloberst

Request for Preferred Promotion for First Lieutenant Horst Carganico (one page only) – dated July 26, 1942, on blank paper with typed comments, signed by the Commander of the 5th Air Fleet, Colonel General Hans-Jürgen Stumpff. Various initials and block stamps in the lower half show the document arrived in Berlin on August 1 and was reviewed by numerous officers over the next seven days.

Wilhelm Crinius
Fighter Pilot

"He is tough, but he fights with calculation and deliberation."

Second Lieutenant Wilhelm Crinius was born on December 1, 1920 at Hohenhausen in Lipper Bergland, North-Rhine Westphalia. He joined the *Luftwaffe* in January 1940 and underwent fighter pilot training. In February 1942, Private First Class Crinius was assigned to the 3rd Squadron, 53rd Fighter Wing "Ace of Spades" (*Jagdgeschwader 53 "Pikas"*), based in Sicily. On April 1, he was promoted to corporal; the following month, his unit transferred to the Eastern Front. He won the Iron Cross 2nd Class on April 30, 1942. Crinius shot down his first two enemy aircraft – Il-2 Sturmoviks – in five minutes on June 9, 1942 and 3 LaGG-3 fighters on June 23, 1942. He received the Iron Cross 1st Class on June 25, 1942. On July 8, he shot down two Russian Douglas A-20 Boston twin-engine bombers attacking a bridge west of Voronezh, but during the fight, his Messerschmitt Me 109F-4 was hit by Russian anti-aircraft fire. He made a belly-landing between the lines, in which his aircraft was totally destroyed, but he was rescued by a German army patrol and returned to his unit.

Crinius claimed his 15th aerial victory on August 1, an LaGG-3. On August 12, he shot down three Mikoyan-Gurevich MiG-3 fighters to record his 25th, 26th and 27th kills. He scored his 49th victory on August 27 – which was also the 1,000th victory for the 1st Group – and shot down his 50th enemy aircraft the next day. He recorded his 55th victory on September 1 and was promoted to the rank of Technical Sergeant. On September 9, 1942, he received the *Luftwaffe* Honor Goblet. Crinius was adept at shooting down more than one aircraft per mission. On September 10, 14, 16, 17 and 18 he shot down 4 enemy aircraft each day, and on September 23, 1942 was awarded both the Knight's Cross of the Iron Cross and the Oak Leaves to the Knight's Cross (the *Wehrmacht's* 127th awardee), a day after scoring his 100th victory.

In September 1942, Technical Sergeant Crinius' chain of command submitted a report requesting he be made a commissioned officer. First Lieutenant and Squadron Commander Wolfgang Tonne wrote:[53]

> Technical Sergeant Crinius is a likeable, tall, athletic person with good social manners. He has a secure, exact behavior towards both the men under his command and superiors. Also, as far as character is concerned, his attitude is first-rate. He is an open, trustworthy person, with a clear character, who sets his path in a goal-oriented and ambitious way. Technical Sergeant Crinius has good general knowledge and, in comparison with his comrades with the same formal education, he appears superior. As to military discipline, Technical Sergeant Crinius is correct and ambitious. He shows expressed talent as a fighter pilot. He owes his success to his relentless courage. He is tough, but he fights with calculation and deliberation. He excels particularly due to his willingness for battle and is extremely ready for combat. Due to his personal values, Technical Sergeant Crinius promises to become a good officer who will also feel at home in these circles.

Captain, and 1st Group Commander, Klaus Quaet-Faslem, added:

I have only known Technical Sergeant Crinius for four weeks. My over-all impression as to his appearance, behavior, military attitude and form is very good. His accomplishments as a fighter pilot are overwhelming. I believe that he will be a good, alert officer, who is a good example for his comrades and the men under his command.

Captain and acting wing commodore Wolf-Dietrich Wilcke of the 3rd Fighter Wing "Udet" (*Jagdgeschwader 3 "Udet"*) wrote:[54]

I second the opinion of the intermediate superior. Technical Sergeant Crinius has a tall, respectable appearance, with good manners and strong military demeanor. His accomplishments as a pilot are far above the average. In as little time as four months he has attained 84 kills which made him the most successful sergeant-pilot of his fighter group. Engaged as the leader of two and four aircraft, he demonstrated his excellent knowledge in leading his group. Technical Sergeant Crinius promises to become a useful wartime officer. ["84 kills" underlined by a subsequent reviewer]

Promoted to the grade of second lieutenant, as requested in the report, Crinius transferred in November 1942 to Tunisia with the 1st Group, 53rd Fighter Wing. In Africa, he scored another 14 victories, including his only four-engine bomber, a B-17, on December 26 over Bizerte. On December 1, he shot down two Spitfires in four minutes; on December 18, he shot down two P-38 fighters within one minute south of Tunis. By January 4, 1943, he had reached 110 kills with the downing of a Boston bomber. On January 13, 1943, in a fight with RAF Spitfires near La Calle, Crinius' Messerschmitt Me 109G-2 was hit and he was wounded in the thigh. Headed for his

Ernst Udet – after his death, the 3rd Fighter Wing (*Jagdgeschwader 3*) received the honorary title of "Udet."

base, his engine then caught fire and he ditched his stricken aircraft in the Mediterranean Sea. He spent 24 hours in the water before being rescued. Hospitalized for his wounds, he became a prisoner of war. During his career, Wilhelm Crinius flew 400 combat missions and was credited with 114 victories – 100 of which were on the Eastern Front – a sortie-to-victory ratio of 3.51 to 1." Wilhelm Crinius died on April 26, 1997 at Stuhr-Fahrenhorst, Lower Saxony

Luftflottenkommando 4   W.B.K. Detmold
Waffengattung: Fliegertruppe
              Flugzeugführer
Truppenteil: I./ Jagdgeschwader 53

6. Okt. 1942

Ltw. 1.10.42
391/D/10.42

Vorschlag
zur Beförderung zum Kriegsoffizier
gemäß Verfügung Ob.d.L. General der
Jagdflieger Nr.376/42 grün v. 23.7.42.

Name: **Crinius**   Geburtstag: 2.12.1920   Ort: Hohenhausen
Vorname: Wilhelm   Familienstand: ledig   Kinder: keine
Dienstgrad: Feldwebel   Beruf: Bankangestellter
Verwendung: Flugzeugführer (Jagdflieger)   Konfession: ev.

Militärischer Werdegang:

Aktive Dienstzeit: von 26.8.39 bis 12.10.39, von 10.1.40 bis heute
Dienstzeit seit Kriegsbeginn: 26.8.39 - 12.10.39, 10.1.40 bis heute
Längere Dienstverpflichtung auf 3, 4½ oder 12 und mehr Jahre:
              auf 4½ Jahre verpflichtet

Beförderungen und Ernennungen:

zum Gefr.: 1.9.40   zum Uffz.: 1.4.42   zum Feldw.: 1.9.42
Tag der Ernennung zum R.O.A. -.-   bzw. K.O.A. -.-
Hat - nicht - mit=Erfolg - ohne=Erfolg - an einem K.O.N.- Lehrgang
von -.-   bis -.-   teilgenommen.
Offizierwahl hat stattgefunden am: -.-

Bildungsgang: Erziehung im elterlichen Hause, Ostern 1927 bis 1935
              Volksschule Hohenhausen, Ostern 1935 bis 1938 kaufm.
              Berufsschule und Lehrling bei der Spar- und Darlehens-
              kasse Hohenhausen, Ostern 1938 bis November 1938 Bank-
              angestellter bei der Spar- und Darlehenskasse Hohen-
              hausen.

Request for Promotion to Officer for Technical Sergeant Wilhelm Crinius (first page) – written in September 1942, on blank paper with typed comments. October 6, 1942 date stamp shows when the report arrived at the *Luftwaffe* Personnel Office. Underlines on report probably done at that location. Handwritten comment in pencil indicates he was commissioned a lieutenant on October 1, 1942.

Bestrafungen vor Diensteintritt: keine
Bestrafungen nach Diensteintritt: keine
Auszeichnungen: 30.3.42 Frontflugspange für Jäger in Bronze
29.4.42 Frontflugspange für Jäger in Silber
30.4.42 Eisernes Kreuz II. Klasse
25.6.42 Eisernes Kreuz I. Klasse
18.8.42 Frontflugspange für Jäger in Gold

Stand und Beruf des Vaters: Malermeister

Familienname der Mutter: Tölle

Anschrift der nächsten Angehörigen: Wilhelm Crinius, Vater,
Hohenhausen / Lippe, Haus-Nr.217

Außerdienstliche Eignung festgestellt durch: I./ J.G. 53

B e u r t e i l u n g :

   Der Feldwebel C r i n i u s ist eine sympatische, grosse, sportliche Erscheinung mit guten Umgangsformen. Er hat ein sicheres, exaktes Auftreten Untergebenen und Vorgesetzten gegenüber. Auch charakterlich ist seine Haltung einwandfrei. Er ist ein offener, ehrlicher Mensch und klarer Charakter, der zielbewusst und strebsam seinen Weg geht.

   Feldw. Crinius hat ein gutes Allgemeinwissen und macht Kameraden mit gleicher Schulbildung gegenüber den Eindruck der Überlegenheit.

   Militärisch ist Feldw. Crinius korrekt und strebsam.

   Als Jagdflieger zeigt er ausgesprochenes Talent. Seine Erfolge verdankt er seinem rücksichtslosen Draufgängertum. Er ist zäh, kämpft jedoch mit Berechnung und Überlegung. Er zeichnet sich besonders durch Kampfesfreude aus und ist äusserst einsatzfreudig.

   Feldw. Crinius verspricht bei seinem Persönlichkeitswert ein guter Offizier zu werden, der sich auch in diesem Kreise wohlfühlen wird.

Tonne.

Oberleutnant und Staffelkapitän.

Request for Promotion to Officer for Technical Sergeant Wilhelm Crinius (second page) – signed by First Lieutenant, and Squadron Commander, Wolfgang Tonne.

Stellungnahme der Zwischenvorgesetzten:

    Der Feldwebel C r i n i u s ist mir erst seit 4 Wochen bekannt. Der Gesamteindruck in Erscheinung, Auftreten, militärischer Haltung und Form ist sehr gut. Seine jagdfliegerischen Leistungen sind überragend. Ich glaube, dass er ein guter, frischer Offizier, Kameraden und Untergebenen ein Vorbild sein wird.

                          Hauptmann und Gruppenkommandeur.

Stellungnahme des Geschwader-Kommodore :

Jagdgeschwader " Udet "   den 14. September 1942

Stellungnahme

    Ich schliesse mich der Stellungnahme der Zwischenvorgesetzten an. Feldwebel C r i n i u s ist eine grosse, stattliche Erscheinung mit guten Umgangsformen und straffem, militärischem Auftreten. Seine fliegerischen Leistungen sind weit über dem Durchschnitt. In knapp 4 Monaten hat er 84 Abschüsse errungen und ist damit der erfolgreichste Unteroffizier-Flugzeugführer seiner Jagdgruppe. Als Rotten- und Schwarmführer verwendet, bewies er hervorragendes taktisches Können in der Führung seines Verbandes. Feldwebel Crinius verspricht, ein brauchbarer Kriegsoffizier zu werden.

                M. d. F. b.

                        Hauptmann und Geschwader-Kommodore

Request for Promotion to Officer for Technical Sergeant Wilhelm Crinius (third page) – signed by Captain, and 1st Group Commander, Klaus Quaet-Faslem, and also by acting commodore of the 3rd Fighter Wing, Captain Wolf-Dietrich Wilcke.

Adolf Dickfeld
Fighter Pilot

"He sometimes tends towards high-handedness."

Colonel Adolf Dickfeld was born on February 20, 1910 at Jüterborg in Mark Brandenburg. He joined the *Luftwaffe* on March 1, 1937 and was promoted to second lieutenant on December 1, 1939. At the outbreak of the war, Dickfeld was assigned to the 3rd Group, 52nd Fighter Wing (*Jagdgeschwader 52*). He flew missions over France, England, Greece and Crete before the unit transferred to Romania in 1941, in preparation for the invasion of Russia. On June 26, 1941 he scored his first two kills. On August 16, 1941, he recorded his 9th and 10th kills – both Polikarpov I-16 fighters southeast of Kiev, destroyed in one minute – and on October 24 shot down five enemy aircraft in six minutes to record his 16th through 20th victories. By the end of 1941, he had accumulated 37 aerial victories and received the *Luftwaffe* Honor Goblet on December 15, 1941.

On January 25, 1942, Adolf Dickfeld won the German Cross in Gold. Second Lieutenant Dickfeld was awarded the Knight's Cross of the Iron Cross on March 19, 1942 for achieving 47 victories. In addition, he had destroyed 8 aircraft, 11 locomotives, 2 armored vehicles and 2 trucks in ground-attack missions. On May 8, he shot down 11 enemy aircraft, followed by nine on May 14 and 10 on May 18, bringing his total to 100. From May 9 to May 27, 1942, he served as the acting commander of the 8th Squadron, 52nd Fighter Wing. Dickfeld was awarded the Oak Leaves to the Knight's Cross on May 19, 1942 for 101 victories and was promoted to first lieutenant on April 1, 1942. Following a lengthy leave, Dickfeld returned to the front and added a further 14 victories. He was appointed the Commander, 2nd Group, 2nd Fighter Wing "Richthofen" (*Jagdgeschwader 2 "Richthofen"*) on November 7, 1942. The unit was transferred to North Africa, where Dickfeld shot down a Spitfire on December 1 and a P-38 Lightning on December 3 over Tunisia, but was badly injured in a take-off accident at Kairouan on January 8, 1943, when his Focke-Wulf Fw 190A-4 struck an obstacle on the airfield. While recovering from his injuries in that crash, on April 17, 1943 Dickfeld was appointed Commander, 2nd Group, 11th Fighter Wing (*Jagdgeschwader 11*) – based in the Bremen–Helgoland area of northern Germany.

On May 10, 1943, Lieutenant Colonel and Wing Commodore Walter Oesau wrote an efficiency report of Captain Adolf Dickfeld, which stated:[56]

Concerning his character, Captain Dickfeld is trustworthy and correct, and military in his appearance. He is a person of tall, representative figure who possesses very good mental talents and who in his train of thought is very flexible. His military attitude is good. His military demeanor is without reproach and exemplary. Full of élan and cheerfulness, he attacks all tasks. It seems that any difficulties are not a burden to him, but rather give him impetus to go to work. Among his comrades, he is well-liked. His appearance vis-à-vis his superiors is secure and balanced; however, he must also realize that he is being led by a firm hand, because otherwise, he sometimes tends towards high-handedness. His ideological attitude is without criticism. He is rooted in the National Socialist ideology and understands how to impart this to the men under his command in a very good manner. Captain Dickfeld has a good knowledge of weapons and information needed by a fighter pilot. His great successes have made him very secure and with 132 aerial victories he is one of the best fighter pilots of the wing. Captain Dickfeld has proven his great talent for improvisation during the occupation of Tunisia. He is in good control of his group in the air as well as on the ground, even though he had taken command only a short time ago. In any case, Dickfeld possesses the ability to lead a fighter group and with further engagements, he will become a good and capable group leader.

Lieutenant Colonel Oesau also stated that Dickfeld was filling his current position "well" and that after further qualifications would be suitable for promotion. This happened quickly, and Captain Dickfeld was promoted to the grade of major on May 18, 1943. He was later shot down during an attack on Allied bombers and forced to bail out into the sea. He was rescued, but was hospitalized with back injuries. Following his recovery, Dickfeld was appointed *General für Nachwuchs* (literally general in charge of new pilots) and Inspector for Hitler Youth Flyers. He reputedly shot down a P-47 Thunderbolt several weeks before the end of the war while flying the Heinkel He 162 jet aircraft.

Adolf Dickfeld was credited with 136 victories in 1072 combat missions, a sortie-to-victory ratio of 7.88 to 1. He achieved 128 victories over the Eastern Front.[57]

Jagdgeschwader Richthofen Nr.2   Gefechtsstand, den 10.5. 1943
(Dienststelle, Truppenteil)

Feldpost-Nr.: L 17 694

.O.P. Paris

Kriegsbeurteilung
Beurteilungsnotiz

über den Hauptmann (Kr.Offz.) und Gruppenkommandeur
(Dienstgrad, Dienststellung)

Vor- und Familienname: Adolf D i c k f e l d   geb.: 2o.2.191o

Rangdienstalter: 1.1.1943   Dienstalterliste: D

Verheiratet, ledig, verwitwet, geschieden (Zutreffendes unterstreichen)

Jetzige Verwendung: seit 7.11.42 Gruppenkommandeur II./J.G.2, seit 1.4.43
(z. B. Staffelkapitän seit)   in den Bereich des XII.Fliegerkorps zur Führung der
II./J.G.11 kommandiert.

Eignungsbeurteilung:
Hauptmann D i c k f e l d ist charakterlich aufrichtig und in seinem
Auftreten korrekt und soldatisch.
Er ist ein Mann von großer stattlicher Figur, der über sehr gute
geistige Veranlagungen verfügt und in seinen Gedankengängen sehr be-
                                                                b.w.!

Wie wird jetzige Stelle ausgefüllt? _gut_

Geeignet zur Beförderung zum nächsthöheren Dienstgrad? _nach weiterer Eignung_

Erworbene Luftwaffenscheine: LF

Strafen: beim J.G.2 keine

Verwendungsvorschläge: (besondere Eignung, weitere Verwendung)

Kommandeur einer Jagdgruppe

(Unterschrift)

Oberstlt.u.Geschwaderkommodore.
(Dienstgrad und Dienststellung)

6041. 10.42. Kroll & Straus, Berlin SO.36 — Din A 4

Efficiency Report for Captain Adolf Dickfeld (front side) – dated May 10, 1943, on pre-printed form, from the Kroll & Straus firm in Berlin, with typed and handwritten comments. Form has a place for a photo but one was never affixed. Signed by Lieutenant Colonel Walter Oesau, Commodore, 2nd Fighter Wing "Richthofen."

Zusätze zur Beurteilungsnotiz: (Nur bei Vorlage an höhere Dienststellen)

beweglich ist.
Seine soldatische Haltung ist gut. Sein militärisches Auftreten einwandfrei und vorbildlich.
Temperamentvoll und froh geht er an alle Arbeiten heran. Sämtliche Schwierigkeiten scheinen ihm nicht lästig, sondern geben ihm Ansporn zur Arbeit.
Im Kameradenkreis ist D. beliebt. Sein Auftreten gegenüber Vorgesetzten ist sicher und gleichmäßig, jedoch muß er jeweils wissen, daß er von einer bestimmten Hand geführt wird, da er sonst bisweilen zu Eigenmächtigkeiten neigt.
Seine weltanschauliche Haltung ist einwandfrei. Das nationalsozialistische Gedankengut ist ihm eigen und er versteht es, seinen Untergebenen dieses in sehr guter Form zu übermitteln.
Hauptmann D. besitzt gute Waffen- und Fachkenntnisse als Jagdflieger. Seine großen Erfolge haben ihn als solchen sicher gemacht und mit 132 erzielten Luftsiegen war er einer der besten Jagdflieger des Geschwaders gewesen.
Großes Improvisationstalent hat D. bei der Besetzung von Tunesien bewiesen. Seinen Verband hat er in der Luft sowie am Boden fest in der Hand gehabt, obgleich er diesen erst kurze Zeit zuvor übernommen hatte.
D. besitzt auf jeden Fall die Fähigkeit eine Jagdgruppe zu führen und wird bei weiteren Einsätzen ein guter und leistungsfähiger Gruppenkommandeur werden.

Oberstlt. und Geschwaderkommodore.

Efficiency Report for Captain Adolf Dickfeld (back side) – signed a second time by Lieutenant Colonel Walter Oesau.

Erwin Diekwisch
Stuka Pilot

"One can always trust him."

Captain Erwin-Peter Diekwisch was born in Buschhütten, near Siegen in Westphalia on August 12, 1920. He entered the *Luftwaffe* at the end of 1940 and first flew with the Supplemental Stuka Squadron (*Ergänzungs-Sturzkampf-Staffel*) of the 1st Stuka Wing (*Sturzkampfgeschwader 1*), at Schaffen-Diest, Belgium.

On January 16, 1941, Diekwisch's chain of command in the Supplemental Squadron – the wing's operational training unit – submitted an efficiency report on him. First Lieutenant Ernst Reusch, the acting squadron commander, wrote the following:[58]

Mental and physical attributes:

Mental: average.
Physical: strong and with good talent.
Good manners.

Character attributes: Open, lively character with great self-confidence, one can always trust him.

Service utilization: Stuka Student

Special training: Pilot's certificate

Service knowledge and accomplishments: In matters outside of the service good; tries hard. In inside service matters, also satisfactory but he is still lacking service experience.

Leadership: good.

Suited for: Appears to be suitable for promotion to lieutenant under appropriate guidance.

Diekwisch is one of the few officer candidates in the squadron who is already more mature. However, since he is still lacking experience due to his short period in the service, he still needs supervision and guidance.

On February 10, 1941, Lieutenant Colonel Walter Hagen, Commodore *Sturzkampfgeschwader 1*, simply added: "In agreement."

On February 1, 1941, Diekwisch was promoted to second lieutenant, just after his first combat mission over the English Channel. A pilot in the 9th Squadron, *Sturzkampfgeschwader 1*, he continued his exploits in 1941 in the Mediterranean theater. In a night attack against Malta, Diekwisch's Junkers Ju 87 took a direct hit in the engine, and he and his radioman were forced to bail out over the coast of Sicily, but he was subsequently rescued. With "Operation Barbarossa," he began his achievements on the Eastern Front, which resulted in the *Luftwaffe* Honor Goblet on April 1, 1942, the German Cross in Gold on June 2, 1942 and the Knight's Cross of the Iron Cross on October 15, 1942, on achieving his 450th combat mission.[59] Diekwisch was promoted to first lieutenant on February 1, 1943 and to captain on January 1, 1944. He transferred to the 1st Squadron, 5th Ground-Attack Wing (*Schlachtgeschwader 5*), flying missions over Norway and Finland. On February 1, 1945, he assumed command of the 3rd Group, 200th Bomber Wing (*Kampfgeschwader 200*); he was wounded in action in 1945, but survived the war.

Erwin-Peter Diekwisch flew 934 combat missions, mostly in Ju 87s. He destroyed one destroyer, one submarine, two merchant ships, sixty-four tanks (the 28th highest score in the *Luftwaffe*) and five key bridges, in addition to scoring twelve aerial victories.[60]

Ergänzungs-Sturzkampf-Staffel   Schaffen-Diest, 16. 1. 1941
Stuka - Geschwader 1   Ort und Tag
        Dienststelle

Anlage _____ zu „Jagd_____" v. B. Nr. _____ vom _____

Beurteilung *)

des   O. Fähnrich Erwin Diekwisch   D1586
        Dienstgrad, Vor- und Familienname

a) Geistige und körperliche Anlagen: Geistig: Durchschnittlich
                                    Körperlich: Kräftig und gut veranlagt.
                                    Gute Umgangsformen

b) Charaktereigenschaften: Offener, lebhafter Charakter mit grossem Selbstvertrauen, man kann sich auf ihn verlassen.

c) Dienstliche Verwendung: Stuka-Schüler
    z.B.: Flugzeugführer, Hilfsbeobachter, Bordfunker, Flugmotorenschlosser, Horchfunker, Messmann, Geräteverwalter, Krankenträger usw.

d) Besondere Ausbildung: LF-Schein
    z.B.: Abgelegte Prüfung, Militärführerschein, Blindflugausbildung usw.

e) Dienstliche Kenntnisse und Leistungen: Im Aussendienst gut, gibt sich Mühe. Im Innendienst ebenso befriedigend, fehlt aber noch eine Erfahrung im Dienst.

f) Führung: Gut

g) Eignung: 1. Zur Beförderung zum nächsthöheren Dienstgrad:
Erscheint bei entsprechender Aufsicht zum Leutnant geeignet.

    2. Zur Ernennung:
       z.B.: Uffz.-Anw. d. B., Res.-Offz.-Anw.

    3. Für welche Verwendung: Flugzeugführer
       z.B.: Bordmechaniker, Bekl.-Verw., Oberfeldw.

                                                    Oberleutnant u. stellv. Staffelführer
                                                    Unterschrift der Disziplinarvorgesetzten

Rückseite.

*) Zum Vervollständigen und zum Abschliessen der Beurteilung kann auch die Rückseite benutzt werden.

2248 – Wehrmachtformularverlag Pet. Kaiser, Düsseldorf; Sternstr. 63a, Ruf 384 38
Auslieferungslager: Brüssel, 12, rue Montagne-aux-Herbes-Potagères. — Tel. 17.21.80.

Efficiency Report for Officer Candidate Erwin Diekwisch (front side) – dated January 16, 1941, on pre-printed form with typed and one handwritten comment. Signed at bottom by First Lieutenant Ernst Reusch, the acting squadron commander. "D1586" in blue pencil is probably an administrative file number.

Diekwisch ist einer der wenigen Fähnriche bei der Staffel, der schon etwas ausgereifter ist. Da es ihm aber infolge seiner geringen Dienstzeit an Erfahrung fehlt, bedarf er noch der Aufsicht und Anleitung.

Signature: Rudy.
Oberleutnant und stellv. Staffelführer

Sturzkampf - Geschwader 1   Gefechtsstand, den 10.2.1941

Einverstanden:

Signature: Hagen.
Oberstlt. und Geschw.-Kommodore.

Efficiency Report for Officer Candidate Erwin Diekwisch (back side) – signed again by First Lieutenant Ernst Reusch, and also by Lieutenant Colonel Walter Hagen, Commodore, 1st Stuka Wing.

Anton Döbele
Fighter Pilot

"He can be harsh and one-sided in judging the people around him."

Second Lieutenant Anton "Toni" Döbele was born at Ehrensberg in the Waldsee region of Württemberg on November 16, 1910. As a corporal, he participated in the Spanish Civil War with the Condor Legion.[61] On his return to Germany, Döbele underwent fighter pilot training and was posted to the Supplemental Group – an operational training formation – of the 54th Fighter Wing "Green Hearts" (*Ergänzungsgruppe, Jagdgeschwader 54 "Grünherz"*). In autumn 1941, he was assigned to 3rd Squadron, 54th Fighter Wing, based on the northern sector of the Eastern Front, with the 1st Air Fleet. By May 1942, between stints as a fighter pilot instructor, he had achieved 4 aerial victories. He transferred to the 1st Squadron and won the Iron Cross 1st Class on February 3, 1943. Döbele recorded his 15th kill, a LaGG-5 fighter on March 19, 1943 on his 216th combat mission. Döbele claimed 16 victories in July and an additional 24 in August, including three Russian fighters shot down on August 7 to record his 49th through 51st victories, three enemy aircraft shot down on August 7, (58-60) and four dispatched on August 23 (62-65). On September 1, Master Sergeant Döbele claimed his 70th victory, a Petlyakov Pe-2 light bomber. On September 13, 1943, he won the *Luftwaffe* Honor Goblet; his 80th victory (a Yak-9 fighter) occurred on September 14.

On September 16, 1943, Döbele's chain of command submitted him for promotion to commissioned officer, specifically for bravery in the face of the enemy (*wegen Tapferkeit vor dem Feinde*). First Lieutenant and 1st Squadron Commander Walter Nowotny wrote two pieces, one as squadron commander and one as acting group commander:[62]

> The squadron requests the promotion of Master Sergeant Anton Döbele to officer (during wartime) due to his courage against the enemy:
>
> **Reason for consideration:** Master Sergeant Döbele is a mature, experienced fighter pilot with an open, honest and well-grounded character. He possesses great inner élan and sweeps along all his comrades and men under him with his excellent knowledge and accomplishments; by his courage and willingness to serve, he is the type of a leader for difficult engagements. His sense of duty is extremely well-founded and he brings along the necessary understanding to the occupation of officer. Towards superiors he is correct, towards the men under his command he is definite in his secure appearance. Well-liked among his comrades. His military and flying accomplishments are above average, his attitude as a soldier is without reproach. Master Sergeant Döbele possesses initiative and talent for improvisation. He is well-rooted in National Socialist ideology, and at any time he is able to utilize and pass on his national socialistic thinking. Mentally, Döbele is well-gifted, he thinks clearly and critically. Physically of medium build, strong, tough and with stamina. Döbele possesses infantry experience due to his peace time training in the old German Army. Against the enemy, Döbele excels in every situation. In 418 combat missions to date, he has garnered 80 victories and flew numerous ground-attack and fighter-bomber missions.
>
> Due to his refreshing, lively nature, his willingness to serve, his healthy drive, his delight in responsibility, his immaculate soldierly attitude, his leadership attributes, his talent for improvisation and his own initiative, Döbele promises to become a good officer. Sometimes Döbele tends to be critical and he can be harsh and one-sided in judging the people around him, not enough objectivity. In his capacity as older, experienced flight leader, he frequently opposes young officers, but he is eager to learn and accepts admonishment. Some lack of general education and in social behavior should be quickly remedied with good guidance. Master Sergeant Döbele is assessed as above average. On February 3, 1942, he was awarded the Iron Cross First Class. On July 6, 1943, he was recommended for the Honor Goblet, on July 9, 1943 for the German Cross, and on September 11, 1943 for the Knight's Cross of the Iron Cross.

The wing commodore, Hubertus von Bonin, writing six days later, also gave Döbele high praise:

> Master Sergeant Döbele is a really outstanding fighter pilot who, during the most difficult air battles, demonstrated exemplary personal accomplishments and he has swept along his pilots with him in every way. The prerequisites which are still lacking will be attained in a short time under respective guidance. It is recommended

that he be promoted to officer due to his courage against the enemy.

Others shared their enthusiasm, and Döbele received the German Cross in Gold on October 4, 1943.[63] He continued his score with his 90th (an Il-2 Sturmovik) aerial victory on November 4, but his luck finally ran out. Master Sergeant Anton Döbele was killed in aerial combat north of the Smolensk-Vitebsk highway at 10:42 a.m., November 11, 1943, when his Focke-Wulf Fw 190A-4 rammed a Russian Il-2 Sturmovik ground-attack aircraft at an altitude of 300 meters, four minutes after shooting down another Il-2 (a different source says the collision was with another German fighter.) He was posthumously awarded the Knight's Cross of the Iron Cross and, as his superiors had requested the previous September, he was promoted to the grade of second lieutenant on March 26, 1944. At the time of his death, he was credited with 458 combat missions and 94 aerial victories, all of which were recorded on the Eastern Front and included 23 Il-2 Sturmoviks; Döbele had a sortie-to-victory ratio of 4.87 to 1. He is buried at a German Military Cemetery in Vilnius-Vingio, Lithuania. During his service in the 1st Squadron, 54th Fighter Wing, Toni Döbele was a member of the most famous flight in the *Luftwaffe* – that composed of First Lieutenant Walter Nowotny, Master Sergeant Rudi Rademacher, Master Sergeant Karl Schnörrer, and Döbele – who while flying together shot down 450 enemy aircraft in Russia.[64]

1.Staffel *Lfl. 6* O.U., den 16.9.1943
I./Jagdgeschwader 54.

Betr.: Antrag auf Beförderung des Ofw. Anton D ö b e l e
zum Kriegsoffizier wegen Tapferkeit vor dem Feinde.

An

I./Jagdgeschwader 54.

Die Staffel bittet um Beförderung des Ofw. Anton D ö b e l e
zum Kriegsoffizier wegen Tapferkeit vor dem Feinde.

Begründung: Oberfeldwebel Döbele ist ein alter erfahrener Jagdflieger mit offenem, ehrlichem und gefestigtem Charakter. Er besitzt grossen inneren Schwung und reisst alle Kameraden und Untergebene durch seine hervorragenden Kenntnisse und Leistungen, durch seinen Mut und Einsatzfreude mit und ist der Typ eines Führers im harten Einsatz. Er hat ein kolossal ausgeprägtes Pflichtbewusstsein und bringt die nötige Auffassung zum Offiziersberuf mit. Gegen Vorgesetzte korrekt, gegen Untergebene bestimmt mit sicherem Auftreten. Unter Kameraden beliebt. Seine militärischen und fliegerischen Leistungen sind hervorragend, seine soldatische Haltung einwandfrei. Ofw. Döbele besitzt Eigeninitiative und Improvisationstalent. Er steht fest auf dem Boden der nationalsozialistischen Weltanschauung und ist jederzeit in der Lage, das nationalsozialistische Gedankengut zu verwerten und weiterzuvermitteln. Geistig ist Döbele gut ausgerüstet, er denkt klar und kritisch. Körperlich mittel, kräftig, zäh und ausdauernd. Infanteristische Erfahrung besitzt Döbele aus seiner friedensmässigen Ausbildung im Reichsheer. Vor dem Feinde bewährte sich Ofw. Döbele in jeder Lage. Er errang in bisher 418 Feindflügen 80 Abschüsse und flog zahlreiche Tiefangriffe und Jabo-Einsätze.

Auf Grund seines frischen, temperamentvollen Wesens, seiner Einsatzfreude, seines gesunden Ehrgeizes, seiner Verantwortungsfreude, seiner einwandfreien soldatischen Haltung, seiner Führereigenschaften, seines Improvisationstalentes und seiner Eigeninitiative verspricht Döbele ein guter Offizier zu werden.

Döbele ist manchmal zu kritisch veranlagt und in der Beurteilung seiner Mitmenschen zu hart und einseitig, nicht objektiv genug. In seiner Eigenschaft als alter erfahrener Schwarmführer vergisst er sich oft jungen Offizieren gegenüber, lässt sich jedoch gerne belehren und zurechtweisen. Einige Lücken in der Allgemeinbildung und im gesellschaftlichen Umgang lassen sich bei guter Anleitung rasch ausfüllen. Ofw. Döbele ist über dem Durchschnitt veranlagt. Ofw. Döbele wurde am 3.2.1943 mit dem Eisernen Kreuz 1.Klasse ausgezeichnet. Er wurde am 6.7.1943 zum Ehrenpokal, am 9.7.1943 zum Deutschen Kreuz und am 11.9.1943 zum Ritterkreuz des Eisernen Kreuzes vorgeschlagen.

Oberleutnant u.Staffelkapitän

b.w.

Request for Promotion to Officer for Master Sergeant Anton Döbele (front side) – dated September 16, 1943, on blank paper with typed comments. Signed by First Lieutenant, and 1st Squadron Commander, Walter Nowotny. Pencil notations at the top probably made at the *Luftwaffe* Personnel Office, include a small cross (Döbele was killed in action on November 11, 1943).

I./Jagdgeschwader 54   Gefechtsstand, den 16. 9. 43.

An den
Reichsminister der Luftfahrt
und Oberbefehlshaber der Luftwaffe,
L.P. - Amt,
auf dem Dienstwege.

    Meiner Begründung als Staffelkapitän habe ich nichts hinzuzufügen.

(signature)

Oberleutnant u. Führer der Jagdgruppe.

Jagdgeschwader 54   Gefechtsstand, 22.9.1943

    Oberfeldwebel D ö b e l e ist ein ganz hervorragender Jagdflieger, der in härtesten Luftkämpfen vorbildlich persönliche Leistungen gezeigt und seine Flugzeugführer in jeder Beziehung mitgerissen hat.

    Die ihm noch fehlenden Voraussetzungen wird er in Kürze bei entsprechender Anleitung erreichen.

    Es wird gebeten, ihm wegen Tapferkeit vor dem Feinde zum Offizier zu befördern.

(signature)

Request for Promotion to Officer for Master Sergeant Anton Döbele (back side) – signed again by Walter Nowotny and by the 54th Fighter Wing Commodore, Major Hubertus von Bonin.

Alfred Druschel
Stuka Pilot

"Distinct talent for improvisation."

Colonel Alfred Druschel was born February 4, 1917 in Bindsachsen near Büdingen, Hesse. He joined the *Luftwaffe* on April 1, 1936 as an officer candidate and spent his first two years of service at various schools – first in Berlin and Rangsdorf and then training to be an observer at the bomber schools at Tutow and Fassberg. On July 1, 1937, he joined the 20th Air Group (*Fliegergruppe 20*), which on November 1, 1938 became the 2nd Group, 2nd Demonstration Wing (*Lehrgeschwader 2*). He flew a Hentschel Hs 123 during the Polish and French campaigns with the unit's 4th Squadron, participating in ground-attacks against Bzura (Poland) and Eben Emael, Dunkirk and the Weygand Line in the west. Druschel won the Iron Cross 2nd Class on September 27, 1939 and the Iron Cross 1st Class on May 21, 1940. He became the Commander, 4th Squadron on December 6, 1940, and until March 1941 flew fighter-bomber missions against ground targets in England and shipping in the English Channel, as part of the 2nd Air Fleet.

Druschel then flew missions in the Balkan campaign in April 1941 from bases in Bulgaria against targets in southern Yugoslavia and Greece; on April 15, 1941 his Messerschmitt Me 109E crashed on takeoff at Bitolj, Yugoslavia, injuring him. During the campaign against the Soviet Union on the Eastern front, Druschel progressed in both battlefield accomplishments and organizational responsibilities. Colonel General Alfred Keller, the commanding general of the 1st Air Fleet, personally awarded Alfred Druschel the Knight's Cross of the Iron Cross on August 21, 1941, after Druschel reached 200 combat missions. He then assumed command of the 2nd Squadron, in support of the German Army's 3rd *Panzer* Group as it advanced on Minsk, Smolensk and Moscow. Druschel assumed command, on March 1, 1942 of the 1st Group, 1st Stuka Wing (*Sturzkampfgeschwader 1* – renamed *Schlachtgeschwader 1* in November 1943) and from June 11, 1943 to October 18, 1943, he served as the *Geschwader* commander. Captain Druschel won the Oak Leaves to the Knight's Cross (the 118th recipient) on September 3, 1942 after flying 600 combat missions and the Swords to the Oak Leaves (the 24th recipient) on February 19, 1943 after flying 700 combat missions. In early July 1943 during "Operation Citadel," Druschel's ground-attack *Geschwader* supported the southern attack pincer on its drive northward towards Kursk; he flew a Focke-Wulf Fw 190F-2 at the time.[65] In October 1943, Druschel became the Inspector of Day Ground-Attack Units. He was promoted to lieutenant colonel on April 1, 1944 and to colonel on July 1, 1944.

On January 13, 1944, the chain of command for Major Alfred Druschel submitted an officer efficiency report on him. The rater Colonel Hubertus Hitschhold wrote:[66]

Short Assessment: Lieutenant Colonel Druschel is a sincere, open, decent and exuberant character, with very good mental and physical attributes. Always alert and open to ideas, filled with National Socialistic thinking, he demonstrates mature personal values. His expressed leadership qualities, his outstanding tactical understanding, coupled with unwavering readiness for combat and decision-making ability have come to full fruition in his service at the front and have come to be expressed in repeated preferential promotions up to his current service grade, as well as the award of the Swords to the Oak Leaves of the Knight's Cross.

In leadership positions as group commander and squadron commander of ground attack units, Lieutenant Colonel Druschel has excelled as both a superior and comrade. In his current activity as Inspector for Ground Attack Units with the General for Ground-Attack Units, he understands how to make use of his various experiences at the front and his energy, prudence and organizational capabilities.

Strong Traits: Passionate, combat-ready pilot; organizer with distinct talent for improvisation.

Summary Assessment: Above Average.
(Above Average, Average, Below Average)

How well is the current position being fulfilled: Very well fulfilled.
(Use only: Very well fulfilled, well fulfilled, fulfilled, not fulfilled)

Suitable for promotion to the next higher service grade: Yes.

Suitable as: Continue in current position.

Druschel assumed command of the 4th Ground-Attack Wing (*Schlachtgeschwader 4*) on December 28, 1944, but his tenure was short-lived. Some days earlier, the 4th Ground-Attack Wing had flown several ground-attack missions near Bastogne, but had achieved dismal results. The *Geschwader* commander, Lieutenant Colonel Ewald Janssen, was fired and Druschel took command – a mere four days before the planned "Operation Bodenplatte," a massive, surprise, low-level air attack against Allied tactical airfields throughout Holland, Belgium and France. Druschel took off at 8:45 a.m. on January 1, 1945 in his Focke-Wulf Fw 190A-8 from the Bonn-Hangelar airfield near Cologne and flew west with his unit over Zülpich and south of Aachen – their target an Allied airfield at St. Trond, Belgium. At 9:10 a.m., the U.S. 445th Anti-Aircraft-Artillery Battalion, located close to the village of Hürtgen, equipped with 40mm Bofers, fired on seven low-flying German fighters. One of the aircraft may have been Druschel's; his wingman lost sight of him about this time and he never returned from the mission. He was listed as missing in action. A recent book asserts that on January 5, 1945, the body of a *Luftwaffe* colonel was recovered and buried next to his Fw 190 near the village of Höfen south of Monschau, but his final resting place has never been officially established.[67]

Alfred Druschel flew over 800 ground-attack missions in an Hentschel Hs 123, a Messerschmitt Me 109 and in various models of the Focke-Wulf Fw 190. He also shot down 7 enemy aircraft.[68]

General der Schlachtflieger Rangsdorf, den 13.1. 1944
(Dienststelle, nicht Feldpostnummer)

Kriegs-Beurteilung zum 1.Februar 1944

für Offz. ausschl. San.-, Vet.-Offz.

über den

Oberstleutnant (Tr.O.)	noch nicht festgesetzt	Alfred	Druschel
Dienstgrad¹⁾	R.D.A. (Ordn. Nr.) und Dienstalterliste	Vorname	Name

4.2.1917	verheiratet, ledig, verwitwet, geschieden	kv
geboren am	(Zutreffendes unterstreichen)	Wehrdiensttauglichkeit²⁾ (kv, gv Feld, gv H, tropentgl., tropenuntgl.)

aktiver Offizier
Zivilberuf (falls vorhanden)   Flugpl.Kdo.Tutow
Inspizient Schlachtflieger   W.B.K. Wiesbaden
jetzige Verwendung seit 11.10.43   Friedensdienststelle und W.B.K.³⁾

gem. D.(Luft) 2000 Ziff. V, 2
Anlaß der Vorlage⁴⁾

Deutsche Auszeichnungen des jetzigen Krieges mit Verleihungsdaten und Angabe, ob und zu welchen Auszeichnungen vorgeschlagen: E.K.II,E.K.I,Ehrenpokal,Ritterkreuz,Eichenlaub zum R.Kr.,Schwerter z.Eichenlaub d.Ritterkr.d.E.K.,Anhänger z.Frontflugspange i.Gold, Medaille "Winterschlacht" i.O. 41/42

¹) Genaue Angabe, ob Tr.-Offz., Erg.-Offz., Offz. z. D., Res.-Offz., Kr.-Offz. z. V.-Offz. — ²) In zweifelhaften Fällen neu festzustellen. — ³) Dienststelle, welche Friedensgebührnisse zahlt und zuständiges Wehrbezirkskommando. — ⁴) z.B.: Versetzung zur III./K.G. 2, terminmäßige Vorlage zum 1. 5. 43.

Kurze Beurteilung (Persönlichkeitswert, nationalsozialistische Haltung, Bewährung vor dem Feinde, dienstliche Leistungen, geistige und körperliche Anlagen und Eignung, infanteristische Erfahrungen, wann und wo erworben):

Oberstlt.Druschel ist ein gerader, offener, anständiger u.lebensfroher Charakter, mit sehr guten geistigen u.körperlichen Anlagen.Stets frisch u.aufgeschlossen,durchdrungen vom nat.soz.Gedankengut, zeigt ausgereifte Persönlichkeitswerte. Seine ausgeprägten Führereigenschaften, sein hervorragendes taktisches Verständnis, verbunden mit rücksichtsloser Einsatz- und Entschlußfreudigkeit, sind im Fronteinsatz voll zur Entfaltung und in wiederholter vorzeitiger Beförderung bis zu dem jetzigen Dienstgrad, sowie in der Auszeichnung mit den Schwertern zum Eichenlaub des Ritterkreuzes d.E.Kr. zum Ausdruck gekommen.
In der truppendienstlichen Führung als Gruppenkommandeur u.Geschwaderkommomore eines Schlachtgeschwaders hat sich Oberstlt.D. als Vorgesetzer u.Kamerad hervorragend bewährt. In seiner jetzigen Tätigkeit als Inspizient für Schlachtfliegerverbände beim General der Schlachtflieger hat er seine vielseitigen Fronterfahrungen mit Tatkraft und Umsicht und Organisationsvermögen zu verwerten verstanden.
Starke Seiten: Passionierter, einsatzfreudiger Flugzeugführer, Organisator mit ausgeprägtem Improvisationstalent.
Schwache Seiten:

Zusammenfassendes Urteil   über Durchschnitt.
(über Durchschnitt, Durchschnitt, unter Durchschnitt):

Wie wird jetzige Stelle ausgefüllt? (Es sind nur die   Sehr gut ausgefüllt.
Ausdrücke „sehr gut ausgefüllt", „gut ausgefüllt", „ausgefüllt", „nicht ausgefüllt" zu verwenden)

Geeignet zur Beförderung zum nächsthöheren Dienstgrad?   geeignet.

B 3614. M.-V. 7. 8. 43

Efficiency Report for Lieutenant Colonel Alfred Druschel (front side) – dated January 13, 1944, on preprinted form, with typed comments.

Eignung
für welche nächsthöhere Verwendung⁵)?
für welche besondere oder anderweitige Verwendung⁶)?
Vorschlag für Verwendung in nächster Zeit⁷)?   noch Belassung in bisheriger Stelle

Sprachkenntnisse (keine Schulkenntnisse)
a) abgelegte Prüfungen: ---
   (z. B.: Dolmetscherprüfung 1. 10. 42)
b) Beherrschung der Sprache: ---
   (z. B.: durch Aufenthalt im Ausland)

Eröffnung zu welchen Punkten, wann, wie
(mündlich oder schriftlich) und durch wen?

Strafen sind mit vollem Straftenor sowie Vermerk über Vollstreckung abschriftlich als Anlage der Kriegsbeurteilung beizuheften.

Dem Beurteilenden bekannt seit
                       unterstellt seit

Ausbildung
a) erworbene Scheine: L. F.
   (L. F., E. L. F., L. B. usw.)
b) Sonderausbildung: ---
   (z. B. Bild Offz., Techn. Offz., Meß-Offz.,
   Funk-Drahtnachr.-Offz., W. K. S.)

_____   Oberst und General der Schlachtflieger
      Unterschrift   Dienstgrad und Dienststellung

Beitrag des Chefs des Generalstabes der vorgesetzten Kommandobehörde (nur bei Genst.-Offz. in Stabsstellungen und zur Dienstleistung zum Generalstab kommandierten Offizieren):

Zusätze vorgesetzter Dienststellen:

---

⁵) Gilt für alle Offz., für Truppen-Offz. hinsichtlich Eignung zur Führung des nächsthöheren Verbandes, für Genst.-Offz. hinsichtlich Eignung zum Chef oder I a, I c der Luftfl., Flieger-Korps, Flak-Korps, Fl.-Div., Flak-Div., zur Versetzung in den Genst., zur Kommandierung in den Genst. — ⁶) z. B.: Höherer Adjutant, Erzieher, Lehrer auf Spezialgebieten, auf Grund von Sprachkenntnissen im Attachédienst; für Genst. Offz hinsichtlich Eignung für Verwendung im Quartiermeisterdienst, im Ic-Dienst, im Transportwesen, als Lehrer für Genst.-Lehrgang (Taktik bzw. Qu.-Dienst); besondere Anlagen für Kriegsgeschichte, Wehrwirtschaft. — ⁷) z. B.: „noch halbjährige Belassung in bisheriger Stelle" oder „alsbaldige Verwendung als Geschw.-Kommodore".

Efficiency Report for Lieutenant Colonel Alfred Druschel (back side) – signed by Colonel Hubertus Hitschhold.

Hans Ehlers
Fighter Pilot

"Of particular note is that on October 8, 1943, after he had completely depleted his ammunition, he rammed a four-engine bomber."

Major Hans Ehlers was born in Hennestedt near Itzehoe in Holstein on July 15, 1914. He served in the Spanish Civil War as a member of the ground crew in Adolf Galland's squadron of the 88th Fighter Group [J/88]. After receiving flight training at Salzwedel and Werneuchen on his return to Germany, Ehlers joined the 2nd Squadron, 3rd Fighter Wing (*Jagdgeschwader 3*) on December 7, 1939 and scored his first two aerial victories – Spitfires, southeast of Valenciennes, France – on May 18, 1940. However, he was forced to make an emergency landing and was taken prisoner. Reunited with his unit after Dunkirk, his aerial troubles continued. Technical Sergeant Ehlers shot down a Spitfire west of Calais without incident on August 26, 1940, but on September 5, 1940, during the Battle of Britain (as part of the 2nd Air Fleet), his Messerschmitt Me 109E crashed into a Spitfire over Canterbury, and he had to nurse the stricken aircraft back to base. On April 4, 1941, he transferred to the 3rd Squadron; his unit deployed to Russia, where he scored 11 kills in 1941, including two on June 26, two on August 15 and two on August 30, which was the 1,000th victory of *Jagdgeschwader 3*.

His unit redeployed to the Western Front on December 12, 1941 and was designated in Holland as the 6th Squadron, 1st Fighter Wing (*Jagdgeschwader 1*). On June 19, 1942, while flying a Focke-Wulf Fw 190A-2, he shot down two Spitfires over Zeebrügge, Belgium; he shot down a B-17 Flying Fortress on December 6, 1942. By the end of June 1943, Ehlers had reached 25 aerial victories. Promoted to second lieutenant on July 1, 1943, he transferred to the 2nd Squadron in July and became the acting squadron commander on August 17, 1943. On October 8, 1943, flying a Focke-Wulf Fw 190A-6, after his weapons malfunctioned, he rammed a B-17 Flying Fortress over Kalle; Ehlers had to then quickly bail out of his crashing plane. *Reichsmarschall* Hermann Göring personally presented Ehlers the German Cross in Gold on October 24 at Deelen, Holland. On November 1, Ehlers assumed command of the 3rd Squadron, 1st Fighter Wing.

On January 16, 1944, Ehlers' chain of command in *Jagdgeschwader 1* submitted a special report requesting a preferred promotion. Captain Alfred Grislawski, the acting group commander, wrote:[69]

Second Lieutenant Ehlers is a sincere and straight character whose actions are dictated by strength and his willingness for combat. He comes from a simple way of life and shows spirit and élan in the execution of the tasks demanded from him. Due to his long period of service as a sergeant, he has great infantry experience.[70] He is leading his squadron with circumspection and energy. In all his work, he personally stands together with his men, and in doing so, he always has an enthusiastic following. He is greatly talented as a fighter pilot and was very successful due to his risk-taking and willingness for combat. Good tactical understanding makes it possible for him to lead his pilots effectively against the enemy. His mental attributes are average. However, he masters all tasks within his sphere of activity. Physically, he is very strong, athletically trained and can be burdened greatly. He is rooted in National Socialist ideology. He possesses the necessary talent for improvisation.

Lieutenant Colonel Walter Oesau, the *Geschwader* commodore, added:

> I place particular great value on Second Lieutenant Ehlers, due to his decent and straight character. He has understood how to win over his squadron, is leading his unit with energy and strength, and is an example for his pilots as a flyer and soldier. Ehlers has excelled particularly through his willingness for combat in the fight against four engine bombers. Due to his tactical understanding, he succeeds in leading his squadron from success to success. Of particular note is that on October 8, 1943, after he had completely depleted his ammunition, he rammed a four-engine bomber and has proven though this decision a particularly high degree of courage. Due to his great troop leadership, through his exemplary training work and his outstanding courage, I consider Second Lieutenant Ehlers worthy of preferential promotion in his troop leadership position.

On April 13, 1944, he shot down a B-17 Flying Fortress and a P-51 Mustang but was lightly wounded in a forced belly-landing of his Focke-Wulf Fw 190A-8 at Gutersdorf. On April 17, 1944, he was named Commander, 1st Group, 1st Fighter Wing. Hans Ehlers received the Knight's Cross of the Iron Cross on June 9, 1944, after chalking up 53 aerial victories. After a rest away from the front, he returned to action in November. On December 27, 1944, on a mission to protect ground troops in the area of Dinant-Rochefort during the Battle of the Bulge, his Focke-Wulf Fw 190A-8 was shot down in combat with Allied fighters. It was the twelfth time that Ehlers was shot down; unlike the previous eleven, this one was fatal.

Hans Ehlers totaled 55 victories, of which 23 were four-engine bombers. He was submitted for a posthumous award of the Oak Leaves to his Knight's Cross, but this was never approved.[71]

```
Generalkommando I. Jagdkorps                    O.U., den 16. Januar 1944
Jagdgeschwader 1                                Wehrmachtteil:  Luftwaffe.
W.B.K.: Salzwedel
Vorgeschlagen gem:
Waffengattung:  Fliegertruppe
                Flugzeugführer.
```

V o r s c h l a g

zur bevorzugten Beförderung eines Offiziers (Leutnant und
Staffelkapitän) in Truppenführerstellung (Hauptmann) gem. R.d.L.u.
Ob.d.L., Lp. Az. 21 Nr. 71849/42 (2 I.D).

```
Vor- und Zuname:       Hans  E h l e r s
Geburtsdatum:          15. 7. 1914
Jetziger Dienstgrad:   Leutnant (Kr.O.)               Obl. 1.3.41
Rangdienstalter:       1. 1. 1939
Eingesetzt als:        Staffelkapitän seit 12.8.43
Geeignet zum:          - - -
Aktiver Wehrdienst seit 1.8.39:

     1. 8.39 - 17. 9.39    Flzgf.Sch. Salzwedel
    18. 9.39 - 15.11.39    Jagdfl.Sch. Werneuchen, Schülerkp.
    16.11.39 -  6.12.39    Erg.Jagdgr.2, Merseburg
     7.12.39 -  3. 4.41    2./J.G. 3
     4. 4.41 - 14. 1.42    3./J.G. 3
    15. 1.42 - 10. 8.43    6./J.G. 1
    11. 8.42 -             3./J.G. 1
```

Beförderung in den einzelnen Offiziers-Dienstgraden:

```
     1. 7.43   zum Leutnant (Kr.O.)
```

Teilnahme an welchen Kämpfen (Verwendung im mobilen Einsatz):

```
    10. 1.40 - 10. 5.40    Sicherung d. deutschen Westgrenze
    11. 5.40 - 15. 2.41    Verwendung im Operationsgebiet d.Westfront
                           11. 5.40 -  4. 6.40  Durchbruch zum Ärmelkanal
                            5. 6.40              Schlacht in Flandern und Artois
    16. 2.41 - 30. 4.41    Verwendung im Heimatkriegsgebiet
     1. 5.41 -  1. 6.41    Verwendung im Operationsgebiet der Westfront
                            (Einsatz gegen England)
     2. 6.41 - 21. 6.41    Sicherung des Generalgouvernements
    22. 6.41 - 15. 9.41    Verwendung im Operationsgebiet der Ostfront
    16. 9.41 - 11.12.41    Verwendung im Heimatkriegsgebiet
    12.12.41 - 12. 7.43    Verwendung im Operationsgebiet der Westfront
                            (Einsatz gegen England)
    13. 7.41 - 11. 8.43    Einsatz in der Tagjagd im besetzten Westgebiet
    12. 8.41 -              - " -
```

-2-

Request for Preferred Promotion for Second Lieutenant Hans Ehlers (front side) – dated January 16, 1944, on blank paper with typed comments. Pencil notations probably made at the *Luftwaffe* Personnel Office.

– 2 –

Beurteilung.

Lt. Ehlers ist ein aufrichtiger und gerader Charakter, dessen Handeln durch Einsatzwillen und Härte bestimmt wird. Er ist von einfacher Lebensart und zeigt Frische und Schwung bei der Durchführung ihm übertragener Aufgaben. Aufgrund seiner langen Dienstzeit als Unteroffizier verfügt er über große infanteristische Erfahrungen. Seine Staffel führt er mit Umsicht und Energie. Bei allen Arbeiten steht er selbst mit seinen Leuten zusammen und hat dadurch immer eine freudige Gefolgschaft. Er ist ein gut veranlagter Jagdflieger und hat infolge seines Draufgängertums und seiner Einsatzfreudigkeit große Erfolge. Gutes taktisches Verständnis befähigt ihn, seine Flugzeugführer wirksam an den Feind zu bringen. Seine geistige Veranlagung ist durchschnittlich. Doch meistert er alle in seinem Wirkungsbereich anfallenden Aufgaben. Körperlich ist er kräftig, sportlich durchgebildet und äußerst belastbar. E. steht auf dem Boden der nationalsozialistischen Weltanschauung. Er verfügt über ausreichendes Improvisationsvermögen.

I.V.

Grislawski
Hauptmann.

Stellungnahme des Geschwaderkommodore:

Ich schätze Lt. E h l e r s auf Grund seines anständigen und geraden Charakters ganz besonders. Er hat es verstanden, seine Staffel für sich zu gewinnen, führt seine Einheit mit Energie und Härte und ist seinen Flugzeugführern in fliegerischer und soldatischer Hinsicht ein Vorbild.

E. hat sich durch besondere Einsatzfreudigkeit im Kampfe gegen die viermot. Kampfflugzeuge hervorgetan. Bedingt durch sein taktisches Verständnis, gelingt es ihm, seine Staffel von Erfolg zu Erfolg zu führen.

B e s o n d e r s h e r v o r z u h e b e n i s t, daß er am 8.10.43, nachdem er sich völlig verschossen hatte, ein viermot. Kampfflugzeug rammte und durch diesen Entschluß einen besonders hohen Grad von Tapferkeit bewiesen hat.

Ich halte den Lt. E h l e r s auf Grund seiner guten Truppenführung, seiner vorbildlichen Erziehungsarbeit und seiner hervorragenden Tapferkeit würdig zur bevorzugten Beförderung in seine Truppenführerstelle.

Oesau
Oberstleutnant

Request for Preferred Promotion for Second Lieutenant Hans Ehlers (back side) – signed by Captain Alfred Grislawski, the acting 1st Group Commander, and by Lieutenant Colonel and Commodore, 1st Fighter Wing, Walter Oesau.

Siegfried Engfer
Fighter Pilot

"His appearance is modest and reserved."

First Lieutenant Siegfried Engfer was born April 27, 1915 at Neuhof in the Dramburg region of eastern Pomerania. He joined the Army in 1935 and served in the infantry before transferring to the *Luftwaffe* in 1937. Engfer transferred to the 9th Squadron, 3rd Fighter Wing (*Jagdgeschwader 3*) in May 1941. However, he sustained a serious injury in an accident on June 4, which kept him from combat duties until spring 1942. Operating over the Eastern Front, Engfer claimed his first victory on March 12, 1942, when he shot down a Russian R-5 tactical reconnaissance biplane. During August 1942, he claimed 15 victories, including his 20th, a LaGG-3 fighter, on August 18. The following month, he scored 24 victories, including his 30th (a P-2), on September 2, his 40th (a MiG-1 fighter near Stalingrad) on September 10 and his 50th (an Il-2 Sturmovik over Stalingrad) on September 15. He ended the month by receiving the *Luftwaffe* Honor Goblet on September 30. Technical Sergeant Siegfried Engfer was awarded the Knight's Cross of the Iron Cross on October 2, 1942 for 52 aerial victories.

On January 20, 1943, Major Wolf-Dietrich Wilcke, the commodore of the 3rd Fighter Wing, submitted a special recommendation for promotion to commissioned officer for Master Sergeant Engfer. Wilcke wrote:[72]

> I request that Master Sergeant Siegfried Engfer be promoted to officer due to his courage against the enemy. As to the evaluation, I agree with the opinion of his group commander dated December 12, 1942. As an officer, Engfer will use his talents to lead young fighter pilots against the enemy to a still greater extent. His appearance is modest and reserved. He takes care to advance himself and will continue to develop the bearing and understanding of an officer.

On May 28, 1943, Engfer transferred to Supplemental Fighter Group East (*Ergänzungs-Jagdgruppe Ost*) – an operational training formation – as a fighter pilot instructor. While there, he suffered a serious illness, which prevented his return to combat duty or flying for the remainder of the war. He was credited with 59 kills in 348 combat missions, all of which occurred on the Eastern Front and that included 25 Il-2 Sturmoviks. He had a sortie-to-victory ratio of 5.89 to 1. Engfer, nicknamed "Leather Pants" (*Lederstrumpf*) by his comrades, probably died in April 1946 under mysterious circumstances, when he disappeared from a train traveling from Vienna to Munich.[73]

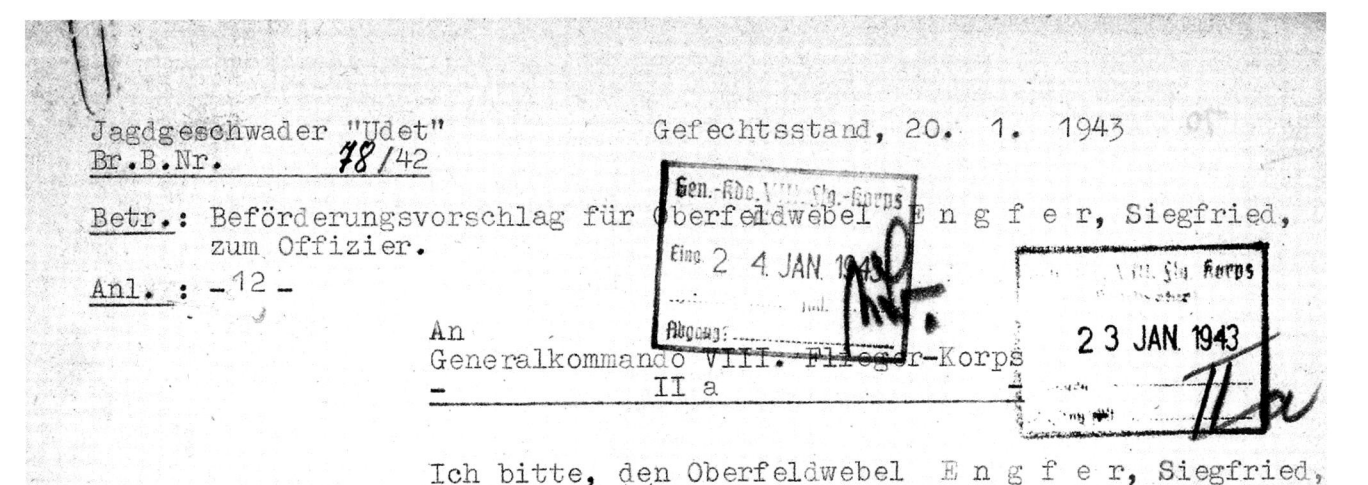

Jagdgeschwader "Udet" Gefechtsstand, 20. 1. 1943
Br.B.Nr. 78/42

Betr.: Beförderungsvorschlag für Oberfeldwebel E n g f e r, Siegfried, zum Offizier.

Anl.: -12-

An
Generalkommando VIII. Flieger-Korps
— II a

Ich bitte, den Oberfeldwebel E n g f e r, Siegfried, wegen Tapferkeit vor dem Feinde zum Offizier zu befördern. Hinsichtlich der Beurteilung schliesse ich mich der Stellungnahme seines Gruppenkommandeurs vom 4. 12. 1942 an.
Engfer wird sein Talent, junge Jagdflieger erfolgreich an den Fein zu führen, als Offizier mit noch grösserem Nachdruck auswerten können. Sein Auftreten ist bescheiden und zurückhaltend. Er gibt si Mühe, vorwärts zu kommen, und wird allmählich in die Haltung und Auf fassung eines Offiziers hineinwachsen.

Major und Geschwader – Kommodore

Request for Promotion to Officer for Master Sergeant Siegfried Engfer (one side only) – dated January 20, 1943, and signed by the Commodore, 3rd Fighter Wing, Major Wolf-Dietrich Wilcke. Stamp at top of page shows document arrived at the headquarters 8th Air Corps either on January 23 or 24.

Waldemar Felgenhauer
Reconnaissance Pilot

"Not totally free of personal ambition."

Captain Waldemar Felgenhauer was born September 2, 1914 at Rastatt, Baden. He entered the *Reichswehr* on April 1, 1932 and was assigned to the 2nd Artillery Regiment. Felgenhauer transferred to the *Luftwaffe* on December 10, 1933 and initially received communications and gunnery training on the 37 mm cannon. Felgenhauer was promoted to staff sergeant on March 1, 1935 and then received general flight training at Magdeburg from April 24, 1935 to December 15, 1935. From December 17, 1935 to March 7, 1936, he underwent fighter pilot training at Schleissheim. He then transferred to the 1st Group, 165th Bomber Wing (*Kampfgeschwader 165*) in Kitzingen and two months later moved to the 2nd Squadron, 123rd Reconnaissance Group (*Aufklärungsgruppe 123*) in Würzburg.

From November 11, 1936 to May 10, 1937, Felgenhauer was temporarily transferred to *Sonderkommando Rügen*, the code name for the *Luftwaffe's* participation in the Spanish Civil War as the Condo Legion, and was assigned to A/88, the reconnaissance group. While in Spain, he was promoted to technical sergeant, flew 71 combat reconnaissance missions and won the Spanish Cross in Silver with Swords, as well as the Spanish "Cruc de Guerra Medaglia de compagna." He was promoted to master sergeant on his return to Germany on June 1, 1937. During World War II, back again with the 2nd Squadron, 123rd Reconnaissance Group, he flew three combat missions on the Western Front in 1939, winning the Iron Cross 2nd Class on December 1; he was promoted to officer candidate on February 1, 1940. During the French campaign in 1940, he flew an additional twelve combat missions and received the Iron Cross 1st Class on June 6, 1940. He was promoted to first lieutenant on May 1, 1940. During the Battle of Britain, from June 24, 1940 to February 18, 1941, Felgenhauer continued his superlative performance by flying a further 23 combat reconnaissance missions, as part of the 3rd Air Fleet.[74] Between March 9, 1941 and March 13, 1942, Waldemar Felgenhauer flew an additional 66 combat missions over the Mediterranean Sea and Africa. He received the Operational Flying Clasp for Reconnaissance in Silver on April 5, 1941, the *Luftwaffe* Honor Goblet on May 30, 1941 and the Operational Flying Clasp for Reconnaissance in Gold a day later.

On May 17, 1941, Major and Squadron Commander Hans von Obernitz submitted a special report requesting a transfer to the regular, peacetime, *Luftwaffe* career officer status for Waldemar Felgenhauer (who was at the time classified as a First Lieutenant of Reserves). In the report, he provided details about Felgenhauer on the front side of the report, to include that he was married, a protestant, had no disciplinary actions against him, and wrote his subjective opinion on the reverse:[75]

Evaluation:

Personal values: Alert and intelligent, very correct in all of his actions, well educated and flexible, a good comrade.

Character attributes: Open and sincere, morally pure, helpful, not totally free of personal ambition.

Mental disposition: Sufficient for continued effort to further educate himself.

Military disposition: Good soldier with sufficient knowledge of military procedures and training. Very good factual knowledge, suitable as Technical Officer. Excellent, reliable pilot.

Physical attributes: Healthy, strong and athletic.

Additional comments (particularly regarding performance in the face of the enemy, in the current service position and regarding suitability for promotion to the next higher service grade): From the beginning of the war, in uninterrupted operations against the enemy, he belongs with the most successful and most experienced pilots of his unit.

On November 11, 1941, Felgenhauer received the Italian "La Medaglia d' argento al valor Militaire 'sul campo,'" but his most significant award came on January 14, 1942 when he was presented the Knight's Cross of the Iron Cross. He continued to fly in combat until April 21, 1942, when he was transferred to the Supplemental Long-Range Reconnaissance Group (*Ergänzungs Fernaufklärungsgruppe*) – an operational training unit – at Weimar-Nohra, where he became a flight instructor. He remained a flight instructor for the duration of the war, finishing the conflict as a captain. After World War II, he joined the new German Air Force and again became a captain. Waldemar Felgenhauer died on November 16, 1963 in Würzburg, Bavaria.[76] He is buried at the *Hauptfriedhof* in Würzburg (Field 5, Row 48, Grave 17.)

2.(F)/123.   O.U., den 17.5.1941.
....
(Truppenteil bzw. Dienststelle.)

                              V o r s c h l a g .
                              ─────────────────

            zur Überführung des (Kriegsoffiziers) **Oblt. Felgenhauer**
            zu den aktiven Friedensoffizieren .

Familienname, Vorname: Felgenhauer,   Waldemar

geb. am: 9.2.1914.   zu: Rastatt/Bad.   Konfession: evang.

Verheiratet, ~~ledig,-verwitwet,-geschieden:~~ +)

Dienstgrad: Oblt. Kr.   Rangdienstalter: 1.5.40.

Diensteintritt: 1.4.32.

Militärische Dienstzeiten(bei Unterbrechungen) u. Werdegang:

1.4.34. z. Oberflieger bef., 1.11.34. z. Gefreiten bef., 1.3.35.z. Unteroffizier bef., 1.3.37.z. Feldwebel bef.,1.6.37.z.Oberfeldwebel bef.,1.2.40. z. Offiziers-Anwärter ern., 1.5.40. z. Oberleutnant Kr. bef.

jetzige Verwendung: Flugzeugführer, Fluglehrer C 2

für welche weitere Verwendungen geeignet: Flugzeugführer.

Bestrafungen vor Diensteintritt: " K e i n e "

Bestrafungen während der milit. Dienstzeiten: " K e i n e "

Bildungsgang (Schulabschluss): Volksschule, Fortbildungsschule.

Zivilberuf: Motorenschlosser

Beruf des Vaters: Reichsbank - Oberzählmeister

Erworbene Lw.-Scheine: E.L.F., Blindflug 2, Kfz. Führerschein 2,3.

+)Nichtzutreffendes ist zu streichen.   Beurteilung:

Request for Transfer for First Lieutenant Waldemar Felgenhauer from Wartime Officer to Career Status (front side) – dated May 17, 1941, on blank paper with typed comments.

Beurteilung:

1. **Persönlichkeitswert:** Frisch und interessiert, sehr korrekt in seiner ganzen Lebenshaltung, wohlerzogen und gewandt, guter Kamerad.

2. **Charakterliche Eignung:** Offen und gerade, innerlich sauber, hilfsbereit, nicht ganz frei von persönlichem Ehrgeiz.

3. **Geistige Veranlagung:** Ausreichend bei fortdauerndem Bestreben, sich weiterzubilden.

4. **Militärische Veranlagung:** Guter Soldat mit ausreichenden Kenntnissen im militärischen Innen- und Ausbildungsdienst. Fachlich sehr gute Kenntnisse, geeignet als T.O. Ausgezeichneter, zuverlässiger Flugzeugführer.

5. **Körperliche Veranlagung:** Gesund, kräftig und sportlich.

6. **Sonstiges (insbesondere über Bewährung vor dem Feinde, in der jetzigen Dienststellung und über Eignung zur Beförderung zum nächsthöheren Dienstgrad):**

   Von Kriegsbeginn an in ununterbrochenem Einsatz vielfach vor dem Feinde bewährt gehört er zu den erfolgreichsten und erfahrensten Flugzeugführern seiner Einheit.

Major und Staffelkapitän.

Request for Transfer for First Lieutenant Waldemar Felgenhauer from Wartime Officer to Career Status (**back side**) – signed by Major and Squadron Commander Hans von Obernitz.

Leopold Fellerer
Night Fighter Pilot

"Untiring willingness for action, coupled with an iron will for victory."

Captain Leopold Fellerer was born in Wiener-Neustadt, Austria on June 7, 1919. Initially trained as a bomber pilot, he came to the 2nd Group, 1st Night Fighter Wing (*Nachtjagdgeschwader 1*) as a technical officer on November 18, 1940. He shot down his first enemy aircraft on the night of February 10/11, 1941, during an RAF Bomber Command raid on Hannover. Fellerer transferred to the 4th Squadron on June 4, which became the 5th Squadron, 2nd Night Fighter Wing (*Nachtjagdgeschwader 2*) on November 1, 1941.

On November 14, 1941, Captain Walter Ehle, Commander, 2nd Group, *Nachtjagdgeschwader 1*, wrote an efficiency report on Second Lieutenant Leopold Fellerer, stating:[77]

Leopold Fellerer (tall officer in the center). Note "Kill" markings on the tail of his Messerschmitt Me 110.

> Tall, commanding appearance. Open, sincere and calm character. Secure and energetic demeanor at the front. Healthy ambition and good mental capabilities make him self-reliant and definitely reliable in his way of handling matters. Good squadron officer who, due to his extensive technical interests and his talent for organization, is especially suited to be a squadron or group technical officer. Very well gifted for aviation, passionate, smart, decisive pilot and night fighter, untiring willingness for action, coupled with an iron will for victory, has several times already been successful in night fighting. He is a capable officer, who with further guidance will some day be able to fully assume the position of squadron commander of night fighters.

Fellerer's unit was redesignated a third time on October 1, 1942 to the 11th Squadron, *Nachtjagdgeschwader 1*. Nine days later, Fellerer assumed command of the 3rd Squadron, *Nachtjagdgeschwader 1*. Following the trend of redesignations, this unit became the 5th Squadron, *Nachtjagdgeschwader 5* on December 1. By this time, Fellerer had scored 11 nighttime victories and had received the *Luftwaffe* Honor Goblet on November 16, 1942.

Fellerer assumed command on December 21, 1943, of the 2nd Group, 5th Night Fighter Wing (*Nachtjagdgeschwader 5*, later to be designated the 3rd Group, 6th Night Fighter Wing [*Nachtjagdgeschwader 6*]), at which point he had achieved 18 aerial victories. In January 1944, he was assigned a daytime mission and promptly shot down two B-17 Flying Fortresses. His greatest night of the war occurred on January 20/21, 1944, when he claimed five four-engine bombers that were part of a 769-aircraft RAF Bomber Command attack against Berlin.[78] Fellerer received the German Cross in Gold on February 5, 1944. Captain Leopold Fellerer was awarded the Knight's Cross of the Iron Cross on April 8, 1944, having reached a score of 34 kills. Fellerer flew several types of aircraft including the Messerschmitt Me 110G-4. He survived the war, scoring 41 aerial victories in 450 combat missions, a sortie-to-victory ratio of 10.97 to 1. Thirty-nine of his kills were at night. But his destiny remained linked to the air. After the war, he joined the new Austrian Air Force and attained the grade of lieutenant colonel. Leopold Fellerer died July 18, 1968 at Mautern/Krems, when his Cessna crashed.[79]

F 805

II./ Nachtjagdgeschwader 1   Gefechtsstand, den 14. 11. 1941

B e u r t e i l u n g s n o t i z

über den

Leutnant Leopold F e l l e r e r.

    Grosse, stattliche Erscheinung, Offener, ehrlicher und ruhiger Charakter. Sicheres und energisches Auftreten vor der Front. Von gesundem Ehrgeiz geleitete gute geistige Veranlagung machen ihn in seinen Handlungsweisen selbstbewusst und unbedingt zuverlässig.

    Guter Staffeloffizier, der auf Grund seines grossen technischen Interesses und seines Organisationstalents sich besonders als Staffel- oder Gruppen T.O. eignet.

    Fliegerisch sehr gut veranlagter, passionierter, schneidiger, entschlossener Flugzeugführer und Nachtjäger, der in unermüdlicher Einsatzfreude, die gepaart ist mit einem eisernen Willen zum Sieg, bereits einige Male erfolgreich in der Nachtjagd gewesen ist.

    L. ist ein befähigter Offizier der bei weiterer Förderung später einmal die Stellung eines Staffelkapitäns in der Nachtjagd voll ausfüllen wird.

Hauptmann und Gruppenkommandeur.

Efficiency Report for Second Lieutenant Leopold Fellerer (one page only) – dated November 14, 1941, on blank paper with typed comments. Signed by Captain Walter Ehle, Commander, 2nd Group, 1st Night Fighter Wing. "F805" penciled at the top is probably an administrative file number.

Karl Fitzner
Stuka Pilot

"Mentally very alert with the best ability to comprehend."

Captain Karl Fitzner was born on July 4, 1915 in Düsseldorf, North Rhine-Westphalia. He entered the *Luftwaffe* in 1935 and underwent flight training. In 1938-1939, Fitzner deployed to Spain with the Condor Legion, initially with the 5th Squadron, 88th Fighter Group (*Jagdgruppe 88* [J/88]) and then with the Stuka squadron in the 88th Bomber Group (*Kampfgruppe 88* [K/88]), receiving the Spanish Cross in Gold with Swords.[80] On his return to Germany, Fitzner served briefly as an instructor in a Stuka school; he then served with the 1st Squadron, 77th Stuka Wing (*Sturzkampfgeschwader 77*) in both the Polish and French campaigns under the 3rd Air Fleet. Fitzner was commissioned a second lieutenant on January 1, 1941. He then deployed to the Balkans and hence to Russia for the German invasions. Fitzner fought in the difficult aerial battles over the Crimea and at Stalingrad, as part of the 8th Air Corps, 4th Air Fleet. He received the *Luftwaffe* Honor Goblet on April 2, 1942 and the German Cross in Gold on August 21, 1942. Karl Fitzner won the Knight's Cross of the Iron Cross on November 27, 1942 as the Commander, 1st Squadron, 77th Stuka Wing, having flown 565 combat missions.

On February 26, 1943, Captain Helmut Bruck, Commander, 1st Group, 77th Stuka Wing, filed an efficiency report on Second Lieutenant Fitzner. The hand-written report read, in part:[81]

Aptitude evaluation: Calm and reflective. Mentally very alert with the best ability to comprehend. Physically [original unreadable]. Works diligently and independently. Sincere comrade. [Original unreadable] particularly gifted. Has excelled in over 550 flights against the enemy. Was awarded the Knight's Cross of the Iron Cross and the Operational Flying Clasp in Gold with Pendant to Bomber Pilots. Fought in Spain.

How is the current position being fulfilled? Very well!

Eligible for promotion to the next higher grade? Yes!

Recommendations for service (special aptitude, further uses): Equally well-suited as a Technical Officer or Commander of a Stuka Squadron.

First Lieutenant Karl Fitzner was killed in action on July 8, 1943, when his Junkers Ju 87 – while in its attack dive – received a direct enemy anti-aircraft shell hit and exploded in mid-air over Ssyrzewo, near Bjelgorod during the Battle of Kursk, flying in the 4th Air Corps. By his death, he had flown over 600 combat missions, primarily in the Junkers Ju 87 dive bomber. He received a posthumous promotion to captain.[82]

I./Sturzkampfgeschwader 77   Gefechtsstand, den 26.2.43

Feldpostnummer L 35747

Beurteilungsnotiz

über den .... Leutnant d. R. .... Gruppen-T.O. ....

Vor- und Zuname: .... Karl Fitzner .... geb.: 4.7.1915

Verheiratet, ledig, verwitwet, geschieden (Zutreffendes unterstr.)

Rangdienstalter: ..... 1.1.41 .... Dienstalterliste: 1.7.35

Eignungsbeurteilung: *[handwritten]*

Wie wird jetzige Stelle ausgefüllt? ..... *[handwritten]*

Geeignet zur Beförderung zum nächsthöheren Dienstgrad? ..... Ja!

Erworbene Dr.-Scheine: ..... E.L.F.

Strafen: ..... Keine!

Verwendungsvorschläge: (besondere Eignung, weitere Verwendung) *[handwritten]*

[signature]
(Unterschrift)

Hauptmann und Gruppenkommandeur.
(Dienstgrad u. Dienststellung).

Efficiency Report for Second Lieutenant (Reserve) Karl Fitzner (one page only) – dated February 26, 1943 on blank paper, with typed categories of the report and handwritten comments. Signed by Captain and Commander, 1st Group, 77th Stuka Wing, Helmut Bruck.

Erwin Fleig
Fighter Pilot

"As an acting squadron commander, he is an exemplary officer on the ground and in the air."

Second Lieutenant Erwin Fleig was born December 6, 1912 in Freiburg im Breisgau, Baden. He joined the 1st Squadron, 51st Fighter Wing (*Jagdgeschwader 51*) in June 1940 as a technical sergeant. He shot down his first enemy aircraft during the Battle of Britain on August 11, 1940 west of Dover, England. He added a Hurricane over Canterbury on August 18, 1940 and a Spitfire over Grays Thurrock on August 31, 1940. On September 2, 1940, Fleig downed another Spitfire three miles east of Canterbury. On September 18, 1940, he shot down two Spitfires in twenty minutes. He dispatched another Spitfire on October 17, 1940 and added a Hurricane on December 1, 1940. On May 8, 1941, Fleig reached his ninth kill, a Hurricane over Dungeness.

But his successes came with a price. On July 28, 1940, after engaging in aerial combat, Fleig made an emergency landing of his Messerschmitt Me 109E-1 near Wissant, France. And on September 9, 1940 he made a belly-landing at Abbeville, France that almost totally destroyed his aircraft. During this time, Fleig served as the wingman ("Katschmarek" in *Luftwaffe* slang) for Werner Mölders, the commodore of *Jagdgeschwader 51*. Erwin Fleig received the Knight's Cross of the Iron Cross on August 8, 1941 as a second lieutenant after amassing 26 kills, including two on July 2, 1941, two on July 15, and two on July 17. By the end of the year, he had reached 45 aerial victories. In March, Fleig assumed command of the 2nd Squadron, 51st Fighter Wing "Mölders" (*Jagdgeschwader 51 "Mölders"*) and on March 28, 1942 shot down his 50th enemy aircraft, an I-301 fighter twelve miles south of Staraja Russa.

The previous day, Major Hannes Trautloft, Commander, 54th Fighter Wing "Green Heart" (*Jagdgeschwader 54 "Grünherz"*), submitted a cover letter to the 1st Air Corps requesting a preferred promotion to first lieutenant for Erwin Fleig, whose unit was temporarily attached to the 54th Fighter Wing. Trautloft wrote the following explanation:[83]

The 54th Fighter Wing is submitting enclosed herewith a request of the 1st Group, Fighter Wing "Mölders" for preferential promotion of Second Lieutenant (Wartime Officer) Erwin Fleig, 1st Group, Fighter Wing "Mölders."

Lieutenant Fleig has distinguished himself through outstanding courage as a fighter pilot. Besides his 50 aerial victories, he has repeatedly proven his constant willingness for engagement in battle during numerous low-level attacks. As an acting squadron commander, he is an exemplary officer on the ground and in the air. Due to his mature character, his age and outstanding courage, the recommendation for preferential promotion and addition to the active officer corps is seconded.

Fleig shot down his 60th enemy aircraft on April 30, 1942. On May 29, 1942, after shooting down a MiG-3, his aircraft was struck by enemy ground fire; Fleig was forced to abandon his damaged Messerschmitt Me 109F-2 and bail out. He did, but came down behind enemy lines near Poddorje and was captured by the Russians. He returned to Germany many years later. Erwin Fleig died on March 1, 1986 in Freiburg.

Erwin Fleig shot down 66 enemy aircraft, of which 57 were over the Eastern Front, in 506 combat missions, a sortie-to-victory ratio of 7.66 to 1.[84]

Jagdgeschwader 54.   Gefechtsstand, 27. März 1942.

<u>Br.B.Nr. 25/42 geh.</u>

Geheim

```
                    Generalkommando
                    des I. Fliegerkorps
                Nr.: 2088 g  2 . MRZ. 1942
                    Anl.: 4  durch:
```

An

       Generalkommando I. Fliegerkorps

                - IIa -

In der Anlage überreicht J.G.54 ein Gesuch der I./J.G. Mölders um bevorzugte Beförderung des Leutnants (Kr.O.) Erwin F l e i g, I./J.G.Mölders.

Leutnant Fleig hat sich <u>durch ganz besondere Tapferkeit als Jagdflieger ausgezeichnet</u>. Neben <u>5o Luftsiegen</u> hat er seine stete Einsatzbereitschaft bei zahlreichen Tiefangriffen wiederholt unter Beweis gestellt. In seiner Staffelführung ist er auf der Erde und in der Luft <u>ein vorbildlicher Offizier.</u> Auf Grund seines ausgereiften Charakters, seines Lebensalters und seiner hervorragenden Tapferkeit wird der Vorschlag auf bevorzugte Beförderung des Lt. Fleig und die Übernahme in das aktive Offizierkorps wärmstens befürwortet.

                                          Trautloft

                                 Major und Geschwaderkommodore.

Anlg.: - 4 -

Cover letter for a Request for Preferred Promotion for Second Lieutenant Erwin Fleig (one page only) – dated March 27, 1942, on blank paper, with typed comments. Signed by Major Hannes Trautloft, Commodore, 54th Fighter Wing. Red stamp shows the report arrived at the 1st Air Corps the following day.

Ernst Frömming

Fallschirmjäger

"Over Crete, he conducted his first jump into enemy territory, without prior training."

Major Ernst Frömming was born on February 4, 1911 in Rotenburg an der Wümme near Stade in Lower Saxony. He entered the German Army on May 1, 1930 and initially served in the 18th Infantry Regiment. Frömming then transferred to the engineers and was promoted through the enlisted ranks, making master sergeant on June 1, 1938. He fought in the French campaign in 1940 with the Army's 34th Engineer Battalion, winning the Iron Cross 2nd Class on June 12, 1940 and receiving the Iron Cross 1st Class on November 12, 1940. He transferred to the *Luftwaffe* on March 24, 1941 and joined the Paratroop Engineer Battalion (*Fallschirm-Pionier-Bataillon*), jumping into Crete on May 20, 1941 as part of the German airborne invasion of the island. Landing in Prison Valley south of Kirtomados, the engineers battled the 8th Greek Regiment. Frömming was then tabbed as a future commissioned officer and was promoted to second lieutenant on November 1, 1941 and first lieutenant the same day! On February 15, 1942, Ernst Frömming became a platoon leader in the Paratroop Engineer Battalion, but did not remain there long and one week later became the acting commander of the 13th Company (Engineer) of the 1st Paratroop Training Regiment (*Fallschirmjäger-Ausbildung-Regiment 1*). He fought with this unit in Russia.

Frömming's chain of command recommended him for an accelerated promotion to captain on April 4, 1943. Ernst Liebach, Frömming's immediate commander, wrote:[85]

Of average height, strong appearance. Fully adaptable to all physical demands.

Mentally of good average with good comprehension and clear judgment. Good talent for organizing. Open, immaculate character with mature nature. Expressed perception of duty with great joy of responsibility and readiness for service. Upright soldierly attitude with secure and definitive appearance while at the front. Well-rooted engineer technical knowledge and accomplishments with good tactical talent and clearness. Specially merited as instructor.

Vis-à-vis his superiors he is correct and behaves with military bearing. In the circle of his comrades, he is well-liked. Towards the men under his command, he keeps the upper hand and treats them sternly, but justly. Because of his uplifting élan and his great care for his men, he is well liked and respected. Well-rooted in National Socialist ideology. He has proven often that he knows how to master difficult situations. His social situation is in good order. Presents a good, immaculate appearance in situations outside of the service.

First Lieutenant Frömming came up from the ranks from active duty sergeant. Already during the Western Campaign of 1940, as staff sergeant and platoon leader, he excelled and was awarded the Iron Cross 2nd and 1st Class. On March 24, 1941 he was transferred to the paratroops, and over Crete he conducted his first jump into enemy territory without prior training. For his particularly courageous behavior, as well as his accomplishments in face of the enemy during these battles and on the Newa on the Eastern Front in 1941, he received the Honorary Salver of the *Reichsmarschall*. Effective November 1, 1941, he was promoted to First Lieutenant, and on February 21, 1942 he took over the 13th Company (Engineers) of the 1st Parachute Training Regiment. Within the shortest time, he understood how to transform this company into a fully capable reserve company. It was his accomplishment that the reserves, from which the company came, were not only well-trained, but excelled through a very particular spirit of readiness for service and team spirit.

Since October 8, 1942, Frömming was the commander of this company in the rear operational area of the Eastern Front for security and operations against partisans. In January 1943, he took over the 2nd Company, Parachute Engineer Battalion and served with this unit at the front northeast of Smolensk. At the time he took over this unit, it was severely weakened due to constant fighting under difficult conditions, as well as due to the leadership of the company, which was not always fitting the circumstances. With his far-reaching leadership, constant concern for the welfare for his troops and his uplifting personality, he succeeded to completely change the unit in a very short time. When the company conducted a night attack on March 25 to March 26, 1943 north of Massejenki – to regain the previously lost strongpoint – at the forefront of the infantry companies, it was to his credit that the unit demonstrated masterful success and outstanding aggressive spirit. Above that, his company fulfilled in an exemplary way many mine and obstacle operations of all kinds, often under enemy fire. Frömming was always a shining example of personal courage for his troops.

Within the framework of the rated period, he has successfully led a paratroop company for close to seven months in the conditions of the winter war in the East in battle in front of the enemy and he has fully proven himself for over a year as company leader. Therefore, he is being recommended for preferential promotion to Captain. In consideration of his age, the simultaneous immediate award of a preferential date of rank is also being recommended.

Brigadier General Richard Heidrich, the division commander, added on May 5, 1943:

In agreement and seconding this petition. First Lieutenant Ernst Frömming, Parachute Engineer Battalion is, without reservation, suitable for preferential promotion to captain.

Ten days later, Lieutenant General Kurt Student, 11th Air Corps Commander, added:

The preferential promotion of First Lieutenant Frömming to captain is being seconded by me.

He was promoted to captain on May 21, 1943. After fighting in Russia, the unit moved to the defense of Sicily, where Frömming's company destroyed 146 bridges and laid 5,000 mines to delay the Allied advance on the island. He then withdrew to Italy, where in November 1943, Frömming became the acting commander of the 1st Paratroop Engineer Battalion (*Fallschirm-Pionier-Bataillon 1*), which subsequently moved to the Cassino area. On March 16, 1944, Frömming's troops helped repel the 5th Indian Brigade from seizing Hill 236, while on March 19, Frömming's paratroopers denied the 1st Battalion, 4th Essex Regiment their attack objective of Hill 435. Frömming won the German Cross in Gold on March 26, 1944. He was promoted to major on May 31, 1944, and assumed full command of the battalion on June 13, 1944. Major Ernst Frömming received the Knight's Cross of the Iron Cross on November 18, 1944 for his leadership of the battalion in Italy. Ernst Frömming died August 18, 1959 in Rotenburg an der Wümme.[86] He is buried there at the *Friedhof Lindenstrasse* (Block 2, Row 6, Grave 27).

Fallschirmpionierbataillon   O.U., den 30. 4. 1943

Gen.Kdo.XI.Flieger-Korps

W.B.K. Koblenz

<u>V o r s c h l a g</u>
zur bevorzugten Beförderung.

gem. R.d.L.u.Ob.d.L., L.P., Nr. 71 489/42)2,ID) II.Ang.
v. 22.12.42, Abschnitt A.

für Oblt. (Kr.O.) Ernst F r ö m m i n g.

<u>Dienststellung:</u> Kompanie-Chef
<u>Rangdienstalter:</u> 1.2.1942
<u>Beförderungsdaten zu den beiden letzten Offz.-Dienstgraden:</u>
   Leutnant (Kr.O.) m.Wirkung v. 1.11.1941 ohne R.D.A.
   Oberleutnant (Kr.O.) m.W.v. 1.11.1941 u.R.D.A.v.1.2.42.
<u>Geburtsdatum:</u> 4.2.1911
<u>Auszeichnungen:</u>
   E.K. 2. und 1. Klasse im Westfeldzug 1940,
   Erdkampfabzeichen der Lw. am 5.9.1942,
   Ehrenschale des Herrn Reichsmarschalls am 7.12.42

<u>Begründung:</u>
   A) <u>Allgemeine Leistungen:</u>
     Mittelgroße kräftige Erscheinung. Allen körperlichen Anforderungen voll gewachsen.

     Geistig guter Durchschnitt mit guter Auffassungsgabe und klarem Urteil. Organisatorisch gut begabt.

     Offener einwandfreier Charakter mit gereiftem Wesen. Ausgeprägtes Pflichtbewußtsein mit großer Verantwortungsfreudigkeit und Einsatzbereitschaft.

     Straffe soldatische Haltung mit sicherem und bestimmtem Auftreten vor der Front. Wohlfundierte pioniertechnische Kenntnisse und Leistungen bei guter taktischer Begabung und Übersicht. Besonders bewährt als Ausbilder.

     Vorgesetzten gegenüber korrekt und militärisch. Im Kameradenkreise sehr beliebt. Setzt sich Untergebenen gegenüber durch und behandelt sie streng aber gerecht. Wegen seines mitreißenden Schwungs und seiner großen Fürsorge bei seinen Männern beliebt und geachtet.

- 2 -

Request for Preferred Promotion for First Lieutenant Ernst Frömming (first page) – dated April 30, 1943, on blank paper, with typed and handwritten comments.

– 2 –

Steht auf dem Boden der nationalsozialistischen Weltanschauung.

Hat oft bewiesen, daß er schwierige Lagen zu meistern versteht.

Geordnete wirtschaftliche Verhältnisse.

Gute Umgangsformen bei einwandfreiem außerdienstlichem Verhalten.

B) Einzelangaben:

Oblt. Frömming ist aus dem aktiven Unteroffizierstand hervorgegangen. Er hat sich schon im Westfeldzug 1940 als Oberfeldwebel und Zugführer besonders ausgezeichnet und wurde mit dem E.K. 2. und 1. Klasse ausgezeichnet. Am 24.3.1941 kam er zur Fallschirmtruppe und führte über Kreta seinen ersten Absprung zugleich als Feindsprung ohne vorherige Ausbildung durch. Für sein besonders tapferes Verhalten sowie seine vor dem Feind gezeigten Leistungen bei diesen Kämpfen und im Ostfeldzug 1941 an der Newafront erhielt er die Ehrenschale des Herrn Reichsmarschalls. Mit Wirkung vom 1.11.1941 wurde er zum Oberleutnant befördert und übernahm am 21.2.1942 die 13. (Pi.)/ Fsch.Jg.Ausb.Rgt.1. Er verstand es in kürzester Zeit, diese Kp. zu einer voll leistungsfähigen Ergänzungskompanie zu machen. Es war sein Verdienst, daß der Ersatz, der aus der Kp. hervorging, nicht nur gut ausgebildet war, sondern sich durch einen ganz besonderen Geist der Einsatzbereitschaft und Kameradschaft auszeichnete.

Seit dem 8.10.1942 war Fr. als Chef dieser Kp. im Operationsgebiet der Ostfront zur Sicherung und zur Bandenbekämpfung eingesetzt. Im Januar 1942 übernahm er die 2./Fsch.Pi.Btl. und war mit dieser an der Front nordostwärts Smolensk eingesetzt. Bei der Übernahme war die Kp. infolge der ständigen Einsätze unter schwierigen Verhältnissen sowie der bis dahin nicht immer sachgemäßen Führung der Kp. durch seinen Vorgänger stark mitgenommen. Durch sachgemäße Führung, ständige Fürsorge und durch seine mitreißende Persönlichkeit gelang es ihm, die Kp. in kürzester Zeit völlig umzuwandeln. Wenn die Kp. bei dem Nachtangriff vom 25. zum 26.3.1943 nördlich Massejenki ihre Aufgabe, Zurückeroberung der verloren gegangenen Stützpunkte, an der Spitze der Jäger-Kompanien mustergültig löste und sich hierbei durch einen ganz besonderen Angriffsschwung auszeichnete, so war dieses sein Verdienst. Darüber hinaus hatte die Kompanie zahlreiche Minen- und sonstige Sperraufträge aller Art zum größten Teil unter feindlicher Feuereinwirkung vorbildlich ausgeführt. Stets war Fr. hierbei seiner Kp. ein leuchtendes Vorbild an persönlicher Tapferkeit.

Im Sinne der Bezugsverfügung hat er eine Fallschirmpionierkompanie seit fast 7 Monaten unter den Bedingungen des Winterkrieges im Osten vor dem Feinde im Kampf erfolgreich geführt und sich seit über einem Jahr als Kompanieführer voll bewährt. Er wird daher zur bevorzugten Beförderung zum Hauptmann vorgeschlagen. Aufgrund seines Lebensalters wird gem. Abschnitt C, Ziffer 1, 2. Absatz, der Bezugsverfügung gleichzeitig die sofortige Verleihung eines Rangdienstalters vorgeschlagen.

Major und Btl.-Kommandeur

Request for Preferred Promotion for First Lieutenant Ernst Frömming (second page) – signed by Major Ernst Liebach, Commander, Paratroop Engineer Battalion.

Stellungnahme des Divisionskommandeurs:

Einverstanden und befürwortet.

Oberleutnant Ernst F r ö m m i n g Fallsch.Pi.-Btl.
ist zur bevorzugten Beförderung zum H a u p t m a n n
uneingeschränkt geeignet.

Div.Gef.St., den 5. Mai 1943

[signature]
Generalmajor und Divisionskommandeur.

Gen.Kdo.XI.Fliegerkorps den 15.5.1943
Der Kommandierende General

Bevorzugte Beförderung des Oblt. Frömming zum Hauptmann wird von mir befürwortet.

[signature] Student
General der Flieger

Request for Preferred Promotion for First Lieutenant Ernst Frömming (third page) – signed by Brigadier General Richard Heidrich, Commander, 1st Paratroop Division, and Lieutenant General Kurt Student, 11th Air Corps Commander.

Wilhelm Fulda
Glider Pilot/Fighter Pilot

"While with the 3rd Squadron, Air-Landing Wing, he received the Knight's Cross of the Iron Cross from the Führer due to his courage in combat."

Captain Wilhelm Fulda was born in Antwerp, Belgium on May 21, 1909. He began his *Luftwaffe* career on November 1, 1935 and became a DFS-230 glider pilot. He flew a glider for "Assault Group Stahl" that seized a bridge over the Albert Canal north of Eben Emael, winning the Iron Cross 2nd Class on May 12, 1940 and the 1st Class a day later. He joined the 3rd Squadron, 1st Air-Landing Wing (*Luftlandegeschwader 1*) on August 8, 1940. During the German invasion of Greece, Second Lieutenant Wilhelm Fulda was awarded the Knight's Cross of the Iron Cross for leading an assault glider group that landed 52 paratroop engineers on the Isthmus of Corinth in an attempt to seize a key bridge on April 26, 1941. During this operation, he not only piloted a glider in a difficult landing at the bridge, but also led all 12 DFS 230 gliders in the mission. After the 2nd Paratroop Regiment (*Fallschirmjäger Regiment 2*) landed, Fulda took acting command of a *Fallschirmjäger* platoon on the ground in the attack. The German engineers captured the bridge, but British officers exploded the demolition charges on the bridge by shooting at them. The paratroopers lost 63 killed and 174 wounded; the Germans captured 900 British, Australian and New Zealand troops, and 1,450 Greek soldiers.

From September 4, 1942 to February 4, 1943, he led the 1st Towing Squadron of the 2nd Air-Landing Wing (*Luftlandegeschwader 2*), equipped with Gotha Go-242 transport gliders. During this period, his unit – as part of the 8th Air Corps – flew re-supply missions in support of the beleaguered German 6th Army surrounded in the Stalingrad pocket. The following month, Fulda's group flew in support of the German air bridge between the Crimea and the Kuban. He was promoted to first lieutenant on February 1, 1943.

Fulda then transferred to the fighter arm and led the 2nd Group, 301st Fighter Wing (*Jagdgeschwader 301*), assuming command on November 26, 1943. He was promoted to captain on January 1, 1944.

On May 1, 1944, Fulda's chain of command submitted an efficiency report on his performance. Major and acting *Geschwader* commodore, Manfred Mössinger, wrote the following:[87]

Short Evaluation (Personal values, National Socialist attitude, accomplishments before the enemy, service accomplishments, mental and physical attributes and suitability, infantry experience, when and how obtained): Fulda is of tall, slender appearance with good military attitude. Physically he can be fully utilized and is up to all service-connected demands. Mentally alert and well-gifted. His character tendencies are without criticism. Fresh and always ready for combat, he fulfills his tasks which are required of him as a group leader. Fulda understands how to sweep along his men through his example. While with the 3rd Squadron, Air-Landing Wing, he received the Knight's Cross of the Iron Cross from the *Führer* due to his courage in combat. As a fighter pilot in day and night operations, he has continued to excel. Fulda is firmly rooted in National Socialism and understands to relay these ideas to others.

Strong Traits: Fully expressed leadership qualities, very talented pilot, shows willingness for combat.

Summarized evaluation: above average
(Above Average, Average, Below Average)

How is the current position being fulfilled? Very well fulfilled.
(Use only: Very well fulfilled, well fulfilled, fulfilled, not fulfilled)

Suitable for promotion to next higher service grade? Without reservation.

Suitable as: Remain in the current service position

Known to the person submitting this review: since September 1, 1943

Subordinated to the person submitting this review: since November 1, 1943

Brigadier General Joachim-Friedrich Huth, the 7th Fighter Division Commander, added: "In agreement. Proven officer and good unit leader."

On August 28, 1944, Fulda took command of the 1st Group, 302nd Fighter Wing (*Jagdgeschwader 302*, which later became the 3rd Group, *Jagdgeschwader 301*), equipped with Focke-Wulf Fw 190A-8 fighters. From November 25, 1944 to April 19, 1945 – when the unit was disbanded – Fulda was the Commander, 1st Group, 400th Fighter Wing (*Jagdgeschwader 400*), a unit equipped with the Messerschmitt Me 163 rocket fighter, operating out of Brandis near Leipzig. He survived the war. Wilhelm Fulda died on August 8, 1977 in Hamburg. His varied career included shooting down one four-engine bomber.[88]

Jagdgeschwader 301   Gef.Stand, den 1.5.1944
  Dienststelle, nicht Feldpostnummer

Kriegs-Beurteilung zum 1. Juni 1944
für Offz. ausschl. San.-, Vet.-Offz.

über den

Hptm. (Kr.O.)   Bef.Dat.1.1.44(1)D   Wilhelm   Fulda
  Dienstgrad   *R.D.A. (Ordn. Nr.) und*   *Vorname*   *Name*
Flieg.Tr.   *Dienstalterliste*
21.5.09   verheiratet, ledig, verwitwet, geschieden   kv. tdf.
  geboren am   *(Zutreffendes unterstreichen)*   *Wehrdiensttauglichkeit*
                                                     (kv, gv Feld, gv H., tropentgl., tropenuntgl.)

          Segelflug- Schulführer
                  Zivilberuf (falls vorhanden)
Gruppenkommandeur II/JG 301   WBK Coesfeld/ Westf.
m.d.W.d.Gb.Verwendung seit 1.12.43   *Friedensdienststelle und W R K*
          terminmässige Vorlage zum 1.6.44
                  Anlaß der Vorlage

Deutsche Auszeichnungen des jetzigen Krieges mit Verleihungsdaten und Angabe, ob und zu welchen Auszeichnungen vorgeschlagen: EK II u. I.Kl. am 13.5.40 Ritterkreuz des EK am 22.6.41

---

1) Genaue Angabe, ob Tr.-Offz., Erg.-Offz., Offz. z. D., Res.-Offz., Kr.-Offz., z.V.-Offz.
2) In zweifelhaften Fällen neu festzustellen.
3) Dienststelle, welche Friedensgebührnisse zahlt und zuständiges Wehrbezirkskommando.
4) z. B.: Versetzung zur III./K. C. 2, terminmäßige Vorlage zum 1.5. 43.

Kurze Beurteilung:
(Persönlichkeitswert, nationalsozialistische Haltung, Bewährung vor dem Feinde, dienstliche Leistungen, geistige und körperliche Anlagen und Eignung, infanteristische Erfahrungen, wann und wo erworben)

F. ist eine grosse, schlanke Erscheinung mit guter soldatischer Haltung. Körperlich ist er voll belastbar u. allen truppendienstlichen Anforderungen gewachsen. Geistig rege u. gut veranlagt. Seine charakterliche Veranlagung ist ohne Tadel. Frisch u. immer einsatzfreudig erfüllt er seine Aufgaben, die an ihn als Gruppenkommandeur gestellt werden. F. versteht es, seine Männer durch sein Vorbild mitzureissen.
~~Starke Seiten:~~ Beim 3./Luftlandegeschw. erhielt er auf Grund seines tapferen Einsatzes vom Führer das Ritterkreuz des E.K. Als Jagdflieger im Tag-u. Nachteinsatz hat er sich weiterhin bewährt.
F. steht auf dem Boden des Nationalsozialismus u. versteht es, ~~sixxxxx~~
~~Schwache Seiten:~~ dieses Gedankengut Anderen zu vermitteln.
Starke Seiten: Ausgeprägte Führereigenschaften, fliegerisch sehr gut begabt, einsatzfreudig.

Zusammenfassendes Urteil:
(über Durchschnitt, Durchschnitt, unter Durchschnitt)   über Durchschnitt

Wie wird die jetzige Stelle ausgefüllt?
(Es sind nur die Ausdrücke „sehr gut ausgefüllt", „gut ausgefüllt",
„ausgefüllt", „nicht ausgefüllt" zu verwenden)   sehr gut ausgefüllt

Geeignet zur Beförderung zum nächsthöheren Dienstgrad?
                                                             uneingeschränkt geeignet

Lager-Nr. 1278 Heß, Braunschweig-München-Berlin 09 48

Efficiency Report for Captain Wilhelm Fulda (front side) – dated May 1, 1944, on pre-printed form from the Hess firm in Braunschweig.

Eignung
für welche nächsthöhere Verwendung ⁵)?
für welche besondere oder anderweitige Verwendung ⁶)?   } Verbleib in derzeitiger
Vorschlag für Verwendung in nächster Zeit ⁷)?   } Dienststellung

Sprachkenntnisse (keine Schulkenntnisse)
a) abgelegte Prüfungen:
(z. B.: Dolmetscherprüfung 1. 10. 42)   keine
b) Beherrschung der Sprache:
(z. B.: durch Aufenthalt im Ausland)

Eröffnung zu welchen Punkten, wann, wie
(mündlich oder schriftlich) und durch wen?   keine

Strafen   keine
sind mit vollem Straftenor sowie Vermerk über Vollstreckung abschriftlich als Anlage der Kriegsbeurteilung beizuheften.

Dem Beurteilenden bekannt seit   1.9.43
                      unterstellt seit 1.11.43

Ausbildung
a) erworbene Scheine:
(L.F., E.L.F., L.B. usw.)   L.F. u. Bl.III
b) Sonderausbildung:
(z. B. Bild.-Offz., Techn. Offz., Meß-Offz.,
Funk-Drahtnachr.-Offz., W. K. S.)

Unterschrift   Major u. Geschwaderkommodore
                                        Dienstgrad und Dienststellung m.d.W.d.G.b.

Beitrag des Chefs des Generalstabes der vorgesetzten Kommandobehörde:
(nur bei Genst.-Offz. in Stabsstellungen und zur Dienstleistung zum Generalstab kommandierten Offizieren)

Zusätze vorgesetzter Dienststellen:
7. Jagddivision   Div.Gef.Stand, 14.5.44

            Einverstanden. Bewährter Offizier und guter Verbandsführer.

                                        Generalmajor und Divisionskommandeur

⁵) Gilt für alle Offz., für Truppen-Offz. hinsichtlich Eignung zur Führung des nächsthöheren Verbandes, für Genst.-Offz. hinsichtlich Eignung zum Chef oder Ia, Ic der Luffl., Flieger-Korps, Flak-Korps, Fl.-Div., Flak-Div., zur Versetzung in den Genst., zur Kommandierung in den Genst.
⁶) z. B.: Höherer Adjutant, Erzieher, Lehrer auf Spezialgebieten, auf Grund von Sprachkenntnissen im Attachédienst; für Genst.-Offz. hinsichtlich Eignung für Verwendung im Quartiermeisterdienst, im Ic-Dienst, im Transportwesen, als Lehrer für Genst.-Lehrgang (Taktik bzw. Qu.-Dienst); besondere Anlagen für Kriegsgeschichte, Wehrwirtschaft.
⁷) z. B.: „noch halbjährige Belassung in bisheriger Stelle" oder „alsbaldige Verwendung als Geschw.-Kommodore".

Efficiency Report for Captain Wilhelm Fulda (back side) – signed by Major Manfred Mössinger, acting commodore of the 301st Fighter Wing, and by Brigadier General Joachim-Friedrich Huth, 7th Fighter Division Commander.

Robert Gast
Fallschirmjäger

"Alert and open to new ideas."

Second Lieutenant Robert Gast was born March 28, 1920 at Kapsweyer in the Rhineland-Pfalz. He entered the *Luftwaffe* and joined the 7th Company, 2nd Paratroop Regiment (*Fallschirmjäger-Regiment 2*) on January 1, 1940. Gast was promoted to private first class on January 1, 1941 and to corporal on January 1, 1942. Fighting with the unit on the Eastern Front, he won the Iron Cross 2nd Class on March 17, 1942 south of Kharkov along the Donez and Mius Rivers and was promoted to staff sergeant on April 1, 1942. Gast received the Iron Cross 1st Class on January 2, 1943 and was designated an officer candidate shortly thereafter. From April 28, 1943 to June 12, 1943, he attended an officer candidate basic course and then entered an officer candidate platoon leader course at the *Luftwaffe's* Ground Combat School. His training chain of command submitted what we would term an academic efficiency report, with the commander of the training company providing most of the input on July 28, 1943. It read, in part:[89]

1. **Character and personal values:** Gast possesses a mature, open character. He is calm and modest.

2. **Attitude towards the National Socialist State:** Well-rooted in National Socialist ideology.

3. **Mental aptitude:** Alert and open to new ideas. Possesses good general education and expresses himself well

4. **Physical attributes:** Of medium height, slender, he has endurance and toughness. Very good soldier appearance.

5. **Leadership:** Very good.

6. **Behavior outside of the service:** Nothing negative is known.

7. **Service Aptitude:**

Appearance at the front and command voice: Very calm and modest. Clear commander's voice.

Accomplishments as a leader: Gast is absolutely fully aware of his duty and he is reliable as a leader of a battalion.

Decision-making ability and confronting critical situations: Tackles critical situations calmly. He does not let himself be taken by surprise nor be taken aback.

8. **Service knowledge:**
Service in battle: possesses good knowledge with good adaptability.

Marksmanship: good

Weapon's knowledge: good

Tactics: Tactical knowledge is satisfactory.

Military science: Good

Practical knowledge of particular weapons: Familiar to a good extent with all weapons studied during training.

9. **Fitness Judgment:**

To officer: Yes

For which position in a ground combat unit: Platoon Leader

For which position as a non-commissioned officer: n/a

The training battalion commander, a captain, offered: "In agreement." Brigadier General and Commander of the Ground Combat School Alfred Sturm signed the report, but added no comment of his own.

Robert Gast was promoted to second lieutenant on July 24, 1943. He was assigned to the 7th Paratroop Regiment (*Fallschirmjäger-Regiment 7*), 2nd Paratroop Division (*2. Fallschirmjäger-Division*), where, on July 1, 1944, he became the acting commander of the 9th Company. The 2nd Paratroop Division entered Brest, France on August 9, 1944. The Allied assault on the city began on August 29, when RAF heavy bombers struck Brest at night, and bombers from the U.S. 8th Air Force hit the fortress the next day. Then the U.S. 2nd, 8th and 29th Infantry Divisions began their assault. Hitler ordered Bernard Ramcke, the fortress commander, to hold to the last man, and the 7th Paratroop Regiment was positioned in the eastern sector of the city. However, the American attack was relentless.[90] Gast and his unit were forced to surrender on September 18, 1944. He was awarded the Knight's Cross of the Iron Cross on October 6, 1944.[91]

Erdkampfschule der Luftwaffe
für K. O. A.
J. a. O. A. – Jugführerlehrgang
Batl.

O. U., den 28. VII. 1943

Beurteilung

Dienstgrad, Vor- und Zuname: Feldwebel Robert G a s t .

Aktiver Truppenteil: 7./Fallschirmjäger-Rgt. 2

Wehrersatzdienststelle: Ludwigshafen

Teilnahme am Lehrgang vom 15.6. bis 31.7.43

Alter: 23 Jahre.

1. Charakter u. Persönlichkeitswert: G. besitzt einen gefestigten, offenen Charakter. In seinem Wesen ist er ruhig und bescheiden.

2. Einstellung zum n. s. Staat: Steht fest auf dem Boden der n.s. Weltanschauung.

3. Geistige Veranlagung: Geistig rege und interessiert veran-lagt. Besitzt gute Allgemeinbildung und gute Ausdrucksform.

4. Körperliche Veranlagung: Von mittelgroßer, schlanker Gestalt, ist er ausdauernd und zäh. Sehr gute soldatische Haltung.

5. Führung: Sehr gut

6. Außerdienstliches Verhalten: Nichts Nachteiliges bekannt.

7. Dienstliche Befähigung:
   a) Auftreten vor der Front und Kommandosprache: Sehr ruhiges und bescheidenes Auftreten, klare Kdo.-Sprache.
   b) Leistungen als Führer: G. ist absolut pflichtbewußt und zuverlässig als Führer mit einer tadellosen Haltung.
   c) Entschlußfähigkeit und Einstellung zu krit. Lagen: Kritische Lagen werden ohne Verzögerung in aller Ruhe angepackt. Läßt sich nicht überraschen noch verblüffen.

8. Dienstliche Kenntnisse:
   a) Gefechtsdienst: Verfügt über gute Kenntnisse mit gutem Anpassungsvermögen
   b) Schießen: Gut
   c) Waffenlehre: Gut
   d) Taktik: Taktisches Verständnis ist ausreichend.
   e) Wehrwesen: Gut
   f) Praktische Kenntnis der einzelnen Waffen: Alle im Lehrgang durchgenommenen Waffen werden gut beherrscht.

Wenden!

Efficiency Report for Technical Sergeant Robert Gast (front side) – dated July 28, 1943, on pre-printed form, with typed and handwritten comments.

9. Eignungsurteil:

a) zum Offizier: _____ Ja _____

b) zu welcher Verwendung in der Erdkampftruppe: Zugführer.

c) zu welcher Verwendung in Unteroffiziersstellungen: _____

[signature]
Hauptmann u. Komp.-Chef.

Stellungnahme des Batl.-Kommandeurs: Einverstanden.

[signature]
~~Major~~ (Hptm.) u. Batl.-Kommandeur.

O. U., den 29. JULI 1943 1943

[signature]
Generalmajor u. Kommandeur der
Erdkampfschule.

Efficiency Report for Technical Sergeant Robert Gast (back side) – signed by a captain, a major and Brigadier General Alfred Sturm, Commander of the Ground Combat School.

Walter Gericke
Fallschirmjäger

"Major Gericke has fully proven himself as a battalion commander."

Colonel Walter Gericke was born on December 23, 1907 in Bilderlahe near Marienburg in Lower Saxony. He entered the German Police in 1929; four years later, he was assigned to the Land Police Group "General Göring." Promoted to second lieutenant on April 1, 1933, he became a first lieutenant in the Police on August 31, 1935 and took command of the 2nd Company of the Regiment "General Göring." Now in the *Luftwaffe*, on September 1, 1937, Gericke assumed command of the 11th Company of the 4th Paratroop Battalion of the regiment; he was promoted to captain on March 1, 1938. Gericke transferred to command the 4th Company of the 1st Paratroop Regiment (*Fallschirmjäger Regiment 1*).

On April 10, 1940, Gericke – still in command of the 4th Company – won the Iron Cross 2nd Class, while seizing a key Danish bridge at Storstromme near Vordingborg which linked the islands of Falster and Seeland at whose end was the Danish capital, Copenhagen – during the German invasion of Denmark; on May 10, 1940, Gericke and the 4th Paratroop Company jumped into Zwijndrecht and fought at Dordrecht, Holland in an attempt to seize key bridges over the Maas River, and Gericke received the Iron Cross 1st Class on May 12, 1940. He then became the liaison officer to Lieutenant General Stumpff in Drontheim, Norway in support of the airborne transport effort to support German forces far to the north at Narvik.

On January 21, 1941, Captain Gericke became the executive officer of the 4th Battalion, 1st Paratroop Assault Regiment (*Fallschirmjäger-Sturm-Regiment 1*), the regiment's heavy mortars, anti-tank guns, heavy machine-guns and engineers. During the German airborne invasion of Crete on May 20, 1941, his unit air-landed with the mission of seizing the airfield at Máleme. He assumed temporary command of the regiment, when Brigadier General Eugen Meindl was seriously wounded. Missing most of their heavy weapons, Gericke's battalion crossed the Tavronitis River and gained a toehold on the key heights of Hill 107. The attack finally succeeded (Gericke was ably assisted by three other officers, Josef Barmetler, Dr. Heinrich Neumann and Horst Trebes), which opened the way for a German victory on the island, although the battalion had 120 men killed in action, attesting to the ferocity of the fighting. For this achievement, Adolf Hitler awarded Captain Walter Gericke (and the other three officers) the Knight's Cross of the Iron Cross on June 14, 1941.

Gericke and his unit then deployed to Russia, where he fought first near Stalino in the Ukraine and later along the Wolchow River southeast of Leningrad. The *Luftwaffe* promoted Walter Gericke to major on August 1, 1942; shortly thereafter, the battalion became the demonstration battalion at the *Luftwaffe* Ground Combat School at Mourmelon le Grand, France. Gericke, in addition to his normal command duties, became the leader of the company commanders' course at the school. At the beginning of 1943, the battalion was officially separated from the regiment. Following a reorganization – it remained a demonstration unit – to a paratroop infantry battalion, Gericke assumed command of this new formation, the 2nd Battalion, 6th Paratroop Regiment (*Fallschirmjäger Regiment 6*) on July 1, 1943.

On July 17, 1943, the commander of the 11th Air Corps, Kurt Student, submitted a request to the *Luftwaffe* High Command to advance Walter Gericke's date of rank to an earlier calendar date (and thus make him eligible earlier for promotion to lieutenant colonel.) The request read:[92]

Under the provision of regulations, the 11th Air Corps requests an improvement in the date of rank of Major (Tr. O) Walter Gericke, Commander of the 2nd Battalion, 6th Paratroop Regiment. Major Gericke was awarded the Knight's Cross of the Iron Cross on June 14, 1941 as a battalion commander during the operation in Crete. Since this time, Major Gericke has fully proven himself as a battalion commander. An improvement in his date of rank is warmly approved by me.

Gericke's battalion, subordinated directly to the 11th Air Corps (instead of to a traditional regiment) moved from France to Foggia, Italy. On September 9, 1943, Gericke led an airborne attack on the Italian Supreme Command Headquarters at Monte Rotundo (15 miles northeast of Rome), after Italy changed sides in the war. The Germans captured 2,500 Italian soldiers at the mountain headquarters, losing 56 paratroopers – their major target, Marshal Badoglio was not present during the raid. Gericke received the German Cross in Gold for this action on September 15. In October 1943, the *Luftwaffe* created the 4th Paratroop Division, and the 2nd Battalion, 6th Paratroop Regiment served as the base for the formation of the 11th Paratroop Regiment (*Fallschirmjäger Regiment 11*). Gericke assumed acting command of the unit.

On January 18, 1944, in the fight against the Allied seaborne invasion at Anzio-Nettuno, Gericke distinguished himself in preventing the Allies from breaking out of the beachhead. He was mentioned in the *Wehrmacht* dispatches on June 10, 1944 for heroism and achievement in Italy; he was promoted to lieutenant colonel on July 1, 1944. On September 17, 1944, Lieutenant Colonel Walter Gericke received the Oak Leaves to the Knight's Cross of the Iron Cross for his stellar defensive combat in Italy, to include the defense of Futa Pass. Gericke was promoted to colonel on January 30, 1945. He finished the war as an acting division commander of the 11th Paratroop Division and later the 21st Paratroop Division.

After spending one year as a prisoner of war, Gericke returned to Germany. In 1956, he entered the *Bundeswehr*, rising to the grade of Major General and the command of the 1st Air Landing Division. He retired on March 31, 1965. Walter Gericke died on October 19, 1991 in Alsfeld.[93]

```
Generalkommando                                    den 17.7.1943
XI.Fliegerkorps          23. JULI 1943
IIa Az. 21 d
Bezug: 1.) R.d.L.u.Ob.d.L. LP Nr. 71 489/42 (2,ID) II.Ang.v.22.12.42.
       2.) R.d.L.u.Ob.d.L. LP Nr. 14 391/43 (2,ID) v. 10.3.1943.
Betr.: Rangdienstalterverbesserung für Major (Tr.O.) G e r i c k e,
       Walter.
             An
             Reichsluftfahrtministerium -L.P.2.ID-

       Gem.o.a.Bezug 2) Ziffer 2 beantragt das Gen.Kdo.
eine Rangdienstalterverbesserung für den Major (Tr.O.) G e r i c k e,
Walter, Kdr.d.II./Fsch.Jg.Rgt. 6.
       Major Gericke wurde am 14.6.1941 als Btls.Kdr.
beim Kreta-Einsatz mit dem Ritterkreuz des Eisernen Kreuzes ausge-
zeichnet. Seit dieser Zeit hat sich Major Gericke als Btl.Kdr. wei-
terhin voll bewährt.
       Eine Rangdienstalterverbesserung wird von mir
wärmstens befürwortet.

                                         Der Kommandierende General
```

Request for Advancement of Date of Rank for Walter Gericke (one side only) – dated July 17, 1943 and signed by Lieutenant General Kurt Student, Commander, 11th Air Corps.

Siegfried Gerstner
Fallschirmjäger

"A healthy degree of self-confidence and ambition."

Major Siegfried Gerstner was born November 16, 1916 in Passau, Bavaria. He joined the Army on December 12, 1936 and served with the 54th Mountain Engineer Battalion. On September 1, 1938, Gerstner was promoted to second lieutenant and transferred to the 82nd Mountain Engineer Battalion. He served with this unit in the Polish campaign in 1939 and the Norwegian campaign in 1940, winning the Iron Cross 2nd Class on February 1, 1940 and the Iron Cross 1st Class on June 1, 1940. Gerstner transferred to the *Luftwaffe* on August 1, 1940 as a first lieutenant and became a platoon leader in the 7th Paratroop Engineer Battalion (*Fallschirm-Pionier-Bataillon 7*). On April 16, 1941, he assumed command of the 4th Company in the same battalion and jumped into Crete during the German airborne invasion of the island. Gerstner's company, which had jumped into the western part of Prison Valley six miles southwest of Khaniá, encountered heavy resistance from the 8th Greek Regiment. He received the *Luftwaffe* Honor Goblet on August 1, 1941 for his exploits on the island.

Gerstner next fought in Russia, where the engineer battalion repelled numerous Russian attacks while successfully defending their positions at Ssinzawino and the "Wasps' Nest" on the Newa River east of Leningrad. He was wounded in action on October 28, 1941, but returned to duty and received the German Cross in Gold on June 1, 1942. He was subsequently pulled up to the staff of the 7th Air Division. Gerstner was promoted to captain on February 1, 1943 and assumed acting command of the 2nd Paratroop Engineer Battalion on February 16, 1943. He commanded this unit until January 7, 1944, when he was severely wounded in heavy fighting near Kirowograd and transported to a hospital.

On January 15, 1944, Gerstner's chain of command recommended him for accelerated promotion. Major General Gustav Wilke, acting division commander (the word "acting" seems to have been written in later by the actual division commander, Bernhard Ramcke!) wrote the following:[94]

> Captain Gerstner joined the 54th Mountain Engineer Battalion of the Army on December 1, 1936. After seeing service as a platoon leader and company commander, on August 1, 1940 he arrived at the Parachute Engineer Battalion as a company commander. After further engagement as the O I on the staff of the 7th Air Division, Captain Gerstner was made the acting commander of the 2nd Parachute Engineer Battalion on February 16, 1943, during the formation of the 2nd Paratroop Division. From March 8, 1943 to April 3, 1943 he attended the Battalion Commander's School and was rated "well qualified" as commander of a Parachute Pioneer Battalion.
>
> Captain Gerstner participated in the operations during the campaigns in Poland and Norway, and he jumped into Crete. On the Eastern Front, he was engaged during the winter of 1941 on the Newa, during the winter of 1942/43 on the central front, and during the winter of 1943/44 as Battalion Commander and Division Engineer Leader during the heavy defensive and offensive battles east of Shitomir and south-east of Kirowograd. His promotion to be the Commander of the 2nd Parachute Engineer Battalion has already been requested.
>
> Captain Gerstner is of short, strong, very wiry appearance with friendly, sincere presence. Open, definitely reliable character with a healthy degree of self-confidence and ambition. Good concept of his profession. Expressed personality with excellent leadership qualities. Mentally above average, he possesses good clarity and great flexibility. Very good understanding and know-how. Clear orders. Captain Gerstner understood how to train and educate the 2nd Parachute Engineer Battalion under the most difficult circumstances. He has led this battalion very successfully during the engagements in the battle for Rome and in the particularly difficult defensive and attack battles east of Shitomir and south-east of Kirowograd, until he was transferred to a field hospital on January 6, 1944 due to being wounded in action.
>
> Captain Gerstner has functioned very well in his position as acting battalion commander of the 2nd Parachute Engineer battalion and has full aptitude for the grade of Major. Therefore, he is being recommended for preferential promotion to this service rank.

Major General Ramcke, who had been temporarily away from the division due to serious illness, wrote on the application: "I agree to this recommendation in its full contents."

Finally, on January 30, 1944, the 11th Air Corps Commander, Lieutenant General Kurt Student, weighed in and wrote: "The preferential promotion to major is warmly recommended by me."

Siegfried Gerstner was promoted to major on February 7, 1944. He again took command of the 2nd Paratroop Battalion in March 1944. During the battle for Brest in August and September of 1944, he initially commanded this battalion and then assumed command of the 2nd Battalion, 7th Paratroop Regiment. Siegfried Gerstner was awarded the Knight's Cross of the Iron Cross on September 13, 1944. He was captured by U.S. troops on September 18, 1944. He rejoined the new German *Bundeswehr* after the war and retired as a colonel on March 31, 1975.[95]

2. Fallschirm-Division   Gef.Stand, 15. 1. 1944

Vorschlag

zur bevorzugten Beförderung

gem. R.d.L.u.Ob.d.L. LP Nr. 71489/42 (2, ID) II. Angel. vom 22.12.42

für Hauptmann (Tr.O.) G e r s t n e r, Siegfried

Dienststellung: Führer des Fallschirm-Pionier-Bataillons 2
Rangdienstalter: 1. 2. 1943 (100)
Beförderungsdaten zu den beiden   Oberleutnant: 1. 8. 1940
letzten Offiziers-Dienstgraden: Hauptmann: 1. 2. 1943
Geburts-Tag: 16. 11. 1916
Auszeichnungen: 1.2.40 Eisernes Kreuz 2.Klasse
                 1.6.40 Eisernes Kreuz 1.Klasse
                 1.8.41 Ehrenpokal der Luftwaffe
                 1.6.42 Deutsches Kreuz in Gold

B e g r ü n d u n g :

A.) Allgemeine Leistungen

Hptm. Gerstner ist am 1.12.1936 beim Gebirgs-Pionier-Batl. 54 in die Wehrmacht eingetreten. Er kam nach Verwendung als Zugführer und später Kompanie-Chef am 1.8.1940 beim Fallschirm-Pionier-Bataillon als Kompanie-Chef zur Fallschirm-Truppe. Nach späterer Verwendung als O I im Stabe der Flieger-Division 7 wurde Hptm. G. ab 16.2.1943 bei Aufstellung der 2. Fallschirm-Division mit der Führung des Fsch.Pi.Batl. 2 beauftragt.
Vom 3.3.1943 - 3.4.1943 besuchte er die Batl.-Führer-Schule und wurde als zum Kommandeur eines Fsch.Pi.Batl. "gut geeignet" beurteilt.
Hptm. Gerstner hat an den Einsätzen beim Polen- und Norwegen-Feldzug und nach Fallschirm-Absprung am Kreta-Feldzug teilgenommen.
An der Ostfront wurde er im Winter 41 an der Newa, im Winter 1942/43 im Mittelabschnitt und im Winter 1943/44 als Batl.-Kommandeur und Divisions-Pi-Führer bei den schweren Abwehr- und Angriffskämpfen ostwärts Shitomir und südostwärts Kirowograd eingesetzt. Seine Ernennung zum Kommandeur des Fallschirm-Pionier-Batl. 2 wurde bereits beantragt.

B.) Einzelangaben

Hauptmann Gerstner ist eine kleine, kräftige, sehr drahtige Erscheinung mit freundlichem, verbindlichem Wesen. Offener, unbedingt zuverlässiger Charakter mit gesundem Selbstbewußtsein und Ehrgeiz.
Gute Berufsauffassung. Ausgesprochene Persönlichkeit mit vorzüglichen Führereigenschaften.
Geistig über den Durchschnitt veranlagt besitzt er gute Übersicht und große Wendigkeit. Sehr gutes taktisches Verständnis und Können. Klare Befehlsgebung.

Request for Preferred Promotion for Captain Siegfried Gerstner (front side) – dated January 15, 1944, on blank paper, with typed and handwritten comments.

– 2 –

Hptm. Gerstner hat es verstanden, das Fsch.Pi.Batl.2 unter schwierigsten Umständen auszubilden und zu erziehen. Er hat dieses Batl. bei den Einsätzen im Kampf um Rom und bei den besonders schweren Abwehr- und Angriffskämpfen ostwärts Shitomir und südostwärts Kirowograd mit besonderem Erfolg geführt, bis er auf Grund der erneuten Verwundung am 6.1.1943 in ein Lazarett überführt werden mußte.

Hauptmann Gerstner hat seine Stelle als Bataillons-Führer des Fsch.-Pi.Batl. 2 sehr gut ausgefüllt und besitzt volle Eignung zum Major. Er wird deshalb zur bevorzugten Beförderung zu diesem Dienstgrad vorgeschlagen.

Die Voraussetzungen gem. Bezugsverfügung Abschnitt A 1 b) sind erfüllt.

Wilke.
Generalleutnant und Kommandeur

[handwritten endorsement]
Ramcke.
Generalleutnant u. Kommandeur
der 2. Fallsch. Jägerdivision.

Generalkommando XI.Fliegerkorps   O.U., den 30. Januar 1944
Der Kommandierende General

Eine bevorzugte Beförderung zum Major wird von mir warm befürwortet.

Student
General der Flieger.

Request for Preferred Promotion for Captain Siegfried Gerstner (back side) – signed by Major General Gustav Wilke, acting commander for the 2nd Paratroop Division, Major General Bernard Ramcke, Commander, 2nd Paratroop Division, and Lieutenant General Kurt Student, Commander, 11th Air Corps.

Franz Grassmel
Fallschirmjäger

"Sometimes a little stubborn."

Lieutenant Colonel Franz Grassmel was born January 8, 1906 in Mochow, Brandenburg. He entered Police service in 1928 and transferred to the Army in 1935. For the next five years, Grassmel served in several Army anti-tank battalions, and participated in the Polish campaign in 1939 and the French campaign in 1940.

First Lieutenant Grassmel reached a seminal moment in his life when he attended the airborne school on June 14, 1940. From there he assumed command of the 14th Company (Anti-tank) of the 1st Paratroop Regiment (*Fallschirmjäger-Regiment 1*).

The following recommendation for promotion, dated November 28, 1940, requests promotion for Franz Grassmel to the grade of captain. The report was written by Colonel Bruno Bräuer, the commander of the 1st Paratroop Regiment. Although the report misspells Grassmel's last name, it is quite complimentary about this new *Luftwaffe* officer, when it states:[96]

> First Lieutenant Grasmehl possesses an open, upright and mature character. Good mental capabilities. Sometimes a little stubborn. Trustworthy, conscientious and dutiful. Good physical condition. Since August 1, 1940, Grasmehl has been engaged as Company Commander of the 14th Company. His practical knowledge and highly developed awareness of responsibility as well as his untiring zeal assure him the success in the leadership of his company. Energetic and goal-oriented, he has taken the company to a high level of training. Correct, modest and responsive to his superiors; strict but just towards the men under his command. Well-liked among his comrades. Fills his position well. Without reservation, suitable for promotion to the next higher service grade.

On May 20, 1941, Captain Grassmel and his company were part of the massive German airborne attack against the island of Crete; his unit was part of the second assault wave, jumping into drop zones just outside the town of Heráklion. Grassmel fought bravely, personally leading two anti-tank guns against the western gate of the town and was awarded both the Iron Cross 2nd Class and the Iron Cross 1st Class on June 10, 1941 (He would receive the Crete cuff title on May 20, 1942). On June 1, 1942 he was named the acting commander of the 3rd Battalion, 4th Paratroop Regiment (*Fallschirmjäger-Regiment 4*) and officially assumed command one month later. He and his unit would serve in combat in Russia for two periods (September 29, 1941-November 17, 1941 with the German 16th Army at Leningrad and November 5, 1942-March 28, 1943 with the German 9th Army near Rzev). He would be awarded a German Cross in Gold on June 15, 1943 for these actions, but it had come with a cost – on December 18, 1942, Grassmel was wounded in action.

After Russia, Grassmel and his battalion jumped into Sicily in July 1943 as part of the attempt to stop the Allied invasion of the island. South of Catania, defending at the Bottaceto Ditch, Grassmel's unit held out until August before being forced to withdraw to the Italian mainland. Major Grassmel's greatest day as a soldier came on March 19, 1944 at the Second (some sources categorize it as the Third) Battle of Cassino. Four days previously, 460 Allied bombers dropped

1,000 tons of bombs on the Italian town of Cassino and its German defenders and followed the aerial attack with an 8-hour artillery barrage in which 890 guns fired 195,696 rounds. The same day, Grassmel became the acting commander of the 4th Paratroop Regiment. The bombardment was not enough to dislodge the paratroopers, and after 96 hours of heavy ground combat – centered around the Continental Hotel – a combined New Zealand, Indian and American armored thrust along the "Cavendish Road" attempted to turn the northern flank of the German positions through the mountains and seize the Albaneta Farm. In their way stood Grassmel's 4th Regiment. The 35-armored-vehicle-attack bogged down in the midst of accurate German anti-tank fire and judicious use of anti-tank mines; German sources claim 29 vehicles were destroyed or damaged, while other sources put the losses at 22. In either case, the attack failed; Grassmel was awarded the Knight's Cross of the Iron Cross on April 8, 1944.

On August 18, 1944, Major Grassmel became the acting commander of the 20th Paratroop Regiment (*Fallschirmjäger-Regiment 20*). His unit, which became part of the 7th Paratroop Division (*7. Fallschirmjäger-Division*), fought in Venlo and Overbeck, Holland, Weissenburg and Hagenau, France and later in the Reichswald in Germany as part of the 1st Parachute Army. Wounded again on February 10, 1945, his unit helped thousands of German soldiers and civilians escape westward – away from the Soviets – over the Weser River near the end of the war. Promoted to lieutenant colonel on March 12, 1945, he received the Oak Leaves to the Knight's Cross on May 8, 1945.

After the war, Grassmel spent almost two years as a prisoner of war. A veteran of both the epic *Fallschirmjäger* attack at Crete and the epic *Fallschirmjäger* defense at Cassino, Franz Grassmel died on June 30, 1985 at Stade an der Elbe, Lower Saxony.[97] He is buried at the *Friedhof Geestberg* (Section 11, Grave 97).

1. Flieger-Division 7   den 28. November 1940.
X 2. Fallschirm-Jäger Rgt.1   Wehrmachtteil Luftwaffe
X 3. W.B.K.: Bad Kissingen
4. Vorgeschlagen gem.: D.R.d.L.und Ob.d.L., Luftwaffenpersonalamt,
                     (21)o.10.10 Nr. 67 466/10.40 (3 IA) vom
                     28.10.40.

V o r s c h l a g

zur Beförderung eines Offiziers (D.B.) zum nächsthöheren Dienstgrad.

Vor und Zuname: G r a s m e h l , Franz
Geburtsdatum: 8.1.1906
Jetziger Dienstgrad: Oberleutnant d.R.
Rangdienstalter: 1. Oktober 1937
6. **Eingesetzt als:** Kompanie-Chef
7. **Geeignet zum:** Kompanie-Chef
Aktiver Wehrdienst seit 1.8.39: von 1.8.39 bis 31.7.40 Festungs-
                               Panzer-Abw. Abt. 545, seit 1.8.40
                               Chef 14./Fallschirm-Jäger Rgt.1
Teilnahme an welchen Kämpfen: ----
Wird vorgeschlagen zur Beförderung zum: Hauptmann

Kurze Beurteilung durch den Rgt.-Kommandeur:

      Oberleutnant Grasmehl besitzt einen offenen, graden und ausgereiften Charakter. Gute geistige Veranlagung. Manchmal etwas stur. Zuverlässig, gewissenhaft und pflichtbewußt. Körperlich gut veranlagt.

      G. ist ab 1.8.1940 als Kompanie-Chef der 14.Kompanie eingesetzt. Gute praktische Kenntnisse, hohes Verantwortungsbewußtsein, sowie unermüdlicher Eifer sichern ihm den Erfolg in der Führung seiner Kompanie.

      Energisch und zielbewußt hat er die Kompanie auf einen guten Ausbildungsstand gebracht.

      Gegenüber Vorgesetzten korrekt, bescheiden und zuvorkommend, gegenüber Untergebenen streng aber gerecht.

      Im Kameradenkreise beliebt.

      Füllt seine Stelle gut aus.

      Zum nächsthöheren Dienstgrad uneingeschränkt geeignet.

Request for Promotion for First Lieutenant (Reserve) Franz Grassmel (one page only) – dated November 28, 1940, on blank paper, with typed comments. Signed by Colonel Bruno Bräuer, Commander, 1st Paratroop Regiment. Grassmel's name is incorrectly spelled [Grasmehl] in the report. Remarks made later in pencil indicate he was promoted to captain on January 1, 1941.

Alfred Gross

Fighter Pilot

"Keeps rather to himself."

Second Lieutenant Alfred Gross was born October 4, 1919 in Alt-Placht near Templin in Brandenburg. Nicknamed "Fred," he served as a flight instructor with Supplementary Group East (*Ergänzungs Gruppe Ost*) until the fall of 1943, when he was transferred to the 5th Squadron, 54th Fighter Wing "Green Hearts" (*Jagdgeschwader 54 "Grünherz"*). Gross chalked up his first aerial victory in October and served as wingman to Horst Ademeit, achieving 14 kills and winning both the Iron Cross 2nd and 1st Classes. By the end of the year, his score had risen to 20. In April 1944, he was transferred to the 9th Squadron, 54th Fighter Wing on the Western Front. By this time he had 39 aerial victories – including four in one day – and had been awarded the *Luftwaffe* Honor Goblet on April 24.

On May 6, 1944, the 3rd Group, 54th Fighter Wing submitted a special efficiency report on Alfred Gross that requested a promotion to Second Lieutenant as a wartime officer. Werner Schroer, the group commander, forwarded the report – the bulk of which was written by First Lieutenant Eugen-Ludwig Zweigart, the 9th Squadron Commander. Zweigart remarked:[98]

> Gross possesses good mental capabilities. Tall physique, enduring and tough. Decent, upright character, but keeps rather to himself. Leadership qualities are present. Immaculate behavior vis-à-vis superiors, well-liked by his comrades. Good military knowledge and accomplishments. Lively interest in service-related matters and good comprehension of service. Gross is an excellent fighter pilot. In his missions, most recently as a flight leader, he demonstrated dash, courage and great risk-taking at the same time without losing prudence. In the East, he accomplished 39 kills in 127 combat missions at the front in hard air battles. Gross was awarded the Iron Cross 1st Class and the Operational Clasp for Fighters in Gold.

During the Normandy invasion in June, Gross served as the Commander, 8th Squadron. On June 29, Captain Emil "Bully" Lang brought Gross with him from the 54th Fighter Wing to the 26th Fighter Wing "Schlageter" (*Jagdgeschwader 26 "Schlageter"*). On August 27, 1944, Gross was detailed to serve on the staff of the 2nd Group. But this posting was short-lived; on September 3, 1944, while serving as the wingman to the 2nd Group Commander Captain Lang, he shot down a Spitfire in his Focke-Wulf Fw 190A-8 near St. Trond, Belgium, but was bounced by sixteen P-51 Mustangs from the 338th Fighter Squadron of the 55th Fighter Group. The 338th Squadron Commander bore down on Gross's aircraft, which was at an altitude of 600 feet, shooting it down. Gross bailed out, but was seriously wounded in the action. Although he survived, his wounds did not permit future frontline duty. Lang was not so fortunate and died in the same engagement. Alfred Gross died September 19, 1947 in Tönning/Holstein.

He flew 175 combat missions and shot down 52 enemy planes, 39 in the East, a sortie-to-victory ratio of 3.36 to 1.[99]

III./Jagdgeschwader 54   O.U., den 6.5.1944

<u>V o r s c h l a g</u>

<u>zur Beförderung zum ~~Truppen-bzw.~~-Kriegsoffizier</u>

Zur Beförderung zum Leutnant (KO.) wird vorgeschlagen:

<u>Dienstgrad</u>:	Oberfähnrich (Kr) (d.R.)
<u>Familienname</u>:	G r o ß
<u>Vorname</u>:	Alfred
<u>Geburtsdatum</u>:	4.10.1919 zu Alt - Placht
<u>Wehrersatzdienststelle</u>:	W.B.K. Neuruppin
<u>Truppendienststelle</u>:	III./J.G. 54, 8.Staffel
<u>Heimatanschrift</u>:	Wustrau Kr. Ruppin, Gartenstr. 47
<u>Wehrtauglichkeitsgrad</u>:	k.v.

Sämtliche geforderten Voraussetzungen sind erfüllt.

Außerdienstliche Eignung beantragt:

      W.B.K. Neuruppin

<u>"Sonderaktion Offiziernachwuchs"</u>

      Major und Gruppenkommandeur.

Request for Promotion to Officer for Officer Candidate Alfred Gross (front side) – dated May 6, 1944, on blank paper, with typed comments. Signed by Major Werner Schroer, Commander, 3rd Group, 54th Fighter Wing.

Kurze Beurteilung.

G. hat gute geistige Anlagen. Er ist körperlich groß, ausdauernd und zäh. Ehrlicher, aufrichtiger Charakter, geht jedoch wenig aus sich heraus. Führeranlagen sind vorhanden. Einwandfreies Benehmen gegenüber Vorgesetzten, bei Kameraden gern gesehen. Gute militärische Kenntnisse und Leistungen. Reges dienstliches Interesse und gute Diensauffassung. G. ist ein ausgezeichneter Jagdflieger. Er zeigte bei seinen Einsätzen, die er zuletzt als Schwarmführer flog, Schneid, Mut und großes Draufgängertum, ohne dabei die Umsicht zu verlieren. Im Osten konnte er in harten Luftkämpfen bei 127 Frontflügen 39 Abschüsse erzielen. G. wurde mit dem E.K. I und der Frontflugspange für Jäger in Gold ausgezeichnet.

Zweigart
Oberleutnant und Staffelführer.

Request for Promotion to Officer for Officer Candidate Alfred Gross (back side) – signed by First Lieutenant Eugen-Ludwig Zweigart, the 9th Squadron Commander.

Hans Grünberg
Fighter Pilot

"In his nature are hidden leadership qualities."

First Lieutenant Hans "Specker" Grünberg was born on July 8, 1917 at Gross-Fahlenwerder in the Soldin area of Pomerania. He joined the 5th Squadron, 3rd Fighter Wing (*Jagdgeschwader 3*) in May 1942 and shot down his first enemy plane – a Russian DB-3 twin-engine bomber – on August 19. By the end of the year, Grünberg had shot down 11 aircraft. He achieved his 20th victory on April 23, 1943, when he shot down a Russian I-16 fighter, and his 30th victory, on May 31, when he shot down a Yak-4 twin-engine fighter. Grünberg's most successful day on the Eastern Front came on July 5, 1943, when he downed seven Russian Il-2 Sturmovik ground-attack aircraft in three missions to record his 37th through 43rd victories. He scored his 50th kill on July 12, 1943. He bailed out when he suffered engine failure following aerial combat with Yak-1 fighters on 16 July (he bailed out four times during his time in Russia). He scored his 61st and last victory on the Eastern Front on August 1, 1943. Grünberg then flew with the 5th Squadron, *Jagdgeschwader 3 "Udet"* on homeland defense duties based in Germany. He was awarded the *Luftwaffe* Honor Goblet on August 8, 1943 and the German Cross in Gold on September 27, 1943 as a technical sergeant.

On December 20, 1943, Grünberg's chain of command submitted a special report requesting promotion to commissioned officer, based on his bravery in the face of the enemy. His acting group commander Captain Heinrich Sannemann wrote the following:[100]

> Officer Candidate/Master Sergeant Grünberg is an open and sincere human being of immaculate character. He always showed a calm and modest appearance and demonstrated a clear and educated philosophy of life. In his nature are hidden leadership qualities, which will grow with the demands directed towards him. His general mental aptitude is above average. Physically, he is also well-gifted.
>
> The general service knowledge and accomplishments by G. [Grünberg] are outstanding. As a soldier, he keeps his distance and attitude vis-à-vis his superiors. He proved himself a passionate fighter pilot, who under the most difficult missions has remained courageous and victorious. His flight knowledge was proven, not only in the Eastern Campaign but also in battle with British air forces near Malta and in the defense against substantial Anglo-American flights over the occupied areas in the West. In total, up to now he has shot down 62 enemy airplanes in the East and one four-engine enemy bomber and one enemy fighter in the West. However, both most recent shoot-downs have not yet been confirmed.
>
> Officer Candidate/Master Sergeant Grünberg was named an officer candidate on October 1, 1943 and since then has proven himself worthy in every respect. His mature character and diverse demonstrated leadership qualities justify the promotion to wartime officer due to his courage against the enemy.

Colonel Wolf-Dietrich Wilcke, Commodore, 3rd Fighter Wing "Udet", added the following short summary on January 1, 1944:

I second the evaluation of the group commander. Officer Candidate/Master Sergeant Grünberg is fully suitable for promotion to Second Lieutenant (Wartime Officer).

Finally, Brigadier General Max Ibel, commander of the 2nd Fighter Division (*2. Jagddivision*) wrote on January 21, 1944:

In agreement. Due to his outstanding accomplishments, I consider Officer Candidate/Master Sergeant Grünberg suitable for promotion to second lieutenant without reservation.

Master Sergeant Grünberg recorded his first four-engine bomber kill on February 24, 1944, when he claimed a USAAF B-24 – probably from the 2nd Bomb Division, 8th Air Force attack against Gotha and Eisenach – near Bad Hersfeld as his 64th aerial victory. On May 9, 1944, Grünberg was appointed commander of the 5th Squadron, 3rd Fighter Wing "Udet". He claimed his 70th victory on May 29, when he shot down a USAAF B-17 Flying Fortress from the 1st Bomb Division, 8th Air Force near Stettin. Second Lieutenant Hans Grünberg received the Knight's Cross of the Iron Cross on June 9, 1944, after achieving 77 aerial victories.

At the end of 1944, Grünberg was transferred to the 1st Group, 7th Fighter Wing (*Jagdgeschwader 7*), flying Messerschmitt Me 262 jet fighters. On November 21, he was appointed the 1st Squadron Commander, based at Lechfeld. While returning from a combat mission against USAAF bombers on April 17, 1945, he was surprised by USAAF P-51 Mustangs and shot down over Plzen-Bory, but survived after bailing out. His last victory was on April 19, when he shot down a USAAF B-17 Flying Fortress of the 3rd Air Division, 8th Air Force over Bohemia, but he again had to bail out of his Me 262 near Prague. On April 17, 1945, Grünberg was ordered to report to Reim for duty with *Jagdverband 44* commanded by Major General Adolf Galland. He served out the remainder of the war with this unit. Grünberg was credited with 82 victories in 550 combat missions, a sortie-to-victory ratio of 6.71 to 1. He recorded 61 victories over the Eastern Front (including 27 Il-2 Sturmoviks) and 21 over the Western Front (including 10 four-engine bombers). Five of these Western Front kills (3 B-17 Flying Fortresses and 2 Lancasters) were achieved while piloting the Messerschmitt Me 262 jet fighter. He also destroyed 27 trucks, one locomotive and one armored reconnaissance vehicle in ground-attack missions.[101] Hans Grünberg died on January 16, 1998 in Ellerau/Hamburg.

II./ Jagdgeschwader Udet   Gefechtsstand, den 20.12.1943

Beurteilung

Fahnenjunker-Oberfeldwebel (Kr.) G r ü n b e r g ist ein offener und ehrlicher Mensch mit einwandfreiem Charakter. Er zeigte stets ein ruhiges und bescheidenes Wesen und offenbarte eine anschauliche und gebildete Lebensauffassung. In seiner Natur verbergen sich Führereigenschaften, die mit den Anforderungen, die an ihn gerichtet werden, wachsen. Seine allgemeine geistige Veranlagung liegt über dem Durchschnitt. Körperlich ist er ebenfalls gut veranlagt.

Die allgemeinen dienstlichen Kenntnisse und Leistungen des G. sind hervorragend. Als Soldat bewahrte er seinen Vorgesetzten gegenüber Abstand und Haltung.

Er zeigte sich als passionierter Jagdflieger, der sich auch bei oft schweren Einsätzen tapfer und erfolgreich schlug. Sein fliegerisches Können stellte er nicht nur im Ostfeldzug, sondern auch im Kampf mit britischen Luftstreitkräften bei Malta und bei der Abwehr anglo=amerikanischer Großeinflüge in den besetzten Westgebieten unter Beweis. Insgesamt schoß er bisher 61 Feindflugzeuge im Osten und ein 4-motoriges Feindflugzeug und einen Feindjäger im Westen ab. Die beiden letzteren Abschüsse wurden jedoch noch nicht zuerkannt.

Fahnenjunker-Oberfeldwebel (Kr.) Grünberg wurde am 1.10.43 zum K.O.A. ernannt und hat sich inzwischen weiterhin in jeder Hinsicht sehr gut bewährt. Seine charakterliche Reife und die mehrfach hervorgetretenen Führereigenschaften rechtfertigen die Beförderung zum Kriegsoffizier wegen Tapferkeit vor dem Feinde.

Hauptmann u. stellv. Gruppenkommandeur.

b.w.

Request for Promotion to Officer for Officer Candidate Hans Grünberg (front side) – dated December 20, 1943, on blank paper, with typed comments. Signed by Captain Heinrich Sannemann, acting commander of the 2nd Group, 3rd Fighter Wing.

Jagdgeschwader Udet					Gefechtsstand, 1.1.1944.

    Ich schließe mich der Beurteilung des Gruppen=
kommandeurs an. Fahnenjunker-Oberfeldwebel (Kr.)
G r ü n b e r g ist zur Beförderung zum Leutnant (Kr.)
voll geeignet.

					Oberst und Geschwaderkommodore.

2. Jagddivision
 - Kommandeur -					Stabsquartier, den 21.1.1944

    E i n v e r s t a n d e n.
    Aufgrund seiner hervorragenden Leistungen halte ich
Fhj.-Oberfeldwebel (Kr.) G r ü n b e r g uneingeschränkt zur Beförderung zum Leutnant für geeignet.

Request for Promotion to Officer for Officer Candidate Hans Grünberg (back side) – signed by Colonel Wolf-Dietrich Wilcke, Commodore, 3rd Fighter Wing, and by Brigadier General May-Josef Ibel, Commander, 2nd Fighter Division.

Andreas Hagl
Fallschirmjäger

"He is no longer able to withstand the hardships of war."

Captain Andreas Hagl was born April 21, 1911 in Farchant-Garmisch in Bavaria. He entered the Army on October 10, 1931 with the 19th Infantry Regiment in Munich. As a Staff Sergeant, Hagl joined the *Luftwaffe* on April 17, 1937 and volunteered to become a paratrooper; he then joined the 2nd Battalion, 1st Paratroop Regiment (*Fallschirmjäger-Regiment 1*) and fought in the Polish campaign. By then a technical sergeant, Hagl won the Iron Cross 2nd Class on October 13, 1939. In 1940, Hagl fought in the campaign in Holland, helping to seize the key railroad bridge over the Maas River at Moerdijk as a platoon leader, and was wounded on May 22, 1940. On July 9, 1940, he received the Iron Cross 1st Class. A month later, Hagl became an officer candidate and transferred to the 3rd Paratroop Regiment (*Fallschirmjäger-Regiment 3*). After receiving his commission to second lieutenant on November 1, 1940, he became a platoon leader in the 2nd Company. During the German airborne invasion of Crete, Hagl's unit jumped into Prison Valley and began a difficult fight against the 10th New Zealand Brigade southwest of Khaniá. On landing, the 1st Battalion Commander (Captain Friedrich von der Heydte) attempted to make contact with the 3rd Battalion and used Hagl's platoon to spearhead the effort. On May 26, Hagl assumed command of the entire 2nd company; he was seriously wounded that day in the right thigh by hand grenade shrapnel, but continued to lead the company. On June 10, 1941, Hagl assumed command of the regiment's 7th Company. He received the Wound Badge in Silver on July 5, 1941 and the Knight's Cross of the Iron Cross on July 7, 1941.

Hagl was wounded again on October 8, 1941, while the regiment was deployed and fighting in Russia. This began a lengthy period of hospital stays and rear area postings during recovery and rehabilitation. These assignments included time at Braunschweig in the 3rd Paratroop Regiment's depot, on the staff of the 1st Supplementary Paratroop Regiment – an operational training unit – and a return to a reserve hospital in Bonn. On May 15, 1944, Captain Hagl (he had been promoted on May 1, 1943) became a supply officer in the 1st Paratroop Division (*1. Fallschirmjäger-Division*) in Italy.

On July 28, 1944, Hagl's chain of command submitted an efficiency report on him. This report was completed entirely by his regimental commander Colonel Ludwig Heilmann, who had known Hagl for almost four years:[102]

Short Evaluation (Personal values, National Socialist attitude, accomplishments before the enemy, service accomplishments, mental and physical attributes and suitability, infantry experience, when and how obtained): Captain Hagl is a sincere, honest officer with an exemplary National Socialist attitude. He has proven himself in action against the enemy in an excellent way. His service capabilities are somewhat limited due to having been wounded. In spite of that, he still accomplishes more than many a healthy officer. He is no longer able to withstand the hardships of war.

Strong Traits: Personal readiness for action without reservation.

Weak Traits: None known.

Summary Assessment: Average.
(Above Average, Average, Below Average)

How well is the current position being fulfilled: Very well fulfilled.
(Use only: Very well fulfilled, well fulfilled, fulfilled, not fulfilled)

Suitable for promotion to the next higher service grade: Yes.

Suitable as: Commander of a Replacement Battalion.

Known to the person submitting this review: since August 1, 1940.

There are conflicting reports concerning the death of Andreas Hagl. The most reliable published source states that Hagl fell in action on July 28, 1944 (the day of this report). Another account, in the *Volksbund Deutsche Kriegsgräberfürsorge* organization – a group dedicated to the maintenance and preservation of German military cemeteries – states that Andreas Hagl was killed in action on April 29, 1945 near San

Vito di Laguzzano in the province of Vicenza and is buried at the German Military Cemetery at Costermano, Italy (Section 2, Grave 554). Still another source states that Hagl died in April 1945 at the hands of Italian partisans in northern Italy after being captured. Given the location of Costermano (near Lake Garda in northern Italy) and the procedures used to re-inter German military graves after the war, it is more likely that Hagl died somewhere in northern Italy, but the date of his death remains obscure.[103]

What is clear is that although seriously wounded numerous times during the war, Andreas Hagl continued to fight until he could fight no more.

Luftwaffe Efficiency & Promotion Reports

Fallschirmjaeger-Regiment 3   Gef.Stand _____, den 28.7. 1944
  Dienststelle, nicht Feldpostnummer

Kriegs-Beurteilung zum 1. August 1944
für Offz. ausschl. San.-, Vet.-Offz.
über den

Hptm.(Kr.O.)   1. 4. 1942   Andreas   H a g l
  Dienstgrad   R.D.A. (Ordn.Nr.) und   Vorname   Name
                Dienstalterliste

21. 4. 1911   verheiratet, ledig, verwitwet, geschieden   ?
  geboren am   (Zutreffendes unterstreichen)   Wehrdiensttauglichkeit
                                                 (kv, gv Feld, gv H., tropentgl., tropenuntgl.)

              Schneider   W B K:
              Zivilberuf (falls vorhanden)
Nachkdo.Fhr.1.Fsch.Jg.Div.s.15.5.44   Braunschweig
  jetzige Verwendung seit   Friedensdienststelle und W.B.K.

              terminmaessige Vorlage zum 1.8.1944
                        Anlaß der Vorlage

Deutsche Auszeichnungen des jetzigen Krieges mit Verleihungsdaten und Angabe, ob und zu welchen Auszeichnungen vorgeschlagen: Erinnerungsmedaille f.d.1.10.38 m/Spange; E.K.2.Kl. am 13.10.1939; Verw.Abz. in Schwarz am 22.5.40; E.K.1.Kl. am 9.7.41; Ritterkreuz zum E.K. am 9.7.1941; Aermelband "Kreta" am 20.5.1943;Verw. Abz. in Silber am 5.7.1941

¹) Genaue Angabe, ob Tr.-Offz., Erg.-Offz., Offz. z.D., Res.-Offz., Kr.-Offz., z.V.-Offz.
²) In zweifelhaften Fällen neu festzustellen.
³) Dienststelle, welche Friedensgebührnisse zahlt und zuständiges Wehrbezirkskommando.
⁴) z.B.: Versetzung zur III./K.G. 2, terminmäßige Vorlage zum 1.5.43.

Kurze Beurteilung:
(Persönlichkeitswert, nationalsozialistische Haltung, Bewährung vor dem Feinde, dienstliche Leistungen, geistige und körperliche Anlagen und Eignung, infanteristische Erfahrungen, wann und wo erworben)

Hptm. H a g l ist ein aufrichtiger, biederer Offizier mit vorbildlicher nationalsozialistischer Haltung. Vor dem Feinde hat er sich hervorragend bewährt. Seine dienstlichen Leistungen sind durch Folgen einer Verwundung etwas beschränkt. Trotzdem leistet er noch mehr als mancher gesunde Offizier. Den Strapazen eines Krieges ist er nicht mehr gewachsen.

Starke Seiten: Rücksichtslose persönliche Einsatzbereitschaft.

Schwache Seiten: Nicht aufgetreten.

Zusammenfassendes Urteil: Durchschnitt.
(über Durchschnitt, Durchschnitt, unter Durchschnitt)

Wie wird die jetzige Stelle ausgefüllt?   Sehr gut.
(Es sind nur die Ausdrücke „sehr gut ausgefüllt", „gut ausgefüllt", „ausgefüllt", „nicht ausgefüllt" zu verwenden)

Geeignet zur Beförderung zum nächsthöheren Dienstgrad?   Ja.

Efficiency Report for Captain Andreas Hagl (front side) – dated July 28, 1944, on pre-printed form from the Hess firm in Braunschweig, with typed comments.

Eignung
für welche nächsthöhere Verwendung⁵)?   Eignet sich zum Kommandeur eines Ers.-Btl.
für welche besondere oder anderweitige Verwendung⁶)?
Vorschlag für Verwendung in nächster Zeit⁷)?

Sprachkenntnisse (keine Schulkenntnisse)
a) abgelegte Prüfungen: Keine
(z. B.: Dolmetscherprüfung 1. 10. 42)
b) Beherrschung der Sprache:
(z. B.: durch Aufenthalt im Ausland)

Eröffnung zu welchen Punkten, wann, wie   Keine
(mündlich oder schriftlich) und durch wen?

Strafen
sind mit vollem Straftenor sowie Vermerk über Vollstreckung abschriftlich als Anlage der Kriegsbeurteilung beizuheften.

Dem Beurteilenden bekannt seit   1.8.40.
~~unterstellt seit~~

Ausbildung
a) erworbene Scheine: Fallschirmschuetzenschein
(L. F., E. L. F., L. B. usw.)
b) Sonderausbildung: Keine
(z. B. Bild.-Offz., Techn. Offz., Meß-Offz.,
Funk-Drahtnachr.-Offz., W. K. S.)

[signature]   Oberst u. Regimentskommandeur.
Unterschrift   Dienstgrad und Dienststellung

Beitrag des Chefs des Generalstabes der vorgesetzten Kommandobehörde:
(nur bei Genst.-Offz. in Stabsstellungen und zur Dienstleistung zum Generalstab kommandierten Offizieren)

Zusätze vorgesetzter Dienststellen:

---

⁵) Gilt für alle Offz., für Truppen-Offz. hinsichtlich Eignung zur Führung des nächsthöheren Verbandes, für Genst.-Offz. hinsichtlich Eignung zum Chef oder Ia, Ic der Luftfl., Flieger-Korps, Flak-Korps, Fl.-Div., Flak-Div., zur Versetzung in den Genst., zur Kommandierung in den Genst.
⁶) z. B.: Höherer Adjutant, Erzieher, Lehrer auf Spezialgebieten, auf Grund von Sprachkenntnissen im Attachédienst; für Genst.-Offz. hinsichtlich Eignung für Verwendung im Quartiermeisterdienst, im Ic-Dienst, im Transportwesen, als Lehrer für Genst.-Lehrgang (Taktik bzw. Qu.-Dienst); besondere Anlagen für Kriegsgeschichte, Wehrwirtschaft.
⁷) z. B.: „noch halbjährige Belassung in bisheriger Stelle" oder „alsbaldige Verwendung als Geschw.-Kommodore".

Efficiency Report for Captain Andreas Hagl (back side) – signed by Colonel Ludwig Heilmann, Commander, 3rd Paratroop Regiment.

Reino Hamer
Fallschirmjäger

"He sweeps the men under his command along with him."

Major Reino Hamer was born on August 29, 1916 in Rastede near Oldenburg. He joined the *Luftwaffe* on December 1, 1936 and initially served with several anti-aircraft units. Promoted to second lieutenant on March 1, 1939, he served as a battery commander in the 32nd Anti-Aircraft Regiment (*Flak-Regiment 32*) in the Norwegian campaign in 1940. Hamer was promoted to first lieutenant on March 1, 1941, attended airborne school and became a platoon leader in the Paratroop Anti-Aircraft Machine-Gun Battalion (*Fallschirm-Fla-MG-Bataillon*). In November, he became a company commander in the battalion – which deployed to the Leningrad front – and received the Iron Cross 2nd Class on December 1, 1941. During 1942, Hamer attended several tactical schools in Germany before assuming command of the anti-tank company of the 100th *Luftwaffe* Field Battalion on December 1, 1942 as it fought on the southern sector of the Eastern Front. On February 1, 1943, Hamer won the Iron Cross 1st Class and became the Commander, 2nd Company, 6th Paratroop Regiment (*Fallschirmjäger-Regiment 6*) on March 1, 1943.

On October 29, 1943, Hamer's chain of command submitted him for an accelerated promotion to captain. In it, his battalion commander Captain Oswald Finzel said:[104]

> First Lieutenant Hamer is an officer who fully and completely satisfies the conditions for preferential promotion based on service requirements. In his position as company commander, his accomplishments are greatly above average. He is an alert, energetic, idealistic and enthusiastic officer, who approaches the tasks demanded from him in an unburdened and courageous way, while at the same time making cool and sound decisions. In difficult situations, he is always in complete command. Direct and secure in his demeanor and speech, he sweeps the men under his command along with him. He understands how to lead his troops during duty and also during times of rest with a free spirit, cleanliness in basic attitudes and readiness for service. His very good service accomplishments, his good infantry knowledge and experience in the winter campaigns of 1941/42 and 1942/43 on the Eastern Front and his nature as a leader qualify him to be a very good officer who may also be employed as an acting battalion commander with further training.
>
> First Lieutenant Hamer has been the acting commander of the company since October 1, 1941 and from December 1, 1942 has been the company commander. In the battles at Petroschino on the Newa, he has led his company in an outstanding manner and he was extensively involved in the fighting of Battle Group Matthaeas near Woroschilowgrad-Makar-Ja-Nerowka and at the break-through at Krassnowka on the Donez. Since the establishment of the 1st Battalion, 6th Paratroop Regiment (Assault), he was in charge of the 2nd Company. In the battles around Rome, he deployed his soldiers, many of whom were very young, in an exemplary manner and contributed very significantly to the quick success which the paratroopers attained.

Major Ernst Liebach, Hamer's regimental commander, also had extremely positive comments on the officer:

> First Lieutenant Hamer is a mature, distinguished character, who has fully proven his above-average leadership in guiding his company in the most difficult engagements in the East. In the periods between the engagements, he has accomplished valuable teaching and training tasks in the formation of new troops. With his character attributes, his highly developed concept of service and his leadership qualities, he ranks high above the average of his peers as a company commander. His preferential promotion is recommended most sincerely.

The acting division commander Brigadier General Walter Barenthin also supported the promotion by stating:

> After discussion with the Commander of the 2nd Paratroop Division Major General Ramcke, the preferential promotion according to the determination of a date of rank is recommended. The conditions of the *Luftwaffe* regulations of December 22, 1942 are completely fulfilled.

Finally, the commander of the 11th Air Corps, Lieutenant General Kurt Student, simply added: "Recommended!"

Reino Hamer was promoted to captain and given a date of rank of October 1, 1943. He returned to the Eastern Front in December 1943 and fought in several defensive battles along the Dnepr, Bug and Dniester Rivers. Still in Russia, he became the commander of the 1st Battalion, 6th Paratroop Regiment on March 1, 1944. As losses mounted, Captain Hamer assumed acting command of a battle group composed of the remnants of the regiment. Leaving Russia in May 1944, Hamer then took command of the newly-formed 1st Battalion, 7th Paratroop Regiment (*Fallschirmjäger-Regiment 7*) on June 1, 1944. He then deployed to Brest, France, where he received the German Cross in Gold on July 12, 1944 and was promoted to major on August 1, 1944. Major Reino Hamer received the Knight's Cross of the Iron Cross on September 5, 1944 for his actions in Russia the previous May. He was taken prisoner on September 19, 1944, when American forces captured Brest. Hamer survived the war, joined the new German Army in 1956, rose to the grade of colonel and retired in 1977. Reino Hamer died July 24, 1992 in Ubstadt near Bruchsal in Baden.[105]

I./Fallsch. Jg. Rgt. 6 (Sturm)   O. U., am 29. Oktober 1943
Abt. IIa   Az. 21

V o r s c h l a g

zur

b e v o r z u g t e n   B e f ö r d e r u n g

Gemäß R.d.L. u. Ob.d.L. LP Nr. 71 489/42 (2 ID)
II. Ang. v. 22.12.42 Abschnitt

für   Oberleutnant (Tr.O.)   H a m e r   Reino
           Dienstgrad   Name   Vorname

Dienststellung: Kompanie-Chef

Rangdienstalter: 1. 3. 41 (26)

Beförderungsdaten zu den
beiden letzten Offz.-Dienstgraden: zum Leutnant (Tr.O.) 1. 3. 39
                                        " Oberleutnant (Tr.O.) 1. 3. 41

Geburtsdatum: 29. 8. 1918

Auszeichnungen: Ostmedaille, Erdkampfabzeichen der Lw.
                    E.K.II. u. E.K.I. Klasse

B e g r ü n d u n g :

A) **Allgemeine Leistungen**
    Oblt. Hamer ist ein Offizier, auf den die Bedingungen für die bevorzugte Beförderung auf Grund der Dienststellung (Bezugsverfügung-A 1 a und A 4) voll und ganz zutreffen. In seiner Stellung als Kompanie-Chef liegen seine Leistungen erheblich über dem Durchschnitt. Er ist ein frischer, schwungvoller, begeisterter Offizier voller Ideale, der unbeschwert und draufgängerisch an ihm gestellte Aufgaben herangeht und trotzdem kühl und sicher abwägt. Er ist auch in schwierigen Verhältnissen immer Herr der Lage. Bestimmt und sicher in Auftreten und Sprache reißt er seine Untergebenen mit. Er versteht in Dienst und Freizeit seiner Kompanie Frische, Sauberkeit der Grundhaltung und Einsatzfreudigkeit zu verleihen. Seine sehr guten dienstlichen Leistungen, die guten infanteristischen Kenntnisse und Erfahrungen aus den Winterfeldzügen 1941/42 und 1942/43 im Osten und seine Führernatur qualifizieren ihn zu einem sehr guten Offizier, der bei weiterer Ausbildung auch als Bataillonsführer zu verwenden ist.

B) **Einzelangaben**
    Oblt. Hamer führt seit dem 1. 10. 41 eine Kompanie und ist seit dem 1. 12. 42 Kompanie-Chef. Er hat seine Kompanie in den Gefechten bei Petroschino an der Newa hervorragend geführt und hatte erheblichen Anteil an den Gefechten der Kampfgruppe Matthaeas bei Woroschilowgrad-Makarow-Ja-Nerowka und deren Durchbruch bei Krassnowka am Donez. Seit Aufstellung des I./Fallsch. Jg. Rgt. 6 (Sturm) führt er die 2. Kompanie. Bei den Kämpfen um Rom hat er seine zum Teil sehr jungen Soldaten hervorragend eingesetzt und trug sehr wesentlich zu dem schnellen Erfolg bei, den die Fallschirmtruppe erringen konnte.

                                                  Hauptmann u. stellv. Btl.-Kdr.

Request for Preferred Promotion for First Lieutenant Reino Hamer (front side) – dated October 29, 1943, on blank paper, with typed and handwritten comments. Signed by Captain Oswald Finzel, Commander, 1st Battalion, 6th Paratroop Regiment.

Stellungnahme des Rgts.-Führers:

Oblt. H a m e r ist ein gereifter vornehmer Charakter, der durch die Führung seiner Kompanie in schwierigen Einsätzen im Osten seine über dem Durchschnitt liegenden Führereigenschaften voll unter Beweis gestellt hat. In den Zeiten zwischen den Einsätzen hat er bei den Neuaufstellungen wertvolle Erziehungs- und Ausbildungsarbeit geleistet. Als Leiter eines K.O.A.-Schulungslehrganges hat er sich erneut bewährt. Als Kompanie-Chef steht er mit seiner charakterlichen Veranlagung, seiner hohen Berufsauffassung und seinen Führereigenschaften weit über dem Durchschnitt seiner übrigen Kameraden. Seine bevorzugte Beförderung gem. R.d.L.u.Ob.d.L.,LP Nr. 71 489/42 (2, ID) II. Ang. v. 22.12.42, Abschnitt A.,1.,a) unter gleichzeitiger Festsetzung eines RDA. wird wärmstens befürwortet.

Major und Rgts.-Führer.

Stellungnahme des Divisionsführers:

Nach Rücksprache mit dem Kommandeur der 2.Fallsch.Jg.Div., Generalleutnant R a m c k e , wird die bevorzugte Beförderung unter Festsetzung eines Rangdienstalters befürwortet. Die Bedingungen des Erlasses R.d.L.u.Ob.d.L.,LP Nr. 71 489/42 (2, ID) II.Ang. v. 22.12.42, Abschnitt A.,1.,a) sind voll erfüllt.

I. V.

Generalmajor und Divisionsführer.

Gen.Kdo. XI.Fliegerkorps
Der Kommandierende General

O.U., 14.11.1943

Request for Preferred Promotion for First Lieutenant Reino Hamer (back side) – signed by Major Ernst Liebach, acting commander of the 6th Paratroop Regiment, Brigadier General Walter Berenthin, acting division commander, and Lieutenant General Kurt Student, Commander, 11th Air Corps.

Friedrich-August von der Heydte
Fallschirmjäger

"Distinguished himself through prudent leadership of his battalion and ruthless personal action."

Lieutenant Colonel Dr. Friedrich-August von der Heydte was born on March 30, 1907 in Munich, Bavaria. He entered the *Reichswehr* as an officer candidate on April 1, 1925 with the 19th Infantry Regiment. One year later, he transferred to the 18th Cavalry Regiment but soon thereafter obtained permission to leave the service to pursue academic studies. This he did, studying law and philosophy at the universities of Munich, Berlin, Vienna, Graz and Innsbruck (and joining the Catholic Society – which was the source of his later nickname), not returning to the Army until 1935, when he joined the 2nd Cavalry Regiment. Von der Heydte was promoted to second lieutenant on August 1, 1936 and was posted to the 15th Cavalry Regiment. Two months later he made first lieutenant. In 1937, von der Heydte was named Commander, 2nd Company, 6th Anti-Tank Detachment (*Panzer-Abwehr-Abteilung 6*), was promoted to captain on October 1, 1938 and won the Iron Cross 2nd Class on September 27, 1939 with the unit on the West Wall. In January 1940, von der Heydte joined the division staff of the 246th Infantry Division; he would subsequently be assigned to the staff of the 227th Infantry Division on July 2, 1940.

Although he received the Iron Cross 1st Class on September 26, 1940, von der Heydte volunteered to transfer to the *Luftwaffe* on October 25, 1940. He attended airborne school and was then named Commander, 1st Battalion, 3rd Paratroop Regiment (*Fallschirmjäger-Regiment 3*) on December 10, 1940. The battalion jumped into Crete on May 20, 1941, landing in Prison Valley and seizing the village of Agia. Captain von der Heydte received the Knight's Cross of the Iron Cross on July 9, 1941 for his actions in Crete and was promoted to major on August 1, 1941. His unit then deployed to Russia and the siege of Leningrad. Von der Heydte received the German Cross in Gold on March 9, 1942 for these exploits and also took command of the Paratroop Demonstration Battalion (*Fallschirmjäger-Lehr-Bataillon*) at Döberitz. However, North Africa beckoned and von der Heydte deployed there to command a battle group of Paratroop Regiment Ramcke from August 1942 to January 1943. He distinguished himself in the defensive battles at El Alamein and for personally leading a night attack on December 16, 1942 at Nofilia. On February 1, 1943, Major von der Heydte became the division operations officer (Ia) for the 2nd Paratroop Division (*2. Fallschirmjäger Division*).

On July 7, 1943, the commanding general of the 11th Air Corps, Kurt Student, submitted a request for an accelerated promotion for Major von der Heydte. Student wrote:[106]

> The corps command applies for a preferential promotion of Major Friedrich-August Freiherr von der Heydte, 2nd Paratroop Division.
>
> Major Freiherr von der Heydte excelled in the campaign in Crete as a battalion commander with outstanding courage. For that he was awarded the Knight's Cross of the Iron Cross on July 9, 1941. From October 4, 1941 to November 16, 1941, he took part in the battles at the Newa and was awarded the German Cross in Gold for additional, repeated examples of his courage. As the commander of the 1st Battalion 3rd Paratroop Regiment from December 16, 1941 to February 15, 1943, particularly from August 3, 1942 to January 11,

170

1943, he participated with the 1st *Luftwaffe Jägerbrigade* in operations in North Africa (battles in the El Alamein defensive positions and the withdrawal of Rommel's Army up to Buerat). During those battles, Major von der Heydte distinguished himself through prudent leadership of his battalion and ruthless personal action.

Since February 16, 1942, Major von der Heydte has been with the 2nd Paratroop Division. During the formation of the division, he put his far-reaching knowledge and thorough experience of parachuting to good use for the division and used it to such a great extent that he was able to support the successful establishment and training of the division under the most difficult of circumstances.

Major von der Heydte is, without reservation, qualified for promotion to the next higher service grade. His preferential promotion is most warmly recommended by me.

On a reconnaissance flight to the island of Elba, on September 12, 1943, his plane crashed – killing the pilot and seriously injuring von der Heydte. After partially recuperating, von der Heydte assumed command of the newly formed 6th Paratroop Regiment (*Fallschirmjäger-Regiment 6*) and deployed to Normandy. On June 6, 1944, the Allies invaded and von der Heydte led a determined defense of Carentan against the U.S. 101st Airborne Division. Von der Heydte, who was promoted to lieutenant colonel on August 1, 1944, received the Oak Leaves to the Knight's Cross of the Iron Cross on September 30, 1944 for his actions in Normandy. In December 1944, Lieutenant Colonel von der Heydte was given command of a special battle group and parachuted behind American lines during the Battle of the Bulge. Codenamed "Operation Stösser," his mission was to secure a key crossroads at Baraque Michel, Belgium, ahead of the advancing 12th SS *Panzer* Division. Wounded in the operation, von der Heydte was captured by American troops; he would spend two years as a prisoner of war. After the war, von der Heydte joined the new German air force and rose to the grade of brigadier general (Reserve). Later in life, von der Heydte became a Fellow of the Carnegie Endowment for International Peace. Friedrich von der Heydte, nicknamed the "Rosary Paratrooper," died on July 7, 1994 at Aham an der Vils near Landshut in Bavaria.[107]

Generalkommando　　　　　　　　　　　　　　O.U., 19.7.1943
XI.Fliegerkorps
IIa Az. 21 c 20

Bezug: R.d.L.u.Ob.d.L. LP Nr. 71 489/42 (2,ID) II.Ang.v.22.12.1942.
Betr.: Bevorzugte Beförderung des Major Frhr.v.d. H e y d t e.

An
Reichsluftfahrtministerium -L.P.2 ID-

   Gen.Kdo. beantragt die bevorzugte Beförderung des Major (Tr.O.) Frhr.v.d. H e y d t e, Friedrich-August, 2.Fsch.Jg. Div.
   Major v.d.Heydte hat sich beim Einsatz Kreta als Btl.Kdr. durch hervorragende Tapferkeit ausgezeichnet. Ihm wurde hierfür am 9.7.1941 das Ritterkreuz des Eisernen Kreuzes verliehen.
   Vom 4.10.41-16.11.41 nahm er an den Kämpfen an der Newa teil und wurde für weitere wiederholte Tapferkeitsbeweise mit dem Deutschen Kreuz in Gold ausgezeichnet.
   Als Kdr. des I./Fsch.Jg.Rgt. 3 (Lehr-Btl.) v. 16.12.41-15.2.43 nahm er innerhalb der Lw.Jägerbrigade 1 v. 3.8.42 - 11.1.1943 an dem Einsatz in Nordafrika (Kämpfe in der El-Alamein - Stellung, Rückzugsbewegung der Armee Rommel bis nach Buerat) teil. Auch bei diesen Kämpfen zeichnete sich Major v.d.Heydte durch umsichtige Führung seines Btls. und rücksichtslosen Einsatz seiner Person besonders aus.
   Seit 16.2.1943 ist Major v.d.Heydte Ia bei der 2.Fsch.Jg.Div. Bei dem Aufbau der 2.Fsch.Jg.Div. hat er als Ia sein umfangreiches Wissen und seine gründlichen Kenntnisse des Fallschirmwesens nutzbringend für die Division und mit großer Umsicht verwertet, so daß er den Div.Kdr. bei der unter schwierigsten Verhältnissen erfolgten Aufstellung und Ausbildung der Division in wertvollster Weise unterstützen konnte.
   Major v.d.Heydte ist zur Beförderung zum nächsthöheren Dienstgrad uneingeschränkt geeignet. Seine bevorzugte Beförderung wird wärmstens befürwortet.

Der Kommandierende General

Request for Preferred Promotion for Major Friedrich-August von der Heydte (one page only) – July 19, 1943, on blank paper, with typed comments. Signed by Lieutenant General Kurt Student. Stamped block indicates that the report was received at the *Luftwaffe* Personnel Office on July 26, with an initial appearing to be that of Bruno Loerzer, chief of the office.

Herbert von Hoffer
Ground-Attack Pilot/Fighter Pilot

"He is very sensitive, easily becomes nervous."

Second Lieutenant Herbert von Hoffer was born January 18, 1920 at Karlsbad, Bohemia (now Karlovy Vary in the Czech Republic). In 1941, he attended flight school at the fighter school at Zerbst before his assignment in August 1941 to the Supplemental Fighter Squadron at Lippstadt (*Jagdflieger-Ergänzungsstaffel*). From September 1941 to March 1943, von Hoffer served on the Eastern Front with the 2nd Group, 2nd Demonstration Wing (*Lehrgeschwader 2*), which became the 2nd Group, 1st Ground-Attack Wing (*Schlachtgeschwader 1*). He won the *Luftwaffe* Honor Goblet on September 21, 1942. On February 13, 1943, Sergeant von Hoffer won the German Cross in Gold with the 2nd Squadron, 1st Ground-Attack Wing. He was also wounded once in action during this time while the unit was subordinated to the 8th Air Corps (4th Air Fleet).

From April 12 to June 19, 1942, Technical Sergeant von Hoffer attended an officer candidate school at the 4th Air War School (*Luftkriegschule 4*) at Fürstenfeldbruck. Upon graduation, the commander of the school Brigadier General Herbert Sonnenburg completed an efficiency report on von Hoffer. Sonnenburg wrote:[108]

Personality attributes and character suitability: Due to internal inhibitions, von Hoffer is not fully developed. At the same time, he works independently, has natural freshness, is always ready to be of assistance and is helpful. He is very sensitive, easily becomes nervous. At times it will be hard for him to apply the same severity to men under his command as he applies it to himself. Consistently working on himself, he accomplishes his best in a task demanded from him. His being is characterized by his quiet, calm, modest attitude. Because of his strong sense of justice, he quickly wins over the confidence of the men under his command. He is suited to become a wartime officer.

Mental attributes: Von Hoffer is mentally alert and possesses a good talent for comprehension. His general knowledge is good. However, his thinking is still only slightly matured, but he endeavors to deepen it and to further educate himself.

Physical attributes: Due to shrapnel, his athleticism is somewhat restricted. However, he applies his full being toward accomplishments and at the same time demonstrates personal toughness and good accomplishments.

Military accomplishments and suitability: At the front he still shows slight awkwardness, and due to his inhibitions, he cannot always accomplish what he set out to do. In general, he is lacking experience. During schooling, he strives hard to follow the instructions and showed at the end of the training course decent accomplishments after great initial difficulty. His presentation was prepared with diligence and well-presented as to sentence structure as well as contents. His accomplishments are worthy of recognition.

Result of examination regarding pilot capabilities: useful for military flight

Recommended use: as pilot

Suitable for: Recommended as suitable for wartime officer. Participant is willing to enter an officer career with limited service time.

Von Hoffer returned to combat in Russia from June 1943 to May 1944, first with the 2nd Ground-Attack Wing (*Schlachtgeschwader 2*), and later with the 5th Squadron, 1st Ground-Attack Wing (which later became the 5th Squadron, 77th Ground-Attack Wing [*Schlachtgeschwader 77*]). Promoted to second lieutenant on January 1, 1944, he assumed command of the 5th Squadron, flying Focke-Wulf Fw 190s, and received the Knight's Cross of the Iron Cross on August 8, 1944, as his unit supported the 8th Air Corps (4th Air Fleet) in southern Russia. From June to December 1944, von Hoffer served in a series of flight instructor positions with the 101st Ground-Attack Wing (*Schlachtgeschwader 101*) – based in France – and the 102nd Ground-Attack Wing (*Schlachtgeschwader 102*). In January 1945, he also served briefly at the *Luftwaffe* Gunnery School at Vaerlöse. In February and March 1945, von Hoffer returned to combat with the 10th Ground-Attack Wing (*Schlachtgeschwader 10*) – flying against Soviet forces in Hungary – before spending the final month of the war flying the Messerschmitt Me 163 *Komet* rocket fighter in the 400th Fighter Wing (*Jagdgeschwader 400*). During the war, von Hoffer flew over 700 combat missions. He shot down 9 enemy aircraft in addition to destroying numerous ground targets. In the 1950s, von Hoffer, now with the name Hoffer-Sulmthal, joined the Austrian air force, and reached the grade of major. Herbert von Hoffer died in a military air crash on September 1, 1967 at Zeltweg, Austria.[109]

Luftkriegsschule 4   K   Fürstenfeldbruck, 19.6.43

G e h e i m

Der Feldwebel v. H o f f e r , Herbert
geb. am 18.1.20

Feldp.-Nr. L 42 379, Lgpa. Breslau

hat am 15. Lehrgang für Kriegs-Offz.-Nachwuchs
vom 12.4. bis 19.6.43 teilgenommen.

B e u r t e i l u n g

1.) Persönlichkeitswert und charakterliche Eignung:

v. Hoffer kommt durch innere Hemmungen nicht voll zur Entfaltung. Dabei arbeitet er selbständig, ist von natürlicher Frische, stets hilfsbereit und zuvorkommend. Sehr sensibel, wird leicht nervös. Es wird ihm manchmal schwer werden, die gleiche Härte wie gegen sich, auch gegen Untergebene anzuwenden. Stets an sich arbeitend, leistet er in einer ihm gestellten Aufgabe sein Bestes. Sein Wesen ist gekennzeichnet durch seine stille, ruhige, bescheidene Haltung. Das Vertrauen seiner Untergebenen wird durch seinen starken Gerechtigkeitssinn schnell erworben. Zum Kriegsoffizier geeignet.

2.) Geistige Veranlagung:

v. Hoffer ist geistig regsam und besitzt eine gute Auffassungsgabe. Sein Allgemeinwissen ist gut. Sein Denken ist jedoch noch wenig geschult, doch ist er bemüht, sich zu vertiefen und weiterzubilden.

3.) Körperliche Veranlagung:

Sportlich durch Geschoßsplitter etwas behindert. Er setzt sich jedoch mit seiner ganzen Person für eine Leistung ein und zeigt dabei eigene Härte und gute Leistungen.

4.) Militärische Leistungen und Eignung:

Vor der Front zeigt er sich noch etwas unbeholfen und kann sich infolge seiner Hemmungen nicht immer durchsetzen. Im wesentlichen fehlt es jedoch an Übung. Im Unterricht gibt er sich Mühe, zu folgen und zeigte am Schluß des Lehrgangs nach anfänglich großen Lücken brauchbare Leistungen. Sein Vortrag ist mit Fleiß vorbereitet und wie im Satzbau so auch inhaltlich gut vorgetragen. Seine Leistungen sind anzuerkennen.

Efficiency Report for Officer Candidate Herbert Hoffer (front side) – dated June 19, 1943, on blank paper with typed comments.

5.) <u>Ergebnis der Untersuchung auf Fliegertauglichkeit:</u>
    wehrfliegertauglich

6.) <u>Vorgeschlagene Verwendung:</u>
    Flugzeugführer.

7.) <u>Fliegerische Ausbildung:</u>
    Flugzeugführer (L.F.-Schein)

8.) <u>Als geeignet für:</u>
    Geeignet für die Übernahme als Kriegsoffizier dem R.L.M. (L.P.) vorgeschlagen!

9.) <u>Besondere Bemerkungen:</u>
    Auszeichnungen: E.K. II u.I, Frontflugspange in Gold, Ostmedaille, Deutsches Kreuz in Gold.
    Verwundungen: Verwundetenabzeichen in Schwarz
    Verheiratet: —

10.) <u>Teilnehmer ist bereit, die Offizierlaufbahn</u>
     mit begrenzter Dienstzeit einzuschlagen.

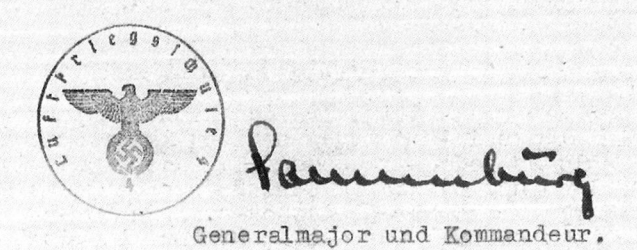

Generalmajor und Kommandeur.

Efficiency Report for Officer Candidate Herbert von Hoffer (back side) – signed by the Commander of the 4th Air War School, Brigadier General Herbert Sonnenburg.

Franz Hrdlicka
Fighter Pilot

"He has read the Führer's Mein Kampf."

Captain Franz Hrdlicka was born in Maxdorf near Brünn in Moravia on October 15, 1920. He entered the *Luftwaffe* on November 15, 1939 and became an officer candidate. From the beginning of 1940, he served in the Supplemental Fighter Group (*Ergänzungs-Jagdgruppe*) – the operational training formation – of the 77th Fighter Wing (*Jagdgeschwader 77*), based at Götzendorf, and then in the 5th Squadron and took part in the Balkan campaign and the invasion of Crete. He scored his first victory – an I-16 fighter – on July 6, 1941, his second – a MiG-3 fighter – on August 6, and his third – an SB-2 bomber – on August 12, but on September 22, 1941, he crashed on landing at Tschaplinka in the Ukraine in his Messerschmitt Me 109E-7 and was injured. He returned to the front on September 25 and raised his score to 27, before being seriously wounded in aerial combat on August 6, 1942 in his Messerschmitt Me 109F-4. Hrdlicka received the *Luftwaffe Honor Goblet* on September 13, 1942. Again he spent time convalescing, but returned to command the 5th Squadron in February 1943 in the skies over Tunisia. He reached his 28th victory on March 12, 1943, and by August 19, 1943 he had registered 36 kills. He won the German Cross in Gold on August 23, 1943.[110]

Franz Hrdlicka next moved to homeland defense in the skies over Germany and in August 1944 was the acting commander of the 1st Group, 2nd Fighter Wing "Richthofen" (*Jagdgeschwader 2 "Richthofen"*). On September 27, 1944, he was shot down in combat with a Spitfire near Arnhem and had to bail out wounded from his Messerschmitt Me 109G-6. He received the Knight's Cross of the Iron Cross on October 18, 1944, having amassed 44 aerial victories and soon thereafter was transferred to be the Commander, 1st Squadron, *Jagdgeschwader 2 "Richthofen"*. He assumed full command of the 1st Group, *Jagdgeschwader 2 "Richthofen"* in February 1945.

Franz Hrdlicka was killed in action on March 25, 1945 over Betzenrod, Hesse in aerial combat with U.S. fighters. He was submitted for the award of the Oak Leaves after his death, but the approval for the award cannot be documented. His remains were not found until September 8, 1951. He was subsequently buried at Tutzing on Lake Starnberg in Bavaria.[111]

Franz Hrdlicka flew over 500 combat missions; the exact total of his aerial victories is not certain, but probably about 60, of which 27 were over the Eastern Front and 2 were four-engine bombers.[112]

The efficiency report on Hrdlicka comes from early in his career. On April 11, 1941, the acting commander of the Supplemental Fighter Group of *Jagdgeschwader 77*, First Lieutenant Ernst-Albrecht Schultz, submitted a recommendation to promote Franz Hrdlicka to second lieutenant. He wrote:[113]

Character: A decent soldier who has taken his deferment greatly to heart, very ambitious and reliable.

Mental attributes: Not particularly intelligent, but very striving.

Physical attributes: Somewhat awkward, but has good promise.

Attitude and appearance: Still somewhat insecure due to a lack of experience.

Service accomplishments: According to the demands of the service. Accomplishments as a pilot have greatly improved.

Service use: fighter pilot student

Attitude towards the National Socialist state: He has read the *Führer's* "*Mein Kampf*," possesses the basic knowledge of the National Socialist ideology and is in a position to relate it to others.

Promotion to the next higher service grade: yes

A lieutenant colonel added: "The application for promotion to Lieutenant is being seconded."

Erg. Jagdgruppe 77   Gefechtsstand, den 11.4.41
Br.B.Nr. 403/41 geh.

Betr.: Vorschlag zur Beförderung zum Leutnant.

R.d.L.u.Ob.d.L.
Berlin.

Zur Beförderung zum Leutnant wird in Vorschlag gebracht:

Familienname: H r d l i c k a   Vorname: Franz

geb.am: 15.10.20   zu M a x d o r f   Konfession: kath.

Dienstgrad: Fähnrich   verwendet als: Flugzeugführer

Diensteintritt am: 15.11.1939   verh./led.: ledig

Ernennung zum Oberfähnrich: Kinder:

Offz.-Anwärter wann? 1.4.40

Wehrbezirks-Kdo. d.Wohnortes: B r ü n n

Bestrafungen vor Diensteintritt: keine

Bestrafungen nach Diensteintritt: keine

Zum Offizier gewählt am: 10.4.1941

Beruf vor Diensteintritt: Schüler

Stand und Beruf des Vaters: Landwirt

Mutter geborene: G r i t z b a c h

Anschrift der Eltern bzw. des Vormundes: Franz H r d l i c k a,
          Maxdorf 33, Post Brünn 20

Bildungsgang: s.Personalnachweis

Militärischer Werdegang: s.Wehrpass

Begründung:

Request for Promotion to Officer for Officer Candidate Franz Hrdlicka (first side) – dated April 11, 1941.

Beurteilung:

1. **Charakter:** Anständiger Soldat, der sich seine Zurückstellung sehr zu Herzen genommen hat, sehr ehrgeizig und zuverlässig.

2. **Geistige Veranlagung:** Nicht besonders intelligent aber sehr strebsam.

3. **Körperliche Eignung:** Etwas unbeholfen, hat aber gute Anlagen.

4. **Haltung und Auftreten:** Noch etwas unsicher wegen mangelnder Übung.

5. **Dienstliche Leistungen:** Entsprechend den Anforderungen des Dienstes. Fliegerische Leistungen haben sich sehr gebessert.

6. **Dienstliche Verwendung:** Jagdschüler

7. **Einstellung zum Nationalsozialistischen Staat:** Er hat das Buch des Führers "Mein Kampf" gelesen, er beherrscht die Grundzüge des nationalsozialistischen Gedankengutes und ist in der Lage, es anderen zu vermitteln.

8. **Beförderung zum nächsthöheren Dienstgrad:** Ja.

Oblt.u.m.d.W.d.G.d.Gr.Kdrs.b.

Request for Promotion to Officer for Officer Candidate Franz Hrdlicka (second side) – signed by First Lieutenant Ernst-Albrecht Schultz, acting Replacement Group commander.

Der Beförderungsvorschlag zum Leutnant wird befürwortet:

I.A.

Oberstleutnant.

Laut R.d.L.u.Ob.d.L. Nr. 5185/41 geh. (IIa) vom 13.2.1941 ist für die Weiterreichung die L.In. 3 zuständig.

Request for Promotion to Officer for Officer Candidate Franz Hrdlicka (third side) – signed by a lieutenant colonel.

Eberhard Jacob
Stuka Pilot

"Man of character."

Major Eberhard Jacob was born January 18, 1917 in Taulkinnen, East Prussia. In 1939 and 1940, he served as a pilot and group adjutant in the 2nd Group, 2nd Stuka Wing "Immelmann" (*Sturzkampfgeschwader 2 "Immelmann"*) in both the Polish and French campaigns. Jacob received the Iron Cross 2nd Class on September 28, 1939 and the Iron Cross 1st Class on July 7, 1940. In May 1941, he assumed command of the 4th Squadron, 2nd Stuka Wing "Immelmann," participated in seriously damaging the British aircraft carrier *Formidable* off Crete on May 26, 1941 and was awarded the Operational Flying Clasp for Bombers in Gold on October 13, 1941. In January 1942, he transferred to the 3rd Stuka Wing (*Sturzkampfgeschwader 3*) and took command of the 7th Squadron. Flying combat missions over the Mediterranean Sea and North Africa, Jacob won the *Luftwaffe* Honor Goblet on March 18, 1942 and the German Cross in Gold on April 24, 1942. On November 1, 1942, he assumed duties as the Operations Officer (Ia) on the staff of Air Commander Africa (*Fliegerführer Afrika*) and Air Commander Tunisia (*Fliegerführer Tunis*). He held these positions until May 1943, when Germany was forced to withdraw from Africa.

Jacob then transferred to the Eastern Front, where he became the Commander, 3rd Group, *3rd* Stuka Wing. Jacob led this unit in the skies over the Caucasus and Crimea from June 18, 1943 to October 15, 1943. During this period, he was wounded in July and received the Operational Flying Clasp for Bombers in Gold with Pendant on September 18, 1943. He then returned to Berlin, where he became a liaison officer from the staff of General of Ground-Attack Units (*General der Schlachtflieger*) to the *Luftwaffe* Operations Staff and on the Operations Staff itself. Captain Eberhard Jacob received the Knight's Cross of the Iron Cross on February 29, 1944 for actions as the 3rd Group Commander. He was promoted to major on May 1, 1944.

Near the end of the war, on March 29, 1945, less than a month before the Soviets closed in on the German capital, the Operations Officer and the Chief of the *Luftwaffe* Operations Staff, Lieutenant Colonel Kurt von Greiff and Brigadier General Eckhard Christian, respectively, submitted an officer efficiency report in Berlin on Major Eberhard Jacob. Lieutenant Colonel von Greiff wrote:[114]

Short Evaluation (Personal values, National Socialist attitude, accomplishments before the enemy, service accomplishments, mental and physical attributes and suitability, infantry experience, when and how obtained)**:** Man of character with a big heart and good disposition. Quiet temperament, always indefatigable and in good spirits. Mentally very agile, with good general knowledge. Thinks clearly and logically, acts independently and responsibly. Personal leadership lives up to any demands.

Without formal academy training, he was accepted into the General Staff of the *Luftwaffe*; due to his diligence and ability for rapid comprehension, he quickly mastered the sizeable workload of the Operations Department of the Operations Staff. He relays his opinions clearly and objectively to his superiors, and he understands how to convincingly present them to the officers under him. His appearance is sure and correct.

As the commander of a Stuka group, he excelled in an outstanding manner (Knight's Cross winner). Fully rooted in National Socialism.

A comrade, who is very well liked, full of humor, always ready to help others.

Will be able to perform very well as a troop commander as well as a General Staff officer.

Summary Assessment: Above Average.
(Above Average, Average, Below Average)

How well is the current position being fulfilled: Very well fulfilled.
(Use only: Very well fulfilled, well fulfilled, fulfilled, not fulfilled)

Suitable for promotion to the next higher service grade: Not possible.

Suitable as: Wing Commodore of a Stuka wing, Operations Officer of an Air Corps or Air Division.

Known to the person submitting this review: since October 5, 1943.

Subordinated to the person submitting this review: since April 29, 1944.

Brigadier General Christian added, "Good soldier and General Staff Officer, who deserves special advancement."

Eberhard Jacob survived the war.[115] He died on February 27, 1982 at Bad Orb in Hesse. He is buried there at the *Stadtfriedhof* (Section 27, Grave 143/144).

Lw. Führungsstab Ia   H.Qu., den 29. 3.   1945
(Dienststelle, nicht Feldpostnummer)

Kriegs-Beurteilung zum   1. April   1945
für Offz. ausschl. San.-, Vet.-Offz.
über den

Major i.G.	1.5.44 A 1	Eberhard	Jacob
Dienstgrad¹⁾	R.D.A. (Ordn. Nr.) und Dienstaltersliste	Vorname	Name

18.1.1917   verheiratet, ledig, verwitwet, geschieden   kv.
geboren am   (Zutreffendes unterstreichen)   Wehrdiensttauglichkeit²⁾
                                                          (kv, gv Feld, gv H, tropentgl., tropenuntgl.)

-/-
Zivilberuf (falls vorhanden)

Hilfsoffz.Ia op 1 seit 29.4.44
Gruppenltr. " jetzige Verwendung seit 15.1.45   Fl.Pl.Kdo.Stolp/Reitz; WBK Stolp/R.
                                                    Friedensdienststelle und W.B.K.³⁾

Termin 1.4.45 gem. D (Luft) 2000
Anlaß der Vorlage⁴⁾

Deutsche Auszeichnungen des jetzigen Krieges mit Verleihungsdaten und Angabe, ob und zu welchen
Auszeichnungen vorgeschlagen: 28.9.39 EK II, 7.7.40 EK I, 13.10.41 FFSp.in Gold,
18.3.42 Ehrenpokal, 1.5.42 DK in Gold, 9.6.42 Erinnerungsmed.Afrika,
14.7.43 Verw.Abz.in Schwarz, 18.9.43 Anh.(4oo) z.FFSp., 29.2.44 Ritter-
1.9.44 KVK II m. Schw.   kreuz

¹⁾ Genaue Angabe, ob Tr.-Offz., Erg.-Offz., Offz. z. D., Res.-Offz., Kr.-Offz. z. V.-Offz. — ²⁾ In zweifelhaften Fällen neu
festzustellen. — ³⁾ Dienststelle, welche Friedensgebührnisse zahlt und zuständiges Wehrbezirkskommando. — ⁴⁾ z. B.:
Versetzung zur III./K.G. 2, terminmäßige Vorlage zum 1. 5. 43.

Kurze Beurteilung (Persönlichkeitswert, nationalsozialistische Haltung, Bewährung vor dem
Feinde, dienstliche Leistungen, geistige und körperliche Anlagen und Eignung, infanteristische
Erfahrungen, wann und wo erworben):

Charaktervoller Mann mit viel Herz und Gemüt. Im Temperament ruhig,
immer unverdrossen und wohlgelaunt. Geistig sehr rege, mit gutem
Allgemeinwissen. Denkt klar und logisch, handelt selbständig und verantwortungsbewusst. Führerpersönlichkeit, die jeder Belastung gewachsen ist.
Ohne Akademieausbildung in den Generalstab der Luftwaffe übernommen,
hat er sich in das umfangreiche Arbeitsgebiet des Ia op 1 der Füh-
rungsabteilung auf Grund seines Fleisses und seiner schnellen Auffassungsgabe schnell eingearbeitet. Vertritt seine Ansichten klar
und sachlich gegen Vorgesetzte und versteht es, sie gegen untergeord-
nete Dienststellen überzeugend zur Geltung zu bringen. Im Auftreten
sicher und korrekt.
Als Kommandeur einer Sturzkampfgruppe durch Tapferkeit hervorragend
bewährt (Ritterkreuzträger). Steht voll auf dem Boden des Nationalsozialismus.
Besonders beliebter, humorvoller, stets hilfsbereiter Kamerad.
Wird als Truppenkommandeur, wie als Genst.Offz. stets besonders Gutes
leisten.

J388

Zusammenfassendes Urteil   Über dem Durchschnitt
(über Durchschnitt, Durchschnitt, unter Durchschnitt):

Wie wird jetzige Stelle ausgefüllt? (Es sind nur die   Sehr gut
Ausdrücke „sehr gut ausgefüllt", „gut ausge-
füllt", „ausgefüllt", „nicht ausgefüllt" zu verwenden)

Geeignet zur Beförderung zum nächsthöheren Dienstgrad?   steht noch nicht heran.

B 3614. M.-V 7. 3. 44

Efficiency Report for Major Eberhard Jacob (front side) – dated March 29, 1945, on pre-printed form, with typed comments. "J388" in blue pencil is probably an administrative file number.

Eignung
für welche nächsthöhere Verwendung⁵)?   Geschwaderkommodore eines Schlachtgeschwaders,
für welche besondere oder anderweitige Verwendung⁶)?   Ia eines Fliegerkorps oder einer Flieger-Division
Vorschlag für Verwendung in nächster Zeit⁷)?

Sprachkenntnisse (keine Schulkenntnisse)
  a) abgelegte Prüfungen:
     (z. B.: Dolmetscherprüfung 1. 10. 42)
  b) Beherrschung der Sprache:
     (z. B.: durch Aufenthalt im Ausland)

Eröffnung zu welchen Punkten, wann, wie
  (mündlich oder schriftlich) und durch wen?

Strafen sind mit vollem Straftenor sowie Vermerk über Vollstreckung abschriftlich als Anlage der Kriegsbeurteilung beizuheften.

Dem Beurteilenden bekannt seit   5.10.43
                   unterstellt seit 29.4.44

Ausbildung
  a) erworbene Scheine: LF
     (L. F., E. L. F., L. B. usw.)
  b) Sonderausbildung:
     (z. B. Bild-Offz., Techn. Offz., Meß-Offz.,
     Funk-Drahtnachr.-Offz., W. K. S.)

_____   Oberstlt. i.G. und Chef Ia
       Unterschrift   Dienstgrad und Dienststellung

Beitrag des Chefs des Generalstabes der vorgesetzten Kommandobehörde (nur bei Genst.-Offz. in Stabsstellungen und zur Dienstleistung zum Generalstab kommandierten Offizieren):

Zusätze vorgesetzter Dienststellen:

Der Chef des Lw. Führungsstabes

Guter Soldat und Generalstabsoffizier, der besonderer Förderung wert ist.

                                      Generalmajor.

Efficiency Report for Major Eberhard Jacob (back side) – signed by the Operations Officer and the Chief of the *Luftwaffe* Operations Staff, Lieutenant Colonel Kurt von Greiff and Brigadier General Eckhard Christian, respectively. "J389" in blue pencil is probably an administrative file number.

Karl Janke
Stuka Pilot

"He lacks the talent to sweep the soldiers along with him and to create enthusiasm for something."

Major Karl Janke was born February 7, 1912 in Sparsen near Neustettin. He began his military career on October 1, 1931 in the Army, serving in a signal battalion. Janke transferred to the *Luftwaffe* in 1935. After flight training, Janke joined the 2nd Group, 163rd Stuka Wing (*Sturzkampfgeschwader 163*, which in April 1939 was designated the 3rd Group, 2nd Stuka Wing "Immelmann" [*Sturzkampfgeschwader 2 "Immelmann"*]). Flying with the 8th Squadron, he flew in the Polish and French campaigns. In May 1940, he was shot down over Belgium and suffered a fractured skull. His injuries grounded him until October, but he resumed flying and served in the Greek campaign and the invasion of the Soviet Union. On September 16, 19, 21, 22, 23, 25 and 27, the *Luftwaffe's* 1st Air Fleet conducted bombing attacks against the ships of the Red Banner Baltic Fleet harbored at the Soviet naval base at Kronstadt (an island in the Gulf of Finland.) The ships, which included the battleships *October Revolution* (*Oktyabrskaya Revolyutsiya*) and *Marat*, and the heavy cruiser *Kirov*, were guarded by over 1,000 anti-aircraft guns. On September 25, the 3rd Group – commanded by Captain Ernst-Siegfried Steen and including First Lieutenant Karl Janke – attacked and seriously damaged the *Kirov*. Steen was killed in the attack, while Janke won the *Luftwaffe* Honor Goblet on October 20, 1941.

Some weeks earlier, on October 2, Janke's chain of command submitted an efficiency report on him. First Lieutenant Wilhelm Kaiser, the 3rd Group Adjutant (filling in for the fallen group commander) wrote the following:[116]

Character: First Lieutenant Janke is an open, upright, decent and straight-forward character. He is dutiful and willing to help. He is liked in the circle of his comrades.

Personal values: Depressed somewhat due to his overly developed pessimism. As a result, he is lacking the necessary dash with which to sweep others along.

Conduct before the enemy: In the campaigns against Poland, France, the Balkans and Russia as pilot and at last as an acting squadron commander, he has excelled through great courage and bravery.

Accomplishments during service: As an acting squadron commander, he is conscientious. However, he lacks the talent to sweep the soldiers along with him and to create enthusiasm for something.

Possibilities for utilization: [left blank]

Punishments: none

Captain, and 1st Group Commander, 2nd Stuka Wing "Immelmann", Bruno Dilley, added comments later, on July 1, 1942:

Captain Janke has been with the group from March 25, 1942 to May 31, 1942. Nothing is to be added to the above evaluation.

Janke received the German Cross in Gold on December 2, 1941. On June 15, 1942, he assumed command of the 5th Squadron, but transferred to the command of the 7th Squadron a month later. Captain Karl Janke received the Knight's Cross of the Iron Cross on November 16, 1942 as the 7th Squadron Commander, after flying his 460th combat mission. In January 1943, unable to fly due to the effects of his previous wounds and injuries, Janke transferred to be a tactics instructor and chief inspector at the 9th Air War School (*Luftkriegschule 9*) and remained there until the end of the war. After the conflict, Janke became a ship captain. Karl Janke died December 22, 1981 in Hamburg.

Karl Janke was credited with flying 500 combat missions, which included sinking a 5,000-ton merchant ship, and destroying 32 tanks, 3 armored trains and 3 key bridges.[117]

III./Sturzkampfgeschwader IMMELMANN 2   Gefechtsstand, 2.10.41

Beurteilungs-Notizen

für

Oberleutnant Karl J a n k e .

vom 1.8.38 bis 24.9.41 bei der III./Sturzkampfgeschwader IMMELMANN 2.

Charakter: Oblt. Janke ist ein offener, aufrechter, anständiger und gerader Charakter. Er ist pflichtbewußt und hilfsbereit. Im Kameradenkreise ist er beliebt.

Wert der Persönlichkeit: Krankt etwas an übertriebenem Pessimismus. Dadurch fehlt ihm der notwendige mitreißende Schwung.

Bewährung vor dem Feinde: In den Feldzügen gegen Polen, Frankreich, Südosten und Sowjetrußland hat er sich als Flugzeugführer und zuletzt als Staffelführer durch großen Mut und durch Tapferkeit ausgezeichnet.

Dienstliche Leistungen: Als Staffelführer ist er gewissenhaft. Es fehlt ihm aber das Vermögen, die Soldaten mitzureißen und für etwas zu begeistern.

Verwendungsmöglichkeit:

Strafen: keine.

A.B.

Kaiser

Oberleutnant und Adjutant

I./Sturzkampfgeschwader IMMELMANN 2   Gefechtsstand, 1.7.42.

Hptm. Janke befand sich vom 25.3.42 - 31.5.42 bei der Gruppe. Vorstehender Beurteilung ist nichts hinzuzufügen.

Hauptmann u. Gruppenkommandeur

Efficiency Report for First Lieutenant Karl Janke (one page only) – dated October 2, 1941, on blank paper with typed comments. Signed by First Lieutenant Wilhelm Kaiser, the group adjutant, and by Captain Bruno Dilley, Commander, 1st Group, 2nd Stuka Wing.

Peter Jenne
Fighter Pilot

"Unwavering spirit for battle."

Captain Peter Jenne was born on May 5, 1920 at Wittenberg, Saxony. He entered the *Luftwaffe* on November 15, 1939 and joined the 42nd Aviation Training Regiment at Salzwedel. He continued his training and rose through the enlisted ranks, culminating in his promotion to second lieutenant on April 1, 1941. In the summer of 1942, Jenne was serving with the 1st Squadron, 1st Destroyer Wing (*Zerstörergeschwader 1*) on the Eastern Front, flying a Messerschmitt Me 110 twin-engine fighter in ground-attack missions as part of the 8th Air Corps (4th Air Fleet). He achieved considerable success in this role destroying 12 tanks, 10 artillery pieces and eight rocket launchers. Jenne received the Iron Cross 2nd Class on June 20, 1942, the Iron Cross 1st Class on August 4, 1942, the Operational Clasp for Fighters in Gold on September 13, 1942, the *Luftwaffe* Honor Goblet on November 20, 1942 and the German Cross in Gold on April 1, 1943. It was hard fighting, including flying in support of the German 6th Army at Stalingrad in December 1942. On January 20, 1943, Jenne destroyed his Me 110 in a crash landing at a forward, snow-covered airfield, in an incident that claimed the life of his radio operator.

Peter Jenne was promoted to first lieutenant on April 1, 1943. The unit was designated the 1st Squadron, 26th Destroyer Wing "Horst Wessel" (*Zerstörergeschwader 26 "Horst Wessel"*) in July 1943. Jenne assumed the position of 1st Squadron Commander on October 9, 1943. The unit was later transferred to Germany to perform home defense duties, and Jenne again excelled. He shot down a B-17 Flying Fortress on December 20 – during the 8th Air Force's mission against Bremen. On December 22, 1943, he shot down two B-24 Liberator bombers from the 2nd Bomb Division in a five-minute period over the Netherlands. On April 1, 1944, Jenne received an accelerated promotion to captain. In July 1944, his unit was designated the 1st Squadron, 6th Fighter Wing (*Jagdgeschwader 6*) and re-equipped with Focke-Wulf Fw 190 single-engine fighters. On September 12, 1944, Jenne was appointed commander of the 12th Squadron, 300th Fighter Wing "Wild Boar" (*Jagdgeschwader 300 "Wilde Sau"*). He became the 1st Group Commander on January 1, 1945.

On January 28, 1945, the chain of command in *Jagdgeschwader 300 "Wilde Sau"* submitted an efficiency report on Jenne, necessitated by the change of command (*Kommodorewechsel*) in the 300th Fighter Wing. Lieutenant Colonel and Wing Commodore Walter Dahl wrote the following:[118]

Short Evaluation (Personal values, National Socialist attitude, accomplishments before the enemy, service accomplishments, mental and physical attributes and suitability, infantry experience, when and how obtained): Tall, slender appearance, spirited, full of temperament, an officer with straight attitude and demeanor of a soldier, very eager to serve, fighter's nature, convinced National Socialist. In more than 250 engagements, he has proven himself in an excellent manner as a destroyer pilot and later as a day-time fighter pilot. The shooting down of 5 enemy fighter planes and 10 four-engine bombers reveal his unwavering spirit for battle. Even after he was shot down during an air battle, when he could only save himself by jumping out with a parachute, during which he encountered serious back injuries, he insisted to be sent back to fight immediately after his recovery. Since then, he succeeded in shooting down two additional four-engine bombers.

Strong Traits: Great willingness for action, outstanding talent for flying.

Weak Traits: Not applicable.

Summary Assessment: Above Average.
(Above Average, Average, Below Average)

How well is the current position being fulfilled: Well fulfilled.
(Use only: Very well fulfilled, well fulfilled, fulfilled, not fulfilled)

Suitable for promotion to the next higher service grade: Yes, after continued accomplishments.

Suitable as: Group Commander.

Known to the person submitting this review: since February 1943.

Subordinated to the person submitting this review: since October 8, 1944.

The incoming acting commodore of *Jagdgeschwader 300*, Major Kurd Peters, made a brief, but final, notation several weeks later:

Concluded due to a hero's death on March 2, 1945. Nothing to add to the submitted evaluation.

Jenne was awarded the Knight's Cross of the Iron Cross on February 2, 1945, after achieving 17 aerial victories in addition to his previous ground-attack accomplishments. In an encounter with enemy fighters on March 2, 1945 over Schmerwitz, Brandenburg, Jenne was shot down in his Messerschmitt Me 109G-10 and died in the ensuing crash. Peter Jenne was credited with at least 17 victories, of which 14 were on the Western Front and included 12 four-engine bombers.[119]

Luftwaffe Efficiency & Promotion Reports

Jagdgeschwader 300   Gef.St., den 28.Jan. 1945
(Dienststelle, nicht Feldpostnummer)

Kriegs-Beurteilung zum _____ 194_
für Offz. ausschl. San.- Vet.-Offz.

über den

Hptm.(Tr.O.)   1.4.44   Peter   Jenne
Dienstgrad 1)   R. D. A. (Ordn. Nr.) und   Vorname   Name
                Dienstalterliste

5. 6. 20   verheiratet, ledig, verwitwet, geschieden   kv.
geboren am   (Zutreffendes unterstreichen)   Wehrdiensttauglichkeit 2)
                                                    (kv, gv Feld, gv H, tropentgl., tropenuntgl.)

           k e i n e n
            Zivilberuf (falls vorhanden)

                                            Flak Hannover-Buchholz
Gruppenkommandeur   W.B.K. Berlin IX
jetzige Verwendung seit 21.1.45   Friedensdienststelle und W. B. K. 3)

        Kommodorewechsel
         Anlaß der Vorlage 4)

Deutsche Auszeichnungen des jetzigen Krieges mit Verleihungsdaten und Angabe, ob und zu welchen Auszeichnungen vorgeschlagen: E.K.II.Kl. 20.6.42, E.K.I.Kl.4.8.42 Ehrenpokal 20.11.42, Deutsches Kreuz in Gold 1.4.43 Fr.Fl.Sp.Gold 13.9.42

1) Genaue Angabe ob Tr.-Offz., Erg.-Offz., Offz. z. D., Res.-Offz., Kr.-Offz., z. V.-Offz. — 2) In zweifelhaften Fällen neu festzustellen. 3) Dienststelle, welche Friedensgebührnisse zahlt und zuständiges Wehrbezirkskommando. — 4) z. B. Versetzung zur III./K.G. 2, terminmäßige Vorlage zum 1, 5, 43.

Kurze Beurteilung (Persönlichkeitswert, nationalsozialistische Haltung, Bewährung vor dem Feinde, dienstliche Leistungen, geistige und körperliche Anlagen und Eignung, infanteristische Erfahrungen, wann und wo erworben):

Große, schlanke Erscheinung, frisch, temperamentvoll, ein Offz.mit gerader Haltung u.soldatischer Einstellung, sehr einsatzfreudig, Kämpfernatur, überzeugter Nationalsozialist. In mehr als 250 Einsätzen hat er sich als Zerstörer u.später als Tagjäger hervorragend bewährt. Der Abschuß von 5 feindl.Jägern und 10 4-mot.Kampfflugzg. verrät seinen unverwüstlichen Kampfgeist. Obwohl er während eines Luftkampfes abgeschossen wurde, sich durch Fallschirmabsprung noch retten konnte, dabei aber eine nicht unerhebliche Rückgratverletzung sich zugezogen hat, drängte er nach seiner Genesung sofort wieder zum Einsatz. Dabei gelang ihm der Abschuß von weiteren zwei 4-mot. Kampfflugzeugen.   (Fortsetzung siehe Anlage)

Starke Seiten:

Große Einsatzfreude, hervorragende fliegerische Begabung.

Schwache Seiten:

                                            J924
entfällt.

Zusammenfassendes Urteil
(über Durchschnitt, Durchschnitt, unter Durchschnitt):   über Durchschnitt

Wie wird jetzige Stelle ausgefüllt? (Es sind nur die Ausdrücke „sehr gut ausgefüllt" „gut ausgefüllt" „ausgefüllt", „nicht ausgefüllt" zu verwenden)   gut ausgefüllt

Geeignet zur Beförderung zum nächsthöheren Dienstgrad?   ja,
                                                         nach weiterer Bewährung

E. Sommer, Ahlen V 43

Efficiency Report for Captain Peter Jenne (front side) – dated January 28, 1945, on pre-printed form from the E. Sommer firm, with typed comments. "J924" in blue pencil is probably an administrative file number.

191

Eignung
  für welche nächsthöhere Verwendung ⁵)? Gruppenkommandeur
  für welche besondere oder anderweitige Verwendung ⁶)?
  Vorschlag für Verwendung in nächster Zeit ⁷)? Gruppenkommandeur

Sprachkenntnisse (keine Schulkenntnisse)
  a) abgelegte Prüfungen:
     (z. B.: Dolmetscherprüfung 1. 10. 42)
  b) Beherrschung der Sprache:
     (z. B.: durch Aufenthalt im Ausland) keine

Eröffnung zu welchen Punkten, wann, wie
  (mündlich oder schriftlich) und durch wen? keine

Strafen sind mit vollem Straftenor sowie Vermerk über Vollstreckung abschriftlich als Anlage der Kriegsbeurteilung beizuheften. keine

Dem Beurteilten bekannt seit } Februar 1943
                 unterstellt seit   8.10.44

Ausbildung
  a) erworbene Scheine:
     L. F., E. L. F., L. B. usw.)
  b) Sonderausbildung:
     z. B. Bild-Offz., Techn. Offz., Meß-Offz.,   E L F , B L F II
     Funk-Drahtnachr.-Offz., W/K/S.)   keine

....   Oberstleutnant u. Geschw.-Kommodore
       Unterschrift   Dienstgrad und Dienststellung

Beitrag des Chefs des Generalstabes der vorgesetzten Kommandobehörde (nur bei Genst.-Offz. in Stabsstellungen und zur Dienstleistung zum Generalstab kommandierten Offizieren):

Abgeschlossen anläßlich des Heldentodes am 2.3.45.

Vorliegender Beurteilung nichts hinzuzufügen.

                                                  Major und Geschwaderkommodore.
                                                  m.d.W.d.G.b.

Zusätze vorgesetzter Dienststellen:

---

⁵) Gilt für alle Offz., für Truppen-Offz. hinsichtlich Eignung zur Führung des nächsthöheren Verbandes, für Genst.-Offz. hinsichtlich Eignung zum Chef oder Ia, 1 c der Luftfl., Flieger-Korps, Flakkorps, Fl.-Div., Flak-Div., zur Versetzung in den Genst., zur Kommandierung in den Genst. — ⁶) z. B.: Höherer Adjudant, Erzieher, Lehrer auf Spezialgebieten, auf Grund von Sprachkenntnissen im Attachedienst; für Genst.-Offz. hinsichtlich Eignung für Verwendung im Quartiermeisterdienst, im Ic-Dienst, im Transportwesen, als Lehrer für Genst.-Lehrgang (Taktik bzw. Qu.-Dienst); besondere Anlagen für Kriegsgeschichte, Wehrwirtschaft. — ⁷) z. B.: „noch halbjährige Belassung in bisheriger Stelle" oder „alsbaldige Verwendung als Geschw.-Kommodore".

Efficiency Report for Captain Peter Jenne (back side) – signed by Lieutenant Colonel Walter Dahl, Commodore, 300th Fighter Wing, and by Major Kurd Peters, acting wing commodore.

Karl Kennel
Destroyer Pilot/Fighter Pilot

"He is well liked due to his calm, but also humorous and very friendly manner."

Major Karl Kennel was born on January 17, 1914 at Pirmasens in the Pfalz. Originally a policeman in Ludwigshafen, he joined the *Luftwaffe* on May 9, 1935. He underwent military training at Schleissheim before learning to fly at Weimar and Oldenburg. In May 1938, Kennel was assigned to the 132nd Fighter Wing "Richthofen" (*Jagdgeschwader 132 "Richthofen"*), but then transferred to a Destroyer unit. At the beginning of World War II, Corporal Kennel was serving with the 1st Group, 26th Destroyer Wing "Horst Wessel" (*Zerstörergeschwader 26 "Horst Wessel"*), operating twin-engine Messerschmitt Me 110 fighters out of Varel, Germany, on the North Sea coast. He gained his first victory over a French aircraft over Dunkirk. During the ensuing French campaign, he flew 48 missions in support of ground forces and also added two further kills to his total, winning the Iron Cross 2nd Class on May 26, 1940 and the Iron Cross 1st Class on June 24, 1940.

Karl Kennel then flew with the 2nd Group, 2nd Destroyer Wing (*Zerstörergeschwader 2*), flying 30 fighter-bomber missions against airfields and naval targets in southern England as part of the 3rd Air Fleet in the Battle of Britain. In the spring 1941, he participated in the invasion of the Balkans. He was promoted to second lieutenant on June 1, 1941. During the invasion of Russia, Kennel continued to primarily fly ground-attack missions. He received the *Luftwaffe* Honor Goblet on September 9, 1941. During 1942, the unit was re-equipped with Me 210 twin-engine fighter-bombers. On March 16, 1942, Kennel was awarded the German Cross in Gold. In April 1942, Kennel was appointed Squadron Commander with the Supplemental Destroyer Group (*Ergänzungs-Zerstörer-Gruppe*) – an operational training formation – based at Deblin-Irena, and led this unit until September.

On October 6, 1942, Captain Gerhard Weyert, the 2nd Group Commander, 2nd Destroyer Wing, submitted a lengthy, hand-written report on Second Lieutenant Karl Kennel, which read:[120]

> Second Lieutenant Kennel is a slender person of medium height with a very refreshing and alert demeanor. As to his character, he is open, conscientious and trustworthy, and he is in possession of very healthy ambition. Even though he is a wartime officer, he has always striven successfully to close any knowledge gaps through diligence and zeal. Mentally, he is alert and active. His general knowledge is average, his military know-how is good. As an officer, Second Lieutenant Kennel possesses personal values and capabilities which result in very positive qualifications. His comprehension can be called very good; his demeanor and attitude are definite, correct and self-confident. As a pilot, Lieutenant Kennel demonstrates a high degree of know-how, extensive experience and unwavering courage and risk-taking in combat, coupled with clever thoughtfulness and clear thinking. He always accomplished his many combat missions with the highest degree of success. As to his philosophy, Second Lieutenant Kennel is well-rooted in National Socialism. His social behavior is immaculate.

Among his comrades, he is well liked due to his calm, but also humorous and very friendly manner. To summarize, Second Lieutenant Kennel is a very useful officer of whom a lot of good things should be expected in the future, due to his character attributes and his definite capabilities. As a pilot, he is in position to lead a larger unit; however, as an officer he has to gather some more experience in troop leadership so that his excellent talents can be brought fully to fruition as a squadron commander at a later date.

In October 1942, First Lieutenant Kennel was appointed commander of the 5th Squadron, 1st Ground-Attack Wing (*Schlachtgeschwader 1*), operating over the middle and southern areas of the Eastern Front. These operations included missions out of the Crimea in October and in support of the surrounded German 6th Army in Stalingrad in January 1943. The unit was equipped with Focke-Wulf Fw 190s configured as fighter-bombers. On September 19, 1943, Captain Karl Kennel was awarded the Knight's Cross of the Iron Cross for flying 500 combat missions and achieving 28 aerial victories. In November 11, 1943, he was appointed the commander of 1st Group, 152nd Ground-Attack Wing (*Schlachtgeschwader 152*), based first at Deblin-Irena and then at Prossnitz (now Prostejov, Czech Republic). In the summer of 1944, Kennel transferred once again and was appointed the acting commander of 2nd Group, 2nd Ground-Attack Wing "Immelmann" (*Schlachtgeschwader 2 "Immelmann"*) on July 29, 1944. He assumed full command on August 11, 1944. Captain Karl Kennel was awarded the Oak Leaves to the Knight's Cross (the 666th *Wehrmacht* soldier to be so honored) on November 25, 1944 for 800 combat missions. He was promoted to major on January 30, 1945 and survived the war. Karl Kennel flew 957 combat missions and recorded 34 aerial victories. Three of his victories were recorded over the Western Front.[121] Karl Kennel died on July 1, 1999 at Pirmasens. He is buried there at the *Waldfriedhof* (Section 2a, Row 1, Grave 44).

II./Zerstörergeschwader 2   O.U., 6.10. 1942
(Dienststelle, Truppenteil)

Feldpostnummer: L 41733

Luftgaupostamt: Wien   Lichtbild

Beurteilungsnotiz

über

den   Leutnant , Flugzeugführer
(Dienstgrad, Dienststellung)

Karl Kennel   geb.: 17.1.1914
(Vor- und Zuname)

Kr.O. R.D.A. 1.10.1940

verheiratet, ledig, verwitwet, geschieden (Zutreffendes unterstreichen)

Jetzige Verwendung: (z. B. Staffelkapitän seit) Flugzeugführer seit 28.4.1942

(Eignungsbeurteilung nächste Seite)

Efficiency Report for Second Lieutenant Karl Kennel (first page) – dated October 6, 1942, on pre-printed form with handwritten comments.

Eignungsbeurteilung:

Lt. Kennel ist ein schlanker, mittelgrosser Mensch mit einem sehr frischen und gewecktem Wesen. Charakterlich ist er aufgeschlossen, gewissenhaft und zuverlässig, und besitzt einen gesunden Ehrgeiz. Obwohl er Kriegsoffizier ist, hat er sich stets mit Erfolg bemüht, seine Lücken durch Fleiss und Strebsamkeit zu schliessen. Geistig ist er geweckt und rege. Sein Allgemeinwissen ist durchschnittlich, seine militärischen Kenntnisse sind gut.

Als Offizier besitzt Lt. Kennel Persönlichkeitswerte und Fähigkeiten, die ihm eine sehr positive Qualifikation geben. Seine Auffassung ist als sehr gut zu bezeichnen, sein Auftreten und seine Haltung ist bestimmt, korrekt und selbstbewusst.

Als Flugzeugführer zeigt Lt. Kennel sicheres Können, umfangreiche Erfahrung und ein äusserst unerschrockenen Mut und kühnes Draufgängertum in Verbindung mit ruhiger Umsicht und klarem Denken. Seine vielen Feindflüge führte er stets mit bestem Erfolg durch.

Weltanschaulich ist Lt. Kennel im Nationalsozialismus gefestigt. Sein gesellschaftliches Benehmen ist einwandfrei. Im Kameradenkreis ist er durch seine

Efficiency Report for Second Lieutenant Karl Kennel (second page).

14

Wie wird jetzige Stelle ausgefüllt? Sehr guter Staffeloffizier und Flugzeugführer

Geeignet zur Beförderung zum nächsthöheren Dienstgrad? Zum Oblt. geeignet.

Erworbene Lw.-Scheine: E.L.F., Bl. II.

Strafen: Keine

Verwendungsvorschläge: Staffeloffizier im Zerstörerverband.

Weyert Hptm.

(Unterschrift)

Hauptmann und Gruppenkommandeur.

(Dienstgrad und Dienststellung)

Zusätze zur Beurteilungsnotiz: (Nur bei Vorlage an höhere Dienststellen)

ruhiger aber doch humorvoller und sehr kameradschaftlicher ist sehr beliebt.

Im ganzen ist Lt. Kennel ein sehr brauchbarer Offizier, von dem auf Grund seiner charakterlichen Vorteile und seiner ausgeprägten Fähigkeiten noch viel Gutes zu erwarten sein wird. Als Flugzeugführer ist er durchaus in der Lage, eine grössere Einheit zu führen, als Offizier jedoch muss er noch etwas Erfahrung in der Truppenführung sammeln, um seine wertvollen Anlagen als späterer Staffelkapitän voll zur Auswirkung bringen zu können.

Weyert Hptm.

Efficiency Report for Second Lieutenant Karl Kennel (third page) – signed twice by Captain Gerhard Weyert, the 2nd Group Commander, 2nd Destroyer Wing.

Alfred Kindler
Bomber Pilot

"He is an example for his squadron."

Captain Alfred Kindler was born September 4, 1915 at Mauschdorf, Silesia. He joined the 2nd Bomber Wing "Wooden Hammer" (*Kampfgeschwader 2 "Holzhammer"*) in 1939 and over the course of the next three years flew 230 combat missions over Poland, France, the Balkans and England. First Lieutenant Kindler served as the commander of the 5th Squadron, 2nd Bomber Squadron from October 6 to October 20, 1941. When the 6th Squadron Commander was killed in action on October 20, Kindler assumed command of the 6th Squadron the following day. Kindler won the *Luftwaffe* Honor Goblet and on February 7, 1942, he received the German Cross in Gold as a first lieutenant.[122] He was promoted to captain on April 20, 1942.

On July 31, 1942, the 2nd Bomber Wing launched an attack on Birmingham, England, but actually dropped their 14 tons of high explosive and 34 tons of incendiaries on targets in Wolverhampton, some twelve miles away. At 3:08 a.m., Captain Kindler's Dornier Do 217E-4 was hit by British anti-aircraft fire over New Market and crashed. Kindler and his entire crew survived, but were taken prisoner.

On August 3, 1942, just three days after Kindler and his crew were posted missing in action, the chain of command in the 2nd Bomber Wing submitted an efficiency report on him. Captain Walter Bradel, the 2nd Group Commander, wrote in part:[123]

Evaluation of suitability: Tall, strong appearance. Humorous, open nature. Good mental and physical attributes. Decent, true character, excels due to his modest understanding of duty. Because of his courage and willingness for action, he is an example for his squadron. Good soldier with immaculate exterior and inner demeanor. His service knowledge and accomplishments are well balanced; he has good general knowledge. In his contact with superiors, he is correct and polite. Very well liked by his comrades and men under his command due to his helpfulness and untiring care for them. He is definitely capable of conducting the most difficult missions on his own. Firmly rooted in National Socialist ideology.

As a pilot ready for combat, he has proven himself in an outstanding manner in a total of 216 combat missions in the air war against Poland, France, Yugoslavia and Greece, and against England, and he was awarded the Iron Cross 2nd and 1st Class, the *Luftwaffe* Honor Goblet for special accomplishments in air war, the Operational Flying Clasp for Bombers in Gold and the German Cross in Gold.

How is the current position being fulfilled? Is being fulfilled very well.

Suitable for promotion to the next higher service grade? Not yet eligible.

Suggestions for use as: Not applicable. Captain Kindler has been missing since July 31, 1942 (combat mission against England).

Lieutenant Colonel Hans von Koppelow, standing in as the acting wing commodore, stated: "Nothing to be added."

Captain Alfred Kindler was awarded the Knight's Cross of the Iron Cross on September 24, 1942. He survived the war. Alfred Kindler died August 30, 2000 in Mühltal/Trautheim, Hesse.[124]

II./Kampfgeschwader 2   Gefechtsstand, den 3.8.42

Feldpostnummer : L 38 354 ,
             LGPA.: Amsterdam ü./Bentheim.

B e u r t e i l u n g s n o t i z

über den Hauptmann (Tr.O.), Flugzeugführer und Staffelkapitän
Vor- und Zuname : Alfred K i n d l e r   geb.: 4.9.15 R.D.A.: 1.4.4?
Verheiratet, ledig, verwitwet, geschieden.
Jetzige Verwendung: War Staffelkapitän der 6./K.G.2 seit 21.10.41
Eignungsbeurteilung :

   Große, kräftige Erscheinung. Heiteres, aufgeschlossenes Wesen.
Gute geistige und körperliche Veranlagung. Anständiger, ehrlicher Charakter, zeichnet sich durch gediegene Pflichtauffassung aus. Durch seinen Mut und seine Einsatzfreude ist er das Vorbild seiner Staffel. Guter Soldat mit tadelloser äußerer und innerer Haltung. Seine dienstlichen Kenntnisse und Leistungen sind ausgeglichen; er verfügt über gutes Allgemeinwissen. In seinem Verhalten gegenüber Vorgesetzten ist er korrekt und taktvoll. Bei seinen Kameraden und Untergebenen wegen seiner Hilfsbereitschaft und seiner unermüdlichen Fürsorge sehr beliebt Ist durchaus befähigt, schwierige Aufträge selbständig durchzuführen.
   Steht auf dem Boden der nationalsozialistischen Weltanschauung.
   Hat sich als einsatzfreudiger Flugzeugführer auf insgesamt 216 Feindflügen im Luftkrieg gegen Polen, Frankreich, Jugoslawien und Griechenland und gegen England hervorragend bewährt und wurde mit dem E.K. 2. u. 1.Klasse, dem Ehrenpokal für besondere Leistungen im Luftkrieg, der Frontflugspange in Gold und dem Deutschen Kreuz in Gold ausgezeichnet.
Wie wird jetzige Stelle ausgefüllt? Wurde sehr gut ausgefüllt.
Geeignet zur Beförderung zum nächsthöheren Dienstgrad? Steht noch nicht
                                                            heran.
Erworbene Lw.-Scheine: ELF-Schein/Land, Blindflug II, Beob.-Schein/Land
Strafen : Keine.
Verwendungsvorschläge: Entfällt. Hptm. Kindler ist seit dem 31.7.42
                vermißt. (Feindflug gegen England.)

                                   Hauptmann und Kommandeur.

Efficiency Report for Captain Alfred Kindler (front side) – dated August 3, 1942, on blank paper with typed comments. Signed by Captain and Commander, 2nd Group, 2nd Bomber Wing, Walter Bradel. Report notes that Kindler has been missing in action since July 31, 1942.

Stellungnahme des Geschwaderkommodore:

Nichts hinzuzufügen.

Gefechtsstand, den 8.8.1942   Oberstleutnant b.m.d.W.d.G.d.Kommodore

Efficiency Report for Captain Alfred Kindler (back side) – signed by Lieutenant Colonel Hans von Koppelow, standing in as the acting wing commodore, 2nd Bomber Wing.

August Lambert
Ground-Attack Pilot

"He was mentioned several times in official Wehrmacht dispatches."

First Lieutenant August Lambert was born February 18, 1916 in Kleestadt near Dieburg in Hesse. Master Sergeant Lambert flew his first combat mission on April 28, 1943 in southern Russia with the 2nd Group, 1st Ground-Attack Wing (*Schlachtgeschwader 1*). By early 1944 – with the unit designated the 2nd Group, 2nd Ground-Attack Wing "Immelmann" (*Schlachtgeschwader 2 "Immelmann"*) – flying in a Focke-Wulf Fw 190A-5 in the 5th Squadron, he scored 70 aerial victories in just three weeks. This included shooting down 12 aircraft on April 17, 1944 and 14 enemy planes on May 6, 1944. Showing great versatility, Lambert also destroyed 7 enemy tanks in ground-attack missions on April 11, 1944. Lambert received the *Luftwaffe* Honor Goblet on January 17, 1944 and was mentioned in *Oberkommando der Wehrmacht* dispatches on April 18, May 5 and May 8, 1944. He received the Knight's Cross of the Iron Cross on May 14, 1944, after flying 300 combat missions.

Earlier in his career, Lambert's chain of command believed he was not ready for promotion. But after events of the previous two months, their opinion changed. On May 7, 1944, Major Heinz Frank, the group commander, submitted a request to the *Luftwaffe* Air Ministry for promotion for Lambert. Frank wrote:[125]

> The deferment of promotion for Second Lieutenant Lambert, 2nd Group, 2nd Ground-Attack Wing "Immelmann" to First Lieutenant, requested with the letter from 2nd Group, 2nd Ground-Attack Wing "Immelmann" dated December 14, 1943, is herewith being cancelled.

> During the defensive battles in the Crimea, Second Lieutenant Lambert has proven himself in an outstanding way, so that he was mentioned several times in official *Wehrmacht* dispatches. By now he is fully deserving of being promoted to First Lieutenant.

Lambert then assumed duties as a flight instructor with *Schlachtgeschwader 151* in Austria. He won the German Cross in Gold on October 1, 1944. In March 1945, Lambert became the commander of the 8th Squadron, 77th Ground-Attack Wing (*Schlachtgeschwader 77*). On April 17, 1945, Lambert's Focke-Wulf Fw 190F-8 took off from an airfield at Kamenz, northeast of Dresden, armed for a ground attack against Soviet armor. However, some 60-80 P-51D Mustangs of the 55th Fighter Group had been escorting 410 B-17 Flying Fortresses of the 3rd Air Division in the Dresden area. After completing their escort mission, the American fighters descended to low-level to attack targets of opportunity at the Riesa/Canitz, Bautzen and Kamenz airfields. At Kamenz, the Mustangs spotted the German aircraft on the airfield preparing for take-off. Sixteen Focke-Wulfs were destroyed and six pilots killed, including Lambert. The *Luftwaffe* ace had managed to fly twelve miles in an effort to escape, but his plane finally crashed a mile from Hoyerswerda. *Luftwaffe* troops buried him the following day at Hutberg near Kamenz. He is buried at the German military cemetery at Kamenz-*St. Justfriedhof* in an end grave.

The most successful *Schlacht* pilot in the *Luftwaffe*, in terms of enemy aircraft destroyed, First Lieutenant August Lambert flew 350 combat missions, in which he shot down 116 Russian aircraft. He also destroyed over 100 vehicles in ground attacks. After his death, Lambert's chain of command submitted him for the Oak Leaves, but this request was not approved.[126]

II./Schlachtgeschwader 2 Immelmann   Gef.St., den 7. Mai 1944

Betr.: Lt. (Kr.O.) L a m b e r t (August), geb. am 18.2.1916.
Bezug: Hiesiges Schreiben vom 14.12.1943.

An

R.d.L. und Ob.d.L.
   - L. P. -

B e r l i n.

Die mit Schreiben II./S.G.2 Immelmann vom 14.12.1943 beantragte Zurückstellung des Lt. L a m b e r t II./S.G.2 Immelmann von der Beförderung zum Oberleutnant wird aufgehoben.
Lt. Lambert hat sich bei den Abwehrkämpfen auf der Krim hervorragend bewährt, sodaß er mehrfach im Wehrmachtbericht genannt wurde. Er ist nunmehr vollauf würdig zum Oberleutnant befördert zu werden.

Major und Gruppenkommandeur.

Request for Promotion for Second Lieutenant August Lambert (one page only) – dated May 7, 1944, on blank paper, with typed comments. Signed by Major Heinz Frank, Commander, 2nd Group, 2nd Ground-Attack Wing. Stamp shows the request reached the *Luftwaffe* headquarters on May 17 and was reviewed by many officials.

Emil Lang
Fighter Pilot

"Demands of himself first."

Captain Emil "Bully" Lang was born on January 14, 1909 at Talheim (near Sontheim) in the Neckar region of Württemberg. He was a well-known track-and-field athlete and professional civilian pilot with *Lufthansa* before World War II. At the outbreak of the war, Lang was serving with a transport unit. In 1942, he was accepted for fighter pilot training and was subsequently posted to the 54th Fighter Wing "Green Heart" (*Jagdgeschwader 54 "Grünherz"*), based on the Eastern Front, and assigned to the 1st Squadron. He gained his first three kills in March. In April, he transferred to the 5th Squadron. His early exploits included winning the Iron Cross 2nd Class on June 13, receiving the Operational Flying Clasp for Fighters in Gold on June 25, shooting down 3 Bell P-39 Airacobras and 1 Curtiss P-40 Tomahawk on August 1 and earning the Iron Cross 1st Class on August 2, 1943. By August 20, he had been appointed squadron commander. In October and November, Lang claimed 101 victories, recording 68 victories during October, including ten on October 13 and twelve on October 21, for which he was awarded the *Luftwaffe* Honor Goblet on October 27. On November 3, Lang claimed 18 victories over the Kiev region. He received the Knight's Cross of the Iron Cross on November 22, with 119 aerial victories. Three days later, Lang was awarded the German Cross in Gold.

On April 9, 1944, First Lieutenant Lang was appointed commander of the 9th Squadron, 54th Fighter Wing, engaged in homeland defense over Germany. On April 11, 1944, he received the Oak Leaves to the Knight's Cross (the 448th awarded). In June, Lang claimed 15 victories, including his 150th kill (a P-47 Thunderbolt) on June 14, four P-51 Mustangs shot down in four minutes on June 20, and another four P-51s downed in four minutes on June 24. Captain Lang was appointed 2nd Group Commander, 26th Fighter Wing "Schlageter" (*Jagdgeschwader 26 "Schlageter"*) on June 28, 1944.[127] On July 9, 1944, Lang shot down three RAF Spitfire fighters in five minutes; on August 15, he downed two P-47 Thunderbolts in one minute; on August 25, he vanquished three P-38 Lightning twin-engine fighters in five minutes, and on August 26, he dispatched three Spitfires. On September 3, 1944, Lang experienced mechanical trouble with his aircraft and when he finally took off from Melsbroek, he had difficulty raising the undercarriage. Ten minutes later Allied fighters (some sources state American Mustangs, another Thunderbolts, and still another RAF Spitfires) intercepted the flight. It appears that an enemy round hit his hydraulic system, causing the wheels to drop.[128] Lang was last seen diving vertically with his undercarriage extended at an altitude of 200 meters. His Focke-Wulf Fw 190A-8 hit the ground and exploded near St. Trond, Belgium.

On September 28, 1944, Lang's chain of command submitted a request for a supplemental (posthumous) promotion to major. Lieutenant Colonel and commodore of *Jagdgeschwader 26 "Schlageter,"* Josef "Pips" Priller wrote:[129]

Captain Lang was transferred to the wing on June 29, 1944 and tasked with the leadership of the 2nd Group. In him, the group obtained a leader who lifted up the unit in a unique exemplary way and, due to his untiring personal accomplishments in the air and on the ground, he proved in an outstanding manner to be fighter and leader. Captain Lang took over the group during a time of the hardest engagements at the invasion front, where unavoidable losses created large holes. With his élan and leadership talent, he understood in the shortest time how to relay strength and confidence to the last of his group and in his personal unwavering engagement he was a shining example for everyone. Through his outstanding great passion for flying, coupled with a relentless will for action, he not only attained outstanding success for himself, but also gave to his group the prerequisite for outstanding success in every way through his tactical correct leadership of the unit in the air. In 13 missions engaging the enemy, he succeeded in scoring 28 victories. His group was the first one to reach 100 victories since the invasion.

With that accomplishment, he became one of the most successful leaders and was mentioned in the *Wehrmacht* dispatches. Up to now, he has downed 173 planes.

Captain Lang is a fully matured character, serious and calm in his demeanor, yet definite and energetic when strength was needed. Very good attitude as an officer. Demands of himself first. He understands how to reach the men under his command correctly. Captain Lang possesses an exemplary concept of service, has initiative and talent for improvisation to a large degree, well rooted in the National Socialist ideas.

Captain Lang has been missing in action since September 3, 1944.

Due to his great capabilities and exemplary success, I consider Captain Lang eligible for a supplemental [posthumous] promotion to Major (Wartime Officer) and request the promotion according to the regulations regarding the promotion of soldiers who have fallen or are missing during the war.

The commander of the 2nd Fighter Corps (*II. Jagdkorps*) Major General Alfred Bülowius added:

I concur with the supplemental [posthumous] promotion of Captain Emil Lang to Major (Wartime Officer).

Despite these recommendations and Lang's record of achievement, he was not posthumously promoted. Emil Lang was credited with 173 victories in 403 combat missions, a sortie-to-victory ratio of 2.33 to 1. He recorded 144 victories in the East and 29 victories in the West, 28 of which were claimed over the Invasion Front (the highest total of a German ace) making him the 27th overall highest-scoring *Luftwaffe* fighter ace.[130] He is buried at the German Military Cemetery at Lommel, Belgium in a communal grave.

Beförderungsvorschlag für Offiziere (Kr.O.)

Vorschl.Dienststelle: JAGDGESCHWADER "SCHLAGETER" NR. 26
Höh.Kdo.Behörde   : Generalkommando II. Jagdkorps Datum: 28.9.1944
W.B.K.   : München II   Waffengattung: Fl.Tr.

Es wird vorgeschlagen zum Hauptmann (Kr.O.) mit Wirkung vom 1.8.1944
==

Vor- und Zuname   : Emil L a n g   Geb.Dat.: 14.1.1909
Jetziger Dienstgrad: Hauptmann (Kr.O.) befördert am: 1.4.44 RDA.: ./.
eingesetzt als   : Gruppenkommandeur
                      in Truppenführerstellung
                      auf Planstelle (Stabsoffz.Stelle) gem.KSTN. 1142 (L) (F.B.)
Geeignet zum   : Gruppenkommandeur (seit 3.9.44 vermißt).
Art und Dauer der Verwendung im derzeitigen mobilen Einsatz einschl.
Uk-Stellung und Arbeitsurlaub oder sonstigen Urlaubs über 3 Monate:

von:	bis:	Dienststelle:	Dienststellung:
26. 8.39	30. 9.40	Fl.H.Komp. Gablingen	Flugzeugführer
1.10.40	6. 4.42	Lz.Gruppe 7, München	Flugzeugführer
7. 4.42	2. 7.42	Flzgf.Überf.Sch.Prenzlau	Flugzeugführer
3. 7.42	14. 8.42	Jagdflieger Vorschule 1	Jagdschüler
15. 8.42	5. 1.43	1./Jagdfliegerschule 5	Jagdschüler
6. 1.43	10. 2.43	Jagdgruppe Ost	Jagdflugzeugführer
11. 2.43	12. 4.44	II./Jagdgeschwader 54	Staffelführer
13. 4.44	28. 6.44	III./Jagdgeschwader 54	Staffelkapitän
29. 6.44	3. 8.44	II./Jagdgeschwader 26	Gruppenkommandeur

Strafen: keine
Auszeichnungen:

24.10.40 Kriegsverdienstkreuz 2. Klasse mit Schwertern
23. 3.43 Frontflugspange für Jäger in Bronze
14. 5.43 Frontflugspange für Jäger in Silber
25. 6.43 Frontflugspange für Jäger in Gold
13. 6.43 Eisernes Kreuz II. Klasse
 2. 8.43 Eisernes Kreuz I. Klasse
27.10.43 Ehrenpokal für besondere Leistungen im Luftkrieg
25.11.43 Deutsches Kreuz in Gold
22.11.43 Ritterkreuz des Eisernen Kreuzes
11. 4.44 Eichenlaub zum Ritterkreuz des Eisernen Kreuzes.

Beurteilung durch den Disziplinarvorgesetzten:

    Hauptmann (Kr.O.) L a n g wurde am 29.6.1944 zum Geschwader versetzt und mit der Führung der II./J.G. 26 beauftragt. Mit ihm bekam die Gruppe einen Führer, der in einmalig vorbildlicher Weise seinen Verband hochriß und durch seine unermüdlichen persönlichen Leistungen in der Luft und am Boden sich als Kämpfer und Führer vorzüglich auszeichnete. Hptm. Lang übernahm die Gruppe in einer Zeit des härtesten Einsatzes an der Invasionsfront, wo unvermeidliche Verluste große Lücken gerissen hatten. Durch seinen Schwung und seine Führerkraft verstand er es in kürzester Zeit Festigkeit und Vertrauen bis zum Letzten seiner Gruppe zu geben und

b.wenden

Request for Supplemental Promotion for Captain Emil Lang (front side) – dated September 28, 1944, on blank paper, with typed comments.

war im persönlich rücksichtslosen Einsatz allen leuchtendes Vorbild. Durch seine überaus große fliegerische Passion, gepaart mit schonungslosem Einsatzwillen brachte er nicht nur für sich hervorragende Erfolge, sondern gab auch durch seine taktisch richtige Führung des Verbandes in der Luft der Gruppe die Voraussetzung zu vorzüglichem Breitenerfolg. Allein in 13 Einsätzen mit Feindberührung an der Invasionsfront erzielte er 28 Abschüsse. Seine Gruppe erreichte als erste den 100. Abschuß seit der Invasion.

Er stempelte sich dadurch zu einem der erfolgreichsten Führer und fand durch Nennung im Wehrmachtsbericht Anerkennung. Er erzielte bisher 173 Abschüsse.

Hptm. Lang ist ein voll ausgereifter Charakter, ernst und ruhig im Wesen, jedoch bestimmt und energisch wo Härte gefordert. Sehr gute Einstellung als Offizier. Fordert von sich zuerst. Er versteht es, seine Untergebenen richtig anzufassen.

Hptm. Lang besitzt vorbildliche Dienstauffassung, hat Eigeninitiative und Improvisationstalent in großem Maße, steht fest auf d Boden der nationalsozialistischen Idee.

Hptm. Lang wird seit dem 3.9.1944 nach Luftkampf vermißt.

Ich halte Hptm. Lang auf Grund seiner großen Fähigkeiten und seiner vorbildlichen Erfolge zur nachträglichen Beförderung zum Major (Kr.O.) geeignet und bitte um Beförderung gemäß der Verordnung über die Beförderung während des Krieges gefallener und vermißter Soldaten.

Priller

Oberstleutnant und Geschwaderkommodore.

Der Kommandierende General   Korpsgefechtsstand, 2. Okt.19
des II. Jagdkorps

Ich befürworte die nachträgliche Beförderung des Hauptmann Emil L a n g zum Major (Kr.O.).

Generalleutnant

Request for Supplemental Promotion for Captain Emil Lang (back side) – signed by Lieutenant Colonel Josef "Pips" Priller, Commodore, 26th Fighter Wing, and by Major General Alfred Bülowius, Commander, 2nd Fighter Corps.

Karl-Heinz Langer
Fighter Pilot

"After the encirclement of Stalingrad, showed unusual courage on numerous combat missions out of the fortress."

Major Karl-Heinz Langer was born in Görlitz, Saxony on April 19, 1914. On May 26, 1941, he became the adjutant for the 3rd Group, 3rd Fighter Wing (*Jagdgeschwader 3*) and scored his first aerial victory on July 14, 1941 on the Eastern Front. On September 5, 1942 he was injured making an emergency landing in his Messerschmitt Me 109F-4 at Krasnojarskij. On December 17, 1942, inside the Stalingrad encirclement, Langer's Me 109G-2 rolled at the Pitomnik airfield, injuring him again.[131] On June 1, 1943, Langer assumed command of the 7th Squadron, 3rd Fighter Wing "Udet." He had only 11 victories by this point in the war.

In the fall of 1943, his career took off when his unit transferred to homeland defense over Germany, where on the afternoon of October 14, 1943, he shot down a B-17 Flying Fortress during the massive 8th Air Force 229-bomber second attack on Schweinfurt, but during the combat was shot down himself in his Messerschmitt Me 109G-6 and wounded.[132] While in the *Geschwader*, Langer often served as the wingman for the wing commodore Wolf-Dietrich Wilcke before the latter's death. Langer then spent time as a flight instructor before assuming acting command of the 3rd Group, 3rd Fighter Wing "Udet" on May 21, 1944. He followed that by winning the German Cross in Gold on July 26, 1944 and the *Luftwaffe* Honor Goblet on August 12, 1944.

On July 24, 1944, Major Heinz Bär, the acting commodore of *Jagdgeschwader 3 "Udet,"* submitted a special request for a preferred promotion for Captain Karl-Heinz Langer. Bär wrote:[133]

> Captain Karl-Heinz Langer has belonged to the Wing since May 26, 1941 and, therefore, is one of the officers who have served in the Wing for the longest time. You can always depend on him no matter where he stood. He has: led his squadron in an excellent manner, made it possible for the now-fallen commodore, Colonel Wilcke, to succeed in numerous aerial victories due to his courageous, unselfish protection [as wingman]; after the encirclement of Stalingrad, showed unusual courage on numerous combat missions out of the fortress and has taken care of the new pilots in an excellent manner in just a short time. However, his best accomplishments were at the Invasion Front. At the beginning of the invasion, on May 20, 1944, he was tasked as the stand-in commander of the 3rd Group, *Jagdgeschwader "Udet."* While other groups could not conduct their fighter-bomber missions due to severe enemy action, Langer again and again was able to bomb on target due to his clever leadership and hard, decisive risk-taking. Most of the missions saw him at the front of his pilots. The success of his exemplary willingness for combat showed in the good attitude and steadfast behavior of his group; even the most difficult invasion missions could not adversely affect their military spirit. Next to his successes – 21 aerial victories during 412 enemy flights, two of which were kills at the invasion front – his decent personality, respected by superiors and the men under his command, being well-liked, and being definitely trustworthy are present. Due to his accomplishments against the enemy, his exemplary troop leadership in combat and the personality values, I request his preferential promotion to Major (Tr.O.)

During "Operation Bodenplatte," on January 1, 1945, Langer destroyed two Spitfires on an Allied airfield at Eindhoven, Holland. He was awarded the German Cross in Gold the same day. The group returned to the Eastern Front the following month, and Langer also functioned as the *Geschwader* Adjutant. On April 20, 1945, Major Karl-Heinz Langer received the Knight's Cross of the Iron Cross. Langer flew 486 combat missions, of which 15 were fighter-bomber missions and 57 were ground-attack. He shot down 30 aircraft, of which 10 were in the West (including 4 four-engine bombers). He also destroyed 5 enemy aircraft on their airfields, as well as over 40 vehicles, 3 rocket launchers and one locomotive. Karl-Heinz Langer died on May 6, 1955 in Remscheid.[134]

Request for Preferred Promotion for Captain Karl-Heinz Langer (one page only) – dated July 24, 1944, on blank paper, with typed comments. Signed by Major Heinz Bär, acting commodore of the 3rd Fighter Wing. Stamps show that the report arrived at the 2nd Fighter Corps on July 25 and at the *Luftwaffe* Personnel Office on August 2.

Erich Leie
Fighter Pilot

"Has excelled in his current assignment."

Lieutenant Colonel Erich Leie, nicknamed "Tiger-Leie," was born on September 10, 1916 at Kiel in Schleswig-Holstein. On March 21, 1940, he was assigned to the 3rd Group, 2nd Fighter Wing "Richthofen" (*Jagdgeschwader 2 "Richthofen"*). He claimed his first victory on May 14, eight miles east of Sedan, France, when he shot down a RAF Blenheim twin-engine bomber.[135] By October 1940, Leie was serving in the wing staff and formed a close flying relationship with *Luftwaffe* ace Helmut Wick, the wing commodore. On October 29, 1940, First Lieutenant Leie shot down a Hurricane over Portsmouth. Leie downed two Hurricanes south of Portsmouth in a one-minute time span on November 7, 1940. On November 10, 1940, Leie shot down a Spitfire east of Portland, while Wick was doing the same. On November 11, 1940, flying again with Wick, Leie shot down a Hurricane and a Spitfire in five minutes over Portland, while Wick was adding another 3 kills of his own. A day later (November 12) Leie shot down two Hurricanes over Southampton, while Wick was downing five British fighters on the same mission. Finally, on November 28, 1940, Leie shot down a Spitfire south of the Isle of Wight. Wick scored two kills in the same dogfight, but was shot down and disappeared into the Atlantic.

Leie recorded his 12th victory on June 22, 1941, when he shot down a RAF Spitfire fighter between St. Omer and Arques, serving as the wing adjutant. He added two more Spitfires in a two-minute period on June 24. Erich Leie was awarded the Knight's Cross of the Iron Cross on August 1, 1941, following 21 victories on the Channel Front. On August 12, 1941, the wing commodore, Major Walter Oesau, and First Lieutenant Leie, flying together, went wild over the English Channel, dispatching 8 Spitfires between them. By the end of 1941, Leie's victory total had climbed to 32, including six RAF Spitfires shot down on July 23, and his 30th victory on November 8, another Spitfire, shot down over the Somme Estuary. Nineteen forty-two saw him continue as a Spitfire-killer, as he shot down one on January 26, another on April 25, two more on May 1, another on May 19, one more on June 2, another (his 40th aerial victory) on June 3 and a final Spitfire on June 5. On May 4, 1942, First Lieutenant Leie was appointed Commander, 1st Group, 2nd Fighter Wing "Richthofen."

Erich Leie (center, nearest painting of Adolf Hitler) receives congratulations from Field Marshal Hugo Sperrle. Officer next to Leie is Rudolf Pflanz, also a Knight's Cross recipient. Officer on the far right appears to be Knight's Cross with Oak Leaves winner Egon Mayer. All three men were in the 2nd Fighter Wing and all were awarded the Knight's Cross on August 1, 1941, which could be the date of this photo.

On August 13, 1942, Field Marshal Hugo Sperrle, Commander, 3rd Air Fleet (*Luftflotte 3*), wrote a cover letter to a preferential promotion request to captain for First Lieutenant Erich Leie. In this short letter, Sperrle wrote:[136]

> The enclosure presents the evaluation note with the proposal for preferential promotion of First Lieutenant Erich Leie, who is tasked as the acting commander of the 1st Group, 2nd Fighter Wing. First Lieutenant Leie has excelled in his current assignment and in his former position a wing adjutant. Up to now, he has succeeded in 42 shoot-downs and was awarded the Knight's Cross of the Iron Cross on August 2, 1941.
>
> I second this proposal.

On August 19, he participated in the air-battle over Dieppe, claiming another RAF Spitfire fighter as his 42nd victory. However, he was shot down and wounded during this engagement, but successfully bailed out of his Focke-Wulf Fw 190A-3 seven miles southwest of Abbeville.

After a stay in the hospital, Leie resumed command of the 1st Group on October 2, 1942. On November 9, 1942, he received the German Cross in Gold. On January 6, 1943, Leie was named Commander, 1st Group, 51st Fighter Wing "Mölders" (*Jagdgeschwader 51 "Mölders"*) based on the Eastern Front. Leie, now flying a Focke-Wulf Fw 190A-5, successfully led the group during the offensive operations leading up to "Operation Citadel," the Battle of Kursk during July 1943. Flying a Focke-Wulf Fw 190A-5, he shot down an Il-2 Sturmovik on July 13 as his 50th kill and another Sturmovik on August 12 as his 75th aerial victory. On November 6, 1943, Major Leie shot down four enemy aircraft to record his 97th through 100th victories. He was granted a lengthy spell of leave and returned to frontline duty at the end of March, but managed only three kills prior to being shot down in aerial combat with Russian fighters on July 6. He bailed out of his stricken aircraft over Russian lines but was fortunate in that his parachute was blown back over German lines. By October 1944, Leie's victory total stood at 114. He was elevated to command the 77th Fighter Wing "Ace of Hearts" (*Jagdgeschwader 77 "Herzas"*) on December 29, 1944. Erich Leie was killed on March 7, 1945 four miles south of Schwarzwasser, Czechoslovakia, (now Cerná Voda, Czech Republic), when he collided with a crashing Russian Yak 9 fighter and failed to survive a low level bail-out from his Messerschmitt Me 109G-14. He received a posthumous promotion to lieutenant colonel and was recommended for the award of the Oak Leaves to the Knight's Cross, but the decoration was never approved.

Erich Leie was credited with 118 victories in over 500 combat missions, a sortie-to-victory ratio of about 4.23 to 1. He recorded 76 victories over the Eastern Front, including 32 Sturmovik ground-attack aircraft. Of his 42 confirmed victories recorded over the Western front, 30 were Spitfires, and one was a four-engine bomber.[137] He is listed among the dead at a cemetery in Valasske Mezirici in the Czech Republic.

Geheim!

Luftflottenkommando 3   Den 13. August 1942
Az. 21 p / Adj.(IIa)
Nr. 12940 /42 geh.

Betr.: Vorschlag auf bevorzugte Beförderung des Oblt.(Tr.O.)
       L e i e (Erich), m.d.W.d.G.b.d.Kdr.I./J.G.2.
Anlg.: -1- Beurt.(i.v.U.)

An den
   Reichsminister der Luftfahrt und
   Oberbefehlshaber der Luftwaffe - L.P.1 Kurierstelle
         B e r l i n .

In der Anlage wird eine Beurteilungsnotiz mit Vorschlag zur bevorzugten Beförderung für Oblt.(Tr.O.) L e i e (Erich), mit der Führung der I./J.G.2 beauftragt, vorgelegt.

Oblt. Leie hat sich in seiner jetzigen Verwendung und in seiner früheren Stelle als Geschwader-Adjutant bewährt. Er hat bisher 42 Abschüsse erzielt und wurde am 2.8.41 mit dem Ritterkreuz des Eisernen Kreuzes ausgezeichnet.

Ich befürworte den Vorschlag.

                                                Generalfeldmarschall.

Request for Preferred Promotion for First Lieutenant Erich Leie (one page only) – dated August 13, 1942, on blank paper, with typed comments. Signed by Field Marshal Hugo Sperrle, Commander, 3rd Air Fleet. Stamps show that the report arrived at the *Luftwaffe* Personnel Office on August 17.

Ludwig Leingärtner
Stuka Pilot

"Has fully distinguished himself as an officer with great willingness for combat against the enemy."

Captain Ludwig Leingärtner was born December 22, 1919 at Bittenbrunn near Neuberg/Donau in Bavaria. At the outbreak of the war, Leingärtner was serving in the German Labor Service, but quickly entered the *Luftwaffe* on October 1, 1939. He flew his first combat missions with the 4th Group (Stuka), 1st Demonstration Wing (*Lehrgeschwader 1*), which became the 1st Group, 5th Stuka Wing (*Sturzkampfgeschwader 5*) on January 27, 1942. On January 22, 1943, Leingärtner received the *Luftwaffe* Honor Goblet for his ground attack successes on the Eastern Front.

On April 5, 1943, Colonel General Alfred Keller, commander of the 1st Air Fleet (*Luftflotte 1*), wrote a short cover letter for a packet to the *Luftwaffe* High Command in Berlin concerning a promotion and date of rank for Second Lieutenant Leingärtner. Keller's letter read:[138]

For the reasons expressed in the application as well as the opinion by the Air Commander 1, the application is being seconded, particularly because Leingärtner has fully distinguished himself as an officer with great willingness for combat against the enemy.

The horsepower provided by the air fleet commander was effective, and Leingärtner soon made first lieutenant. On May 19, 1943, he won the German Cross in Gold. He assumed command of the 2nd Squadron, 1st Ground-Attack Wing (*Schlachtgeschwader 1*) on June 20, 1943. He won the Knight's Cross of the Iron Cross on February 5, 1944 as the Commander, 2nd Squadron, 1st Ground-Attack Wing. On April 4, 1944, after a well deserved leave at home, Ludwig Leingärtner began his return trip to the front, when the Junkers Ju 52 transport aircraft in which he was a passenger was shot down by enemy fighters north of Torgau. At his death, Ludwig Leingärtner had flown 540 combat missions.[139]

Geheim

Luftflottenkommando 1   O.U., den 5. April 1943
II Nr. 1744/43 geh. IIa
Az.: 21

Betr.: Beförderung Ltn. (Tr.O.) L e i n g ä r t n e r (Ludwig)
       I./Sturzkampfgeschwader 5.

An den
Reichsminister der Luftfahrt u.
Oberbefehlshaber der Luftwaffe
- L.P. -
B e r l i n .

Anliegend wird ein Antrag der I./Stuka 5 um anderweitige Festsetzung des R.D.A. von

Ltn. (Tr.O.) L e i n g ä r t n e r (Ludwig)

mit der Bitte um Entscheidung vorgelegt.

Aus den in dem Antrag sowie der Stellungnahme des Fliegerführers 1 angeführten Gründen wird der Antrag befürwortet, insbesondere, da sich L. als tapferer und einsatzfreudiger Offizier vor dem Feinde voll bewährt hat.

8 Anlagen.   Der Chef der Luftflotte 1
                          und Befehlshaber Ost.

                                  Keller
                               Generaloberst.

Request for Promotion for Second Lieutenant Ludwig Leingärtner (one page only) – dated April 5, 1943, on blank paper, with typed comments. Signed by Colonel General Alfred Keller, Commander, 1st Air Fleet. Red stamp shows the request arrived at the *Luftwaffe* Personnel Office on April 8, and it was initialed by Brigadier General Werner von Rudloff.

Lothar Linke

Night Fighter Pilot

"Possesses good social manners."

First Lieutenant Lothar Linke was born on October 23, 1909 at Liegnitz in Silesia. Prior to World War II, he was a flying instructor. At the outbreak of the war, Master Sergeant Linke was serving with the 3rd Squadron, 76th Destroyer Wing (*Zerstörergeschwader 76*). He participated in the invasions of Poland and Norway, and recorded his first victory on April 19, 1940, when he shot down an RAF Blenheim twin-engine bomber near Stavanger in Norway. Linke transferred to the night fighters in August 1940 and following transition training, he was posted to the 4th Squadron, 2nd Group, 1st Night Fighter Wing (*Nachtjagdgeschwader 1*).

On January 18, 1941, Linke's chain of command in *Nachtjagdgeschwader 1* submitted a special efficiency report requesting he be promoted to second lieutenant. First Lieutenant Helmuth Lent, the 6th Squadron Commander, wrote:[140]

> Master Sergeant Linke is a mature, decisive man who is gifted with a healthy ambition and who, due to his age and his maturity, possesses good social manners. With a high sense of responsibility which characterizes his understanding of service, he possesses good initiative. With above average talent for comprehension and general knowledge as well as physical appearance, he has demonstrated during the course of the war that he will be a full-fledged officer and superior in every respect. His courage shown since the beginning of the war as a destroyer pilot, and most recently as a night fighter, and his healthy dare-devil nature have been proven through his many engagements, his aerial victories and the awarding of the Iron Cross 2nd and 1st Classes. In view of his superior knowledge and his experience in aviation, he is respected by his superiors and the men under his command.

Captain Walter Ehle, the 2nd Group Commander, *Nachtjagdgeschwader 1*, added his own remarks:

> I am in full agreement with the evaluation of the Squadron Captain regarding Master Sergeant Linke. Master Sergeant Linke, by reason of his character, his unquestionable attitude as a soldier and his proven fighting spirit in many missions is suitable to be a wartime officer in every respect.

Major Wolfgang Falck, the wing commodore, simply added: "In full agreement!"

Linke gained his first night victory on the night of May 11/12, 1941, when he shot down a RAF Wellington twin-engine bomber (which was on an RAF Bomber Command mission against Hamburg) near Osterfelde, Germany. On November 1, 1941, Linke's squadron was designated the 5th Squadron, 2nd Night Fighter Wing (*Nachtjagdgeschwader 2*). By this time, Linke had accumulated two victories by day and a further two victories at night. By the end of 1942, Linke had increased his victory total to 11, the last a Halifax bomber. Fifth Squadron again underwent redesignation, becoming the 11th Squadron, *Nachtjagdgeschwader 2* on October 1, 1942. He received the *Luftwaffe* Honor Goblet on January 25, 1943, and on February 27, 1943, Linke was appointed 12th Squadron Commander. On the night of May 4/5, 1943, he shot down four RAF bombers (two Halifaxes, a Lancaster and a Wellington) on an RAF Bomber Command 596-aircraft raid of Dortmund to record his 20th through 23rd aerial victories.[141] On the night of May 13/14, 1943, after downing two RAF Lancaster four-engine bombers, Lothar Linke was shot down when his Messerschmitt Me 110G-4 was hit by return fire northwest of Lemmer, the Netherlands, which started an engine fire. He and his radio operator, Master Sergeant Czybulka, bailed out, but Linke struck the tail unit of the aircraft and fell to his death. First Lieutenant Lothar Linke was posthumously awarded the German Cross in Gold on May 29, 1943 and the Knight's Cross of the Iron Cross on September 19, 1943.[142] He was credited with 27 aerial victories in over 100 combat missions, a sortie-to-victory ratio of about 2.70 to 1. He recorded 24 victories at night, including 12 four-engine bombers and one DeHaviland Mosquito.[143] Lothar Linke is buried in the German Military Cemetery at Ysselsteyn, Netherlands (Field AR, Row 4, Grave 92).

314/8

Luftflottenkommando 2   O. U. , den 18. 1. 41
II./Nachtjagdgeschwader 1
W.B.K. Breslau II   L u f t w a f f e .
Vorgeschlagen gem:

a) Bes.Anl.14 zum Mob.-Plan (L), Abschnitt 3, B.
b) L.Dv.1000, Abschnitt 3.
c) Bes.Lw.Bestimmungen Nr.27, Ziff. 770.
d) R.d.L.u.Ob.d.L., L.P.-Amt 2, Az.22 a 12 (K)
    Allg.Nr. 70005/40 (2, II) v. 18.11.40, Abschnitt D, Ziff. II, 5.

K 3/2

Waffengattung: Fliegertruppe.

     Betr.: Vorschlag zur Beförderung zum Leutnant (Kriegsoffizier).

     Auf dem Dienstwege an
         R. d. L. u. Ob. d. L. (L.P.),   B e r l i n

     Zur Beförderung zum Leutnant (Kriegsoffizier) wird in Vorschlag gebracht:

Familienname, Vorname: L i n k e , Lothar
geb.am: 23.10.09   zu: Liegnitz   Konf.: ev.
Dienstgrad: Oberfeldwebel d.Res.   verwendet als: Flugzeugführer
Diensteintritt am: 1.3.34   verh., led.: verh.
Ernennung zum R.O.A. bzw. Kriegs-Offz.-Anw. wann: 20.12.40
Kinder: keine
Bestrafung vor Diensteintritt: keine
Bestrafung nach Diensteintritt: keine
Zum Offizier gewählt am: 18. 1. 41
Bürgerlicher Beruf: Fluglehrer
Stand und Beruf des Vaters: Lokomotivführer, verstorben 1924
Mutter geborene: Körner
Anschrift der Eltern oder des Vormundes bzw. der Ehefrau:
Ruth L i n k e geb. Richter, Breslau-Wilhelmsruh, Donarweg 14.
Bildungsgang: Erziehung im elterlichen Hause.
                Ostern 1916 - Ostern 1919 Volksschule Liegnitz
                Ostern 1919 - Ostern 1927 Oberrealschule Liegnitz
                                                     (Prima-Reife)
                April 1927 - April 1928 Privatschule in Liegnitz.
Militärischer Werdegang: 1. 3.34 - 31.12.34   3./Fahr-Abt.Rendsburg
                            24. 7.39 - 7. 9.40   3./Zerstörergeschwader 76
                            ab 8. 9. 40   6./Nachtjagdgeschwader 1.

                                                                                    Be-

Request for Promotion to Officer for Master Sergeant (Reserve) Lothar Linke (first page) – dated January 18, 1941 on blank paper with typed comments. Pencil comment indicates Linke was promoted on March 1, 1941. Underlines in red pencil probably done at the *Luftwaffe* Personnel Office. "K" in red pencil could be the initial of Gustav Kastner-Kirdorf, head of the office during this period.

Beförderungen und Ernennungen:

```
z. Gefr. d.Res.    am   1. 1. 39
z. Uffz. d.Res.    am   1. 4. 39
z. Feldw.d.Res.    am  25. 8. 39
z. Obfw. d.Res.    am   1. 7. 40
z. K.O.A.          am  20.12. 40
```

Begründung, Beurteilung:

Obfw. Linke ist ein ausgereifter, zielbewußter, mit gesundem Ehrgeiz ausgestatteter Mann, der infolge seines Alters und seiner Reife gute Umgangsformen besitzt. Bei hohem Verantwortungsgefühl, das seine Diensterfassung kennzeichnet, besitzt er gute Initiative.

Bei überdurchschnittlicher Auffassungsgabe und Allgemeinbildung sowie guter körperlicher Veranlagung hat er im Laufe des Krieges gezeigt, daß er in jeder Hinsicht einen vollwertigen Offizier und Vorgesetzten abgeben wird. Seine von Beginn des Krieges an als Zerstörer und in letzter Zeit als Nachtjäger gezeigte Tapferkeit und sein gesundes Draufgängertum worden bewiesen durch seine vielen Einsätze, seine Abschüsse und seine Auszeichnung mit dem E.K. II und I. Wegen seines überlegenen Könnens und seiner fliegerischen Erfahrung ist er bei seinen Vorgesetzten und Untergebenen geachtet.

Oberleutnant und Staffelkapitän
6./Nachtjagdgeschwader 1

Mit der Beurteilung des Staffelkapitäns über den Obfw. L i n k e einverstanden.

Obfw. Linke ist auf Grund seines Charakters, seiner einwandfreien soldatischen Einstellung und seines in vielen Einsätzen bewiesenen kämpferischen Geistes in jeder Beziehung zum Kriegsoffizier geeignet.

Hauptmann und Gruppenkommandeur
II./Nachtjagdgeschwader 1

Voll einverstanden!

5.2.41.

Major und Geschwaderkommodore.

Request for Promotion to Officer for Master Sergeant (Reserve) Lothar Linke (second page) – signed by First Lieutenant Helmut Lent, Commander, 6th Squadron, Captain Walter Ehle, Commander, 2nd Group, and Major Wolfgang Falck, Commodore, 1st Night Fighter Wing.

Helmut Lipfert
Fighter Pilot

"He is a shining example for his squadron."

Captain Helmut Lipfert was born on August 6, 1916 at Lippelsdorf near Saalfeld, Thuringia. After serving in the Army, he joined the *Luftwaffe* in 1941 and was assigned to the 52nd Fighter Wing (*Jagdgeschwader 52*) following flying training. On his arrival at Simovniki in Russia, Lipfert was assigned to the 6th Squadron on December 16, 1942. Two days later, he made a belly-landing in his Messerschmitt Me 109G-2. He gained his first victory on his 18th combat mission on January 30, 1943, shooting down a Russian LaGG-5 fighter near Mal Balabinka. Lipfert won the Iron Cross 2nd Class on March 12, 1943, the Operational Flying Clasp for Fighters in Gold on April 26, 1943 and the Iron Cross 1st Class on April 29, 1943. He achieved his 20th victory, a Yak-1 fighter, on September 5, 1943 near Taranovka. The following day, Lipfert assumed acting command of the 6th Squadron. By the end of 1943, his score had reached 80, which included five enemy aircraft shot down on October 8. He received the *Luftwaffe* Honor Goblet on November 14, 1943, shortly after his 50th kill – an Il-2 Sturmovik.

On December 12, 1943, the chain of command in *Jagdgeschwader 52* submitted a special efficiency report requesting preferential promotion by reason of duty requirements. Captain Erich Barkhorn, 2nd Group Commander, wrote the following:[144]

Short Evaluation (Personal values, National Socialist attitude, accomplishments before the enemy, service accomplishments, mental and physical attributes and suitability, infantry experience, when and how obtained)**:** Mature personality, at the same time open and full of humor. Uncomplicated character. He is harsh against himself and knows how to assert himself. His military appearance is correct. He has worked to complete his knowledge. Physically athletic and flexible. As a fighter pilot, he is passionate, flies cleverly and has attained great success. He is an example for his squadron.

Summarized evaluation: Above average
(Above Average, Average, Below Average)

How is the current position being fulfilled? Well fulfilled.
(Use only: Very well fulfilled, well fulfilled, fulfilled, not fulfilled)

Suitable for promotion to next higher service grade? Yes.

Suitable for which next-higher position: as a Squadron Commander.

Known to the person submitting this review: since December 1942.

Lieutenant Colonel Dietrich Hrabak, 52nd Fighter Wing Commodore, added:

> Second Lieutenant Lipfert is a mature personality; well rooted in his character and decent in his demeanor, he is a shining example for his squadron. Accomplished in numerous aerial fights with the enemy, he has attained 76 kills to date. Second Lieutenant Lipfert is suited for preferential promotion to First Lieutenant.

On January 28, 1944, Lipfert won the German Cross in Gold, with his victory total at 87. He achieved his 100th aerial victory, another Sturmovik, on April 11, 1944, shortly after receiving the Knight's Cross of the Iron Cross on April 5, as he terrorized the skies over the Crimea as the Soviet Army closed in on the German defenders at Sevastopol. Lipfert continued his upward climb and scored his 150th kill, a Yak-7 fighter, on October 24, 1944. During this period, he often tallied more than one enemy aircraft in a day, dispatching – for example – three Yak-1s in nine minutes on May 7 (over Sevastopol), three Russian fighters in five minutes on July 19, and two Il-2 Sturmoviks in one minute on October 23. Lipfert scored his 175th kill, a Yakovlev Yak-3 fighter, on January 14, 1945. On February 15, 1945, the *Luftwaffe* appointed Captain Lipfert to the 1st Group Commander, 53rd Fighter Wing "Ace of Spades" (*Jagdgeschwader 53 "Pikas"*). In this role, he claimed his 200th kill, an La-7 fighter, on April 8, 1945. He became the 837th *Wehrmacht* recipient of the Oak Leaves to the Knight's Cross on April 17, 1945, one day after scoring his final victory, a Yak-9.

Helmut Lipfert was credited with a total of 203 aerial victories (200 were in the East), attained in 700 combat missions, a sortie-to-victory ratio of 3.45 to 1. He also destroyed two motor-torpedo boats and 30 trucks in ground-attack missions. Helmut Lipfert, the 15th highest-scoring *Luftwaffe* fighter pilot, died August 10, 1990 at Einbeck. He is buried there at the *Zentralfriedhof* (Section 35, Grave 30).[145]

II./Jagdgeschwader 52   Im Felde, den 15. 12. 1943
Dienststelle, nicht Feldpost-Nr.

Kriegs=Beurteilung zum _____ 194_

für Offz. ausschl. San.-, Vet.-Offz.

über den

Lt.(Kr.O.)   1.8.42   Helmut   Lipfert
Dienstgrad¹)   RDA. - Ordn.-Nr. - u. Dienstalterliste   Vorname   Name

6. 8. 1916   verheiratet, ledig, verwitwet, geschieden   kv., tropentgl.
geb. am   Zutreffendes unterstreichen   Wehrdiensttauglichkeit²)
                                                [kv., gv. Feld, gv. H., tropentgl., tropenuntgl.]

R.A.D.-Führer (Feldmeister)
Zivilberuf - falls vorhanden -

Staffelführer seit 6.9.43   W.B.K. Rudolstadt
jetzige Verwendung seit   Friedensdienststelle und WBK.³)

Bevorzugte Beförderung auf Grund der Dienststellung
Anlaß der Vorlage⁴)

Deutsche Auszeichnungen des jetzigen Krieges mit Verleihungsdaten und Angabe, ob und zu welchen Auszeichnungen vorgeschlagen:
Med.z.Er.a.d.1.1o.38 am 6.11.39, E.K.II am 12.3.43,
E.K.I am 29.4.43, Frontfl.Sp.f.Jg.i.Gold am 26.4.43,
Ehrenpokal f.bes.Leistg.i.Luftkr.am 14.11.43, z.Deutsch.Kreuz i.Gold
eingereicht am 23.10.43, z. Ritterkreuz d.E.K. eingereicht am 13.12.43.

¹) Genaue Angabe, ob Tr. Offz., Erg.Offz., Offz. z D., Res.Offz., Kr.Offz., z.V Offz. — ²) In zweifelhaften Fällen neu festzustellen. — ³) Dienststelle, welche Friedensgebührnisse zahlt, und zuständiges Wehrbezirkskommando. — ⁴) z.B. Versetzung zur III./KG. 2, terminmäßige Vorlage zum 1. 5. 43.

Kurze Beurteilung (Persönlichkeitswert, national-sozialistische Haltung, Bewährung vor dem Feinde, dienstl. Leistungen, geistige und körperl. Anlagen und Eignung, infanter Erfahrungen, wann u. wo erworben):

Reife Persönlichkeit, dabei aufgeschlossen und humorvoll.
Charakterlich unkompliziert. Er ist hart gegen sich selbst und
kann sich durchsetzen.
Militärisches Auftreten korrekt, Kenntnisse hat er vervollkommnet.
Körperlich sportlich und gewandt.
Als Jagdflieger passioniert, fliegt besonnen und hat gute Erfolge
erzielt. Ist seiner Staffel Vorbild.

Starke Seiten: - - -

Schwache Seiten: - - -

Zusammenfassendes Urteil
(über Durchschnitt, Durchschnitt, unter Durchschnitt):   über Durchschnitt

Wie wird die jetzige Stelle ausgefüllt?
(Es sind nur die Ausdrücke „sehr gut ausgef.", „gut aus-   gut ausgefüllt.
gefüllt", „ausgefüllt", „nicht ausgefüllt" zu verwenden)

Geeignet z. Beförderung z. nächsthöheren Dienstgrad?   ja

Best.-Nr. F 860 L Wehrmachtverlag: Emil Reimann, Breslau 1, Altbüßerstr. 10 7 43 B/0022

Efficiency Report for Second Lieutenant Helmut Lipfert (front side) – dated December 15, 1943, on preprinted form from the Emil Reimann firm in Breslau, with typed comments.

Eignung
für welche nächsthöhere Verwendung? ⁵)   als Staffelkapitän
für welche besondere oder anderweit. Verwendung? ⁶)
Vorschlag für Verwendung in nächster Zeit? ⁷)

Sprachkenntnisse (keine Schulkenntnisse)
a) abgelegte Prüfungen: - - -
   [z.B.: Dolmetscherprüfung 1.10.42]
b) Beherrschung der Sprache:
   [z.B.: durch Aufenthalt im Ausland]

Eröffnung zu welchen Punkten, wann, wie   - - -
(mündlich oder schriftlich) und durch wen?

Strafen sind mit vollem Straftenor sowie Vermerk über Vollstreckung abschriftlich als Anlage der Kriegs-
beurteilung beizuheften.

Dem Beurteilenden bekannt seit   Dezember 42
~~unterstellt seit~~

Ausbildung
a) erworbene Scheine: L.F.
   [L.F., E.L.F., L.B. usw.]
b) Sonderausbildung:
   [z.B. Bild-Offz., Techn. Offz., Meß-Offz.,
   Funk-Drahtnachr.-Offz., W.K.S.]

_____   Hauptmann und Gruppenkommandeur.
   Unterschrift   Dienstgrad u. Dienststellung

Beitrag des Chefs des Generalstabes der vorgesetzten Kommandobehörde (nur bei
Genst.-Offz. in Stabsstellungen und zur Dienstleistung zum Generalstab kommandierten Offizieren):

Zusätze vorgesetzter Dienststellen:

Jagdgeschwader 52   Im Felde, den 20. 12. 1943

   Lt. L i p f e r t ist eine ausgereifte Persönlichkeit; gefestigt
in seinem Charakter und anständig in seiner Gesinnung ist er seiner
Staffel ein leuchtendes Vorbild. Vor dem Feinde in zahlreichen Luftkämpfen bewährt, konnte er bisher 76 Abschüsse erzielen.
   Lt. L i p f e r t ist zur bevorzugten Beförderung zum Oberleutnan
voll geeignet.

                                                Oberstleutnant u. Geschwaderkommodore

⁵) Gilt für alle Offz., für Truppen-Offz. hinsichtlich Eignung zur Führung des nächsthöheren Verbandes, für Genst. Offz. hinsichtlich Eignung zum Chef oder Ia, Ic der Luftfl., Flieger-Korps, Flak-Korps, Fl. Div, Flak-Div., zur Versetzung in den Genst., zur Kommandierung in den Genst. — ⁶) z. B: Höherer Adjutant, Erzieher, Lehrer auf Spezialgebieten, auf Grund von Sprachkenntnissen im Attachédienst; für Genst. Offz. hinsichtlich Eignung für Verwendung im Quartiermeisterdienst, im Ic-Dienst, im Transportwesen, als Lehrer für Genst, Lehrgang (Taktik bzw. Qu.Dienst); besondere Anlagen für Kriegsgeschichte, Wehrwirtschaft. — ⁷) z.B.: „noch halbjährige Belassung in bisheriger Stelle", oder „alsbaldige Verwendung als Geschw. Kommodore".

Efficiency Report for Second Lieutenant Helmut Lipfert (back side) – signed by Captain Erich Barkhorn, Commander, 2nd Group, 52nd Fighter Wing, and by Lieutenant Colonel Dietrich Hrabak, 52nd Fighter Wing Commodore.

RATER BIOGRAPHIES

The following are abbreviated biographies of the raters and senior raters, who signed the documents found in this volume. When a rater was also the subject of another document, the reader will find his expanded biography in Part 2, not in this section.

Werner Andres

Lieutenant Colonel Werner Andres was born July 13, 1909. His significant positions included: Commander, 1st Squadron, 3rd Fighter Wing (*Jagdgeschwader 3*), July 1, 1938-January 31, 1940; Commander, 2nd Group, 27th Fighter Wing (*Jagdgeschwader 27*), February 6, 1940-August 8, 1940; Commander, 3rd Group, 3rd Fighter Wing (*Jagdgeschwader 3*), August 1, 1941-May 12, 1942; Commander, Supplemental Group East (*Ergänzungs-Gruppe Ost*), May 23, 1942 – January 31, 1943 and April 1943 – June 30, 1943; Commodore, 1st Supplemental Fighter Wing (*Ergänzungs-Jagdgeschwader 1*), October 15, 1944-December 11, 1944; and Commodore, 2nd Supplemental Fighter Wing (*Ergänzungs-Jagdgeschwader 2*), December 11, 1944-February 1, 1945. On August 28, 1941, Andres was seriously injured in an accident on take-off in his Messerschmitt Me F-2, which completely destroyed the aircraft. He was promoted to lieutenant colonel (*Oberstleutnant*) on July 1, 1944. During the war, he shot down 5 enemy aircraft.[1]

Heinz Bär

Lieutenant Colonel Heinz "Pritzl" Bär was born March 25, 1913 in Sommerfeld near Leipzig in Saxony. Bär's significant positions included: Commander, 12th Squadron, 51st Fighter Wing "Mölders" (*Jagdgeschwader 51 "Mölders"*), July 20, 1941-May 11, 1942; acting commander, 1st Group, 77th Fighter Wing (*Jagdgeschwader 77*), May 12, 1942-June 1943; Commander, Supplemental Group South (*Ergänzungs-Gruppe Süd*), August 19, 1943-January 1944; Commander, 2nd Group, 1st Fighter Wing "Oesau" (*Jagdgeschwader 1 "Oesau"*), March 15, 1944-May 12, 1944; acting commodore, 1st Fighter Wing, May 12, 1944-May 20, 1944; Commodore, 3rd Fighter Wing "Udet" (*Jagdgeschwader 3 "Udet"*), June 7, 1944-February 23, 1945; and Commodore, 2nd Supplemental Fighter Wing (*Ergänzungs-Jagdgeschwader 2*), February 23, 1945-April 27, 1945. He won the Iron Cross 2nd Class on September 29, 1939, the Iron Cross 1st Class on July 6, 1940, the Knight's Cross of the Iron Cross on July 2, 1941, the Oak Leaves to the Knight's Cross on August 14, 1941 and the Swords to the Oak Leaves on February 16, 1942. He also won the *Luftwaffe* Honor Goblet on June 1, 1942 and the German Cross in Gold on June 8, 1942. Bär was recommended for the award of the Diamonds in January 1945, but this was never approved. He was promoted to Second Lieutenant on September 7, 1940 and to Major on March 28, 1943. In 1943, he ran afoul of Hermann Göring and was temporarily demoted to squadron commander. Bär flew 1,000 combat missions and shot down 221 enemy aircraft, a sortie-to-victory ratio of 4.52 to 1. Of these, 96 were in the East, 65 in the Mediterranean Theater and 16 with the Messerschmitt Me 262. He was killed in a small plane accident on April 28, 1957, while performing aerobatics, when he suddenly spun in from a low altitude over Braunschweig-Waggum, Lower Saxony.[2]

Gerhard Barkhorn

Major Gerhard Barkhorn was born on May 20, 1919 at Königsberg, East Prussia. He joined the *Luftwaffe* in 1937 as an officer candidate, and began his flight training in March 1938. On completion of his training, he was assigned to the 3rd Squadron, 2nd Fighter Wing "Richthofen" (*Jagdgeschwader 2 "Richthofen"*). Among his significant wartime positions were: Commander, 4th Squadron, 52nd Fighter Wing (*Jagdgeschwader 52*), May 21, 1941-September 1, 1943; Commander, 2nd Group, 52nd Fighter Wing, September 1, 1943-January 15, 1945; and Commodore, 6th Fighter Wing (*Jagdgeschwader 6*), January 16, 1945-April 10, 1945. Barkhorn received the Iron Cross 2nd Class on October 23, 1940, the Iron Cross 1st Class on December 3, 1940, the *Luftwaffe* Honor Goblet on July 20, 1942 and the German Cross in Gold on September 7, 1942. He was awarded the Knight's Cross of the Iron Cross on August 23, 1942, the Oak Leaves to the Knight's Cross on January 11, 1943 and the Swords on March 2, 1944. He was promoted to Major (*Major*) on May 1, 1944. After the war, Barkhorn was a prisoner of war of the Allies; he was released in September 1945. He joined the new *Bundesluftwaffe* in 1956, commanded Fighter-Bomber Wing 31 "Boelcke" and rose to the rank of major general before retiring in 1976. On January 6, 1983, during a winter storm on an autobahn near Cologne, Barkhorn and his wife were involved in a serious automobile accident. He died in a hospital on January 8, 1983. He is buried at Tegernsee, Bavaria.[3] Gerhard Barkhorn was credited with 301 victories gained in 1104 combat missions (a sortie-to-victory ratio of 3.66 to 1), all of which occurred over the Eastern Front. He was wounded by ground-fire on July 25, 1942.[4]

Walter Barenthin
Brigadier General Walter Barenthin was born January 13, 1888 in Berlin, Brandenburg. He entered the Army in 1909 and became an engineer officer. During World War I, Barenthin served as a regimental adjutant and a company commander in the 25th Pioneer Regiment. He left the Army in 1920 but was reactivated into the Army in 1936 during the expansion of the German armed forces. On April 1, 1941 he transferred to the *Luftwaffe*. His significant positions included: Corps Engineer Leader, 11th Air Corps (*Stopi, XI. Fliegerkorps*), April 1, 1941-October 31, 1942; Commander *Luftwaffe Jäger Regiment "Barenthin"*, November 1, 1942-March 10, 1943; Commander Operational Training and School Units 11th Air Corps, May 1943-September 12, 1943; Commander 3rd Paratroop Division (*3. Fallschirmjäger-Division*), September 13, 1943-February 14, 1944; Commander of Replacement and Training Units Parachute Army, February 15, 1944-December 30, 1944; Commander Paratroop Training and Replacement Division (*Fallschirmjäger-Ausbildungs-und Ersatz-Division*), December 31, 1944-March 31, 1945; and Commander 20th Paratroop Division (*20. Fallschirmjäger-Division*), April 1, 1945-May 9, 1945. His promotions included: Lieutenant Colonel (*Oberstleutnant*), September 1, 1940; Colonel (*Oberst*), April 1, 1942; and Brigadier General (*Generalmajor*), September 1, 1943. Barenthin was wounded in action in Africa on March 10, 1943 and received a German Cross in Gold on May 25, 1943. The British held him as a prisoner of war from 1945 to 1947. Walter Barenthin died February 28, 1959.[5]

Horst Beeger
Major Horst Beeger was born June 8, 1913 in Bautzen, Saxony. His significant positions included: Commander, 3rd Squadron, 1st Group (*Kampf*), 1st Demonstration Wing (*Lehrgeschwader 1*), October 1, 1940-August 19, 1942; and Commander, 3rd Group, 101st Bomber Wing (*Kampfgeschwader 101*), February 1, 1943-August 14, 1943. He won the Knight's Cross of the Iron Cross on November 23, 1941 as a first lieutenant and squadron commander. Horst Beeger flew combat missions over Poland, Norway, France, England and the Mediterranean during the war. He was credited with sinking the cruiser *HMS York*. On April 16, 1941, his Junkers Ju 88 was shot down during a raid on Khalkis harbor in Greece, and he was rescued at sea. Horst Beeger died on March 3, 1998 in Wahnbek/Rastede, Lower Saxony.[6]

Hubertus von Bonin
Lieutenant Colonel Hubertus von Bonin was born in Potsdam, Brandenburg on August 3, 1911. His significant assignments included: Commander, 5th Squadron, 26th Fighter Wing "Schlageter" (*Jagdgeschwader 26 "Schlageter"*), June 28, 1939-December 24, 1939; Commander, 3rd Squadron, 88th Fighter Group [Spain] (*Jagdgruppe 88 [J/88]*), December 5, 1938-May 22, 1939; Commander, 1st Group, 26th Fighter Wing "Schlageter," January 1, 1940-May 9, 1940; Commander, 1st Group, 54th Fighter Wing "Green Hearts" (*Jagdgeschwader 54 "Grünherz"*), May 10, 1940-June 30, 1941; acting commander, 2nd Group, 51st Fighter Wing (*Jagdgeschwader 51*), July 11, 1941-August 8, 1941; Commander, 4th Fighter School (*Jagdfliegerschule 4*), July 11, 1941 October 1, 1941; Commander, 3rd Group, 52nd Fighter Wing (*Jagdgeschwader 52*), October 1, 1941-July 5, 1943; and Commodore, 54th Fighter Wing "Green Hearts," July 6, 1943-December 15,

1943. He was awarded the Knight's Cross of the Iron Cross on December 21, 1942. He also received the Spanish Cross in Gold with Swords. In addition, he won the German Cross in Gold on October 27, 1942. Major Hubertus von Bonin was killed in action over Gorodok, Russia on December 15, 1943 when his Focke-Wulf FW 190A-5 was shot down. He was buried at a German military cemetery at Orsha. Von Bonin was posthumously promoted to lieutenant colonel. Hubertus von Bonin scored 77 aerial victories, including 4 in Spain, 9 in the West and 64 over the Eastern Front. Hubertus von Bonin was one of three brothers who flew for the *Luftwaffe*. Jürgen Oskar von Bonin was killed in action as an observer in a transport wing, while Eckart-Wilhelm von Bonin, a Knight's Cross winner and night fighter, survived.[7]

Walter Bradel

Lieutenant Colonel Walter Bradel was born July 31, 1911 in Breslau-Carlowitz, Silesia. His significant assignments included: Commander, 9th Squadron, 2nd Bomber Wing "Wooden Hammer" (*Kampfgeschwader 2 "Holzhammer"*), September 12, 1940-December 1, 1941; Commander, 2nd Group, 2nd Bomber Wing, December 1, 1941-February 1, 1943; and Commander, 2nd Bomber Wing, January 23, 1943-May 5, 1943. He won the Knight's Cross of the Iron Cross on September 17, 1941. Bradel's promotions included: Major (*Major*), September 1, 1942; and Lieutenant Colonel (*Oberstleutnant*), May 1, 1943. Returning from a bombing mission against Norwich, England on May 5, 1943, his Dornier Do 217K-1 was shot down by an enemy long-range night fighter. The crew tried to make an emergency landing but crashed, killing Bradel, who was flying in the observer position. Walter Bradel is buried at the German Military Cemetery at Ysselsteyn, Netherlands (Block CX, Row 4, Grave 85).[8]

Bruno Bräuer

Lieutenant General Bruno Bräuer was born February 4, 1893 in Willmannsdorf in Silesia. He entered the Army in 1908 and became an infantryman. Bräuer served in World War I with the 155th West Prussian Infantry Regiment, winning the Iron Cross 2nd and 1st Class. He left the Army after the war and entered the Police, where he later became the commander of the 1st Battalion Land Police Group "General Göring," the forerunner of the *Luftwaffe's* Hermann Göring Regiment and later Hermann Göring Division. Bräuer became a paratrooper in 1936 and transferred to the *Luftwaffe*. His significant positions included: Commander, 4th Battalion, Regiment "General Göring," September 1, 1937-April 1, 1938; Commander, 1st Battalion, 1st Paratroop Regiment (*Fallschirmjäger-Regiment 1*), April 1, 1938-November 23, 1938; Commander, 1st Paratroop Regiment (*Fallschirmjäger-Regiment 1*), January 1, 1939-September 6, 1942; Commandant of Fortress Crete (*Kommandant der Festung Kreta*), February 23, 1943-June 1, 1944; and the Commander, 9th Paratroop Division (*9. Fallschirmjäger-Division*), March 2, 1945-April 18, 1945. His promotions included: Lieutenant Colonel (*Oberstleutnant*), January 1, 1938; Colonel (*Oberst*), January 1, 1939; Brigadier General (*Generalmajor*), September 1, 1941; Major General (*Generalleutnant*), September 6, 1942; and Lieutenant General (*General der Fallschirmjäger*), June 1, 1944. He received the Knight's Cross of the Iron Cross on May 24, 1940 and the German Cross in Gold on April 13, 1942. A Greek tribunal sentenced him to death on February 9, 1946 for war crimes on Crete. Bruno Bräuer was executed by a Greek firing squad at Athens-Xaidari, Greece at 5:00 a.m. on May 20, 1947. He is buried at the German Military Cemetery at Máleme, Crete (Block 3, Grave 851.)[9]

Helmut Bruck

Colonel Helmut Bruck was born February 16, 1913 in Kittliztreben/Bunzlau. He entered the *Luftwaffe* as an officer candidate on August 1, 1935 and attended flight school at Magdeburg. His significant assignments included: acting commander, 1st Group, 77th Stuka Wing (*Sturzkampfgeschwader 77*), August 20, 1940-1941; Commander, 1st Group, 77th Stuka Wing, 1941-February 19, 1943; Commodore, 77th Stuka Wing, February 20, 1943-October 18, 1943; Commodore, 77th Ground-Attack Wing (*Schlachtgeschwader 77*), October 18, 1943-December 7, 1944; and Commodore, 151st Ground-Attack wing (*Schlachtgeschwader 151*), December 7, 1944-March 31, 1945. Bruck won the Iron Cross 2nd Class on September 13, 1939, the Iron Cross 1st Class on May 21, 1940, the Knight's Cross of the Iron Cross on September 4, 1941 and the Oak Leaves to the Knight's Cross on December 20, 1943. He also received the German Cross in Gold on October 20, 1942. His promotions included: Captain (*Hauptmann*), April 1, 1941; Major (*Major*), March 1, 1943; Lieutenant Colonel (*Oberstleutnant*), November 1, 1943; and Colonel (*Oberst*), April 1, 1944. He flew 973 combat missions during the war. Helmut Bruck died on August 25, 2001 in Veitlahm/Mainleus near Kulmbach, Bavaria.[10]

Alfred Bülowius

Lieutenant General Alfred Bülowius was born on January 14, 1892 in Königsberg, East Prussia. He joined the Army in 1911 and served in World War I in the 41st Infantry Regiment before transferring to Bomber Wing 3, where he became a pilot. He left the Army in 1920 and briefly served in the Police before rejoining the Army in 1925. For the next nine years he served primarily in an air defense capacity; he transferred to the *Luftwaffe* on September 1, 1934. His significant positions included: Commodore, 1st Demonstration Wing (*Lehr-Geschwader 1*), November 17, 1939-June 18, 1940 and June 21, 1940-October 21, 1940; Higher Flight Training Commander 7, October 21, 1940-January 14, 1941; Higher Commander Bomber and Stuka Schools, Prague, January 15, 1941-August 1, 1942; Commander *Luftwaffe* Command Don, August 2, 1942-October 31, 1942; Commander, 1st Air Division (*1. Flieger-Division*), November 1, 1942-June 25, 1943; Commander, 2nd Air Corps (*II. Fliegerkorps*), June 26, 1943-June 30, 1944; Commander 2nd Fighter Corps (*II. Jagdkorps*), July 1, 1944-October 15, 1944; Commander, 16th Air District (*Befehlshaber Luftgau XVI*), October 16, 1944-January 21, 1945; Commander, 15th Air District (*Befehlshaber Luftgau XV*), January 22, 1945-February 3, 1945; and Commander, Staff Dresden in Air District 3, February 22, 1945-April 1945. His promotions included: Colonel (*Oberst*), January 1, 1939; Brigadier General (*Generalmajor*), June 1, 1941; Major General (*Generalleutnant*), March 1, 1943; and Lieutenant General (*General der Flieger*), December 1, 1944. Bülowius was shot down, wounded in action and captured by the French on June 18, 1940, but was repatriated two days later. He received the Knight's Cross of the Iron Cross on July 4, 1940 and the German Cross in Gold on December 21, 1942. Alfred Bülowius died on August 9, 1968 in Detmold, North Rhine-Westphalia. He is buried at the *Waldfriedhof Kupferberg* in Detmold (Section C, Grave 338).[11]

Eckhard Christian

Brigadier Eckhard Christian was born December 1, 1907 in Berlin-Charlottenburg, Brandenburg. He initially entered the German Navy on April 1, 1926, serving on several warships and specializing in torpedoes. Christian transferred to the *Luftwaffe* on October 1, 1934 with the grade of first lieutenant and received observer training before assuming duties as an aerial observer on the pocket battleship *Admiral Scheer*. His significant positions included: Operations Officer, 10th Air Corps (*X. Fliegerkorps*), March 8, 1940-June 2, 1940; Commander, 2nd Group, 26th Bomber Wing (*Kampfgeschwader 26*), August 21, 1940-January 14, 1941; General Staff Officer, Supreme Command (OKW), January 15, 1941-August 24, 1943; Operations Officer, *Luftwaffe* Operations Staff (*Ia des Luftwaffen-Führungsstabes*), August 25, 1943-August 31, 1944; Chief, *Luftwaffe* Operations Staff (*Chef des Luftwaffen-Führungsstabes*), September 1, 1944-April 22, 1945; and Liaison Officer from *Luftwaffe* High Command (OKL) to OKW Staff North, April 22, 1945-May 8, 1945. Christian received the German Cross in Silver on May 10, 1945. His promotions included: Major (*Major*), June 1, 1940; Lieutenant Colonel (*Oberstleutnant*), March 1, 1942; Colonel (*Oberst*), March 1, 1943; and Brigadier General (*Generalmajor*), September 1, 1944. He received the German Cross in Silver at the end of the war. Eckhard Christian married Gerda Daranowsky, one of Adolf Hitler's secretaries, in 1943, but they later divorced.[12] Eckhard Christian died on January 3, 1985 in Bad Kreuznach, Rhineland-Pfalz. He is buried at Bad Munster am Stein-Ebernburg, *Friedhof Ebernburg* (Section 8, Grave 20).[13]

Walter Dahl

Colonel Walter Dahl was born on March 27, 1916 at Lug in the Bergzabern region of Rhineland-Pfalz. He joined the Army in 1935, initially serving in the infantry before transferring to the *Luftwaffe* and becoming a pilot. Dahl became a flight instructor in 1939; in May 1941, he transferred to the 3rd Fighter Wing (*Jagdgeschwader 3*). His key positions included: Commander, 4th Squadron, 3rd Fighter Wing "Udet" (*Jagdgeschwader 3 "Udet"*), February 13, 1942-April 9, 1942; Commander, 1st Squadron, Supplemental Group, 3rd Fighter Wing "Udet" (*Ergänzungsgruppe, Jagdgeschwader 3 "Udet"*), April 10, 1942; staff, General of Fighters, April 1943-July 20, 1943; Commander, 3rd Group, 3rd Fighter Wing "Udet," July 20, 1943-May 21, 1944; Commodore, 300th Fighter Wing (*Jagdgeschwader 300*), June 27, 1944-December 1944; and Inspector of Day Fighters, January 26, 1945-May 1, 1945. Dahl received the *Luftwaffe* Honor Goblet on December 23, 1941 and German Cross in Gold on December 2, 1942. He was awarded the Knight's Cross of the Iron Cross on March 11, 1944 and the Oak Leaves to the Knight's Cross on February 1, 1945. Colonel Dahl ended the war flying Me 262 jet fighters with the 3rd Group, 2nd Supplemental Fighter Wing. He crashed-landed his Messerschmitt Me 109F-2 on June 24, 1941 and was seriously injured. Walter Dahl shot down 128 enemy aircraft – his first on the opening day of the invasion of Russia in 1941 – in 678 missions, of which about 300 were ground-attack missions. He claimed 30 four-engine bombers and 34 Il-2 Sturmoviks; he achieved a minimum of 2 victories flying the Me 262. Walter Dahl survived the war and died on November 25, 1985 in Heidelberg, Baden-Württemberg, at age 69. He is buried at the *Bergfriedhof* in Heidelberg (Section T, Grave 6).[14]

Karl-Egon von Dalwigk zu Lichtenfels
Captain Karl-Egon von Dalwigk zu Lichtenfels was born March 26, 1915. His significant wartime assignments included: Commander, 16th Squadron, 2nd Bomber Wing "Wooden Hammer" (*Kampfgeschwader 2 "Holzhammer"*), September 5, 1943-January 21, 1944; Commander, 5th Group, 2nd Bomber Wing "Wooden Hammer," January 21, 1944-February 6, 1944; and Commander, 2nd Group, 51st Bomber Wing "Edelweiss" (*Kampfgeschwader 51 "Edelweiss"*), 1944. He was promoted to captain on April 1, 1942.[15]

Bruno Dilley
Major Bruno Dilley was born August 29, 1913 in Gumbinnen, East Prussia. He transferred from the Police to the *Luftwaffe* in 1935 as a second lieutenant. It could be argued that Major Bruno Dilley started World War II – or at least fired its first shots. At 4:34 a.m. on September 1, 1939 Second Lieutenant Bruno Dilley led three Junkers Ju-87B Stuka dive bombers of the 3rd Squadron, 1st Stuka Wing (*Sturzkampfgeschwader 1*), in an attack against the Dirschau Bridge over the Vistula River to destroy the ignition cables for the Polish explosive charges designed to cripple the structure. The German invasion of Poland, the first act of World War II, began six minutes later. His significant operational assignments included: Commander, 1st Stuka School at Wertheim (*Sturzkampffliegerschule 1*), September 1, 1941-October 16, 1941; Commander, 1st Group, 2nd Stuka Wing "Immelmann" (*Stukageschwader 2 "Immelmann"*), October 16, 1941-January 4, 1942; Commodore, 101st Stuka Wing (*Sturzkampfgeschwader 101*), September 1, 1943-October 18, 1943; Commodore, 103rd Ground-Attack Wing (*Schlachtgeschwader 103*), October 18, 1943-October 1943; and Commander, Ground-Attack School – Metz (*Schlachtfliegerschule Metz*), October 1, 1943-1944. He won the Knight's Cross of the Iron Cross on June 4, 1942 and the Oak Leaves to the Knight's Cross on January 12, 1943. He was promoted to Major (*Major*) on September 1, 1943. On April 6, 1941, Dilley was shot down in his Ju-87 over Macedonia during the invasion of Yugoslavia, but he survived and returned to his unit. Dilley joined the *Bundeswehr* in 1956. Bruno Dilley died on August 31, 1968 in Reutlingen, Baden-Württemberg.[16]

Kurt-Bertram von Döring
Brigadier General Kurt-Bertram von Döring was born in Ribbekardt, Silesia on February 18, 1889. He entered the Army in March 1907 and served in World War I as a fledgling fighter pilot. Von Döring left the Army in 1920; from 1923 to 1929 he served as an advisor to the Argentinean and Peruvian air forces. He joined the German *Luftwaffe* on June 1, 1934. Von Döring's most important assignments included: Commander, 1st Group, 132nd Fighter Wing "Richthofen" (*Jagdgeschwader 132 "Richthofen"*), April 1, 1935-April 1, 1936; Commodore, 134th Fighter Wing "Horst Wessel" (*Jagdgeschwader 134 "Horst Wessel"*), April 20, 1936-May 1, 1939; Commodore, 26th Destroyer Wing "Horst Wessel" (*Zerstörergeschwader 26 "Horst Wessel"*), May 1, 1939-December 15, 1939; 2nd Fighter Commander (*Jagdfliegerführer 2*), December 15, 1939-December 1, 1940; Inspector of Fighters, December 19, 1940-August 5, 1941; Fighter Commander Center (*Jagdfliegerführer Mitte*), August 9, 1941-January 31, 1942; Commander, 1st Night Fighter Division (*Nachtjagdgeschwader 1*), February 1, 1942-April 30, 1942; Commander, 1st Fighter Division (*1. Jagd-Division*), May 1, 1942-October 14, 1943; and Commander, 3rd Fighter Division (*3. Jagd-Division*), October 15, 1943-November 9, 1943. He ended the war working in the Air Ministry in Berlin. Just before the invasion of France in 1940, friendly fighters of the 51st Fighter Wing mistakenly shot down von Döring's aircraft, but he was not seriously injured. Von Döring was captured in May 1945 and released from prisoner of war status in 1947. His promotions included: Lieutenant Colonel (*Oberstleutnant*), January 1, 1936; Colonel (*Oberst*), April 1, 1938; Brigadier General (*Generalmajor*), July 19, 1940; and Major General (*Generalleutnant*), November 1, 1941. He received the German Cross in Gold on December 1, 1942. Kurt von Döring died on July 9, 1960 at Kloster Medingen, Saxony.[17]

Walter Ehle
Major Walter Ehle was born April 28, 1912 in Windhuk, German Southwest Africa. He served in the Condor Legion in Spain, winning the Spanish Cross in Gold with Swords. At the beginning of World War II, Ehle was serving as the Commander, 3rd Squadron, 1st Destroyer Wing (*Zerstörergeschwader*

1). His key assignments included: Commander, 2nd Group, 1st Night Fighter Wing (*Nachtjagdgeschwader 1*), October 6, 1940-November 17, 1943. He was killed when his Messerschmitt Me 110G-4 crashed, due to faulty landing lights during the approach to the airfield at Horpmoel, Belgium on November 11, 1943. He received the German Cross in Gold on November 9, 1942 and the Knight's Cross of the Iron Cross on August 29, 1943. He is buried at the German Military Cemetery at Lommel, Belgium (Block 21, Grave 42). Ehle totaled 39 aerial victories, of which 35 were at night.[18]

Wolfgang Falck
Colonel Wolfgang "Wolf" Falck was born on August 19, 1910 at Berlin, Brandenburg. His flying and military career began as a member of the *Reichswehr* in April 1931 when he was selected for training at the clandestine flight school at Schleissheim and later, on Russian territory at Lipezk, south of Moscow. He began his flight training in April 1932. When he came back to Germany, he attended the Infantry School at Dresden for officer training. His significant positions included: Commander, 5th Squadron, 132nd Fighter Wing "Richthofen" (*Jagdgeschwader 132 "Richthofen"*), April 1, 1936-July 1, 1938; Commander, 8th Squadron, 132nd Fighter Wing, July 1, 1938-November 1, 1938; Commander, 5th Squadron, 141st Destroyer Wing (*Zerstörergeschwader 141*), November 1, 1938-April 30, 1939; Commander, 1st Squadron, 76th Destroyer Wing (*Zerstörergeschwader 76*), May 1, 1939-August 31, 1939; Commander, 1st Group, 1st Destroyer Wing (*Zerstörergeschwader 1*), February 19, 1940-June 26, 1940; Commodore, 1st Night Fighter Wing (*Nachtjagdgeschwader 1*), June 26, 1940-July 1, 1943; *Luftwaffe* Operations Staff (*Luftwaffenführungsstab*), July 1, 1943-1943); Operations Officer, *Luftwaffe* Commander Center/*Reich* (*Luftwaffenbefehlshaber Mitte/Reich*), 1943-February 3, 1944; Fighter Commander Balkans (*Jagdfliegerführer Balkan*), 1944; and Commander, *Luftwaffe* training schools, 1944-May 8, 1945. His promotions included: Second Lieutenant (*Leutnant*), October 1, 1934; First Lieutenant (*Oberleutnant*), April 1, 1936; Major (*Major*), July 1, 1940; Lieutenant Colonel (*Oberstleutnant*), January 1, 1943; and Colonel (*Oberst*), July 1, 1943. He received the Knight's Cross of the Iron Cross on October 7, 1940. Post-war, Falck undertook a variety of jobs, attended night school and studied business. In 1961, he was approached by North American Aviation to undertake aviation consultancy work, and in 1966, he joined McDonnell Douglas. On retirement from business in 1986, he lived in St. Ulrich in Austria. Wolfgang Falck flew a minimum of 90 combat missions and shot down seven enemy aircraft.[19]

Oswald Finzel
Captain Oswald Finzel's significant assignments included: Commander, 1st Battalion, 6th Paratroop Regiment (*Fallschirmjäger-Regiment 6*), September 1, 1943-January 1, 1944; Commander, 2nd Battalion, 6th Paratroop Regiment (*Fallschirmjäger-Regiment 6*), January 1, 1944-March 1, 1944; and Commander, 1st Battalion, 2nd Paratroop Regiment (*Fallschirmjäger-Regiment 2*), August 1, 1944-October 1, 1944.[20]

Heinz Frank
Major Heinz "Allan" Frank was born December 12, 1914 in Arnstadt, Thuringia. He entered the *Luftwaffe* in 1934 and then joined the 20th Air Group (*Fliegergruppe 20*), which became the 2nd Group (Stuka), 2nd Demonstration Wing (*Lehrgeschwader 2*) on November 1, 1938. He won the Iron Cross 2nd Class on October 28, 1939, the Iron Cross 1st Class on June 27, 1940, the *Luftwaffe* Honor Goblet on December 22, 1940 and the German Cross in Gold on March 6, 1942. Frank won the Knight's Cross of the Iron Cross on September 3, 1942 as a first lieutenant for flying 500 combat missions. He received the Oak Leaves to the Knight's Cross, the 172nd recipient, on January 8, 1943 for flying his 700th combat mission. Frank's significant wartime assignments included: acting commander, 3rd Squadron, 1st Ground-Attack Wing (*Schlachtgeschwader 1*), January 1943-March 1, 1942; Commander, 3rd Squadron, 1st Ground-Attack Wing (*Schlachtgeschwader 1*), March 1, 1942-March 1943; Commander, Supplemental Ground-Attack Group (*Ergänzungs-Schlachtgruppe*), March 1943-May 31, 1943; acting commander, 2nd Group, 1st Stuka Wing (*Sturzkampfgeschwader 1*), September 24, 1943 October, 1943; Commander, 2nd Group, 2nd Ground-Attack Wing "Immelmann" (*Schlachtgeschwader 2 "Immelmann"*), October 15, 1943-July 1944; Commander, 4th Group, 152nd School Wing (*Schul-Geschwader 152*), July 1944-August 7, 1944; and Commander, 1st Group, 151st School Wing (*Schul-Geschwader 151*), August 7, 1944-October 7, 1944 the last two assignments with training units. He was promoted to Major (*Major*) on June 1, 1943. Frank died in a hospital in Yugoslavia on October 7, 1944 of complications following a shooting accident (His unit was involved in anti-partisan operations in Yugoslavia). Frank is buried in Arnstadt, Thuringia. During the war, Heinz Frank flew 900 combat missions and scored 8

aerial victories, flying Henschel Hs 123, Messerschmitt Me 109 and Focke-Wulf Fw 190 aircraft.[21]

Wilhelm von Friedberg

Colonel Wilhelm von Friedberg's significant assignments included: Commander, 2nd Group, 51st Bomber Wing "Edelweiss" (*Kampfgeschwader 51 "Edelweiss"*), June 22, 1941-April 1, 1942; acting commodore, 51st Bomber Wing "Edelweiss" (*Kampfgeschwader 51 "Edelweiss"*), July 4, 1942-November 30, 1942) acting commodore, 76th Bomber Wing (*Kampfgeschwader 76*), 1943; acting commodore, 1st Night Fighter Wing (*Nachtjagdgeschwader 1*), 1943; and Commander, Flying School C6, 1943. He was promoted to Lieutenant Colonel (*Oberstleutnant*) on January 1, 1943 and to Colonel (*Oberst*) on April 1, 1945. Not a pilot, von Friedberg won the Iron Cross 1st Class. He had won the Iron Cross 2nd Class in World War I.[22]

Kurt von Greiff

Colonel Kurt von Greiff's significant assignments included: Commander, 1st Squadron, 51st Bomber Wing "Edelweiss" (*Kampfgeschwader 51 "Edelweiss"*), 1940; Commander, 1st Group, 51st Bomber Wing "Edelweiss" (*Kampfgeschwader 51 "Edelweiss"*), August 12, 1940-February 14, 1941; Operations Officer [Ia Op 1], 3rd Air Fleet (*Luftflotte 3*), February 15, 1941-May 31, 1941; and Chief Operations Branch, *Luftwaffe* Operations Staff (*Luftwaffen-Führungsstabes*), September 4, 1944-April 28, 1945. He received the German Cross in Gold on January 6, 1943, while a major on the staff of *Luftwaffe* Command Don. He was promoted to Colonel (*Oberst*) on April 1, 1945.[23]

Alfred Grislawski

Captain Alfred Grislawski was born on November 2, 1919 at Wanne-Eickel/Ruhr. He entered the *Luftwaffe* on November 1, 1937. On May 30, 1942, he received the *Luftwaffe* Honor Goblet. Sergeant Grislawski won the Knight's Cross of the Iron Cross on July 1, 1942, after 40 aerial victories and became the 446th recipient of the Oak Leaves to the Knight's Cross on April 11, 1944. His significant assignments included: Commander, 1st Squadron, 1st Fighter Wing (*Jagdgeschwader 1*), November 6, 1943-January 24, 1944; Commander, 8th Squadron, 1st Fighter Wing, March 13, 1944-August 23, 1944; and Commander, 11th Squadron, 53rd Fighter Wing "Ace of Spades" (*Jagdgeschwader 53 "Pikas"*), August 24, 1944-September 26, 1944. His promotions included: Second Lieutenant (*Leutnant*), December 1, 1942; First Lieutenant (*Oberleutnant*), June 1, 1943; and Captain (*Hauptmann*), October 1, 1943. Grislawski was wounded in action at least three times during the war, the last on September 26, 1944, after which he spent the rest of the conflict in a hospital. During the war, he flew 800 combat missions and shot down 133 enemy aircraft, a sortie-to-victory ratio of 6.01 to 1. Twenty-four of his victories were in the West and included 18 four-engine bombers. Alfred Grislawski died on September 19, 2003 in Herne, North Rhine-Westphalia.[24]

Walter Hagen

Brigadier General Walter Hagen was born March 16, 1897 in Kiel, Schleswig-Holstein. He entered the Army in 1915 and served two years in the 13th Hussar Regiment before attending pilot training and subsequently serving in support of the Naval Infantry in Flanders. Shortly after the end of hostilities, Hagen left the Army and for many of the next fifteen years he served as a civilian pilot. On April 1, 1935, he entered the *Luftwaffe* with the grade of captain. His significant positions included: Commander, 1st Group (Stuka), *Trägergruppe 186* (the group scheduled for operations off the aircraft carrier *Graf Zeppelin*), September 1, 1939-July 1, 1940; Commodore, 1st Stuka Wing (*Stuka-Geschwader 1*), June 22, 1940-March 15, 1943; Air Commander 1, Africa (*Fliegerführer 1, Afrika*), February 1, 1943-March 30, 1943; Air Commander Albania (*Fliegerführer Albanien*), September 23, 1943-April 29, 1944; Air Commander Croatia (*Fliegerführer Kroatien*), April 29, 1944-August 29, 1944; Air Commander North Balkans (*Fliegerführer Nordbalkan*), August 29, 1944-January 31, 1945; and Commander, 17th Air Division (*17. Flieger-Division*), February 1, 1945-May 8, 1945. His promotions included: Lieutenant Colonel (*Oberstleutnant*), July 1, 1940; Colonel (*Oberst*), April 1, 1942; and Brigadier General (*Generalmajor*), July 1, 1944. Hagen was injured on March 30, 1943 in a plane crash. On July 21, 1940, he received the Knight's Cross of the Iron Cross and on February 17, 1942 he won the Oak Leaves to the Knight's Cross. Walter Hagen died in Kiel on November 24, 1963.[25]

Hans von Hahn

Major Hans von Hahn was born August 7, 1914 in Frankfurt, Hesse. He entered the German Navy as a sea cadet in 1934 and transferred to the *Luftwaffe* a year later. His key assignments included: Commander, 8th Squadron, 53rd Fighter Wing "Ace of Spades" (*Jagdgeschwader 53 "Pikas"*), September 18,

1939-August 20, 1940; Commander, 1st Group, 3rd Fighter Wing (*Jagdgeschwader 3*), August 27, 1940-January 15, 1942; Commander, 2nd Group, 1st Fighter Wing (*Jagdgeschwader 1*), January 15, 1942-June 20, 1942; and Commodore, 103rd Fighter Wing (School) (*Jagdgeschwader 103*), July 21, 1943-April 1945. He won the Knight's Cross of the Iron Cross on July 9, 1941. He was promoted to Major (*Major*) on November 1, 1942. Hans von Hahn died November 5, 1957 in Frankfurt. He flew over 300 combat missions and shot down 34 enemy aircraft, of which 15 were in the West.[26]

Richard Heidrich

Lieutenant General Richard Heidrich was born July 28, 1896 in Lawalde/Löbau, Saxony. He entered the Army on August 18, 1914 at the beginning of World War I. During that conflict, Heidrich won both the Iron Cross 2nd and 1st Class. Between the wars, Heidrich served in the infantry and was an instructor at the Infantry School in Dresden and the War Academy at Potsdam, before transferring to the *Luftwaffe* on January 1, 1939. His key *Luftwaffe* assignments included: Commander, 3rd Paratroop Regiment (*Fallschirmjäger-Regiment 3*), June 1, 1940-July 31, 1942; Commander, 7th Air Division (*7. Fliegerdivision*), August 1, 1942-April 30, 1943; Commander, 1st Paratroop Division (*1. Fallschirmjäger-Division*), May 1, 1943-November 16, 1944; and Commander, 1st Paratroop Corps (*I. Fallschirmkorps*), November 16, 1944-May 3, 1945. His promotions included: Lieutenant Colonel (*Oberstleutnant*), January 1, 1939; Colonel (*Oberst*), April 20, 1940; Brigadier General (*Generalmajor*), August 4, 1942; Major General (*Generalleutnant*), July 1, 1943; and Lieutenant General (*General der Fallschirmtruppe*), October 31, 1944. Heidrich won the 1939 Clasp to the Iron Cross 2nd Class on May 25, 1941 and the 1939 Clasp to the Iron Cross 1st Class the same day. He received the Knight's Cross of the Iron Cross on June 14, 1941 for actions during the airborne invasion of Crete and the Oak Leaves to the Knight's Cross on February 5, 1944. Richard Heidrich also received the Swords to the Oak Leaves (the 55th recipient) on March 25, 1944. He died on December 22, 1947 at Hamburg-Bahrenfeld.[27]

Ludwig Heilmann

Brigadier General Ludwig "King Ludwig" Heilmann was born August 9, 1903 in Würzburg, Bavaria. Too young to serve in World War I, he entered the Army on February 3, 1921 and stayed on active duty as a non-commissioned officer until February 3, 1933, when he retired. Seventeen months later, he was recalled to Army service, commissioned, and assigned to various infantry positions over the next six years, including attending airborne school in 1940. On August 1, 1940, he transferred to the *Luftwaffe*. His significant *Luftwaffe* assignments included: Commander, 3rd Battalion, 3rd Paratroop Regiment (*Fallschirmjäger-Regiment 3*), August 1, 1940-November 14, 1942; acting commander, 3rd Paratroop Regiment (*Fallschirmjäger-Regiment 3*), November 15, 1942-June 4, 1943; Commander, 3rd Paratroop Regiment, June 5, 1943-November 16, 1944; acting commander, 5th Paratroop Division (*5. Fallschirmjäger-Division*), November 17, 1944-December 21, 1944; and Commander, 5th Paratroop Division (*5. Fallschirmjäger-Division*), December 22, 1944-March 5, 1945. His promotions included: Major (*Major*), August 1, 1940; Lieutenant Colonel (*Oberstleutnant*), April 1, 1942; Colonel (*Oberst*), December 1, 1943; and Brigadier General (*Generalmajor*), December 22, 1944. Heilmann won the Iron Cross 2nd Class on October 2, 1939 and the Iron Cross 1st Class on June 14, 1941, the same day that he was awarded the Knight's Cross of the Iron Cross. He won the German Cross in Gold on February 26, 1942. On March 2, 1944, Heilmann received the Oak Leaves to the Knight's Cross and twenty-two days later, on March 25, 1944, he became the 67th recipient of the Swords to the Oak Leaves. He died on October 26, 1959 at Kempten, Bavaria. He was buried there, but in 1987 his grave was re-used for a newer occupant.[28]

Joachim Helbig

Colonel Joachim Helbig was born September 10, 1915 in Börln/Grimma, Saxony. He joined the German Army's 4th Artillery Regiment in 1935 and transferred to the *Luftwaffe* the following year. His key assignments included: Commander, 4th Squadron, 1st Demonstration Wing (*Lehrgeschwader 1*), June 1940-November 5, 1941; Commander, 1st Group (Bomber), 1st Demonstration Wing, November 5, 1941-January 24, 1943; and Commander, 1st Demonstration Wing, August 14, 1943-May 1, 1945. Helbig received the Iron Cross 2nd Class on September 16, 1939 and the Iron Cross 1st Class on June 20, 1940. On October 6, 1940, he won the *Luftwaffe* Honor Goblet and followed that by receiving the Knight's Cross of the Iron Cross on November 24, 1940. Helbig received the Oak Leaves to the Knight's Cross on January 16, 1942 and the Swords – as the 20th recipient – on September 28, 1942. He was promoted to Colonel (*Oberst*) on July 1, 1944. In September 1944, he was seriously wounded, when his staff car was strafed by enemy fighters in the Eifel. An independent officer, he ran afoul of Field Marshal Wolfram von Richthofen and Albert Kesselring during the war. After the war, he became the manager of a brewery in Berlin. Joachim Helbig died on October 5, 1985 in Malente, Spain in an auto accident.[29]

Hubertus Hitschhold
Brigadier General Hubertus Hitschhold was born July 7, 1912 in Kurwien, East Prussia. He joined the German Army on April 1, 1930 and spent four years in the 2nd Cavalry Regiment. Hitschhold then transferred as a second lieutenant to the *Luftwaffe* on October 1, 1934 and joined the 163rd Stuka Wing "Immelmann". (*Sturzkampfgeschwader 163 "Immelmann"*). His significant assignments included: Squadron Commander, 163rd Stuka Wing "Immelmann" (*Sturzkampfgeschwader 163 "Immelmann"*), October 1, 1936-May 1, 1939; Commander, 1st Group, 2nd Stuka Wing "Immelmann" (*Sturzkampfgeschwader 2 "Immelmann"*), May 1, 1939-October 15, 1941; Commander Stuka School 1 – Wertheim (*Stuka-Schule I*), October 16, 1941-June 17, 1942; Commodore, 1st Ground-Attack Wing (*Schlachtgeschwader 1*), June 18, 1942-June 25, 1943; Air Commander Sardinia (*Fliegerführer Sardinien*), June 26, 1943-November 11, 1943; and General of Ground-Attack Aviation (*General der Schlachtflieger*), November 12, 1943-May 8, 1945. Hitschhold's promotions included: Major (*Major*), July 1, 1940; Lieutenant Colonel (*Oberstleutnant*), February 1, 1943; Colonel (*Oberst*), July 1, 1943; and Brigadier General (*Generalmajor*), January 1, 1945. He received Iron Cross 2nd Class on September 15, 1939, the Iron Cross 1st Class on May 11, 1940, the Knight's Cross of the Iron Cross on July 21, 1940 and the Oak Leaves to the Knight's Cross (as the 57th recipient) on December 31, 1941. Hubertus Hitschhold died on March 10, 1966 in Söcking/Starnberg on Lake Starnberg in Bavaria.[30] He is buried at the Municipal Cemetery in Söcking (Grave 1037-1038).[31]

Dietrich Hrabak
Colonel Dietrich Hrabak was born December 19, 1914 in Gross Deuben/Leipzig, Saxony. He entered the German Navy in April 1934 and transferred to the *Luftwaffe* in November 1935 as an officer cadet. His *Luftwaffe* assignments included: Commander, 1st Squadron, 76th Fighter Wing (*Jagdgeschwader 76*), May 1, 1939-July 6, 1940; Commander, 4th Squadron, 54th Fighter Wing "Green Hearts" (*Jagdgeschwader 54 "Grünherz"*), July 6, 1940-August 5, 1940; Commander, 2nd Group, 54th Fighter Wing, August 5, 1940-November 1, 1942; Commodore, 52nd Fighter Wing (*Jagdgeschwader 52*), November 1, 1942-October 1, 1944; and Commodore, 54th Fighter Wing, October 1, 1944-May 8, 1945. He won the Knight's Cross of the Iron Cross on October 21, 1940 and the Oak Leaves to the Knight's Cross on November 25, 1943. He also received the *Luftwaffe* Honor Goblet on September 28, 1940 and the German Cross in Gold on July 10, 1944. He was promoted to Colonel (*Oberst*) on September 1, 1944. During the war, Dietrich Hrabak flew over 1,000 combat missions and shot down 125 enemy aircraft; 16 victories occurred in the West. Dietrich Hrabak died September 15, 1995 in Pfaffenhofen, Bavaria.[32] He is buried in Fürstenfeldbruck, Bavaria, at the Fürstenfeldbruck *Waldfriedhof* (Section 4, Grave 202).[33]

Joachim-Friedrich Huth
Brigadier General Joachim-Friedrich Huth was born on July 31, 1896 in Neuhof/Salzwedel in Saxony. He entered the Army on July 13, 1914 and served as an infantry platoon leader and company commander before becoming a fighter pilot. In this role, he served in the 14th Fighter Squadron before being seriously wounded on March 23, 1918 – he would spend more than a year in a hospital and would have a leg amputated. Huth left the Army in 1920, after serving in *Freikorps Küttner*.[34] He joined the *Luftwaffe* on March 1, 1934. His assignments included: Commander, 2nd Group, 132nd Fighter Wing "Richthofen" (*Jagdgeschwader 132 "Richthofen"*), August 1, 1938-October 31, 1938; Commander, 1st Group, 1st Destroyer Wing (*Zerstörergeschwader 1*), November 1, 1938-December 14, 1939; Commodore, 26th Destroyer Wing "Horst Wessel" (*Zerstörergeschwader 26 "Horst Wessel"*), December 14, 1939-November 1, 1940; Commander, 2nd Destroyer School, Memmingen (*Zerstörer-Schule 2*), November 2, 1940-July 31, 1941; 2nd Fighter Commander (*Jagdfliegerführer 2*), August 1, 1941-August 16, 1942; acting commander, 4th Fighter Division (*4. Jagd-Division*), August 17, 1942-August 14, 1943; Commander, 4th Fighter Division (*4. Jagd-Division*), August 14, 1943-November 10, 1943; Commander 5th Fighter Division (*5. Jagd-Division*), November 11, 1943-February 5, 1944; Commander, 7th Fighter Division (*7. Jagd-Division*), February 6, 1944-November 30, 1944; acting commander, 2nd Fighter Corps (*II. Jagd-Korps*), November 30, 1944-January 26, 1945; and Commander, 2nd Fighter Corps, January 26, 1945-May 8, 1945. He was awarded the Knight's Cross of the Iron Cross on September 11, 1940. Huth's significant promotions included: Lieutenant Colonel (*Oberstleutnant*), January 1, 1939; Colonel (*Oberst*), November 1, 1940;

Brigadier General (*Generalmajor*), April 1, 1943; and Major General (*Generalleutnant*), July 1, 1944. After the war, Huth joined the new German air force in 1956 and rose to the grade of major general. Joachim-Friedrich Huth died at Koblenz, Rhineland-Pfalz on March 27, 1962.[35]

Max-Josef Ibel
Brigadier General Max-Josef Ibel was born January 2, 1896 in Munich, Bavaria. Ibel entered the Army on July 5, 1915 and served in various engineer units during the war, to include a flamethrower regiment. He retired from the Army as a first lieutenant in 1928 (to train at Lipezk, Russia), but was reactivated in 1931. He joined the *Luftwaffe* on April 1, 1934. His significant *Luftwaffe* assignments included: Commander, 1st Group, 135th Fighter Wing (*Jagdgeschwader 135*), March 1, 1937-October 31, 1938; Commodore, 231st (later 3rd) Fighter Wing (*Jagdgeschwader 231/3*), November 7, 1938-September 26, 1939; Commodore, 27th Fighter Wing (*Jagdgeschwader 27*), September 27, 1939-October 12, 1940; Commander, 4th Fighter School, Fürth (*Jagdfliegerschule 4*), October 13, 1940-June 5, 1941; 3rd Fighter Commander (*Jagdfliegerführer 3*), June 6, 1941-November 30, 1942; Higher Fighter Commander West (*Höherer Jagdfliegerführer West*), December 1, 1942-September 14, 1943; and Commander, 2nd Fighter Division (*2. Jagd-Division*), October 1, 1943-December 31, 1944. His promotions included: Lieutenant Colonel (*Oberstleutnant*), June 1, 1938; Colonel (*Oberst*), July 21, 1940; and Brigadier General (*Generalmajor*), January 1, 1944. He received the Knight's Cross of the Iron Cross on August 22, 1940. Ibel was in charge of the Fighter Control Board on the battlecruiser *Scharnhorst* during "Operation Cerberus," the surprise dash up the English Channel by three major warships of the *Kriegsmarine* – the *Scharnhorst*, *Gneisenau* and heavy cruiser *Prinz Eugen* – February 11-13, 1942. He joined the new German air force in 1957 and rose to the grade of brigadier general. Max-Josef Ibel died on March 19, 1981 at Rheinbach, North Rhine-Westphalia. He is buried at the *Waldfriedhof* (Old Section) in Munich (Section 96, Row W, Grave 40).[36]

Wilhelm Kaiser
Captain Wilhelm Kaiser was born November 30, 1914 in Pockau/Marienberg, Saxony. Nicknamed "His Majesty," he entered the *Luftwaffe* on October 1, 1935 and after attending several flight schools joined the 7th Squadron, 50th Air Group (*Fliegergruppe 50*), which later became the 7th Squadron, 2nd Stuka Wing "Immelmann" (*Sturzkampfgeschwader 2* "*Immelmann*"). During the 1941 Balkan campaign, Kaiser flew as the adjutant for the 3rd Group. In Russia, he flew defensive support missions near Kalinin. From May 1, 1942 to April 1, 1943, Kaiser served as a flight instructor in Austria and Italy, received General Staff training and later served in several staff positions. He received the Knight's Cross of the Iron Cross on February 4, 1942, after flying 130 combat missions. He also won the German Cross in Gold on January 19, 1942. His promotions included: First Lieutenant (*Oberleutnant*), June 1, 1940; and Captain (*Hauptmann*), April 1, 1942. During his career, he flew 180 combat missions in Poland, France, England, the Balkans and Russia. He was shot down on May 22, 1941 over the Mediterranean, and although his gunner was killed, Kaiser was rescued from the sea. Wilhelm Kaiser died on September 24, 1993 in Niedernhausen, Hesse.[37]

Alfred Keller
Colonel General Alfred Keller was born on September 19, 1882 in Bochum, Westphalia. He entered the Army on April 5, 1902. During World War I, he was awarded the *Pour le Mérite* on December 4, 1917 for service as a flyer and the commander of the 1st Bomber Wing (and got his nickname of "Bomben-Keller"). During his tenure, the unit conducted a major raid against Paris on the night of January 30-31, 1918 that caused widespread panic. He left the service in 1920 and pursued several civilian aviation endeavors before returning to the Army on January 1, 1934. One month later, he transferred to the *Luftwaffe*. Keller's significant positions included: Commodore, 154th Bomber Wing "Boelcke" (*Kampfgeschwader 154 "Boelcke"*), July 1, 1934-March 31, 1935; acting commander, 1st Air District (*Luftkreis I*), November 1, 1937-December 31, 1937; Commander 2nd Air District (*Luftkreis II*), January 1, 1938-July 31, 1938; Commander, *Luftwaffe* Command East Prussia (*Luftwaffen-Kommandos Ostpreussen*), August 1, 1938-January 31, 1939; Commander, 4th Air Division (*4. Flieger-Division*), February 1, 1939-October 2, 1939; Commander, 4th Air Corps (*IV. Fliegerkorps*), October 3, 1939-August 19, 1940; Commander, 1st Air Fleet (*Luftflotte 1*), August 20, 1940 June 25, 1943; and finally Commander, National Socialist Flying Corps (*Nationalsozialistischen Fliegerkorps* [NSFK]), June 26, 1943-May 8, 1945.[38] His promotions included: Colonel (*Oberst*), January 1, 1934; Brigadier General (*Generalmajor*), April 1, 1936; Major General (*Generalleutnant*), February 1, 1938; Lieutenant General (*General der Flieger*), April 1, 1939; and Colonel General (*Generaloberst*), July 19, 1940.

He received the Knight's Cross of the Iron Cross on June 24, 1940. He also was awarded the *Luftwaffe* Combined Pilots and Observer Badge in Gold with Diamonds. Alfred Keller died on February 11, 1974 in Berlin.[39]

Albert Kesselring
Field Marshal Albert Kesselring was born November 30, 1885 in Marksteft bei Kitzingen in Lower Franconia, Bavaria. He entered the Army in 1904 and became a field artilleryman. During World War I, he served in the 2nd Bavarian Field Artillery Regiment before being detailed to the General Staff. Kesselring was one of the small number of officers to remain in the *Reichswehr* after the war. After numerous command and staff positions, he transferred to the *Luftwaffe* in 1933. Among his significant positions were: Commander 1st Air Fleet (*Luftflotte 1*), February 1, 1939-January 11, 1940; Commander 2nd Air Fleet (*Luftflotte 2*), January 12, 1940-June 26, 1943; Commander-in-Chief South (*Oberbefehlshaber Süd*), January 10, 1942-February 28, 1943 and May 2, 1945-May 8, 1945; Commander-in-Chief Southwest (*Oberbefehlshaber Südwest*), June 26, 1943-March 9, 1945; Commander-in-Chief Army Group C (*Oberbefehlshaber der Heeresgruppe C*), July 26, 1943-October 23, 1944 and January 15, 1945-March 9, 1945; and Commander-in-Chief West (*Oberbefehlshaber West*), March 10, 1945-May 1, 1945. His promotions included: Brigadier General (*Generalmajor*), October 10, 1934; Major General (*Generalleutnant*), April 1, 1936; Lieutenant General (*General der Flieger*), June 1, 1937; Colonel General (skipped this grade); and Field Marshal (*Generalfeldmarschall*), July 19, 1940. During the Battle of Britain, Kesselring's 2nd Air Fleet was responsible for the bombing of southeast England and the London area. Kesselring fractured his skull in a vehicle accident on October 23, 1944 and spent three months in a hospital. He received the Knight's Cross of the Iron Cross on September 30, 1939, the Oak Leaves on February 25, 1942, the Swords on July 18, 1942 and the Diamonds on July 19, 1944. On March 14, 1940, Kesselring ordered a massive air raid on Rotterdam that killed 980 civilians, and made 70,000 homeless. Sentenced to death and then to 20 years imprisonment for war crimes in 1947, he was released from prison in 1952 due to ill health. He published his memoirs the following year. Albert Kesselring died July 15, 1960 in Bad Nauheim, Hesse.[40] He is buried at the *Stadtfriedhof* in Bad Wiessee, Bavaria.

Ullrich Kessler
Lieutenant General Ullrich Kessler was born November 3, 1894 in Danzig-Langfuhr. He joined the German Navy on April 1, 1914, and in the last year of World War I, received naval aviation training before postings to naval air stations at Helgoland, Zeebrügge and Norderney. He remained in the Navy until September 1, 1933, when he transferred to the *Luftwaffe*. His *Luftwaffe* assignments included: Commodore, 1st Bomber Wing "Hindenburg" (*Kampfgeschwader 1 "Hindenburg"*), November 15, 1939-December 19, 1939; Chief of Staff, 1st Air Fleet (*Luftflotte 1*), January 1, 1940-April 30, 1940; Chief of Staff, 10th Air Corps and Air Commander Drontheim (*X. Fliegerkorps, Fliegerführer Drontheim*), May 1, 1940-June 27, 1940; Chief of Staff for Training (*Chef des Stabes des Ausbildungswesen*), June 28, 1940-February 5, 1942; Air Commander Atlantic (*Fliegerführer Atlantik*), February 5, 1942-March 15, 1944; and *Luftwaffe* Air Attaché to Japan, March 16, 1944-May 15, 1945. He received the Knight's Cross of the Iron Cross on April 8, 1944. He also won the German Cross in Gold on February 16, 1944. His promotions included: Colonel (*Oberst*), April 1, 1937; Brigadier General (*Generalmajor*), April 1, 1939; Major General (*Generalleutnant*), April 1, 1941; and Lieutenant General (*General der Flieger*), September 1, 1944. After the capitulation of Germany, Kessler returned from Japan aboard the U-234 submarine; he surrendered and remained a prisoner of war until mid-1947.[41] In later years, he retired to live in Metzingen; Ullrich Kessler died on March 27, 1983 in Bad Urach.

Hans von Koppelow
Colonel von Koppelow's significant assignments included: Supply Officer [Ib], 5th Air Corps (*V. Flieger-Korps*), October 7, 1940-January 15, 1942; Commander, 3rd Group, 2nd Bomber Wing (*Kampfgeschwader 2*), February 16, 1942-April 30, 1942; Commodore, 2nd Bomber Wing (*Kampfgeschwader 2*), May 1, 1942-January 22, 1943; and Supply Officer [*Oberquartiermeister*], 4th Air Fleet (*Luftflotte 4*), September 6, 1943-April 1945. He received the German Cross in Gold on February 19, 1943. Hans von Koppelow was promoted to Colonel (*Oberst*) on February 1, 1943. He survived the war.[42]

Helmut Leicht
Major Helmut Leicht was born November 2, 1916 in Ludwigsburg, Württemberg. He entered the *Luftwaffe* on April 6, 1936, undergoing officer training at Air War School

at Berlin-Gatow. On July 1, 1938, he reported to the 1st Group, 165th Stuka Wing (*Sturzkampfgeschwader 165*), which was redesignated the 1st Group, 77th Stuka Wing (*Sturzkampfgeschwader 77*) on May 15, 1939. His significant wartime assignments included: Squadron Commander, Supplemental Squadron, 77th Stuka Wing (*Ergänzungsstaffel*), February 6, 1941-June 27, 1941; Commander, 2nd Squadron, 77th Stuka Wing (January 3, 1942-January 10, 1943), acting commander, 1st Group, 77th Stuka Wing, January 11, 1943-April 22, 1943; acting commander, 2nd Group, 77th Stuka Wing, April 23, 1943-October 1, 1943; Commander 2nd Group, 77th Stuka Wing, October 1, 1943-November 9, 1943; and Commander, 3rd Group, 10th Ground-Attack Wing (*Schlachtgeschwader 10*), May 5, 1944-June 26, 1944. His promotions included: Major (*Major*), October 1, 1943. First Lieutenant Helmut Leicht won the Knight's Cross of the Iron Cross on September 3, 1942 after flying 400 combat missions. He also won the German Cross in Gold on July 10, 1942. He was seriously wounded in action on June 28, 1941 and September 9, 1943. On June 26, 1944, his Focke-Wulf Fw 190 was shot down during a ground-attack against a Russian column 12 miles southeast of Vitebsk during the Soviet attack against Army Group Center, and Helmut Leicht was posted missing in action. He was never seen again. On October 24, 1944, Helmut Leicht posthumously became the 631st recipient of the Oak Leaves to the Knight's Cross.[43]

Helmut Lent
Colonel Helmut "Bubi" Lent was born on June 13, 1918 at Pyrehne in the Landsberg region of Warthe/Neumark. He joined the *Luftwaffe* on April 1, 1936 as an officer candidate. He began his military training at the Air War School at Berlin-Gatow, but this was interrupted when he was involved in a motor vehicle accident in which he broke his right leg. From March 1, 1938, Second Lieutenant Lent attended the bomber school at Tutow, receiving training as an observer, but once again was involved in a motor vehicle accident in late June, which resulted in a broken jaw and three weeks in a hospital. His first operational assignment was with the 76th Destroyer Wing (*Zerstörergeschwader 76*). His significant wartime assignments included: Commander, 4th Squadron, 1st Night Fighter Wing (*Nachtjagdgeschwader 1*), July 1, 1941-November 1, 1941; Commander, 2nd Group, 2nd Night Fighter Wing (*Nachtjagdgeschwader 2*), November 1, 1941-October 1, 1942; Commander, 4th Group, 1st Night Fighter Wing, October 1, 1942-August 1, 1943; and Commodore, 3rd Night Fighter Wing (*Nachtjagdgeschwader 3*), August 1, 1943-October 7, 1944. His promotions included: Second Lieutenant (*Leutnant*), March 1, 1937; First Lieutenant (*Oberleutnant*), July 1, 1940; Captain (*Hauptmann*), January 1, 1942; Major (*Major*), January 1, 1943; and Lieutenant Colonel (*Oberstleutnant*), March 1, 1944. Helmut Lent received the Knight's Cross of the Iron Cross on August 30, 1941 and the Oak Leaves (98th recipient) to the Knight's Cross on June 6, 1942. He received the Swords (32nd recipient) to the Oak Leaves on August 2, 1943 and the Diamonds on July 31, 1944 (the 15th recipient). He also won the Narvik Shield, the Operational Flying Clasp for Fighters in Gold, the Operational Flying Clasp for Night Fighters in Gold, the *Luftwaffe* Honor Goblet and the Silver Wound Badge. During the war, Lent was wounded in combat with a British Stirling bomber on the night of October 2-3, 1943. These serious wounds to his left thumb and index finger, as well as superficial injuries to his face, kept him from combat duty until November. He was renowned as an expert marksman. On the night of March 22-23, 1944, Lent downed three RAF Lancaster four-engine bombers using just 22 rounds of ammunition. When he reached his 100th night victory on the night of June 15-16, 1944, he downed three Lancaster bombers in seven minutes using just 57 rounds of ammunition. On October 5, 1944, Lent was attempting to land his Junkers Ju 88G-6 at Paderborn, when an engine failed and the plane's wing hit a power cable. He initially survived the crash, which killed three others aboard. With both legs broken, two days later doctors – fearing gangrene – amputated one of his legs, but he succumbed during the operation in a Paderborn hospital. He received a posthumous promotion to Colonel (*Oberst*). Helmut Lent is credited with 110 victories, including 103 at night, of which 59 were four-engine bombers and one De Haviland Mosquito. He is buried in Stade, Lower Saxony, at the *Alter Garnisonsfriedhof*, in an endgrave.[44]

Ernst Liebach
Colonel Ernst Liebach's significant assignments included: Commander, 1st Paratroop Engineer Battalion (*Fallschirm-Pionier-Bataillon 1*), November 26, 1940-January 1, 1943; acting commander, 6th Paratroop Regiment (*Fallschirmjäger-Regiment 6*), 1943; and Commander, 8th Paratroop Regiment (*Fallschirmjäger-Regiment 8*), June 15, 1944-December 15, 1944 and January 17, 1945-April 1945. He was reported killed in action.[45]

Bruno Loerzer
Colonel General Bruno Loerzer was born January 22, 1891 in Berlin, Brandenburg. Entering the Army in 1911, he subsequently attended pilot training during World War I, later serving in the 26th Fighter Squadron (*Jagdstaffel 26*) and as the commander of the 3rd Fighter Wing (*Jagdgeschwader 3*). A close friend of fellow aviator Hermann Göring (at Verdun, Loerzer flew a reconnaissance plane, while Göring sat in the rear as the observer), Loerzer shot down 44 aircraft and received the *Pour le Mérite*. During the 1920s, he was active in civil aviation and helped form the Lithuanian Air Force. Always well-connected (his brother was a *Gauleiter* of Braunschweig), he assumed duties as the President of the German Air Sports League in 1933 and the National Air Sport Leader in 1935. He rejoined the *Luftwaffe* in 1935 and rose to become: Commodore, 53rd Fighter Wing (*Jagdgeschwader 53*), July 15, 1937-March 31, 1938; Inspector of Fighters, April 1, 1938-January 31, 1939; Commander of the 2nd Air Division (*2. Flieger-Division*), February 1, 1939-October 10, 1939; Commander of the 2nd Air Corps (*II. Fliegerkorps*), October 25, 1939-February 22, 1943; and the Chief of the *Luftwaffe* Personnel Department (*Chef des Luftwaffen-Personalamts*), February 23, 1943-December 20, 1944), before going on the *Führer* Reserve list. His promotions included: Brigadier General (*Generalmajor*), April 1, 1938; Major General (*Generalleutnant*), January 1, 1940; Lieutenant General (*General der Flieger*), July 19, 1940; and Colonel General (*Generaloberst*), February 16, 1943. He received the Knight's Cross of the Iron Cross on May 29, 1940. Bruno Loerzer died in Hamburg on August 22, 1960.[46]

Günther Lützow
Colonel Günther "Franzl" Lützow was born on September 4, 1912 in Kiel, Schleswig-Holstein. He began his flight training at a young age, before transferring from the Army to the *Luftwaffe* as a second lieutenant of infantry in 1934. He began his fighter career in the *Luftwaffe* with the 1st Group, 132nd Fighter Wing "Richthofen" (*Jagdgeschwader 132 "Richthofen"*). Lützow's significant assignments included: Commander, 2nd Squadron, 88th Fighter Group [Spain] (*Jagdgruppe 88* [J/88]), March 19, 1937-September 6, 1937; Commander, 1st Group, 3rd Fighter Wing (*Jagdgeschwader 3*), November 3, 1939-August 21, 1940; Commodore, 3rd Fighter Wing "Udet" (*Jagdgeschwader 3 "Udet"*), August 21, 1940-August 11, 1942; acting commodore, 51st Fighter Wing [dual-hatted due to injury of actual commander] (*Jagdgeschwader 51*), September 1941-November 8, 1941; Inspector of Fighters West, August 11, 1942-November 1942; Commander, 1st Fighter Division (*1. Jagddivision*), November 1942-January 1944; and Commander, 4th Fighter School Division (*4. Fliegerschuldivision*), January 1944-January 1945. He won the Spanish Cross in Gold with Diamonds. Lützow also won the Knight's Cross of the Iron Cross on September 18, 1940 and the Oak Leaves to the Knight's Cross on July 20, 1941. On October 11, 1941, he became the 4th recipient of the Swords to the Oak Leaves. Lützow became known as a principal architect behind the "Fighter Pilots' Mutiny," an attempt to reinstate Adolf Galland, who had been dismissed as *General der Jagdflieger* for his outspokenness against the *Luftwaffe* high command and Göring himself. Göring relieved Lützow of his command of the *4. Fliegerschuldivision* and had him posted to Italy to take over as Fighter Command Upper Italy (*Jagdfliegerführer Oberitalien*), but later granted him approval to join Adolf Galland's Messerschmitt Me 262 special unit, Fighter Unit 44 (*Jagdverband 44*). Lützow was promoted to Colonel (*Oberst*) on April 1, 1943. On April 24, 1945, while flying a Messerschmitt Me 262 in *Jagdverband 44*, Günther Lützow was shot down near Donauwörth, Bavaria. His body was never found. With over 300 combat missions, Lützow scored 110 aerial victories, of which 5 were in Spain and 20 in the West.[47]

Manfred Mössinger
Lieutenant Colonel Manfred Mössinger's significant assignments included: Commander, 3rd Group, 301st Fighter Wing "Wild Boar" (*Jagdgeschwader 301 "Wilde Sau"*), October 1943-November 1943; Commodore, 302nd Fighter Wing "Wild Boar" (*Jagdgeschwader 302 "Wilde Sau"*), November 1943-September 1944; and Commodore, 77th Ground-Attack Wing (*Schlachtgeschwader 77*), February 7, 1945-May 5, 1945. He was promoted to lieutenant colonel (*Oberstleutnant*) on September 1, 1944.[48]

Walter Nowotny
An Austrian by birth, Walter "Nowi" Nowotny was born on December 7, 1920 at Ceske Velenice/Gmünd on the Czechoslovakian/Austrian border. He joined the *Luftwaffe* on October 1, 1939 and soon completed flight school at the 5th Fighter Pilot School at Schwechat near Vienna. Nowotny was then posted to the 54th Fighter Wing "Greenhearts" (*Jagdgeschwader 54 "Grünherz"*) on February 23, 1941 and assigned to the 9th Squadron. His significant wartime

assignments included: Commander, 1st Squadron, 54th Fighter Wing "Green Hearts," October 25, 1942-August 10, 1943; Commander, 1st Group, 54th Fighter Wing "Green Hearts," August 10, 1943-October 1943; Commander, 101st Fighter Wing (*Jagdgeschwader 101*) – an operational fighter-training unit – April 1, 1944-September 1944; and Commander, "Kommando Nowotny" – a consolidation of Messerschmitt Me 262 jet test units – September 1944-November 8, 1944. Walter Nowotny won the Knight's Cross of the Iron Cross on September 4, 1942 and the Oak Leaves to the Knight's Cross on September 4, 1943. He received the Swords to the Oak Leaves on September 22, 1943 (the 37th recipient), and on October 19, 1943 he became the 8th recipient of the Diamonds. However, his victories came at a cost. On July 19, 1941, his Messerschmitt Me 109E-7 was shot down by a Soviet I-153, flown by the future Russian ace Alexandr Avdeev (13 victories, killed in action August 12, 1942) over Riga Bay. After three days and nights at sea in a rubber dinghy, Nowotny finally reached the shore. On August 11, 1942, his Me 109G-2 was hit in an aerial engagement and caught fire, and although Nowotny was able to bring the burning aircraft back to his base for a crash-landing, he suffered some injuries, but the worst was saved for last. By November 7, 1944, Nowotny had claimed three victories in the new jet fighter. He took off in his Me 262 on November 8, 1944, flying against USAAF bombers with a fighter escort. Ground personnel reported hearing combat above the clouds, and Nowotny reported over the radio that he had downed a B-24 four-engine bomber and probably destroyed a P-51 fighter. He then reported an engine failure and made a garbled transmission referring to "burning" over the radio. Ground observers saw his Me 262A-1a dive vertically out of the clouds and crash at Epe, 1 1/2 miles east of Hesepe.[19] He is buried at the *Zentralfriedhof* in Vienna, Austria (Section 14C, Grave 12.) Walter Nowotny flew over 442 missions and achieved 258 victories, a sortie-to-victory ratio of 1.71 to 1. Some 255 of his victories were over the Eastern Front. Of his three victories in the West, two were four-engine bombers and all three were while flying the Messerschmitt Me 262. During his service in the 1st Squadron, 54th Fighter Wing, Walter Nowotny was the leader of the most famous flight in the *Luftwaffe* – composed of himself, Master Sergeant Anton Döbele, Master Sergeant Karl Schnörrer and Master Sergeant Rudi Rademacher – who, while flying together, shot down 450 enemy aircraft in Russia.[50]

Hans von Obernitz
Lieutenant Colonel Hans von Obernitz's significant assignments included: Commander, 123rd Reconnaissance Group (*Aufklärungsgruppe 123*), January 1942-August 1943. He won the German Cross in Gold on January 19, 1942.[51]

Walter Oesau
Colonel Walter "Gulle" Oesau was born on June 28, 1913 at Farnewinkel/Heide in Schleswig-Holstein. He joined the Army in 1933 and served in an artillery regiment. The following year Oesau became an officer candidate, began flight training and transferred to the *Luftwaffe*. He then joined Fighter Wing "Richthofen" and served with the *Luftwaffe* in Spain in the 3rd Squadron, 88th Fighter Wing (*Jagdgruppe 88* [J/88]). While in Spain, he scored 9 aerial victories, was wounded in action and was awarded the Spanish Cross in Gold with Diamonds. On March 1, 1939, Oesau joined the 1st Group, 2nd Fighter Wing "Richthofen." His significant assignments included: Commander, 1st Squadron, 20th Fighter Group (*Jagdgruppe 20*), July 15, 1939-June 25, 1940; Commander, 7th Squadron, 51st Fighter Wing (*Jagdgeschwader 51*), June 25, 1940-August 25, 1940; Commander, 3rd Group, 51st Fighter Wing, August 25, 1940-July 28, 1941; Commander, 2nd Fighter Wing "Richthofen" (*Jagdgeschwader 2 "Richthofen"*), July 28 1941-July 1, 1943; 4th Fighter Commander, Brittany (*Jagdfliegerführer 4 Brittany*), July 1, 1943-November 11, 1943; and Commander, 1st Fighter Wing (*Jagdgeschwader 1*), November 12, 1943-May 11, 1944. He won the Knight's Cross of the Iron Cross on August 20, 1940 and the Oak Leaves to the Knight's Cross on February 6, 1941. On July 16, 1941, he became the 3rd recipient of the Swords to the Oak Leaves. He also won the German Cross in Gold on October 17, 1943. His promotions included: Captain (*Hauptmann*), July 19, 1940; Major (*Major*) July 15, 1941; and Colonel (*Oberst*), May 1, 1944. He had his adverse events as well; on January 9, 1942, his Messerschmitt Me 109F-4 rammed another fighter on the airfield during poor visibility conditions at Brest-Guipavas, France. On May 11, 1944, Oesau, leading three aircraft, took off from Paderborn to intercept Allied bombers. During his attack on the bombers, he was bounced by escorting P-38 Lightnings. In the ensuing combat, his Messerschmitt Me 109G-6 was shot down and he was killed near St. Vith, Belgium. Oesau flew over 300 combat missions and accumulated 127 aerial victories (of which 74 were on the Western Front, including 14 four-engine bombers.)[52]

Theodor Osterkamp

Major General Theo Osterkamp was born April 15, 1892 in Düren-Rölsdorf. He entered the German Navy on August 27, 1914 and became a naval aviator. In 1918, as the commander of the 2nd Navy Fighter Squadron, he won the *Pour le Mérite*. Osterkamp left the service in 1920, but resumed his military career on August 1, 1933, when he entered the *Luftwaffe*. His significant positions included: Commander, 2nd Group, 26th Destroyer Wing (*Zerstörergeschwader 26*), April 1, 1936-November 1, 1937; Commander, 4th Group, 132nd Fighter Wing "Richthofen" (*Jagdgeschwader 132 "Richthofen"*), July 1, 1938-August 1, 1938; Commander, Fighter School Werneuchen, August 1, 1938-August 31, 1939; Commodore, 51st Fighter Wing (*Jagdgeschwader 51*), November 25, 1939-July 22, 1940; 1st Fighter Commander (*Jagdfliegerführer 1*), July 22, 1940-November 9, 1940; 2nd Fighter Commander (*Jagdfliegerführer 2*), January 1, 1941-August 1, 1941; Air Commander Africa (*Fliegerführer Afrika*), August 1, 1941-March 31, 1942; 3rd Higher Flight Training Commander (*Höherer Flieger-Ausbildungs-Kommandeur 3*), July 8, 1942-November 2, 1942; and the 17th Higher Flight Training Commander (*Höherer Flieger-Ausbildungs-Kommandeur 17*), November 3, 1942-February 25, 1943. He was awarded the Knight's Cross of the Iron Cross on August 22, 1940. Osterkamp died on January 2, 1975 in Baden-Baden. He is buried at the *Hauptfriedhof* in Baden-Baden (Section 20). Osterkamp shot down 32 enemy aircraft in World War I and 6 in World War II.[53]

Kurd Peters

Major Kurd Peters was born on August 7, 1914 in Braunschweig. He began the war serving in reconnaissance units. His significant assignments included: Commander, 2nd Group, 300th Fighter Wing (*Jagdgeschwader 300*), November 1943-June 29, 1944; and acting commodore, 300th Fighter Wing, January 1945-March 1945. He received the Knight's Cross of the iron Cross on October 29, 1944. He also won the *Luftwaffe* Honor Goblet on October 5, 1942 and the German Cross in Gold on October 20, 1942. Kurd Peters died on July 24, 1957 at Fürstenfeldbruck in Bavaria. During the war, he flew 170 combat missions and shot down four enemy aircraft, all in the West.[54]

Josef "Pips" Priller

Colonel Josef "Pips" Priller was born on July 27, 1915 at Ingolstadt in Bavaria. In 1935, Priller was serving in the 19th Infantry Regiment in the Army. Officer candidate Priller transferred to the *Luftwaffe* and began his flight training at Salzwedel in October 1936. On April 1, 1937, he was posted to the 1st Group, 135th Fighter Wing (*Jagdgeschwader 135*), which was first designated as the 1st Group, 233rd Fighter Wing (*Jagdgeschwader 233*), and later designated the 1st Group, 51st Fighter Wing (*Jagdgeschwader 51*). Priller's significant positions included: Commander, 6th Squadron, 51st Fighter Wing (*Jagdgeschwader 51*), October 1, 1939-November 20, 1940; Commander, 1st Squadron, 26th Fighter Wing "Schlageter" (*Jagdgeschwader 26 "Schlageter"*), November 20, 1940-December 6, 1941; Commander, 3rd Group, 26th Fighter Wing "Schlageter," December 6, 1941-January 11, 1943; Commodore, 26th Fighter Wing, January 11, 1943-January 28, 1945; and Inspector Fighter Pilots East (*Inspekteur der Jagdflieger Ost*), January 28, 1945-May 8, 1945. Priller received the Knight's Cross of the Iron Cross on October 19, 1940 and the Oak Leaves on July 20, 1941. On July 2, 1944 he became the 73rd recipient of the Swords to the Oak Leaves. He also received the German Cross in Gold on December 20, 1941. Priller had a few near-death experiences; on April 17, 1942, bad weather forced him to make an emergency landing, which resulted in moderate damage to his aircraft, while on December 20, 1942, return fire from enemy bombers forced him to make another belly-landing in his Focke-Wulf Fw 190A-4. During the war, he flew 307 combat missions and scored 101 aerial victories, for a sortie-to-victory ratio of 3.03 to 1. All of his victories occurred in the West and included 68 Spitfires and 11 four-engine bombers. Josef "Pips" Priller died on May 20, 1961 of a heart attack at Böbing, Bavaria. He is buried at the *Westfriedhof* in Augsburg, Bavaria.[55]

Klaus Quaet-Faslem

Lieutenant Colonel Klaus Quaet-Faslem was born September 5, 1913 at Kiel. At the beginning of World War II, Quaet-Faslem was serving as a second lieutenant in the 1st Group (Fighter), 2nd Demonstration Wing (*Lehrgeschwader 2*). His assignments included: Commander, 2nd Squadron, 53rd Fighter Wing "Ace of Spades" (*Jagdgeschwader 53 "Pikas"*), November 21, 1941-August 31, 1942; and Commander, 1st Group, 3rd Fighter Wing (*Jagdgeschwader 3*), August 31, 1942-January 30, 1944. He died in an air accident during bad weather, involving his Messerschmitt Me 109G-6 on January 30, 1944 at Langeleben/Braunschweig. He was posthumously awarded the Knight's Cross of the Iron Cross on June 9, 1944.

He also won the *Luftwaffe* Honor Goblet on September 21, 1942 and the German Cross in Gold on November 16, 1942. Klaus Quaet-Faslem shot down 49 aircraft, including 41 in the East. Of his 7 aerial victories in the west, 2 were four-engine bombers.[56]

Günther Rall
Major Günther Rall was born in Gaggenau/Rastatt, Baden on March 10, 1918. He entered military service as an officer candidate in the Army in 1936. The following year, he entered the War College at Dresden, where he was persuaded to transfer to the *Luftwaffe*. After qualifying as a fighter pilot in 1938, he was sent to the 52nd Fighter Wing (*Jagdgeschwader 52*). He saw his first combat during the Battle of France. Ralls's significant duty positions included: Commander, 8th Squadron, 52nd Fighter Wing (*Jagdgeschwader 52*), July 25, 1940-November 28, 1941 and August 28, 1942-July 5, 1943; Commander, 3rd Group, 52nd Fighter Wing (*Jagdgeschwader 52*), July 6, 1943-April 18, 1944; Commander, 2nd Group, 11th Fighter Wing (*Jagdgeschwader 11*), April 19, 1944-May 12, 1944; and Commodore, 300th Fighter Wing (*Jagdgeschwader 300*), February 20, 1945-May 8, 1945. His promotions included: First Lieutenant (*Oberleutnant*), August 1, 1940; Captain (*Hauptmann*), April 1, 1943; and Major (*Major*), May 1, 1944. He received the Knight's Cross of the Iron Cross on September 4, 1942 and the Oak Leaves to the Knight's Cross on October 26, 1942. On September 12, 1943, Günther Rall became the 34th recipient of the Swords to the Oak Leaves. He also won the *Luftwaffe* Honor Goblet on November 17, 1941 and the German Cross in Gold on December 15, 1941. Rall flew a total of 621 missions and was shot down no less than 8 times, being wounded 3 times. He shot down a total of 275 enemy aircraft to become the third highest scoring *Luftwaffe* fighter pilot, giving him a sortie-to-victory ratio of 2.25 to 1.[57]

Bernhard Ramcke
Lieutenant General Bernhard Ramcke was born January 24, 1889 in Schleswig-Friedrichsberg in Schleswig-Holstein. He entered the Navy in 1905 and served as a junior officer on several heavy cruisers before joining a naval infantry regiment engaged in ground combat in Flanders. Wounded twice, Ramcke received the King of Prussia Military Merit Cross in Gold and the Iron Cross 2nd and 1st Class. Immediately after the war, he joined *Freikorps* von Brandeis in the Baltic States, where he was wounded again, before transferring to the Army on March 10, 1919. He remained in that service for twenty years, serving mostly in various infantry assignments. During the 1939 Polish Campaign, Ramcke won the Clasp to the Iron Cross 2nd Class for his actions at an engagement at Tomaszów. On August 1, 1940, Ramcke transferred to the *Luftwaffe* after completing airborne training. His significant positions include: acting commander, 1st Paratroop Assault Regiment (*Fallschirmjäger-Luftlande-Sturm-Regiment 1*), May 21, 1941-June 18, 1941; acting commander, 1st Paratroop Brigade (*Fallschirmjäger-Brigade 1*), April 1, 1942-February 12, 1943; Commander 11th Air Corps Operational Training Units and Schools (*Kommandeur der Ergänzungs-Einheiten und Schulen des XI. Fliegerkorps*), January 1, 1941-February 12, 1943 [dual-hatted]; acting commander, 90th Light Africa Division, September 8, 1942-September 17, 1942; Commander, 2nd Paratroop Division (*2. Fallschirmjäger-Division*), February 13, 1943-August 11, 1944; and Commandant Fortress Brest (*Kommandant der Festung Brest*), August 11, 1944-September 20, 1944. He received the Knight's Cross of the Iron Cross on August 21, 1941, the Oak Leaves on November 13, 1942, the Swords on September 19, 1944 and the Diamonds on September 19, 1944. Sentenced to 5 years imprisonment for war crimes by a French military tribunal, he was released from prison in 1951. He published his memoirs later that year. Bernhard Ramcke died July 4, 1968 in Kappeln near Schlei in Schleswig-Holstein. He is buried at the Friedrichsberg cemetery.[58]

Ernst-Christian Reusch
Major Ernst-Christian Reusch was born September 10, 1916 in Wiesbaden, Hesse. He flew his first combat mission in the Polish campaign. He won the German Cross in Gold on February 4, 1942 and received the Knight's Cross of the Iron Cross on November 3, 1942 as the commander of the 5th Squadron, 2nd Stuka Wing "Immelmann" (*Sturzkampfgeschwader 2 "Immelmann"*). His assignments included: Commander, 5th Squadron, 2nd Stuka Wing "Immelmann," 1942-1944; Commander, 2nd Group, 1st Ground-Attack Wing (*Schlachtgeschwader 1*), May 1944-1944; and Commander, 3rd Group, 1st Ground-Attack Wing, 1944 January 21, 1945. Ernst-Christian Reusch received severe injuries during an emergency landing on January 21, 1945 and died in a military hospital in Danzig on January 26, 1945. He was buried at Rahmel near Gotenhafen (now Gydnia, Poland). During the war he flew a total of 765 combat missions.[59]

Heinrich Sannemann

Captain Heinrich Sannemann's significant assignments included: Commander, 6th Squadron, 3rd Fighter Wing (*Jagdgeschwader 3*), November 23, 1940-March 31, 1942; and acting commander, 2nd Group, 3rd Fighter Wing, 1943-1944. He won the *Luftwaffe* Honor Goblet on October 17, 1941.[60]

Roman Schneider

Colonel Roman Schneider's significant assignments included: Commander, 122nd Reconnaissance Group (*Aufklärungsgruppe 122*), September 1942-March 20, 1943; and Commander, 101st Long Range Reconnaissance Wing (*Fernaufklärungsgeschwader 101*), 1943. He received the German Cross in Gold on March 1, 1943.[61]

Ernst-Albrecht Schultz

First Lieutenant Ernst-Albrecht Schultz's significant assignments included: acting commander, Supplemental Group, 77th Fighter Wing "Ace of Hearts" (*Jagdgeschwader 77 "Herzas"*), March 1941-June 1941.[62]

Herbert Sonnenburg

Major General Herbert Sonnenburg was born on April 18, 1890 in Königsberg, Prussia. He entered the Army on July 1, 1909 and soon became an officer candidate. Promoted to second lieutenant before World War I, during the conflict he served in the field artillery before becoming a pilot. After the war, he served in various infantry assignments and transferred to the *Luftwaffe* on October 8, 1934. His significant *Luftwaffe* assignments included: Commander, 2nd Group, Bomber Wing "General Wever" (*Kampfgeschwader "General Wever"*), March 12, 1936-September 30, 1937; and Commander, Air War School 4, Fürstenfeldbruck (*Luftkriegschule 4, Fürstenfeldbruck*), October 1, 1940-September 16, 1943. His promotions included: Lieutenant Colonel (*Oberstleutnant*), April 1, 1936; Colonel (*Oberst*), August 1, 1938; Brigadier General (*Generalmajor*), June 1, 1941; and Major General (*Generalleutnant*), April 1, 1944. He spent two years as a prisoner of war and died on October 7, 1966 on Wolfenbüttel, Lower Saxony.[63]

Hugo Sperrle

Field Marshal Hugo Sperrle was born in Ludwigsburg, Württemberg on February 8, 1885, the son of a brewer. He entered the Army on July 6, 1903 and spent the bulk of the pre-war years in the 126th Infantry Regiment. He then underwent flight training and flew with the 42nd Field Aviation Detachment before he was shot down and wounded on February 23, 1916. He returned to flying some months later (and won the Knight's Cross of the Royal House Order of Hohenzollern with Swords [*Ritterkreuz des königlichen Hausordens von Hohenzollern mit Schwertern*]); after the war – and after a short stint in the *Freikorps Lüttwitz* – his career again gravitated to the infantry and in 1933 he became the Commander, 8th Infantry Regiment. Sperrle transferred to the *Luftwaffe* as a colonel on March 1, 1934. His significant *Luftwaffe* assignments included: Higher Air Commander 2, Berlin, April 1, 1935-December 30, 1935; Commander 5th Air District, Munich (*Luftkreis 5*), October 1, 1935-March 31, 1938; Commander, Condor Legion [Spain], November 6, 1936-October 31, 1937; Commander 3rd *Luftwaffe* Group, April 1, 1938-January 31, 1939; Commander 3rd Air Fleet (*Luftflotte 3*), February 1, 1939-August 23, 1944; and, simultaneously, Commander *Luftwaffe* West, July 8, 1940-July 23, 1944. Sperrle's promotions included: Brigadier General (*Generalmajor*), October 1, 1935; Major General (*Generalleutnant*), April 1, 1937; Lieutenant General (*General der Flieger*), November 1, 1937; Colonel General (skipped this rank), and Field Marshal (*Generalfeldmarschall*), July 19, 1940. He won the Knight's Cross of the Iron Cross on May 17, 1940. While commander of the Condor Legion, Sperrle ordered the aerial attack on the Basque town of Guernica, in which 1,654 people were killed. He received the Spanish Cross in Gold with Diamonds for his service in Spain. During the Battle of Britain, *Generalfeldmarschall* Hugo Sperrle's *Luftflotte 3* was responsible for attacking the West Country, Midlands and northwest England. After the war, the Allies tried Sperrle at Nürnberg for war crimes, but he was acquitted. He died on April 2, 1953 in Munich, Bavaria.[64] He is buried at the *Soldatenfriedhof* Schwabstadl in Obermeitingen, Bavaria.[65]

Kurt Student

Colonel General Kurt Student was born May 12, 1890 in Birkholz near Züllichau-Schwiebus, Brandenburg. He entered the Army in 1910 and was one of the first officers to receive pilot training in 1913. During World War I he served in several flying units; he was wounded twice in aerial combat (he also crashed once due to an engine defect) and received both the Iron Cross 2nd and 1st Class, and the Knight's Cross of the Royal House Order of Hohenzollern with Swords (*Ritterkreuz des königlichen Hausordens von*

Hohenzollern mit Schwerten). After the war, he remained in the *Reichswehr*, alternating between aviation and infantry duties, before transferring to the *Luftwaffe* on September 1, 1933. Among his significant positions were: Commander, 3rd Air Division (*3. Flieger-Division*), April 1, 1938-July 3, 1938; Commander of Airborne and Air Landing Troops (*Fallschirmjäger und Luftlandetruppen*), July 4, 1938-August 31, 1938; Commander, 7th Air Division (*7. Flieger-Division*), September 1, 1938-September 30, 1940; Commander, 11th Air Corps (*XI. Flieger-Korps*), January 1, 1941-May 31, 1941; Commanding General of Airborne Troops (*Kommandierender General der Fallschirmjäger*), June 1, 1941-February 28, 1944; Commander-in-Chief, 1st Parachute Army (*1. Fallschirm-Armee*), March 1, 1944-November 4, 1944 and April 10, 1945-April 28, 1945; Commander-in-Chief, Army Group H (*Heeresgruppe H*), November 7, 1944-January 25, 1945; and Commander, Army Group "Student" (*Armeegruppe Student*), March 31, 1945-April 10, 1945. While he was named at the end of the war to be Commander-in-Chief of Army Group Vistula, he never actually assumed the command. His promotions included: Brigadier General (*Generalmajor*), April 1, 1938; Major General (*Generalleutnant*), January 1, 1940; Lieutenant General (*General der Flieger* [later *General der Fallschirmtruppe*]), May 29, 1940; and Colonel General (*Generaloberst*), July 13, 1944. He received the Knight's Cross of the Iron Cross on May 12, 1940 and the Oak Leaves to the Knight's Cross on September 27, 1943. Student was almost killed in action on May 14, 1940 when he was shot in the head during the fighting at Rotterdam; he convalesced in hospital and was on sick leave until January 1941. After the war, Student was charged with war crimes that allegedly took place on Crete. He was sentenced to five years imprisonment, but was released after serving two. Kurt Student died on July 1, 1978 at Lemgo, North Rhine-Westphalia.[66] He is buried at the *Friedhof am Obernberg* in Bad Sulzulfen (Section 35, Grave 35).

Hans-Jürgen Stumpff
Colonel General Hans-Jürgen Stumpff was born in Kolberg, West Prussia on June 15, 1889. He joined the Army in 1907 and served in numerous infantry command and staff positions – he was wounded at the start of World War I – before becoming a General Staff officer in 1917. In the conflict, he won both the Iron Cross 2nd and 1st Class. Stumpff remained in the *Reichswehr* after the war, holding several key staff positions in Berlin, including Adjutant of the Chief of the Troop Office and Adjutant of the Chief of the Personnel Office. He transferred as a lieutenant colonel on September 1, 1933 to the *Luftwaffe*. Significant positions in this new service included: Chief of the *Luftwaffe* Personnel Department (*Chef des Luftwaffen-Personalamts*), September 1, 1933-January 31, 1939; Commander, 1st Air Fleet (*Chef der Luftflotte 1*), January 12, 1940-May 10, 1940; Commander, 5th Air Fleet (*Chef der Luftflotte 5*), May 10, 1940-November 6, 1943; *Luftwaffe* Commander Center (*Luftwaffen-Befehlshaber Mitte*), January 6, 1944-February 8, 1944; and Commander-in-Chief, Air Fleet Reich (*Oberbefehlshaber der Luftflotte Reich*), February 9, 1944-May 8, 1945. His promotions included: Brigadier General (*Generalmajor*), April 1, 1936; Major General (*Generalleutnant*), August 1, 1937; Lieutenant General (*General der Flieger*), November 1, 1938; and Colonel General (*Generaloberst*), July 19, 1940. During the Battle of Britain, Stumpff's 5th Air Fleet, headquartered in Norway, had responsibility for bombing northern England and Scotland. He received the Knight's Cross of the Iron Cross on September 18, 1941. In May 1945, Colonel General Stumpff signed the final German surrender to the Soviets at Berlin-Karlshorst as the representative of the *Luftwaffe*. He then spent two years as an Allied prisoner of war. He was then acquitted by a British military tribunal of not protecting Allied airman shot down over Germany from retribution by civilians. Hans-Jürgen Stumpff died March 9, 1968 at Frankfurt am Main, Hesse. He is buried at the *Zentralfriedhof* in Bad Godesberg (Section V, Grave 190.)[67]

Alfred Sturm
Major General Alfred Sturm was born August 23, 1888 in Saarbrücken. He entered the Army in 1905 and became a non-commissioned officer. He began World War I in the 144th Infantry Regiment, before being wounded in 1915. On recovery, he received pilot training and became a pilot in *Jagdstaffel 5* and *Jagdstaffel 89* for the remainder of the war. He remained in the *Reichswehr* until 1928, when he "retired" to receive secret flight training. Reactivated in 1930, he transferred to the *Luftwaffe* on October 1, 1933. Among his significant positions were: Commander, 2nd Paratroop Regiment (*Fallschirmjäger-Regiment 2*), July 1, 1940-September 30, 1942; acting commander, 7th Air Division (*7. Flieger-Division*), May 21, 1941-May 30, 1941; and Commander, *Luftwaffe* Ground Combat Schools (*Kommandeur der Erdkampfschulen der Luftwaffe*), October 1, 1942-January 3, 1945. His promotions included: Colonel (*Oberst*), October

1, 1938; Brigadier General (*Generalmajor*), August 1, 1940; and Major General (*Generalleutnant*), August 1, 1943. He won the Knight's Cross of the Iron Cross on July 9, 1941. At the end of the war, he spent two years as an Allied prisoner of war. Alfred Sturm died on March 8, 1962 in Detmold, North Rhine-Westphalia.[68]

Wolfgang Tonne
Major Wolfgang Tonne was born on February 28, 1918 at Moosbach in the Schleiz region of Thuringia. He joined the *Luftwaffe* in 1937 as an officer cadet. Tonne was posted to the 3rd Squadron, 53rd Fighter Wing "Ace of Spades" (*Jagdgeschwader 53 "Pikas"*) on December 6, 1939 and scored his first aerial success in the 1940 French campaign. He was wounded in aerial combat on July 11, 1941 in his Messerschmitt Me 109F-2 and forced to make a belly-landing. His significant wartime assignments included: Commander, 3rd Squadron, 53rd Fighter Wing, January 24, 1942-April 20, 1943. He received the Knight's Cross of the Iron Cross on September 6, 1942 and the Oak Leaves to the Knight's Cross on September 24, 1942. He also won the *Luftwaffe* Honor Goblet on August 6, 1941 and the German Cross in Gold on August 21, 1942. On April 20, 1943, Wolfgang Tonne was killed in a flying accident caused as he attempted to celebrate his 122nd victory over the airfield at Protville, Tunisia in his Messerschmitt Me 109G-6. He is buried at the German Military Cemetery at Bordj-Cedria, Tunisia. During the war, Wolfgang Tonne recorded 122 victories in 641 missions, a sortie-to-victory ratio of 5.25 to 1.[69]

Hans Trautloft
Colonel Hannes Trautloft was born March 3, 1912 in Gross Obringen/Weimar in Thuringia. During the Spanish Civil War, Trautloft, flying a Heinkel He 51 biplane, scored one of the first German aerial victories on August 25, 1936, but also became the first *Luftwaffe* pilot to be shot down on August 30, 1936. He bailed out, landed near Nationalist forces and returned unharmed to his unit. He received the Spanish Cross in Gold with Swords for his exploits. He had another serious incident on April 22, 1941, when engine failure caused him to make an emergency belly-landing near Pecs, Hungary, and still another when his aircraft was damaged in aerial combat and he was forced to make another belly-landing on June 22, 1941. Trautloft's wartime assignments included: Commander, 2nd Squadron, 77th Fighter Wing "Ace of Hearts" (*Jagdgeschwader 77 "Herz As"*), May 1, 1939-September 19, 1939; Commander, 3rd Group, 51st Fighter Wing (*Jagdgeschwader 51*), September 19, 1939-August 25, 1940; Commodore, 54th Fighter Wing "Green Hearts" (*Jagdgeschwader 54 "Grünherz"*), August 25, 1940-July 5, 1943; Inspector, Fighters East, July 5, 1943-November 27, 1943; Inspector of Day Fighters, November 27, 1943-January 1945; and Commander, 4th Flying School, January 1945-May 8, 1945. He won the Knight's Cross of the Iron Cross on July 27, 1941. He was promoted to Colonel (*Oberst*) on December 1, 1943. From 1957 to 1970, Trautloft served in the new German air force and rose to the rank of major general. He died on January 12, 1995 at Bad Wiessee, Bavaria. During the war, he flew 560 combat missions and scored 57 aerial victories, a sortie-to-victory ratio of 9.82 to 1.[70]

Friedrich Vollbracht
Colonel Friedrich Vollbracht was born in Hamburg on February 8, 1897. He served in the infantry for three years in World War I, before transferring to become a pilot. After flight training, he served in the 5th Fighter Squadron (*Jagdstaffel 5*) and recorded two aerial victories. He joined the *Luftwaffe* as a captain in 1934. Vollbracht's assignments included: Commander, 2nd Group, 134th Fighter Wing (*Jagdgeschwader 134*), November 1, 1937-November 1, 1938; Commander, 2nd Group, 26th Destroyer Wing (*Zerstörergeschwader 26*), November 1, 1938-November 30, 1939; Commodore, 2nd Destroyer Wing (*Zerstörergeschwader 2*), April 1, 1940-September 28, 1940; Commander, Destroyer Supplemental Group Vaerlöse (*Zerstörer-Ergänzungsgruppe Vaerlöse*), September 28, 1940-July 3, 1941; Commander, 1st Night Fighter School (*Nachtjagdschule 1*), July 4, 1941-January 14, 1942; Fighter Commander German Bight (*Jagdfliegerführer Deutsche Bucht*), January 14, 1942-November 16, 1942; and Fighter Commander South France (*Jagdfliegerführer Südfrankreich*), November 16, 1942-September 16, 1944. He won the Knight's Cross of the Iron Cross on October 13, 1940. He was promoted to Colonel (*Oberst*) on March 1, 1942. Friedrich Vollbracht died on August 24, 1968 in Baden-Baden. He is buried at the *Hauptfriedhof* in Baden-Baden (Section 3, Row 1, Grave 13). He had four aerial victories.[71]

Gerhard Weyert
Major Gerhard Weyert's significant positions during the war included: Commander, 11th Squadron, 4th Group (Stuka), 1st Demonstration Wing (*Lehrgeschwader 1*), 1939-November 6, 1939 and May 17, 1940-June 6, 1941; Commander,

2nd Group, 1st Destroyer Wing (*Zerstörergeschwader 1*), November 13, 1942-July 19, 1943; Commander, 3rd Group, 4th Ground-Attack Wing (*Schlachtgeschwader 4*), January 10, 1944-October 15, 1944; and Commander, 2nd Group, 4th Ground-Attack Wing (*Schlachtgeschwader 4*), December 1944-January 27, 1945. Weyert won the Spanish Cross in Gold with Swords as a pilot in the Condor Legion's 88th Fighter Group (*Jagdgruppe 88* [J/88]), in the Spanish Civil War. Weyert won the German Cross in Gold on January 1, 1945. He was promoted to Major (*Major*) on October 1, 1943. During the Allied invasion at Normandy, Weyert and his group flew ground-attack missions against Allied tank concentrations, one of which caused him to make a forced landing at Falaise. The unit then transferred south to bomb French Resistance units attempting to hinder German reinforcements moving from southern France to Normandy.[72]

Wolf-Dietrich Wilcke
Colonel Wolf-Dietrich "Fürst" Wilcke was born in Schrimm in the district of Posen on March 11, 1913. He entered the German Army in 1934 and transferred the following year as an officer candidate to the *Luftwaffe*. He later served briefly with the Condor Legion in Spain and was awarded the Spanish Cross in Bronze with Swords. Among his significant assignments were: Commander, 7th Squadron, 53rd Fighter Wing "Ace of Spades" (*Jagdgeschwader 53 "Pikas"*), September 18, 1939-August 13, 1940; Commander, 3rd Group, 53rd Fighter Wing "Ace of Spades," August 13, 1940-May 18, 1942; and Commodore, 3rd Fighter Wing "Udet" (*Jagdgeschwader 3 "Udet"*), August 12, 1942-March 23, 1944. He received the Knight's Cross of the Iron Cross on August 6, 1941 and the Oak Leaves to the Knight's Cross on September 9, 1942. On December 23, 1942, Wilcke became the 23rd recipient of the Swords to the Oak Leaves. He also won the German Cross in Gold on November 3, 1942. Wilcke was killed in action on March 23, 1944 over Schöppenstedt/Braunschweig, when – after shooting down two enemy aircraft – his Messerschmitt Me 109G-6 was shot down by US fighters. Wilcke flew 732 combat missions during the war and shot down 162 enemy aircraft, a sortie-to-victory ratio of 4.51 to 1. Some 137 of his kills came on the Eastern Front.[73]

Gustav Wilke
Major General Gustav Wilke was born in Deutsch-Eylau, West Prussia on March 6, 1898. He entered the Army in 1916, serving as an officer candidate in the 4th Grenadier Regiment and ending the war as a second lieutenant before leaving the service in 1920. He was reactivated in 1925 and assigned to the 2nd Grenadier Regiment. On October 1, 1935, Wilke transferred to the *Luftwaffe*. Among his significant positions were: Commodore, 1st Demonstration Wing (*Lehr-Geschwader 1*), September 25, 1940-August 31, 1941; Commander *Luftwaffe* Regiment "Wilke," May 1, 1942-September 29, 1942; acting commander, 1st *Luftwaffe* Field Division, September 30, 1942-June 30, 1943; Commander, 1st *Luftwaffe* Field Division, July 1, 1943-October 31, 1943; acting commander, 2nd Paratroop Division (*2. Fallschirmjäger Division*), December 9, 1943-March 31, 1944; Commander, 5th Paratroop Division (*5. Fallschirmjäger Division*), April 1, 1944-August 1944; Commander, 9th Paratroop Division (*9. Fallschirmjäger Division*), September 24, 1944-March 9, 1945; and Commander, 10th Paratroop Division (*10. Fallschirmjäger Division*), March 10, 1945-May 5, 1945. Wilke's promotions included: Colonel (*Oberst*), March 1, 1942; Brigadier General (*Generalmajor*), April 20, 1943; and Major General (*Generalleutnant*), May 1, 1944. He won the Knight's Cross of the Iron Cross on May 24, 1940. At the end of the war, he spent two years as an Allied prisoner of war. Gustav Wilke died on March 14, 1977 in Oberstdorf, Bavaria.[74]

Eugen-Ludwig Zweigart
First Lieutenant Eugen-Ludwig Zweigart was born at Saargemünd in Lothringen on May 3, 1914. He joined the Army in 1935, and later transferred to the *Luftwaffe* and underwent flight training. In the fall of 1940, Staff Sergeant Zweigart was assigned to the 9th Squadron, 54th Fighter Wing "Green Hearts" (*Jagdgeschwader 54 "Grünherz"*). He received the *Luftwaffe* Honor Goblet on October 26, 1942 and the German Cross in Gold on November 17, 1942. On January 22, 1943, Master Sergeant Eugen-Ludwig Zweigart was awarded the Knight's Cross of the Iron Cross as a pilot in the 5th Squadron, *Jagdgeschwader 54 "Grünherz"*.[75]

Lieutenant General Hans-Jürgen Stumpff, Chief of the *Luftwaffe* **Personnel Department,** September 1, 1933-January 31, 1939.

Colonel General Bruno Loerzer, of the *Luftwaffe* **Personnel Department,** February 24, 1943-December 20, 1944.

ENDNOTES

Foreword

[1] French MacLean, *The Cruel Hunters: SS-Sonderkommando Dirlewanger, Hitler's Most Notorious Anti partisan Unit*, Atglen, PA: Schiffer Publishing Co., 1998, 12.

[2] Werner Baumbach, *The Life and Death of the Luftwaffe*, translated by Frederick Holt, New York: Coward-McCann, Inc., 1960, 58.

[3] Adolf Galland, *The First And The Last: The Rise and Fall of the German Fighter Forces, 1938-1945*, translated by Mervyn Savill, New York: Henry Holt and Company, 1954, 3.

[4] Jill Amadio, *Günther Rall: A Memoir – Luftwaffe Ace and NATO General*, Santa Ana, CA: Tangmere Productions, 2002, 34, 92, 98, 155, 243.

Introduction

[1] Rudolf Hofmann, *German Efficiency Report System*, MS# P-134, Königstein, Germany: U.S. Army Europe Historical Division, 1952, 51.

[2] Stephen Thomas Previtera, *The Iron Time: A History of the Knight's Cross*, Richmond, VA: Winidore Press, 1999, 286.

[3] French L. MacLean, *Quiet Flows the Rhine: German General Officer Casualties of World War II*, Winnipeg, Canada: J.J. Fedorowicz, 1996, 22-23. Estimates of the number of Iron Cross 2nd and 1st Class awarded vary. There were likely some 4,950,000 Second Class awards and 450,000 First Class (source: Previtera).

[4] Ernst Obermaier, *Die Ritterkreuzträger der Luftwaffe, Stuka und Schlachtflieger 1939-1945*, Mainz, FRG: Verlag Dieter Hoffmann, 1976, 11.

[5] French L. MacLean, *Quiet Flows the Rhine: German General Officer Casualties of World War II*, Winnipeg, Canada: J.J. Fedorowicz, 1996, 22-23.

[6] Ernst Obermaier, *Die Ritterkreuzträger der Luftwaffe, Stuka und Schlachtflieger 1939-1945*, Mainz, FRG: Verlag Dieter Hoffmann, 1976, 11.

[7] French L. MacLean, *Quiet Flows the Rhine: German General Officer Casualties of World War II*, Winnipeg, Canada: J.J. Fedorowicz, 1996, 22-23.

[8] Ernst Obermaier, *Die Ritterkreuzträger der Luftwaffe, Stuka und Schlachtflieger 1939-1945*, Mainz, FRG: Verlag Dieter Hoffmann, 1976, 11.

[9] French L. MacLean, *Quiet Flows the Rhine: German General Officer Casualties of World War II*, Winnipeg, Canada: J.J. Fedorowicz, 1996, 22-23.

[10] Ernst Obermaier, *Die Ritterkreuzträger der Luftwaffe, Stuka und Schlachtflieger 1939-1945*, Mainz, FRG: Verlag Dieter Hoffmann, 1976, 11.

[11] French L. MacLean, *Quiet Flows the Rhine: German General Officer Casualties of World War II*, Winnipeg, Canada: J.J. Fedorowicz, 1996, 22-23.

[12] Ernst Obermaier, *Die Ritterkreuzträger der Luftwaffe, Jagdflieger 1939-1945*, Mainz, FRG: Verlag Dieter Hoffmann, 1989, 11.

[13] Cajus Bekker, *The Luftwaffe War Diaries*, London: MacDonald & Co., 1967, 383.

[14] Ernst Obermaier, *Die Ritterkreuzträger der Luftwaffe, Jagdflieger 1939-1945*, Mainz, FRG: Verlag Dieter Hoffmann, 1989, 242. The entire Luftwaffe lost 140,000 killed in action and 155,000 missing in action. Source: Wolfgang Dierich, *Kampfgeschwader 51 "Edelweiss": Eine Chronik aus Dokumenten und Berichten 1937-1945*, Stuttgart, FRG: Motorbuch Verlag, 1973, 248-249.

[15] The Russians would clearly disagree with this assertion and at least in one respect their concern seems quite valid. During the war, the Red Air Force produced 800 aces with 15 or more aerial victories. For the most complete history of these Soviet aces, see Hans D. Seidl, *Stalin's Eagles: An Illustrated Study of the Soviet Aces of World War II and Korea*, Atglen, PA: Schiffer Publications, 1998.

[16] Ernst Obermaier, *Die Ritterkreuzträger der Luftwaffe, Jagdflieger 1939-1945*, Mainz, FRG: Verlag Dieter Hoffmann, 1989, 14.

[17] Ernst Obermaier, *Die Ritterkreuzträger der Luftwaffe, Jagdflieger 1939-1945*, Mainz, FRG: Verlag Dieter Hoffmann, 1989, 14.

[18] Ernst Obermaier, *Die Ritterkreuzträger der Luftwaffe, Stuka und Schlachtflieger 1939-1945*, Mainz, FRG: Verlag Dieter Hoffmann, 1976, 11.

[19] Wolfgang Dierich, *Kampfgeschwader 51 "Edelweiss" Eine Chronik aus Dokumenten und Berichten 1937-1945*, Stuttgart, FRG: Motorbuch Verlag, 1973, 292.

[20] Hanfried Schliephake, *The Birth of the Luftwaffe*, Chicago: Henry Regnery Company, 1971, 12.

[21] Hanfried Schliephake, *The Birth of the Luftwaffe*, Chicago: Henry Regnery Company, 1971, 13-21.

[22] Hitler wanted the air force to be named the *Reichsluftwaffe*, but the name never caught on, and it was invariably called just the *Luftwaffe*.

[23] Samuel Mitcham, Jr., *Men of the Luftwaffe*, Novato, CA: Presidio, 1988, 8-11.

[24] Samuel Mitcham, Jr., *Men of the Luftwaffe*, Novato, CA: Presidio, 1988, 10.

[25] Grade shown for each officer is the highest achieved during his period of service at the *Luftwaffe* Personnel Office; for example, Hans-Jürgen Stumpff was a lieutenant colonel in 1933, but by 1937 he had reached the grade of brigadier general.

[26] Kurt Mehner and Reinhard Teuber, *Die Deutsche Luftwaffe 1939-1945 Führung und Truppe*, Norderstedt, Germany; Militair-Verlag Klaus D. Patzwall, 1993, 4.

[27] The fundamental tenets of officer personnel management seem not to have changed from the Imperial Army (prior to and during World War I), through the Reichswehr, to the World War II German Army. Source: Rudolf Hofmann, *German Efficiency Report System*, MS# P-134, Königstein, Germany: U.S. Army Europe Historical Division, 1952, 13.

[28] David Nelson Spires, "The Career of the Reichswehr Officer," PhD Dissertation, University of Washington, 1979, 186-192.

[29] David Nelson Spires, "The Career of the Reichswehr Officer," PhD Dissertation, University of Washington, 1979, 186-192.

[30] Rudolf Hofmann, *German Efficiency Report System*, MS# P-134, Königstein, Germany: U.S. Army Europe Historical Division, 1952, 13.

[31] David Nelson Spires, "The Career of the Reichswehr Officer," PhD Dissertation, University of Washington, 1979, 190-191.

[32] Rudolf Hofmann, *German Efficiency Report System*, MS# P-134, Königstein, Germany: U.S. Army Europe Historical Division, 1952, 14.

[33] Rudolf Hofmann, *German Efficiency Report System*, MS# P-134, Königstein, Germany: U.S. Army Europe Historical Division, 1952, 14.

[34] Rudolf Hofmann, *German Efficiency Report System*, MS# P-134, Königstein, Germany: U.S. Army Europe Historical Division, 1952, 8.

[35] Rudolf Hofmann, *German Efficiency Report System*, MS# P-134, Königstein, Germany: U.S. Army Europe Historical Division, 1952, 14, 21.

[36] Rudolf Hofmann, *German Efficiency Report System*, MS# P-134, Königstein, Germany: U.S. Army Europe Historical Division, 1952, 15.

[37] There was no provision for comments on an officer's religious views. Rudolf Hofmann considered that to be a mistake saying that "sincere confession of Christian principals is worthy of inclusion in the overall evaluation of an officer." Source: Rudolf Hofmann, *German Efficiency Report System*, MS# P-134, Königstein, Germany: U.S. Army Europe Historical Division, 1952, 20, 39.

[38] Rudolf Hofmann, *German Efficiency Report System*, MS# P-134, Königstein, Germany: U.S. Army Europe Historical Division, 1952, 15.

[39] Rudolf Hofmann, *German Efficiency Report System*, MS# P-134, Königstein, Germany: U.S. Army Europe Historical Division, 1952, 21, 22.

[40] In 1938, the German Army Personnel Office inquired senior level commanders concerning introducing a point system in efficiency reporting, but almost without exception this idea was rejected as a point system would tend to obscure the complete picture of an officer. Source: Rudolf Hofmann, *German Efficiency Report System*, MS# P-134, Königstein, Germany: U.S. Army Europe Historical Division, 1952, 35, 36.

[41] Rudolf Hofmann, *German Efficiency Report System*, MS# P-134, Königstein, Germany: U.S. Army Europe Historical Division, 1952, 23, 24, 30, 31.

[42] Rudolf Hofmann, *German Efficiency Report System*, MS# P-134, Königstein, Germany: U.S. Army Europe Historical Division, 1952, 32.

[43] Rudolf Hofmann, *German Efficiency Report System*, MS# P-134, Königstein, Germany: U.S. Army Europe Historical Division, 1952, 32.

[44] Rudolf Hofmann, *German Efficiency Report System*, MS# P-134, Königstein, Germany: U.S. Army Europe Historical Division, 1952, 33.

[45] Rudolf Hofmann, *German Efficiency Report System*, MS# P-134, Königstein, Germany: U.S. Army Europe Historical Division, 1952, 33.

[46] Rudolf Hofmann, *German Efficiency Report System*, MS# P-134, Königstein, Germany: U.S. Army Europe Historical Division, 1952, 38.

[47] John R. Angolia, *For Führer and Fatherland: Military Awards of the Third Reich*, San Jose, CA: Bender Publishing, 1976, 328-330.

[48] John R. Angolia, *For Führer and Fatherland: Military Awards of the Third Reich*, San Jose, CA: Bender Publishing, 1976, 320.

[49] John R. Angolia, *For Führer and Fatherland: Military Awards of the Third Reich*, San Jose, CA: Bender Publishing, 1976, 222.

[50] John R. Angolia, *For Führer and Fatherland: Military Awards of the Third Reich*, San Jose, CA: Bender Publishing, 1976, 223.

[51] John R. Angolia, *For Führer and Fatherland: Military Awards of the Third Reich*, San Jose, CA: Bender Publishing, 1976, 224.

[52] Chris Bishop, *Luftwaffe Squadrons 1939-45*, Stapelhurst, England: Spellmont, 2006, 10.

Rated Officers

[1] *Kriegs-Beurteilung zum 4. April 1944 über den Oberleutnant (Tr. O) Rudolf Franz Joseph Abrahamczik, II. /Kampfgeschwader 51, Hauptmann von Dalwigk, Gefechtsstand, 4. April 1944.*

[2] Sources, Rudolf Abrahamczik: Georg Brütting, *Das waren die deutschen Kampfflieger-Asse 1939-1945*, Stuttgart, FRG: Motorbuch Verlag, 1983, 178; Barry C. Rosch, Luftwaffe Codes, Markings and Units, 1939-1945, Atglen, PA: Schiffer Publishing, 1995, 234-235; Veit Scherzer, *Die Ritterkreuzträger: Die Inhaber des Ritterkreuzes des Eisernen Kreuzes 1939-1945*, Jena, Germany: Scherzers Militairs-Verlag, 2005, 165.

[3] *Beurteilung für den zukünftigen K.O.A. Feldwebel Herbert Bachnick, III. Group, Jagdgeschwader 52, Major Rall, Im Felde, 7.12.1943.*

[4] The American bombers were part of the second USAAF shuttle mission to the USSR, and were based, temporarily, at Mirgorod, Ukraine. Their targets that day were the airfields at Bizau and Zilistea.

[5] Sources, Herbert Bachnick: Roger A. Freeman, *Mighty Eighth War Diary*, London: Jane's, 1981, 319; Ernst Obermaier, *Die Ritterkreuzträger der Luftwaffe, Jagdflieger 1939-1945*, Mainz, FRG: Verlag Dieter Hoffmann, 1989, 83; John Weal, *Jagdgeschwader 52: The Experten*, Aviation Elite Units 15, Oxford, England: Osprey Publishing, 2004, 109.

[6] *Vorschlag zur Überführung des Hauptmann d.R. Josef Barmetler zu den aktiven Friedensoffizieren, Fallschirmjäger-Ersatz-Batl. Stendal, Major und Batl.-Kommandeur, General der Flieger Student, Stendal, 20.4.1943.*

[7] Sources, Josef Barmetler: Peter D. Antill, *Crete 1941: Germany's Lightning Airborne Assault*, Osprey Campaign 147, Oxford, England: Osprey Publishing, 2005, 39; Franz Thomas and Günter Wegmann, *Die Ritterkreuzträger der Deutschen Wehrmacht 1939-1945, Teil II: Fallschirmjäger*, Osnabrück, FRG: Biblio-Verlag, 1986, 10-11.

[8] *Beförderung Oberleutnant Bauer, III./Jagdgeschwader Generaloberst Udet, Major Anders, Gefechtsstand, 16.1.1942.*

[9] Sources, Viktor Bauer: Erwin Lenfeld and Franz Thomas, *Die Eichenlaubträger 1940-1945*, Wiener-Neustedt, Austria: Weilburg Verlag, 1983, 126 ; Ernst Obermaier, *Die Ritterkreuzträger der Luftwaffe, Jagdflieger 1939-1945*, Mainz, FRG: Verlag Dieter Hoffmann, 1989, 52; Jochen Prien, Gerhard Stemmer, Peter Rodeike and Winfried Bock, *Die Jagdfliegerverbände der Deutschen Luftwaffe 1934 bis 1945, Teil 3: Einsatz in Dänemark*

und Norwegen, 9.4. bis 30.11.40, Der Feldzug im Westen, 10.5. bis 25.6.1940, Eutin, Germany: Struve, 390; Jochen Prien, Gerhard Stemmer, Peter Rodeike and Winfried Bock, *Die Jagdfliegerverbände der Deutschen Luftwaffe 1934 bis 1945, Teil 4/I: Einsatz am Kanal und über England, 26.6.1940 bis 21.6.1941*, Eutin, Germany: Struve, 247; Jochen Prien, Gerhard Stemmer, Peter Rodeike and Winfried Bock, *Die Jagdfliegerverbände der Deutschen Luftwaffe 1934 bis 1945, Teil 6/I: Unternehmen "Barbarossa" Einsatz im Osten 22.6. bis 5.12.1941*, Eutin, Germany: Struve, 2003, 151; Jochen Prien, Gerhard Stemmer, Peter Rodeike and Winfried Bock, *Die Jagdfliegerverbände der Deutschen Luftwaffe 1934 bis 1945, Teil 9/I: Winterkampf im Osten 6.12.1941 bis 30.4.1942*, Eutin, Germany: Struve, 33; Jochen Prien, Gerhard Stemmer, Peter Rodeike and Winfried Bock, *Die Jagdfliegerverbände der Deutschen Luftwaffe 1934 bis 1945, Teil 9/II: Vom Sommerfeldzug 1942 bis zur Niederlage von Stalingrad 1.5.1942 bis 3.2.1943*, Eutin, Germany: Struve, 231; Franz Thomas, *Die Eichenlaubträger 1940-1945, Band 1: A-K, L-Z*, Osnabrück, Germany: Biblio-Verlag, 1998, 25; Raymond F. Toliver and Trevor J. Constable, *Das waren die Deutschen Jagdflieger-Asse 1939-1945*, Stuttgart, FRG: Motorbuch Verlag, 1981, 388.

[10] Another source lists the date of award for the German Cross in Gold as April 24, 1942.

[11] *Vorschlag zur Beförderung eines Offiziers (d.B.) zum nächsthöheren Dienstgrad Ludwig Becker, Nachtjagdgeschwader 1, Hauptmann und Gruppenkommandeur Lent, Oberstleutnant Friedberg, Generalleutnant von Döring, Gefechtsstand, 28.10.42*.

[12] Sources, Ludwig Becker: John R. Angolia, *On The Field Of Honor; A History of the Knight's Cross Bearers, Volume 2*, San Jose, CA: Bender Publishing, 1980, 178; Roger A. Freeman, *Mighty Eighth War Diary*, London: Jane's, 1981, 40; Erwin Lenfeld and Franz Thomas, *Die Eichenlaubträger 1940-1945*, Wiener-Neustedt, Austria: Weilburg Verlag, 1983, 219; Martin Middlebrook and Chris Everitt, *The Bomber Command War Diaries*, New York: Viking Penguin, 1987, 232, 276; Ernst Obermaier, *Die Ritterkreuzträger der Luftwaffe, Jagdflieger 1939-1945*, Mainz, FRG: Verlag Dieter Hoffmann, 1989, 56; Mike Spick, *Luftwaffe Fighter Aces: The Jagdflieger and Their Combat Tactics and Techniques*, Mechanicsburg, PA: Stackpole Books, 2003, 151; Franz Thomas, *Die Eichenlaubträger 1940-1945, Band 1: A-K*, Osnabrück, Germany: Biblio-Verlag, 1998, 33; Raymond F. Toliver and Trevor J. Constable, *Das waren die Deutschen Jagdflieger-Asse 1939-1945*, Stuttgart, FRG: Motorbuch Verlag, 1981, 391.

[13] The unit was named in honor of an early Nazi martyr and SA member, Horst Wessel, who was killed during street clashes with communists. His poem became the quasi-anthem of the Nazis: "Die Fahne hoch/Das Horst Wessel Lied".

[14] *Beurteilung über den Hauptmann Friedrich Beckh, II. Gruppe, Jagdgeschwader Horst Wessel Nr 134, Oberstleutnant und Gruppenkommandeur Osterkamp, Oberstleutnant und Geschwaderkommodore von Döring, Oberst Student, Major und Gruppenkommandeur Vollbracht, Werl, 27.8.37*.

[15] Sources, Friedrich Beckh: Gebhard Aders and Werner Held, *Jagdgeschwader 51 "Mölders"*, Stuttgart, FRG: Motorbuch Verlag, 1985, 67, 84, 95, 107; Ernst Obermaier, *Die Ritterkreuzträger der Luftwaffe, Jagdflieger 1939-1945*, Mainz, FRG: Verlag Dieter Hoffmann, 1989, 85; Jochen Prien, Gerhard Stemmer, Peter Rodeike and Winfried Bock, *Die Jagdfliegerverbände der Deutschen Luftwaffe 1934 bis 1945, Teil 4/II: Einsatz am Kanal und über England, 26.6.1940 bis 21.6.1941*, Eutin, Germany: Struve, 106; Jochen Prien, Gerhard Stemmer, Peter Rodeike and Winfried Bock, *Die Jagdfliegerverbände der Deutschen Luftwaffe 1934 bis 1945, Teil 6/I: Unternehmen "Barbarossa" Einsatz im Osten 22.6. bis 5.12.1941*, Eutin, Germany: Struve, 2003, 220-221; Jochen Prien, Gerhard Stemmer, Peter Rodeike and Winfried Bock, *Die Jagdfliegerverbände der Deutschen Luftwaffe 1934 bis 1945, Teil 9/I: Winterkampf im Osten 6.12.1941 bis 30.4.1942*, Eutin, Germany: Struve, 47; Jochen Prien, Gerhard Stemmer, Peter Rodeike and Winfried Bock, *Die Jagdfliegerverbände der Deutschen Luftwaffe 1934 bis 1945, Teil 9/II: Vom Sommerfeldzug 1942 bis zur Niederlage von Stalingrad 1.5.1942 bis 3.2.1943*, Eutin, Germany: Struve, 387.

[16] Jagdgeschwader 51 received the honorary name "Mölders" on December 20, 1941 in honor of World War II fighter ace Werner Mölders, who had commanded the fighter wing until the previous summer. Mölders died in a flying accident on his way to attend the funeral of Ernst Udet.

[17] The green heart was the symbol of Thuringia, the birthplace of the wing's first commander, Hannes Trautloft, and selected by him.

[18] In October 1940, the Italian attack on Greece, through Albania, was repelled, with a Greek counterattack threatening Italian positions in the Balkans. In November, Britain occupied Crete, and Hitler decided to invade Yugoslavia and the Balkans. This would deprive the British of bases for future ground and air operations against Romanian oilfields and indirectly assist Italy by diverting Greek forces from Albania. In March 1941, an anti-German military coup toppled the pro-German Yugoslav government and expedited the attack.

[19] *Beurteilungsnotiz über den Leutnant und Staffelführer Hans Beisswenger, II. Gruppe, Jagdgeschwader 54, Hauptmann und Gruppenkommandeur Hrabak, Im Felde, 4.9.1942*.

[20] Underlines were made in pencil, after the report was written, probably by someone in the Luftwaffe Personnel Department.

[21] Sources, Hans Beisswenger: Erwin Lenfeld and Franz Thomas, *Die Eichenlaubträger 1940-1945*, Wiener-Neustedt, Austria: Weilburg Verlag, 1983, 149; Ernst Obermaier, *Die Ritterkreuzträger der Luftwaffe, Jagdflieger 1939-1945*, Mainz, FRG: Verlag Dieter Hoffmann, 1989, 54; Jochen Prien, Gerhard Stemmer, Peter Rodeike and Winfried Bock, *Die Jagdfliegerverbände der Deutschen Luftwaffe 1934 bis 1945, Teil 6/II: Unternehmen "Barbarossa" Einsatz im Osten 22.6. bis 5.12.1941*, Eutin, Germany: Struve, 2003, 235, 242; Jochen Prien, Gerhard Stemmer, Peter Rodeike and Winfried Bock, *Die Jagdfliegerverbände der Deutschen Luftwaffe 1934 bis 1945, Teil 9/I: Winterkampf im Osten 6.12.1941 bis 30.4.1942*, Eutin, Germany: Struve, 224; Franz Thomas, *Die Eichenlaubträger 1940-1945, Band 1: A-K*, Osnabrück, Germany: Biblio-Verlag, 1998, 39; Raymond F. Toliver and Trevor J. Constable, *Das waren die Deutschen Jagdflieger-Asse 1939-1945*, Stuttgart, FRG: Motorbuch Verlag, 1981, 387; John Weal, *Focke-Wulf Fw 190 Aces of the Russian Front*, Osprey Aircraft of the Aces 6, Oxford, England: Osprey Publishing, 1995, 22-23, 57; John Weal, *Jagdgeschwader 54 "Grünherz,"* Osprey Aviation Elite 6, Oxford, England: Osprey Publishing, 2001, 39, 57, 60, 78.

[22] *Vorschlag zur Beförderung eines Offiziers (d.B.) zum nächsthöheren Dienstgrad Wilhelm Bertram, Kampfgruppe 106, Hauptmann und Gruppenkommandeur Sämischen, Generalleutnant und Fliegerführer Atlantik Kessler, Gefechtsstand, 20.2.42*. Next to the Group Commander's signature block is an interesting phrase translated to "Was written by the officer." Of all the reports in this book, this is only one of two examples of this phrase, which could mean one of two things. It is either a notation that the rater, Sämischen, wrote the evaluation (which was then typed by someone else), or it could mean that the rated officer wrote his own recommendation – on himself – and submitted it to the rater for use in the report.

[23] Sources, Wilhelm Bertram: Georg Brütting, *Das waren die deutschen Kampfflieger-Asse 1939-1945*, Stuttgart, FRG: Motorbuch Verlag,

1983, 181; Barry C. Rosch, *Luftwaffe Codes, Markings and Units, 1939-1945*, Atglen, PA: Schiffer Publishing, 1995, 259; Horst Scheibert, *Die Träger der Ehrenblattspange des Heeres und der Waffen-SS, Die Träger der Ehrentafelspange der Kriegsmarine, Die Inhaber des Ehrenpokals für besondere Leistung im Luftkrieg*, Friedberg, FRG: Podzun-Pallas-Verlag, 1986, 142; Veit Scherzer, *Die Träger des Deutschen Kreuzes in Gold der Luftwaffe 1941-1945*, Bayreuth, FRG: Scherzer's Militair Verlag, 1992, 25.

[24] *Beurteilung, Heinrich Boecker, 3./LG 1, Oberleutnant u. Staffelkapitän Beeger, Orleans-Bircy, 28.12.40.*

[25] Sources, Heinrich Boecker: Georg Brütting, *Das waren die deutschen Kampfflieger-Asse 1939-1945*, Stuttgart, FRG: Motorbuch Verlag, 1983, 182; Veit Scherzer, *Die Träger des Deutschen Kreuzes in Gold der Luftwaffe 1941-1945*, Bayreuth, FRG: Scherzer's Militair Verlag, 1992, 31; Christopher Shores and Brian Cull, *Air War for Yugoslavia, Greece and Crete*, Carrollton, TX: Squadron Signal Publications, 1987, 357; Peter Taghorn, *Die Geschichte des Lehrgeschwaders 1, Band 1 (1936-1942)*, Zweibrücken, Germany: 2004, 232, 267, 455, 457; Peter Taghorn, *Die Geschichte des Lehrgeschwaders 1, Band 2 (1942-1945)*, Zweibrücken, Germany: 2004, 9, 22, 47, 492.

[26] *Vorschlag zur bevorzugten Beförderung für Oberleutnant (Tr.O) Rudolf Boehlein, Fallschirm-Jaeger-Regiment 4, Oberstleutnant und Rgt. Führer Böhmler, Generalleutnant und Divisionskommandeur Heidrich, O.U., 8.11.44.*

[27] Sources, Rudolf Böhlein: Roger Edwards, *German Airborne Troops 1936-1945*, Garden City, NJ: Doubleday & Company, 1974, 116; Ken Ford, *Cassino 1944: Breaking the Gustav Line*, Osprey Campaign 134, Oxford, England: Osprey Publishing, 2004, 63; Bruce Quarrie, *German Airborne Divisions: Mediterranean Theater 1942-45*, Osprey Battle Orders 15, Oxford, England: Osprey Publishing, 2005, 79-80; Franz Thomas and Günter Wegmann, *Die Ritterkreuzträger der Deutschen Wehrmacht 1939-1945, Teil II: Fallschirmjäger*, Osnabrück, FRG: Biblio-Verlag, 1986, 27-28.

[28] The operational intent of the German General Staff was to paralyze Dutch resistance and disrupt the movement of Dutch Army reserves by quickly seizing The Hague, Rotterdam and a few other vital communications' centers, primarily by airborne attacks.

[29] The intent of the German General Staff (manifested in Hitler's "Directive Number 28") for "Operation Mercury" was to occupy the island, which would then serve as an air base against Britain in the Eastern Mediterranean. A costly operation, the paratroopers lost 3,250 killed and 3,400 wounded.

[30] *Vorschlag zur bevorzugten Beförderung für Hauptmann (Tr.O) Rudolf Böhmler, Fallschirm-Jäger-Regiment 3, Oberstleutnant Heilmann, Generalmajor und Divisionskommandeur Heidrich, O.U., 4.5.1943.*

[31] Sources, Rudolf Böhmler: Roger Edwards, *German Airborne Troops 1936-1945*, Garden City, NJ: Doubleday & Company, 1974, 91, 102; Ken Ford, *Cassino 1944: Breaking the Gustav Line*, Osprey Campaign 134, Oxford, England: Osprey Publishing, 2004, 58, 62, 63; James Lucas, *Storming Eagles: German Airborne Forces in World War Two*, London: Arms and Armour Press, 1988, 12, 29, 30; Franz Thomas and Günter Wegmann, *Die Ritterkreuzträger der Deutschen Wehrmacht 1939-1945, Teil II: Fallschirmjäger*, Osnabrück, FRG: Biblio-Verlag, 1986, 29-31.

[32] The unit was named for World War I fighter ace Max Immelmann, the "Eagle of Lille," who was killed in 1916.

[33] *Endgültige Feststellung der ausserdienstlichen Eignung zum Kriegsoffizier Hans-Joachim Brand, Erg. Staffel/St.G. 77, Oberleutnant und Staffelführer Leicht, 22. Juni 1941.*

[34] Proof of Aryan blood crept into almost every facet of German life under National Socialism. In theory, all commissioned officers were required to meet certain German blood standards, although some unique situations did occasionally arise. See: Bryan Mark Rigg's *Hitler's Jewish Soldiers: The Untold Story of Nazi Racial Laws and Men of Jewish Descent in the German Military*.

[35] Sources, Hans-Joachim Brand: Georg Brütting, *Das waren die deutschen Stuka-Asse, 1939-1945*, Stuttgart, FRG: Motorbuch Verlag, 1976, 186; Ernst Obermaier, *Die Ritterkreuzträger der Luftwaffe, Stuka und Schlachtflieger 1939-1945*, Mainz, FRG: Verlag Dieter Hoffmann, 1976, 67; Veit Scherzer, *Die Träger des Deutschen Kreuzes in Gold der Luftwaffe 1941-1945*, Bayreuth, FRG: Scherzer's Militair Verlag, 1992, 37.

[36] *Kriegs-Beurteilung zum 10. Juli 1944 über den Hptm. (Tr.) Werner Breese, 1./Fernaufkl. Geschwader 101, Hauptmann m.d.W.d.G.d.Kdrs.b. Hünsdorff, Oberst Schneider, Grossenhain, 10. Juli 1944.*

[37] Sources, Werner Breese: *Kriegs-Beurteilung zum 10. Juli 1944 über den Hptm. (Tr.) Werner Breese, 1./Fernaufkl. Geschwader 101, Hauptmann m.d.W.d.G.d.Kdrs.b. Hünsdorff, Oberst Schneider, Grossenhain, 10. Juli 1944*; Veit Scherzer, *Die Träger des Deutschen Kreuzes in Gold der Luftwaffe 1941-1945*, Bayreuth, FRG: Scherzer's Militair Verlag, 1992, 39.

[38] Hitler's "Directive Number 17," dated August 1, 1940, gave the following mission to the *Luftwaffe* that led to the battle: "The German Air Force is to overpower the English Air Force with all the forces at its command, in the shortest possible time. The attacks are to be directed primarily against flying units, their ground installations, and their supply organizations, but also against the aircraft industry, including that manufacturing anti-aircraft equipment. After achieving temporary or local air superiority the air war is to be continued against ports, in particular against stores of food, and also against stores of provisions in the interior of the country." Source: H.R. Trevor-Roper, *Blitzkrieg to Defeat: Hitler's War Directives, 1939-1945*, New York: Holt, Rinehart and Winston, 1964, 37-38.

[39] On November 8, 1940 the RAF bombed Munich, the birthplace of the Nazi Party. Hitler demanded revenge and ordered the Luftwaffe to attack an English city. Hermann Göring quickly implemented "Operation Moonlight Sonata," an air attack which sent over 500 bombers against Coventry, a city at the industrial heart of Britain's war production effort. The attack began at about 7:00 pm on November 14 and lasted over 10 hours. *Luftwaffe* bombers dropped over 30,000 incendiary bombs and hundreds of tons of high explosive ordnance. The attack killed 554 people, injured 865 and destroyed 4,330 homes.

[40] *Sonderbeurteilung des Oberleutnant Gerhard Brenner, I. Gruppe, Lehrgeschwader 1, Hauptmann und Gruppenkommandeur Helbig, Gefechtsstand, 14.4.1942.*

[41] Sources, Gerhard Brenner: Cajus Bekker, *The Luftwaffe War Diaries*, London: MacDonald & Co., 1967, 241; Peter Taghorn, *Die Geschichte des Lehrgeschwaders 1, Band 2 (1942-1945)*, Zweibrücken, Germany: 2004, 29, 486, 534.

[42] The *Luftwaffe* Honor Goblet is mentioned in his efficiency report, but not in post-war literature on the award.

[43] *Beurteilung Max Buchholz, I./Jagdgeschwader 3, Hauptmann u. Gruppenkommandeur von Hahn, major und Geschwader-Kommodore Lützow, Gefechtsstand, 2.1.1941.*

[44] "Operation Cerberus" was the name the German Navy gave to the surprise dash up the English Channel by three major warships of the *Kriegsmarine* – the Scharnhorst, Gneisenau and heavy cruiser Prinz Eugen – February 11-13, 1942. The ships, which had previously conducted operations in the North Atlantic, were in Brest – but Hitler felt it was only a matter of time before they were severely damaged by British air attacks or French sabotage. Additionally, he was concerned that the Navy did not have enough strength in Norway to resist a potential British invasion of that coast. Adolf Galland assumed operational control of the

280 *Luftwaffe* fighter aircraft that protected the ships during the run through the English Channel. His younger brother Second Lieutenant Paul Galland, assigned to the 3rd Group, 26th Fighter Wing "Schlageter," in a five minute span personally shot down 4 British Swordfish torpedo-bombers that were attempting to attack the three ships off Gravelines, France. Although the Scharnhorst later struck a mine during the voyage, all ships made it back to German ports.

[45] Sources, Max Buchholz: Ernst Obermaier, *Die Ritterkreuzträger der Luftwaffe, Jagdflieger 1939-1945*, Mainz, FRG: Verlag Dieter Hoffmann, 1989, 96; Jochen Prien, Gerhard Stemmer, Peter Rodeike and Winfried Bock, *Die Jagdfliegerverbände der Deutschen Luftwaffe 1934 bis 1945, Teil 3: Einsatz in Dänemark und Norwegen, 9.4. bis 30.11.40, Der Feldzug im Westen, 10.5. bis 25.6.1940*, Eutin, Germany: Struve, 155; Jochen Prien, Gerhard Stemmer, Peter Rodeike and Winfried Bock, *Die Jagdfliegerverbände der Deutschen Luftwaffe 1934 bis 1945, Teil 6/I: Unternehmen "Barbarossa" Einsatz im Osten 22.6. bis 5.12.1941*, Eutin, Germany: Struve, 2003, 74-79; Jochen Prien, Gerhard Stemmer, Peter Rodeike and Winfried Bock, *Die Jagdfliegerverbände der Deutschen Luftwaffe 1934 bis 1945, Teil 7: Heimatsverteidigung 1. Januar bis 31. Dezember 1942, Einsatz im Westen 1. Januar bis 31. Dezember 1942*, Eutin, Germany: Struve, 2003, 68; Veit Scherzer, *Die Ritterkreuzträger: Die Inhaber des Ritterkreuzes des Eisernen Kreuzes 1939-1945*, Jena, Germany: Scherzers Militairs-Verlag, 2005, 227.

[46] The unit was named in honor of World War I ace, Manfred von Richthofen.

[47] On August 19, 1942, the Allies launched an amphibious raid on Dieppe in northern France. Winston Churchill approved the attack, which would result in 4,384 killed, wounded or missing of the 6,000 men in the landing, to conduct a reconnaissance in force, to test the enemy defenses on a strongly-held coastal sector of France and to discover the level of resistance likely to be met in an attempt to seize a port. In what was the largest single-day air battle to that time, the Royal Air Force flew 2,617 sorties in support of the raid.

[48] *Vorschlag zur Beförderung eines Offiziers (Kr.O.) zum nächsthöheren Dienstgrad Kurt Bühligen, II. Gruppe, Jagdgeschwader Richthofen Nr. 2, Oberleutnant und stellv. Gruppenkommandeur Dickfeld, General der Flieger Loerzer, Generalfeldmarschall Kesselring, Gefechtsstand, 5.12.1942.*

[49] Sources, Kurt Bühligen: *Kriegsbeurteilung über den Hauptmann (Kr.Offz.) Kurt Bühligen, Jagdgeschwader Richthofen Nr. 2, Major und Geschwaderkommodore m.d.W.d.G.b. Egon Mayer, Gefechtsstand, 18.7.1943*; Chris Bishop, *Luftwaffe Squadrons 1939-45*, Stapelhurst, England: Spellmont, 2006, 136; Erwin Lenfeld and Franz Thomas, *Die Eichenlaubträger 1940-1945*, Wiener-Neustedt, Austria: Weilburg Verlag, 1983, 436; Ernst Obermaier, *Die Ritterkreuzträger der Luftwaffe, Jagdflieger 1939-1945*, Mainz, FRG: Verlag Dieter Hoffmann, 1989, 38; Christopher Shores, Hans Ring and William Hess, *Fighters Over Tunisia*, London: Neville Spearman, 1975, 188-192; Raymond Toliver and Trevor J. Constable, *Das waren die Deutschen Jagdflieger-Asse, 1939-1945*, Stuttgart, FRG: Motorbuch Verlag, 1981, 319-320, 388; John Weal, *Jagdgeschwader 2 'Richthofen,'* Osprey Aviation Elite 1, Oxford, England: Osprey Publishing, 2000, 56, 58, 62, 96, 106, 110 & 117; Jochen Prien, Gerhard Stemmer, Peter Rodeike and Winfried Bock, *Die Jagdfliegerverbände der Deutschen Luftwaffe 1934 bis 1945, Teil 4/I: Einsatz am Kanal und über England, 26.6.1940 bis 21.6.1941*, Eutin, Germany: Struve, 122, 124; Jochen Prien, Gerhard Stemmer, Peter Rodeike and Winfried Bock, *Die Jagdfliegerverbände der Deutschen Luftwaffe 1934 bis 1945, Teil 7: Heimatsverteidigung 1. Januar bis 31. Dezember 1942, Einsatz im Westen 1. Januar bis 31. Dezember 1942*, Eutin, Germany: Struve, 2003, 260; Jochen Prien, Gerhard Stemmer, Peter Rodeike and Winfried Bock, *Die Jagdfliegerverbände der Deutschen Luftwaffe 1934 bis 1945, Teil 8/I: Einsatz im Mittelmeerraum November 1941 bis Dezember 1942*, Eutin, Germany: Struve, 2004, 51; Franz Thomas, *Die Eichenlaubträger 1940-1945, Band 1: A-K*, Osnabrück, Germany: Biblio-Verlag, 1998, 89; Tomasz Gronczewski, "Camouflage & Markings: Early Focke-Wulf Fw 190s," HYPERLINK "http://www.ipmsstockholm.org/magazine/2004/08/stuff_eng_profile_fw190a4.htm" *http://www.ipmsstockholm.org/magazine/2004/08/stuff_eng_profile_fw190a4.htm*.

[50] Nidda is 45 minutes north of Frankfurt.

[51] *Antrag auf bevorzugte Beförderung des Oblt. (Tr.O) Carganico und Ernennung zum Kommandeur II./J.G. 5., Luftwaffenkommando 5, Generaloberst Stumpff, Gefechtsstand, 26.7.1942.*

[52] Sources, Horst Carganico: Werner Girbig, *Jagdgeschwader 5 "Eismeerjäger": Eine Chronik aus Dokumenten und Berichten 1941-1945*, Stuttgart, FRG: Motorbuch Verlag, 1976, 342-363; Ernst Obermaier, *Die Ritterkreuzträger der Luftwaffe, Jagdflieger 1939-1945*, Mainz, FRG: Verlag Dieter Hoffmann, 1989, 98; Jochen Prien, *Geschichte des Jagdgeschwaders 77, Teil 1*, Hamburg, Germany: Self-published, 1992, 236, 243, 446; Jochen Prien, Gerhard Stemmer, Peter Rodeike and Winfried Bock, *Die Jagdfliegerverbände der Deutschen Luftwaffe 1934 bis 1945, Teil 3: Einsatz in Dänemark und Norwegen, 9.4. bis 30.11.40, Der Feldzug im Westen, 10.5. bis 25.6.1940*, Eutin, Germany: Struve, 23-24; Jochen Prien, Gerhard Stemmer, Peter Rodeike and Winfried Bock, *Die Jagdfliegerverbände der Deutschen Luftwaffe 1934 bis 1945, Teil 7: Heimatsverteidigung 1. Januar bis 31. Dezember 1942, Einsatz im Westen 1. Januar bis 31. Dezember 1942*, Eutin, Germany: Struve, 2003, 158.

[53] *Vorschlag zur Beförderung zum Kriegsoffizier Wilhelm Crinius, I./Jagdgeschwader 53, Oberleutnant und Staffelkapitän Tonne, Hauptmann und Gruppenkommandeur Quaet-Faslem, Hauptmann und Geschwader-Kommodore Wilcke, September 1942.*

[54] On December 20, 1941, *Jagdgeschwader 3* received the commemorative name "Udet" in honor of Colonel General Ernst Udet, World War I fighter ace and *Luftwaffe* Chief of Supply and Procurement. Udet committed suicide on November 17, 1941, but Hitler attempted to cover-up the cause of Udet's death.

[55] Sources, Wilhelm Crinius: Ernst Obermaier, *Die Ritterkreuzträger der Luftwaffe, Jagdflieger 1939-1945*, Mainz, FRG: Verlag Dieter Hoffmann, 1989, 53; Jochen Prien, *Pik-As: Geschichte des Jagdgeschwaders 53*, Hamburg, Germany: Dr. Jochen Prien, 1991, Teil 2: 568, Teil 3: 1670-16/8; Jochen Prien, Gerhard Stemmer, Peter Rodeike and Winfried Bock, *Die Jagdfliegerverbände der Deutschen Luftwaffe 1934 bis 1945, Teil 8/II: Einsatz im Mittelmeerraum November 1941 bis Dezember 1942*, Eutin, Germany: Struve, 2004, 81.

[56] *Kriegsbeurteilung über den Hauptmann (Kr.Offz.) und Gruppenkommandeur Adolf Dickfeld, Jagdgeschwader Richthofen Nr. 2, Oberstlt. u. Geschwaderkommandeur Oesau, Gefechtsstand, 10.5.1943.*

[57] Sources, Adolf Dickfeld: Ernst Obermaier, *Die Ritterkreuzträger der Luftwaffe, Jagdflieger 1939-1945*, Mainz, FRG: Verlag Dieter Hoffmann, 1989, 50; Jochen Prien, Gerhard Stemmer, Peter Rodeike and Winfried Bock, *Die Jagdfliegerverbände der Deutschen Luftwaffe 1934 bis 1945, Teil 6/II: Unternehmen "Barbarossa" Einsatz im Osten 22.6. bis 5.12.1941*, Eutin, Germany: Struve, 2003, 68, 70, 74, 75; Jochen Prien, Gerhard Stemmer, Peter Rodeike and Winfried Bock, *Die Jagdfliegerverbände der Deutschen Luftwaffe 1934 bis 1945, Teil 8/I: Einsatz im Mittelmeerraum November 1941 bis Dezember 1942*, Eutin, Germany: Struve, 2004, 51; Jochen Prien, Gerhard Stemmer, Peter Rodeike and Winfried Bock, *Die Jagdfliegerverbände der Deutschen Luftwaffe 1934 bis 1945, Teil

9/II: Vom Sommerfeldzug 1942 bis zur Niederlage von Stalingrad 1.5.1942 bis 3.2.1943, Eutin, Germany: Struve, 537.

[58] *Beurteilung des O. Fähnrich Erwin Diekwisch, Ergänzungs-Sturzkampf-Staffel, Oberleutnant u. stellv. Staffelführer Reusch, Oberstlt. Und Geschw.-Kommodore Hagen, Schaffen-Diest, 16.1.1941.*

[59] Another source states the award date for the German Cross in Gold as May 27, 1942.

[60] Sources, Erwin-Peter Diekwisch: Ernst Obermaier, *Die Ritterkreuzträger der Luftwaffe, Stuka und Schlachtflieger 1939-1945*, Mainz, FRG: Verlag Dieter Hoffmann, 1976, 72-73; Veit Scherzer, *Die Träger des Deutschen Kreuzes in Gold der Luftwaffe 1941-1945*, Bayreuth, FRG: Scherzer's Militair Verlag, 1992, 57.

[61] In theory, German military personnel, who volunteered to serve in Spain (for *Luftwaffe* personnel, the tour of duty was generally 6-9 months), were discharged from the German armed forces, but while serving in Spain would be promoted one rank above their previous grade; source: Carlos Caballero Jurado, *The Condor Legion: German Troops in the Spanish Civil War*, Osprey Elite 131, Oxford, England: Osprey Publishing, 2006, 11, 13.

[62] *Antrag auf Beförderung des Ofw. Anton Döbele zum Kriegsoffizier wegen Tapferkeit vor dem Feinde, 1. Staffel, I./Jagdgeschwader 54, Oberleutnant u. Staffelkapitän Nowotny, von Bonin, O.U., 16.9.1943.*

[63] Another source states that the award date for the German Cross in Gold was August 31, 1943.

[64] Sources, Anton Döbele: Ernst Obermaier, *Die Ritterkreuzträger der Luftwaffe, Jagdflieger 1939-1945*, Mainz, FRG: Verlag Dieter Hoffmann, 1989, 101; John Weal, *Focke-Wulf Fw 190 Aces of the Russian Front*, Osprey Aircraft of the Aces 6, Oxford, England: Osprey Publishing, 1995, 68, 72; Veit Scherzer, *Die Träger des Deutschen Kreuzes in Gold der Luftwaffe 1941-1945*, Bayreuth, FRG: Scherzer's Militair Verlag, 1992, 59; John Weal, *Jagdgeschwader 54 "Grünherz,"* Osprey Aviation Elite 6, Oxford, England: Osprey Publishing, 2001, 106.

[65] "Operation Citadel" was the code name for the massive July 1943 German offensive to eliminate the Kursk salient on the Eastern Front. The plan called for a simultaneous attack by the 4th Panzer Army in the south and the 9th Army in the north. To support the 9th Army the *Luftwaffe* allocated the 1st Air Division; the entire 6th Air Fleet was available to support the southern thrust. Together these air units assembled 1,800 aircraft.

[66] *Kriegs-Beurteilung zum 1. Februar 1944 über den Oberstleutnant (Tr.O.) Alfred Druschel, General der Schlachtflieger, Oberst und General der Schlachtflieger Hitschhold, Rangsdorf, 13.1.1944.*

[67] In an interview with former Private First Class Myron MacLean, who was assigned to the U.S. 1st Battalion, 39th Infantry Regiment, 9th Infantry Division, located in the immediate Höfen area in January 1945, he recalled examining a crashed German fighter aircraft, but did not recall any makeshift grave in the area of the wreckage. It is quite possible the grave was never marked.

[68] Sources, Alfred Druschel: John Manrho and Ron Pütz, *Bodenplatte: The Luftwaffe's Last Hope*, Browborough, England: Hikoki Publication, 2004, 48, 63, 64, 278; Ernst Obermaier, *Die Ritterkreuzträger der Luftwaffe, Stuka und Schlachtflieger 1939-1945*, Mainz, FRG: Verlag Dieter Hoffmann, 1976, 31; Jochen Prien, Gerhard Stemmer, Peter Rodeike and Winfried Bock, *Die Jagdfliegerverbände der Deutschen Luftwaffe 1934 bis 1945, Teil 5: Heimatverteidigung 10. Mai 1940 bis 31. Dezember 1941, Einsatz im Mittelmeerraum Oktober 1940 bis November 1941, Einsatz im Westen 22. Juni bis 31. Dezember 1941, Die Ergänzungsjagdgruppen Einsatz 1941 bis zur Auflösung Anfang 1942*, Eutin, Germany: Struve, 2003, 317; John Weal, *Luftwaffe Schlachtgruppen*, Aviation Elite Units 13, Oxford, England: Osprey Publishing, 2003, 34, 35, 52.

[69] *Vorschlag zur bevorzugten Beförderung eines Offiziers (Leutnant und Staffelkapitän) in Truppenführerstellung (Hauptmann) Hans Ehlers, Jagdgeschwader 1, Hauptmann Grislawski, Oberstleutnant Oesau, O.U., 16. Januar 1944.*

[70] The comment "infanteristische Erfahrungen" in the report can be literally translated "infantry experience." In this case, it could also mean in a figurative sense that Ehlers' long experience as an enlisted man would lead him to a certain affinity for ground combat soldiers, i.e., those the *Luftwaffe* was supporting.

[71] Sources, Hans Ehlers: Eric Mombeek, *Defending the Reich: The History of Jagdgeschwader 1 "Oesau"*, Norwich, England: JAC Publications, 1992, 57, 58, 135, 179, 185, 187, 188, 200, 224, 257, 259; Ernst Obermaier, *Die Ritterkreuzträger der Luftwaffe, Jagdflieger 1939-1945*, Mainz, FRG: Verlag Dieter Hoffmann, 1989, 106; Jochen Prien, Gerhard Stemmer, Peter Rodeike and Winfried Bock, *Die Jagdfliegerverbände der Deutschen Luftwaffe 1934 bis 1945, Teil 3: Einsatz in Dänemark und Norwegen, 9.4. bis 30.11.40, Der Feldzug im Westen, 10.5. bis 25.6.1940*, Eutin, Germany: Struve, 155; Jochen Prien, Gerhard Stemmer, Peter Rodeike and Winfried Bock, *Die Jagdfliegerverbände der Deutschen Luftwaffe 1934 bis 1945, Teil 4/I: Einsatz am Kanal und über England, 26.6.1940 bis 21.6.1941*, Eutin, Germany: Struve, 186; Jochen Prien, Gerhard Stemmer, Peter Rodeike and Winfried Bock, *Die Jagdfliegerverbände der Deutschen Luftwaffe 1934 bis 1945, Teil 6/I: Unternehmen "Barbarossa" Einsatz im Osten 22.6. bis 5.12.1941*, Eutin, Germany: Struve, 2003, 74-80; Jochen Prien, Gerhard Stemmer, Peter Rodeike and Winfried Bock, *Die Jagdfliegerverbände der Deutschen Luftwaffe 1934 bis 1945, Teil 7: Heimatsverteidigung 1. Januar bis 31. Dezember 1942, Einsatz im Westen 1. Januar bis 31. Dezember 1942*, Eutin, Germany: Struve, 2003, 77.

[72] *Beförderungsvorschlag für Oberfeldwebel Siegfried Engfer, Jagdgeschwader "Udet", Major und Geschwader-Kommodore Wilcke, Gefechtsstand, 20.1. 1943.*

[73] Sources, Siegfried Engfer: Ernst Obermaier, *Die Ritterkreuzträger der Luftwaffe, Jagdflieger 1939-1945*, Mainz, FRG: Verlag Dieter Hoffmann, 1989, 108.

[74] The Battle of Britain lasted from August 1940 to mid-1941. The *Luftwaffe* raids killed 40,000 people and injured 86,000, destroying 2,000,000 homes. The *Luftwaffe* lost 1,294 aircraft through October 31, 1940 and a further 600 bombers after in the then predominantly night aerial attacks. Source: Chris Bishop, *Luftwaffe Squadrons 1939-45*, Stapelhurst, England: Spellmont, 2006, 38.

[75] *Vorschlag zur Überführung des (Kriegsoffiziers) Oblt. Felgenhauer zu den aktiven Friedensoffizieren, 2.(F)/123, Major und Staffelkapitän von Obernitz, O.U., 17.5.1941.*

[76] Sources, Waldemar Felgenhauer: *Personalnachweis/Dienstlaufbahn, Waldemar Felgenhauer; Offizier-Kriegsstammrolle der 2. Staffel, Aufklärungsgruppe 123, Waldemar Felgenhauer.*

[77] *Beurteilungsnotiz über den Leutnant Leopold Fellerer, II./Nachtjagdgeschwader 1, Hauptmann und Gruppenkommandeur Ehle, Gefechtsstand, 14.11.1941.*

[78] 4.6% of the RAF bomber force was lost in the attack.

[79] Sources, Leopold Fellerer: Martin Middlebrook and Chris Everitt, *The Bomber Command War Diaries*, New York: Viking Penguin, 1987, 124, 465; Ernst Obermaier, *Die Ritterkreuzträger der Luftwaffe, Jagdflieger 1939-1945*, Mainz, FRG: Verlag Dieter Hoffmann, 1989, 110; Veit Scherzer, *Die Träger des Deutschen Kreuzes in Gold der Luftwaffe 1941-1945*, Bayreuth, FRG: Scherzer's Militair Verlag, 1992, 75.

[80] The unit was initially equipped with Junkers Ju 52s and later with Heinkel He 111Bs.

[81] *Beurteilungsnotiz über den Leutnant d.R. Karl Fitzner, I./Sturzkampfgeschwader 77, Hauptmann und Gruppenkommandeur Bruck, Gefechtsstand, 26.2.43.*

[82] Sources, Karl Fitzner: Georg Brütting, *Das waren die deutschen Stuka-Asse, 1939-1945*, Stuttgart, FRG: Motorbuch Verlag, 1976, 195; Ernst Obermaier, *Die Ritterkreuzträger der Luftwaffe, Stuka und Schlachtflieger 1939-1945*, Mainz, FRG: Verlag Dieter Hoffmann, 1976, 78-79; Veit Scherzer, *Die Träger des Deutschen Kreuzes in Gold der Luftwaffe 1941-1945*, Bayreuth, FRG: Scherzer's Militair Verlag, 1992, 79; Peter C. Smith, *Stuka Squadron*, Wellingborough, England: Patrick Stephens, 1990, 157-158.

[83] *Brief an Generalkommando I. Fliegerkorps IIa, Jagdgeschwader 54, Major und Geschwaderkommodore Trautloft, Gefechtsstand, 27. März 1942.*

[84] Sources, Erwin Fleig: Gebhard Aders and Werner Held, *Jagdgeschwader 51 "Mölders"*, Stuttgart, FRG: Motorbuch Verlag, 1985, 109, 210; Ernst Obermaier, *Die Ritterkreuzträger der Luftwaffe, Jagdflieger 1939-1945*, Mainz, FRG: Verlag Dieter Hoffmann, 1989, 111; Jochen Prien, Gerhard Stemmer, Peter Rodeike and Winfried Bock, *Die Jagdfliegerverbände der Deutschen Luftwaffe 1934 bis 1945, Teil 4/II: Einsatz am Kanal und über England, 26.6.1940 bis 21.6.1941*, Eutin, Germany: Struve, 33-41; Jochen Prien, Gerhard Stemmer, Peter Rodeike and Winfried Bock, *Die Jagdfliegerverbände der Deutschen Luftwaffe 1934 bis 1945, Teil 6/I: Unternehmen "Barbarossa" Einsatz im Osten 22.6. bis 5.12.1941*, Eutin, Germany: Struve, 2003, 250-254; Jochen Prien, Gerhard Stemmer, Peter Rodeike and Winfried Bock, *Die Jagdfliegerverbände der Deutschen Luftwaffe 1934 bis 1945, Teil 9/I: Winterkampf im Osten 6.12.1941 bis 30.4.1942*, Eutin, Germany: Struve, 66, 71, 72; Jochen Prien, Gerhard Stemmer, Peter Rodeike and Winfried Bock, *Die Jagdfliegerverbände der Deutschen Luftwaffe 1934 bis 1945, Teil 9/II: Vom Sommerfeldzug 1942 bis zur Niederlage von Stalingrad 1.5.1942 bis 3.2.1943*, Eutin, Germany: Struve, 274.

[85] *Vorschlag zur bevorzugten Beförderung für Oberleutnant (Kr. O) Ernst Frömming, Fallschirmpionierbataillon, Major und Btl. Kommandeur Liebach, Generalmajor und Divisionskommandeur Heidrich, General der Flieger Student, O.U., 30. 4. 1943.*

[86] Sources, Ernst Frömming: Peter D. Antill, *Crete 1941: Germany's Lightning Airborne Assault*, Osprey Campaign 147, Oxford, England: Osprey Publishing, 2005, 46; Ken Ford, *Cassino 1944: Breaking the Gustav Line*, Osprey Campaign 134, Oxford, England: Osprey Publishing, 2004, 62-63; Bruce Quarrie, *German Airborne Divisions: Mediterranean Theater 1942-45*, Osprey Battle Orders 15, Oxford, England: Osprey Publishing, 2005, 79-80; Franz Thomas and Günter Wegmann, *Die Ritterkreuzträger der Deutschen Wehrmacht 1939-1945, Teil II: Fallschirmjäger*, Osnabrück, FRG: Biblio-Verlag, 1986, 63-64.

[87] *Kriegs-Beurteilung zum 1. Juni 1944 über der Hptm. (Kr.O.) Wilhelm Fulda, Jagdgeschwader 301, Major u. Geschwaderkommodore m.d.W.d.G.b. Mössinger, Generalmajor Huth, Gef. Stand, 1.5.1944.*

[88] Sources, Wilhelm Fulda: Ernst Obermaier, *Die Ritterkreuzträger der Luftwaffe, Jagdflieger 1939-1945*, Mainz, FRG: Verlag Dieter Hoffmann, 1989, 115; Georg Schlang, *Die deutschen Lastensegler-Verbände 1937-1945*, Stuttgart, FRG: Motorbuch Verlag, 1985, 21; Christopher Shores and Brian Cull, *Air War for Yugoslavia, Greece and Crete*, Carrollton, TX: Squadron Signal Publications, 1987, 298-299; Georg Tessin, *Verbände und Truppen der deutschen Wehrmacht und Waffen-SS im Zweiten Weltkrieg 1939-1945, Vierzehnter Band: Die Landstreitkräfte: Namensverbände/Die Luftstreitkräfte (Fliegende Verbände)/Flakeinsatz im Reich 1943-1945*, Osnabrück, FRG: Biblio Verlag, 1980, 345; Franz Thomas and Günter Wegmann, *Die Ritterkreuzträger der Deutschen Wehrmacht 1939-1945, Teil II: Fallschirmjäger*, Osnabrück, FRG: Biblio-Verlag, 1986, 65-66.

[89] *Beurteilung Feldwebel Robert Gast, Erdkampfschule der Luftwaffe für K.O.A., Generalmajor und Kommandeur der Erdkampfschule Sturm, O.U., 28. VII, Oktober 1943.*

[90] The U.S. Army suffered 9,831 casualties during the operation to seize the city.

[91] Sources, Robert Gast: Martin Blumenson, *Breakout and Pursuit*, U.S. Army in World War II, The European Theater of Operations, Washington, D.C: Department of the Army, Office of the Chief of Military History, 1961, 387, 634-651, 653; Franz Thomas and Günter Wegmann, *Die Ritterkreuzträger der Deutschen Wehrmacht 1939-1945, Teil II: Fallschirmjäger*, Osnabrück, FRG: Biblio-Verlag, 1986, 67-68.

[92] *Rangdienstalterverbesserung für Major (Tr.O) Walter Gericke, XI. Fliegerkorps, Der Kommandierende General Student, 17.7.1943.*

[93] Sources, Walter Gericke: Peter D. Antill, *Crete 1941: Germany's Lightning Airborne Assault*, Osprey Campaign 147, Oxford, England: Osprey Publishing, 2005, 38, 39, 41, 58; Dietrich Brehde, *Der Blaue Komet: Geschichte des IV. Bataillons des Luftlande-Sturmregiments 1940-1945*, Munich, FRG: Schild Verlag, 1988, 22, 30, 41, 57, 74, 100, 103, 108, 153; Roger Edwards, *German Airborne Troops 1936-1945*, Garden City, NJ: Doubleday & Company, 1974, 154-155; G.C. Kiriakopoulos, *Ten Days to Destiny: The Battle for Crete 1941*, New York: Franklin Watts, 1985, 192; James Lucas, *Storming Eagles: German Airborne Forces in World War Two*, London: Arms and Armour Press, 1988, 14; Veit Scherzer, *Die Ritterkreuzträger: Die Inhaber des Ritterkreuzes des Eisernen Kreuzes 1939-1945*, Jena, Germany: Scherzers Militairs-Verlag, 2005, 309; Franz Thomas and Günter Wegmann, *Die Ritterkreuzträger der Deutschen Wehrmacht 1939-1945, Teil II: Fallschirmjäger*, Osnabrück, FRG: Biblio-Verlag, 1986, 73-75.

[94] *Vorschlag zur bevorzugten Beförderung für Hauptmann (Tr.O) Siegfried Gerstner, 2. Fallschirm-Division, Generalleutnant und Kommandeur Wilke, Generalleutnant und Kommandeur Ramcke, General der Flieger Student, Gefechtsstand, 15.1.1944.*

[95] Sources, Siegfried Gerstner: Peter D. Antill, *Crete 1941: Germany's Lightning Airborne Assault*, Osprey Campaign 147, Oxford, England: Osprey Publishing, 2005, 46, 48; Roger Edwards, *German Airborne Troops 1936-1945*, Garden City, NJ: Doubleday & Company, 1974, 99-100; Franz Thomas and Günter Wegmann, *Die Ritterkreuzträger der Deutschen Wehrmacht 1939-1945, Teil II: Fallschirmjäger*, Osnabrück, FRG: Biblio-Verlag, 1986, 79-80.

[96] *Vorschlag zur Beförderung eines Offiziers (D.B.) zum nächsthöheren Dienstgrad Franz Grasmehl, Fallschirm-Jäger Rgt. 1, Oberst u. Rgts-Kdr Bräuer, 28. November 1940.*

[97] Sources, Franz Grassmel: Peter D. Antill, *Crete 1941: Germany's Lightning Airborne Assault*, Osprey Campaign 147, Oxford, England: Osprey Publishing, 2005, 34; Ken Ford, *Cassino 1944: Breaking the Gustav Line*, Osprey Campaign 134, Oxford, England: Osprey Publishing, 2004, 62-71; John Ellis, *Cassino: The Hollow Victory*, London: André Deutsch Limited, 1984, 221-253; Bruce Quarrie, *German Airborne Divisions: Mediterranean Theater 1942-45*, Osprey Battle Orders 15, Oxford, England: Osprey Publishing, 2005, 79-80; Franz Thomas and Günter Wegmann, *Die Ritterkreuzträger der Deutschen Wehrmacht 1939-1945, Teil II: Fallschirmjäger*, Osnabrück, FRG: Biblio-Verlag, 1986, 85-86.

[98] *Vorschlag zur Beförderung zum Kriegsoffizier Oberfähnrich Alfred Gross, III. / Jagdgeschwader 54, Schroer, Oberleutnant und Staffelführer Zweigart, O.U., 6.5. 1944.*

[99] Sources, Alfred Gross: Donald L. Caldwell, *JG 26: Top Guns of the Luftwaffe*, New York: Orion Books, 1991, 281-282; Ernst Obermaier, *Die Ritterkreuzträger der Luftwaffe, Jagdflieger 1939-1945*, Mainz, FRG: Verlag Dieter Hoffmann, 1989, 123.

[100] *Beurteilung, Fahnenjunker-Oberfeldwebel (Kr.) Grünberg, II./ Jagdgeschwader Udet, Hauptmann u. stellv. Gruppenkommandeur Sannemann, Oberst Wilcke, Ibel, Gefechtsstand, 20.12.1943.*

[101] Sources, Hans Grünberg: Roger A. Freeman, *Mighty Eighth War Diary*, London: Jane's, 1981, 187, 253, 494; Hugh Morgan and John Weal, *German Jet Aces of World War 2*, Osprey Aircraft of the Aces 17, Oxford, England: Osprey Publishing, 1998, 47; Ernst Obermaier, *Die Ritterkreuzträger der Luftwaffe, Jagdflieger 1939-1945*, Mainz, FRG: Verlag Dieter Hoffmann, 1989, 123; Jochen Prien, Gerhard Stemmer, Peter Rodeike and Winfried Bock, *Die Jagdfliegerverbände der Deutschen Luftwaffe 1934 bis 1945, Teil 9/II: Vom Sommerfeldzug 1942 bis zur Niederlage von Stalingrad 1.5.1942 bis 3.2.1943*, Eutin, Germany: Struve, 152.

[102] *Kriegs-Beurteilung zum 1. August 1944 über den Hptm. (Kr. O) Andreas Hagl, Fallschirmjaeger-Regiment 3, Oberst u. Regimentskommandeur Heilmann, Gefechtsstand, 28. 7. 1944.*

[103] Sources, Andreas Hagl: Peter D. Antill, *Crete 1941: Germany's Lightning Airborne Assault*, Osprey Campaign 147, Oxford, England: Osprey Publishing, 2005, 46; Franz Thomas and Günter Wegmann, *Die Ritterkreuzträger der Deutschen Wehrmacht 1939-1945, Teil II: Fallschirmjäger*, Osnabrück, FRG: Biblio-Verlag, 1986, 92-93; Volksbund Deutsche Kriegsgräberfürsorge Website, HYPERLINK "http://www.volksbund.de" *http://www.volksbund. de*, accessed October 20, 2005.

[104] *Vorschlag zur bevorzugten Beförderung für Oberleutnant (Tr.O) Reino Hamer, I./Fallschirmjäger Regiment 6 (Sturm), Hauptmann u. stellv. Btl. Kdr. Finzel, Major und Rgts. Führer Liebach, Generalmajor und Divisionsführer Barenthin, General der Flieger Student, O.U., 29. Oktober 1943.*

[105] Sources, Reino Hamer: Franz Thomas and Günter Wegmann, *Die Ritterkreuzträger der Deutschen Wehrmacht 1939-1945, Teil II: Fallschirmjäger*, Osnabrück, FRG: Biblio-Verlag, 1986, 94-96.

[106] *Bevorzugte Beförderung des Major Frhr.v.d. Heydte, XI. Fliegerkorps, Der Kommandierende General Student, O.U., 19.7.1943.*

[107] Sources, Friedrich von der Heydte: Peter D. Antill, *Crete 1941: Germany's Lightning Airborne Assault*, Osprey Campaign 147, Oxford, England: Osprey Publishing, 2005, 23, 48; Roger Edwards, *German Airborne Troops 1936-1945*, Garden City, NJ: Doubleday & Company, 1974, 157; Franz Thomas, *Die Eichenlaubträger 1940-1945, Band 1: A-K*, Osnabrück, Germany: Biblio-Verlag, 1998, 278; Franz Thomas and Günter Wegmann, *Die Ritterkreuzträger der Deutschen Wehrmacht 1939-1945, Teil II: Fallschirmjäger*, Osnabrück, FRG: Biblio-Verlag, 1986, 114-116.

[108] *Beurteilung Feldwebel von Hoffer, Luftkriegschule 4, Generalmajor Sonnenburg, Fürstenfeldbruck, 19.6.43.*

[109] Sources, Herbert von Hoffer: Ernst Obermaier, *Die Ritterkreuzträger der Luftwaffe, Stuka und Schlachtflieger 1939-1945*, Mainz, FRG: Verlag Dieter Hoffmann, 1976, 94; Veit Scherzer, *Die Träger des Deutschen Kreuzes in Gold der Luftwaffe 1941-1945*, Bayreuth, FRG: Scherzer's Militair Verlag, 1992, 131.

[110] Another source states that the date of the award for the German Cross in Gold was July 12, 1943.

[111] Tutzing is about 45 minutes southwest of Munich.

[112] Sources, Franz Hrdlicka: Ernst Obermaier, *Die Ritterkreuzträger der Luftwaffe, Jagdflieger 1939-1945*, Mainz, FRG: Verlag Dieter Hoffmann, 1989, 137; Jochen Prien, Gerhard Stemmer, Peter Rodeike and Winfried Bock, *Die Jagdfliegerverbände der Deutschen Luftwaffe 1934 bis 1945, Teil 6/II: Unternehmen "Barbarossa" Einsatz im Osten 22.6. bis 5.12.1941*, Eutin, Germany: Struve, 2003, 325, 326, 327, 330; Veit Scherzer, *Die Träger des Deutschen Kreuzes in Gold der Luftwaffe 1941-1945*, Bayreuth, FRG: Scherzer's Militair Verlag, 1992, 137; John Weal, *Jagdgeschwader 2 'Richthofen,'* Osprey Aviation Elite 1, Oxford, England: Osprey Publishing, 2000, 116, 118.

[113] *Vorschlag zur Beförderung zum Leutnant, Franz Hrdlicka, Erg. Jagdgruppe 77, Oblt. u.m.d.W.d.G.d.Gr.Kdrs.b. Schultz, Oberstleutnant Huth, Gefechtsstand, 11.4.41.*

[114] *Kriegs-Beurteilung zum 1. April 1945 über den Major i. G. Eberhard Jacob, Lw. Führungsstab Ia, Oberstlt.i.G. und Chef Ia von Greiff, Generalmajor Christian, H.Qu., 29.3.1945.*

[115] Sources, Eberhard Jacob: Cajus Bekker, *The Luftwaffe War Diaries*, London: MacDonald & Co., 1967, 200; Ernst Obermaier, *Die Ritterkreuzträger der Luftwaffe, Stuka und Schlachtflieger 1939-1945*, Mainz, FRG: Verlag Dieter Hoffmann, 1976, 98; Veit Scherzer, *Die Träger des Deutschen Kreuzes in Gold der Luftwaffe 1941-1945*, Bayreuth, FRG: Scherzer's Militair Verlag, 1992, 143.

[116] *Beurteilungs-notizen für Oberleutnant Karl Janke, III./ Sturzkampfgeschwader Immelmann 2, Oberleutnant und Adjutant Kaiser, Hauptmann u. Gruppenkommandeur Dilley, Gefechtsstand, 2.10.41.*

[117] Sources, Karl Janke: V.I. Achkasov and N.B. Pavlovich, *Soviet Naval Operations in the Great Patriotic War 1941-1945*, Annapolis, Maryland: Naval Institute Press, 1981, 173; Georg Brütting, *Das waren die deutschen Stuka-Asse, 1939-1945*, Stuttgart, FRG: Motorbuch Verlag, 1976, 212, 213, 252; Ernst Obermaier, *Die Ritterkreuzträger der Luftwaffe, Stuka und Schlachtflieger 1939-1945*, Mainz, FRG: Verlag Dieter Hoffmann, 1976, 99; Veit Scherzer, *Die Träger des Deutschen Kreuzes in Gold der Luftwaffe 1941-1945*, Bayreuth, FRG: Scherzer's Militair Verlag, 1992, 144.

[118] *Kriegs-Beurteilung über den Hptm. (Tr.O.) Peter Jenne, Jagdgeschwader 300, Oberstleutnant u. Geschw.-Kommodore Dahl, Major und Geschwaderkommodore m.d.W.d.G.b. Peters, Gefechtsstand, 28. Jan. 1945.*

[119] Sources, Peter Jenne: Roger A. Freeman, *Mighty Eighth War Diary*, London: Jane's, 1981, 155; Ernst Obermaier, *Die Ritterkreuzträger der Luftwaffe, Jagdflieger 1939-1945*, Mainz, FRG: Verlag Dieter Hoffmann, 1989, 140; Veit Scherzer, *Die Träger des Deutschen Kreuzes in Gold der Luftwaffe 1941-1945*, Bayreuth, FRG: Scherzer's Militair Verlag, 1992, 145.

[120] *Beurteilungsnotiz über den Leutnant, Flugzeugführer Karl Kennel, II./Zerstörergeschwader 2, Hauptmann und Gruppenkommandeur Weyert, O.U., 6.10.1942.*

[121] Sources, Karl Kennel: Ernst Obermaier, *Die Ritterkreuzträger der Luftwaffe, Jagdflieger 1939-1945*, Mainz, FRG: Verlag Dieter Hoffmann, 1989, 70; Ernst Obermaier, *Die Ritterkreuzträger der Luftwaffe, Stuka und Schlachtflieger 1939-1945*, Mainz, FRG: Verlag Dieter Hoffmann, 1976, 54; Franz Thomas, *Die Eichenlaubträger 1940-1945, Band 1: A-K*, Osnabrück, Germany: Biblio-Verlag, 1998, 357.

[122] The *Luftwaffe* Honor Goblet is mentioned in his efficiency report but not in post-war literature on the award.

[123] *Beurteilungsnotiz über den Hauptmann (Tr.O.) Alfred Kindler, II./Kampfgeschwader 2, Hauptmann und Kommandeur Bradel, Oberstleutnant b.m.d.w.d.G.d. Kommodore von Koppelow, Gefechtsstand, 3.8.42.*

[124] Sources, Alfred Kindler: Ulf Balke, *Der Luft-Krieg in Europa, Die Operativen Einsätze des Kampf-Geschwaders 2 im Zweiten Weltkrieg, Teil 2*, Koblenz, FRG: Bernhard & Graefe Verlag, 1990, 138, 409, 437; Georg Brütting, *Das waren die deutschen Kampfflieger-Asse 1939-1945*, Stuttgart, FRG: Motorbuch Verlag, 1983, 214; Veit Scherzer, *Die Ritterkreuzträger: Die Inhaber des Ritterkreuzes des Eisernen Kreuzes 1939-1945*, Jena, Germany: Scherzers Militars-Verlag, 2005, 416.

[125] *Brief, Lt. (Kr.O.) August Lambert, II. / Schlachtgeschwader 2 Immelmann, Major und Gruppenkommandeur Frank, Gef. St., 7. Mai 1944.*

[126] Sources, August Lambert: Ernst Obermaier, *Die Ritterkreuzträger der Luftwaffe, Jagdflieger 1939-1945*, Mainz, FRG: Verlag Dieter

Hoffmann, 1989, 153; Ernst Obermaier, *Die Ritterkreuzträger der Luftwaffe, Stuka und Schlachtflieger 1939-1945*, Mainz, FRG: Verlag Dieter Hoffmann, 1976, 108-109; Veit Scherzer, *Die Träger des Deutschen Kreuzes in Gold der Luftwaffe 1941-1945*, Bayreuth, FRG: Scherzer's Militair Verlag, 1992, 187; John Weal, *Luftwaffe Schlachtgruppen*, Aviation Elite Units 13, Oxford, England: Osprey Publishing, 2003, 72, 90, 112.

[127] The unit was named after Albert Leo Schlageter. A World War I veteran, *Freikorps* soldier and Nazi Party member, he was arrested on April 5, 1923 by the French troops in the occupied Ruhr for taking part in sabotage operations. A French military tribunal sentenced him to death by firing squad; he was executed on May 26, 1923.

[128] He may have been the victim of American ace Darrell Cramer, of the 338th Fighter Squadron, 55th Fighter Group, USAAF.

[129] *Beförderungsvorschlag für Offiziere (Kr.O.) Emil Lang, Jagdgeschwader "Schlageter" Nr. 26, Oberstleutnant und Geschwader Kommodore Priller, Generalleutnant Bülowius, 29.9.1944.*

[130] Sources, Emil Lang: Ernst Obermaier, *Die Ritterkreuzträger der Luftwaffe, Jagdflieger 1939-1945*, Mainz, FRG: Verlag Dieter Hoffmann, 1989, 64; Mike Spick, *Luftwaffe Fighter Aces: The Jagdflieger and Their Combat Tactics and Techniques*, Mechanicsburg, PA: Stackpole Books, 2003, 185.

[131] During the Stalingrad campaign, the *Luftwaffe* lost 166 aircraft destroyed in action, 108 aircraft missing in action and 214 aircraft destroyed during landings or take-offs. Some 1,100 aircrew perished in these incidents. Source: Chris Bishop, *Luftwaffe Squadrons 1939-45*, Stapelhurst, England: Spellmont, 2006, 93.

[132] The 8th Air Force lost 60 B-17 Flying Fortress on this mission, each with a ten-man crew.

[133] *Bevorzugte Beförderung von Offizieren – Hauptmann Karl-Heinz Langer, Jagdgeschwader "Udet", Major und Geschwader-Kommodore (m.d.W.d.G.b.) Bär, Gefechtsstand, 24.7.1944.*

[134] Sources, Karl-Heinz Langer: Roger A. Freeman, *Mighty Eighth War Diary*, London: Jane's, 1981, 126; Ernst Obermaier, *Die Ritterkreuzträger der Luftwaffe, Jagdflieger 1939-1945*, Mainz, FRG: Verlag Dieter Hoffmann, 1989, 153; Jochen Prien, Gerhard Stemmer, Peter Rodeike and Winfried Bock, *Die Jagdfliegerverbände der Deutschen Luftwaffe 1934 bis 1945, Teil 9/II: Vom Sommerfeldzug 1942 bis zur Niederlage von Stalingrad 1.5.1942 bis 3.2.1943*, Eutin, Germany: Struve, 232, 234; Veit Scherzer, *Die Träger des Deutschen Kreuzes in Gold der Luftwaffe 1941-1945*, Bayreuth, FRG: Scherzer's Militair Verlag, 1992, 189.

[135] May 14, 1940 became known as the "Day of the Fighter Pilot (*Tag der Jagdflieger*)," when German fighters, protecting German Army crossing sites over the Meuse River, shot down more than 90 attacking British and French aircraft (Source, Samuel Mitcham, Jr., *Men of the Luftwaffe*, Novato, CA: Presidio, 1988, 87).

[136] *Vorschlag auf bevorzugte Beförderung des Oblt. (Tr.O.) Erich Leie, m.d.W.d.G.b d Kdr.I./J.G.2., Luftflottenkommando 3, General-feldmarschall Sperrle, 13. August 1942.*

[137] Sources, Erich Leie: Gebhard Aders and Werner Held, *Jagdgeschwader 51 "Mölders"*, Stuttgart, FRG: Motorbuch Verlag, 1985, 133; Chris Bishop, *Luftwaffe Squadrons 1939-45*, Stapelhurst, England: Spellmont, 2006, 99; Ernst Obermaier, *Die Ritterkreuzträger der Luftwaffe, Jagdflieger 1939-1945*, Mainz, FRG: Verlag Dieter Hoffmann, 1989, 156; Jochen Prien, Gerhard Stemmer, Peter Rodeike and Winfried Bock, *Die Jagdfliegerverbände der Deutschen Luftwaffe 1934 bis 1945, Teil 3: Einsatz in Dänemark und Norwegen, 9.4. bis 30.11.40, Der Feldzug im Westen, 10.5. bis 25.6.1940*, Eutin, Germany: Struve, 131; Jochen Prien, Gerhard Stemmer, Peter Rodeike and Winfried Bock, *Die Jagdfliegerverbände der Deutschen Luftwaffe 1934 bis 1945, Teil 4/I: Einsatz am Kanal und über England, 26.6.1940 bis 21.6.1941*, Eutin, Germany: Struve, 79-80; Jochen Prien, Gerhard Stemmer, Peter Rodeike and Winfried Bock, *Die Jagdfliegerverbände der Deutschen Luftwaffe 1934 bis 1945, Teil 5: Heimatverteidigung 10. Mai 1940 bis 31. Dezember 1941, Einsatz im Mittelmeerraum Oktober 1940 bis November 1941, Einsatz im Westen 22. Juni bis 31. Dezember 1941, Die Ergänzungsjagdgruppen Einsatz 1941 bis zur Auflösung Anfang 1942*, Eutin, Germany: Struve, 2003, 410-411; Jochen Prien, Gerhard Stemmer, Peter Rodeike and Winfried Bock, *Die Jagdfliegerverbände der Deutschen Luftwaffe 1934 bis 1945, Teil 7: Heimatsverteidigung 1. Januar bis 31. Dezember 1942, Einsatz im Westen 1. Januar bis 31. Dezember 1942*, Eutin, Germany: Struve, 2003, 213, 230, 240; Jochen Prien, Gerhard Stemmer, Peter Rodeike and Winfried Bock, *Die Jagdfliegerverbände der Deutschen Luftwaffe 1934 bis 1945, Teil 9/II: Vom Sommerfeldzug 1942 bis zur Niederlage von Stalingrad 1.5.1942 bis 3.2.1943*, Eutin, Germany: Struve, 265; John Weal, *Focke-Wulf Fw 190 Aces of the Russian Front*, Osprey Aircraft of the Aces 6, Oxford, England: Osprey Publishing, 1995, 48, 64, 87.

[138] *Beförderung Ltn. (Tr.O.) Ludwig Leingärtner, Luftflottenkommando 1, Der Chef der Luftflotte 1 und Befehlshaber Ost Generaloberst Keller, O.U., 5. April 1943.*

[139] Sources, Ludwig Leingärtner: Ernst Obermaier, *Die Ritterkreuzträger der Luftwaffe, Stuka und Schlachtflieger 1939-1945*, Mainz, FRG: Verlag Dieter Hoffmann, 1976, 111; Veit Scherzer, *Die Träger des Deutschen Kreuzes in Gold der Luftwaffe 1941-1945*, Bayreuth, FRG: Scherzer's Militair Verlag, 1992, 193.

[140] *Vorschlag zur Beförderung zum Leutnant (Kriegsoffizier) Lothar Linke, II./Nachtjagdgeschwader 1, Oberleutnant und Staffelkapitän Lent, Hauptmann und Gruppenkommandeur Ehle, Major und Geschwaderkommodore Falck, O.U., 18.1.41.*

[141] The attack killed 693 people and injured 1,075; it destroyed 1,218 buildings and seriously damaged another 2,141 (including the Hoesch and Dortmunder Union steel factories). The British lost 5.2% of the attacking bombers. Overall, during the war, RAF Bomber Command destroyed 3,370,000 dwellings in Germany, killing 600,000 people. 50,000 RAF Bomber Command crewmen lost their lives. Source: Peter Hinchliffe, *The Lent Papers: Helmut Lent*, Bristol, England: Cerberus Publishing, 2003, 76.

[142] Another source states that the date of the award of the German Cross in Gold was on April 12, 1943, which would have been before his death.

[143] Sources, Lothar Linke: Martin Middlebrook and Chris Everitt, *The Bomber Command War Diaries*, New York: Viking Penguin, 1987, 154, 383-384; Ernst Obermaier, *Die Ritterkreuzträger der Luftwaffe, Jagdflieger 1939-1945*, Mainz, FRG: Verlag Dieter Hoffmann, 1989, 159; Veit Scherzer, *Die Träger des Deutschen Kreuzes in Gold der Luftwaffe 1941-1945*, Bayreuth, FRG: Scherzer's Militair Verlag, 1992, 198.

[144] *Kriegsbeurteilung über den Lt. (Kr.O.) Helmut Lipfert, II./Jagdgeschwader 52, Hauptmann und Gruppenkommandeur Burkhorn, Oberstleutnant u. Geschwaderkommodore Hrabak, Im Felde, 15.12.1943.*

[145] Sources, Helmut Lipfert: Ernst Obermaier, *Die Ritterkreuzträger der Luftwaffe, Jagdflieger 1939-1945*, Mainz, FRG: Verlag Dieter Hoffmann, 1989, 76; Jochen Prien, Gerhard Stemmer, Peter Rodeike and Winfried Bock, *Die Jagdfliegerverbände der Deutschen Luftwaffe 1934 bis 1945, Teil 9/II: Vom Sommerfeldzug 1942 bis zur Niederlage von Stalingrad 1.5.1942 bis 3.2.1943*, Eutin, Germany: Struve, 498; Veit Scherzer, *Die Träger des Deutschen Kreuzes in Gold der Luftwaffe 1941-1945*, Bayreuth, FRG: Scherzer's Militair Verlag, 1992, 198.

Rater Biographies

[1] Sources, Werner Anders: Jochen Prien, Gerhard Stemmer, Peter Rodeike and Winfried Bock, *Die Jagdfliegerverbände der Deutschen Luftwaffe 1934 bis 1945, Teil 6/I: Unternehmen "Barbarossa" Einsatz im Osten 22.6. bis 5.12.1941*, Eutin, Germany: Struve, 2003, 135, 153; Jochen Prien, Gerhard Stemmer, Peter Rodeike and Winfried Bock, *Die Jagdfliegerverbände der Deutschen Luftwaffe 1934 bis 1945, Teil8/I: Einsatz im Mittelmeerraum November 1941 bis Dezember 1942*, Eutin, Germany: Struve, 2004, 95; Jochen Prien, Gerhard Stemmer, Peter Rodeike and Winfried Bock, *Die Jagdfliegerverbände der Deutschen Luftwaffe 1934 bis 1945, Teil 9/I: Winterkampf im Osten 6.12.1941 bis 30.4.1942*, Eutin, Germany: Struve, 29; Jochen Prien, Gerhard Stemmer, Peter Rodeike and Winfried Bock, *Die Jagdfliegerverbände der Deutschen Luftwaffe 1934 bis 1945, Teil 9/II: Vom Sommerfeldzug 1942 bis zur Niederlage von Stalingrad 1.5.1942 bis 3.2.1943*, Eutin, Germany: Struve, 211; Christian Zweng, *Die Dienststellen, Kommandobehörden und Truppenteile der Luftwaffe 1935-1945, Band 1 Nr. 1-10*, Osnabrück, Germany: Biblio Verlag, 1999, 185.

[2] Sources, Heinz Bär: Franz Kurowski, *Luftwaffe Aces: German Combat Pilots of WWII*, translated by David Johnston, Mechanicsburg, PA: Stackpole, 2004, 77, 83, 105; Ernst Obermaier, *Die Ritterkreuzträger der Luftwaffe, Jagdflieger 1939-1945*, Mainz, FRG: Verlag Dieter Hoffmann, 1989, 30.

[3] Tegernsee is about 60 minutes south of Munich.

[4] Sources, Gerhard Barkhorn: Ernst Obermaier, *Die Ritterkreuzträger der Luftwaffe, Jagdflieger 1939-1945*, Mainz, FRG: Verlag Dieter Hoffmann, 1989, 35; Jochen Prien, Gerhard Stemmer, Peter Rodeike and Winfried Bock, *Die Jagdfliegerverbände der Deutschen Luftwaffe 1934 bis 1945, Teil 9/II: Vom Sommerfeldzug 1942 bis zur Niederlage von Stalingrad 1.5.1942 bis 3.2.1943*, Eutin, Germany: Struve, 503.

[5] Sources, Walter Barenthin: Karl Friedrich Hildebrand, *Die Generale der deutschen Luftwaffe 1935-1945, Band 1 Abernetty-v. Gyldenfeldt*, Osnabrück, FRG, 1990, 45-46; Kurt Mehner and Reinhard Teuber, *Die Deutsche Luftwaffe 1939-1945 Führung und Truppe*, Norderstedt, Germany; Militair-Verlag Klaus D. Patzwall, 1993, 36, 37, 66; Veit Scherzer, *Die Träger des Deutschen Kreuzes in Gold der Luftwaffe 1941-1945*, Bayreuth, FRG: Scherzer's Militair Verlag, 1992, 13.

[6] Sources, Horst Beeger: Georg Brütting, *Das waren die deutschen Kampfflieger-Asse 1939-1945*, Stuttgart, FRG: Motorbuch Verlag, 1983, 180; Veit Scherzer, *Die Ritterkreuzträger: Die Inhaber des Ritterkreuzes des Eisernen Kreuzes 1939-1945*, Jena, Germany: Scherzers Militairs-Verlag, 2005, 188; Christopher Shores and Brian Cull, *Air War for Yugoslavia, Greece and Crete*, Carrollton, TX: Squadron Signal Publications, 1987, 257.

[7] Sources, Hubertus von Bonin: Franz Kurowski, *Luftwaffe Aces: German Combat Pilots of WWII*, translated by David Johnston, Mechanicsburg, PA: Stackpole, 2004, 317; Ernst Obermaier, *Die Ritterkreuzträger der Luftwaffe, Jagdflieger 1939-1945*, Mainz, FRG: Verlag Dieter Hoffmann, 1989, 91; Jochen Prien, Gerhard Stemmer, Peter Rodeike and Winfried Bock, *Die Jagdfliegerverbände der Deutschen Luftwaffe 1934 bis 1945, Teil 6/I: Unternehmen "Barbarossa" Einsatz im Osten 22.6. bis 5.12.1941*, Eutin, Germany: Struve, 2003, 277; Karl Ries and Hans Ring, *Legion Condor, 1936-1939: Eine illustrierte Dokumentation*, Mainz, Germany: Verlag Dieter Hoffmann, 1980, 251, 265-266.

[8] Sources, Walter Bradel: Ulf Balke, *Der Luft-Krieg in Europa, Die operativen Einsätze des Kampf-Geschwaders 2 im Zweiten Weltkrieg, Teil 2*, Koblenz, FRG: Bernhard & Graefe Verlag, 1990, 227, 407, 409, 410, 455; Georg Brütting, *Das waren die deutschen Kampfflieger-Asse 1939-1945*, Stuttgart, FRG: Motorbuch Verlag, 1983, 185-186.

[9] Sources, Bruno Bräuer: Karl Friedrich Hildebrand, *Die Generale der deutschen Luftwaffe 1935-1945, Band 1 Abernetty-v. Gyldenfeldt*, Osnabrück, FRG, 1990, 108-109; Franz Thomas and Günter Wegmann, *Die Ritterkreuzträger der Deutschen Wehrmacht 1939-1945, Teil II: Fallschirmjäger*, Osnabrück, FRG: Biblio-Verlag, 1986, 32-34.

[10] Sources, Helmut Bruck: Ernst Obermaier, *Die Ritterkreuzträger der Luftwaffe, Stuka und Schlachtflieger 1939-1945*, Mainz, FRG: Verlag Dieter Hoffmann, 1976, 45.

[11] Sources, Alfred Bülowius: Karl Friedrich Hildebrand, *Die Generale der deutschen Luftwaffe 1935-1945, Band 1 Abernetty-v. Gyldenfeldt*, Osnabrück, FRG, 1990, 129-130: Peter Taghon, *Die Geschichte des Lehrgeschwaders 1, Band 1 1936-1942*, Zweibrücken, Germany: VDM, 2004, 101.

[12] Christian won Gerda's hand in 1943 over a competitor, SS-Major Erich Kempka. In April 1945, General Christian left Hitler's bunker in Berlin to join *Luftwaffe* chief Hermann Göring in Berchtesgaden, Bavaria, ostensibly to continue the fight, although Christian knew that his wife had opted to remain with the Führer. Gerda was not amused. She remarked after the war: "Well, he went his way and I went mine. But that ended our marriage. I couldn't forgive that kind of desertion. I'm glad I survived, just to be able to divorce the lout."

[13] Sources, Eckhard Christian: Karl Friedrich Hildebrand, *Die Generale der deutschen Luftwaffe 1935-1945, Band 1 Abernetty-v. Gyldenfeldt*, Osnabrück, FRG, 1990, 155-156; James P. O'Donnell, *The Bunker: The History of the Reich Chancellery Group*, Boston: Houghton Mifflin Company, 1978, 120-121.

[14] Sources, Walther Dahl: Ernst Obermaier, *Die Ritterkreuzträger der Luftwaffe, Jagdflieger 1939-1945*, Mainz, FRG: Verlag Dieter Hoffmann, 1989, 72; Jochen Prien, Gerhard Stemmer, Peter Rodeike and Winfried Bock, *Die Jagdfliegerverbände der Deutschen Luftwaffe 1934 bis 1945, Teil 6/I: Unternehmen "Barbarossa" Einsatz im Osten 22.6. bis 5.12.1941*, Eutin, Germany: Struve, 2003, 51, 107; Jochen Prien, Gerhard Stemmer, Peter Rodeike and Winfried Bock, *Die Jagdfliegerverbände der Deutschen Luftwaffe 1934 bis 1945, Teil8/I: Einsatz im Mittelmeerraum November 1941 bis Dezember 1942*, Eutin, Germany: Struve, 2004, 83.

[15] Sources, Karl-Egon von Dalwigk zu Lichtenfels: Ulf Balke, *Der Luft-Krieg in Europa, Die operativen Einsätze des Kampf-Geschwaders 2 im Zweiten Weltkrieg, Teil 2*, Koblenz, FRG: Bernhard & Graefe Verlag, 1990, 412; Peter Taghorn, *Die Geschichte des Lehrgeschwaders 1, Band 2 (1942-1945)*, Zweibrucken, Germany: 2004, 488.

[16] Sources, Bruno Dilley: Cajus Bekker, *The Luftwaffe War Diaries*, London: MacDonald & Co., 1967, 25; Ernst Obermaier, *Die Ritterkreuzträger der Luftwaffe, Stuka und Schlachtflieger 1939-1945*, Mainz, FRG: Verlag Dieter Hoffmann, 1976, 44; Christopher Shores and Brian Cull, *Air War for Yugoslavia, Greece and Crete*, Carrollton, TX: Squadron Signal Publications, 1987, 235.

[17] Sources, Kurt-Bertram von Döring: Karl Friedrich Hildebrand, *Die Generale der deutschen Luftwaffe 1935-1945, Band 1 Abernetty-v. Gyldenfeldt*, Osnabrück, FRG, 1990, 203-204; Franz Kurowski, *Luftwaffe Aces: German Combat Pilots of WWII*, translated by David Johnston, Mechanicsburg, PA: Stackpole, 2004, 46.

[18] Sources, Walter Ehle: Ernst Obermaier, *Die Ritterkreuzträger der Luftwaffe, Jagdflieger 1939-1945*, Mainz, FRG: Verlag Dieter Hoffmann, 1989, 106; Karl Ries and Hans Ring, *Legion Condor, 1936-1939: Eine illustrierte Dokumentation*, Mainz, Germany: Verlag Dieter Hoffmann, 1980, 265-266.

[19] Sources, Wolfgang Falck: Peter Hinchliffe, *The Lent Papers: Helmut Lent*, Bristol, England: Cerberus Publishing, 2003, 82; Ernst Obermaier, *Die Ritterkreuzträger der Luftwaffe, Jagdflieger 1939-1945*, Mainz, FRG: Verlag Dieter Hoffmann, 1989, 109.

[20] Sources, Oswald Finzel: Christian Zweng, *Die Dienststellen, Kommandobehörden und Truppenteile der Luftwaffe 1935-1945, Band 1 Nr. 1-10*, Osnabrück, Germany; Biblio Verlag, 1999, 140, 372, 373.

[21] Sources, Heinz Frank: Ernst Obermaier, *Die Ritterkreuzträger der Luftwaffe, Stuka und Schlachtflieger 1939-1945*, Mainz, FRG: Verlag Dieter Hoffmann, 1976, 43.

[22] Sources, Wilhelm von Friedberg: Peter Hinchliffe, *The Lent Papers: Helmut Lent*, Bristol, England: Cerberus Publishing, 2003, 176-177.

[23] Sources, Kurt von Greiff: Wolfgang Dierich, *Kampfgeschwader 51 "Edelweiss" Eine Chronik aus Dokumenten and Berichten 1937-1945*, Stuttgart, FRG: Motorbuch Verlag, 1973, 296; Kurt Mehner and Reinhard Teuber, *Die Deutsche Luftwaffe 1939-1945 Führung und Truppe*, Norderstedt, Germany; Militair-Verlag Klaus D. Patzwall, 1993, 9; Veit Scherzer, *Die Träger des Deutschen Kreuzes in Gold der Luftwaffe 1941-1945*, Bayreuth, FRG: Scherzer's Militair Verlag, 1992, 100; Christian Zweng, *Die Dienststellen, Kommandobehörden und Truppenteile der Luftwaffe 1935-1945, Band 1 Nr. 1-10*, Osnabrück, Germany; Biblio Verlag, 1999, 168.

[24] Sources, Alfred Grislawski: Ernst Obermaier, *Die Ritterkreuzträger der Luftwaffe, Jagdflieger 1939-1945*, Mainz, FRG: Verlag Dieter Hoffmann, 1989, 63, Veit Scherzer, *Die Ritterkreuzträger: Die Inhaber des Ritterkreuzes des Eisernen Kreuzes 1939-1945*, Jena, Germany: Scherzers Militairs-Verlag, 2005, 325.

[25] Sources, Walter Hagen: Karl Friedrich Hildebrand, *Die Generale der deutschen Luftwaffe 1935-1945, Band 2 Habermehl-Nuber*, Osnabrück, FRG, 1991, 14-15; Kurt Mehner and Reinhard Teuber, *Die Deutsche Luftwaffe 1939-1945 Führung und Truppe*, Norderstedt, Germany; Militair-Verlag Klaus D. Patzwall, 1993, 44.

[26] Sources, Hans von Hahn: Ernst Obermaier, *Die Ritterkreuzträger der Luftwaffe, Jagdflieger 1939-1945*, Mainz, FRG: Verlag Dieter Hoffmann, 1989, 127.

[27] Sources, Richard Heidrich: Karl Friedrich Hildebrand, *Die Generale der deutschen Luftwaffe 1935-1945, Band 2 Habermehl-Nuber*, Osnabrück, FRG, 1991, 47-48; Franz Thomas and Günter Wegmann, *Die Ritterkreuzträger der Deutschen Wehrmacht 1939-1945, Teil II: Fallschirmjäger*, Osnabrück, FRG: Biblio-Verlag, 1986, 99-102.

[28] Sources, Ludwig Heilmann: Karl Friedrich Hildebrand, *Die Generale der deutschen Luftwaffe 1935-1945, Band 2 Habermehl-Nuber*, Osnabrück, FRG, 1991, 51-52.

[29] Sources, Joachim Helbig: Georg Brütting, *Das waren die deutschen Kampfflieger-Asse 1939-1945*, Stuttgart, FRG: Motorbuch Verlag, 1983, 81-100; Franz Kurowski, *Luftwaffe Aces: German Combat Pilots of WWII*, translated by David Johnston, Mechanicsburg, PA: Stackpole, 2004, 24, 33, 39, 41.

[30] Sources, Hubertus Hitschhold: Ernst Obermaier, *Die Ritterkreuzträger der Luftwaffe, Stuka und Schlachtflieger 1939-1945*, Mainz, FRG: Verlag Dieter Hoffmann, 1976, 40.

[31] Böcking/Starnberg is about 30 minutes southwest of Munich.

[32] Sources, Dietrich Hrabak: Ernst Obermaier, *Die Ritterkreuzträger der Luftwaffe, Jagdflieger 1939-1945*, Mainz, FRG: Verlag Dieter Hoffmann, 1989, 59; Jochen Prien, Gerhard Stemmer, Peter Rodeike and Winfried Bock, *Die Jagdfliegerverbände der Deutschen Luftwaffe 1934 bis 1945, Teil 9/I: Winterkampf im Osten 6.12.1941 bis 30.4.1942*, Eutin, Germany: Struve, 216; Jochen Prien, Gerhard Stemmer, Peter Rodeike and Winfried Bock, *Die Jagdfliegerverbände der Deutschen Luftwaffe 1934 bis 1945, Teil 9/II: Vom Sommerfeldzug 1942 bis zur Niederlage von Stalingrad 1.5.1942 bis 3.2.1943*, Eutin, Germany: Struve, 387.

[33] Fürstenfeldbruck is about 30 minutes west of Munich.

[34] The term *Freikorps* was used to name several *paramilitary* organizations that arose in *Germany* as soldiers returned in defeat from World War I. During the period, many German veterans felt disconnected from civilian life and joined the *Freikorps* in search of stability within a military structure, or they joined in an effort to put down numerous Communist uprisings throughout Germany. In addition to fighting in the Ruhr, Bavaria, Berlin and central Germany, several *Freikorps* fought in the Baltic, Silesia and Prussia, sometimes with significant success even against regular troops, before they were officially disbanded in 1920.

[35] Sources, Joachim-Friedrich Huth: Karl Friedrich Hildebrand, *Die Generale der deutschen Luftwaffe 1935-1945, Band 2 Habermehl-Nuber*, Osnabrück, FRG, 1991, 129-130.

[36] Sources, Max-Josef Ibel: Karl Friedrich Hildebrand, *Die Generale der deutschen Luftwaffe 1935-1945, Band 2 Habermehl-Nuber*, Osnabrück, FRG, 1991, 131-132; Ernst Obermaier, *Die Ritterkreuzträger der Luftwaffe, Jagdflieger 1939-1945*, Mainz, FRG: Verlag Dieter Hoffmann, 1989, 138.

[37] Sources, Wilhelm Kaiser: Ernst Obermaier, *Die Ritterkreuzträger der Luftwaffe, Stuka und Schlachtflieger 1939-1945*, Mainz, FRG: Verlag Dieter Hoffmann, 1976, 102; Christopher Shores and Brian Cull, *Air War for Yugoslavia, Greece and Crete*, Carrollton, TX: Squadron Signal Publications, 1987, 358.

[38] The unit was named after World War I fighter ace Oswald Boelcke.

[39] Sources, Alfred Keller: Karl Friedrich Hildebrand, *Die Generale der deutschen Luftwaffe 1935-1945, Band 2 Habermehl-Nuber*, Osnabrück, FRG, 1991, 163-164; Samuel Mitcham, Jr., *Men of the Luftwaffe*, Novato, CA: Presidio, 1988, 131.

[40] Sources, Albert Kesselring: Chris Bishop, *Luftwaffe Squadrons 1939-45*, Stapelhurst, England: Spellmont, 2006, 21; Matthew Cooper, *The German Air Force 1933-1945: An Anatomy of Failure*, London: Jane's, 1981, 16-17; Karl Friedrich Hildebrand, *Die Generale der deutschen Luftwaffe 1935-1945, Band 2 Habermehl-Nuber*, Osnabrück, FRG, 1991, 165-167; Samuel Mitcham, Jr., *Men of the Luftwaffe*, Novato, CA: Presidio, 1988, 85.

[41] Sources, Ullrich Kessler: Karl Friedrich Hildebrand, *Die Generale der deutschen Luftwaffe 1935-1945, Band 2 Habermehl-Nuber*, Osnabrück, FRG, 1991, 168-169.

[42] Sources, Hans von Koppelow: Kurt Mehner and Reinhard Teuber, *Die Deutsche Luftwaffe 1939-1945 Führung und Truppe*, Norderstedt, Germany; Militair-Verlag Klaus D. Patzwall, 1993, 18, 23, 51; Veit Scherzer, *Die Träger des Deutschen Kreuzes in Gold der Luftwaffe 1941-1945*, Bayreuth, FRG: Scherzer's Militair Verlag, 1992, 172; Christian Zweng, *Die Dienststellen, Kommandobehörden und Truppenteile der Luftwaffe 1935-1945, Band 1 Nr. 1-10*, Osnabrück, Germany; Biblio Verlag, 1999, 130, 316.

[43] Sources, Helmut Leicht: Ernst Obermaier, *Die Ritterkreuzträger der Luftwaffe, Stuka und Schlachtflieger 1939-1945*, Mainz, FRG: Verlag Dieter Hoffmann, 1976, 52; Veit Scherzer, *Die Ritterkreuzträger: Die Inhaber des Ritterkreuzes des Eisernen Kreuzes 1939-1945*, Jena, Germany: Scherzers Militairs-Verlag, 2005, 474.

[44] Sources, Helmut Lent: Peter Hinchliffe, *The Lent Papers: Helmut Lent*, Bristol, England: Cerberus Publishing, 2003, 24, 112, 215, 258-260; Ernst Obermaier, *Die Ritterkreuzträger der Luftwaffe, Jagdflieger 1939-1945*, Mainz, FRG: Verlag Dieter Hoffmann, 1989, 23; Veit Scherzer, *Die Ritterkreuzträger: Die Inhaber des Ritterkreuzes des Eisernen Kreuzes 1939-1945*, Jena, Germany: Scherzers Militairs-Verlag, 2005, 476.

[45] Sources, Ernst Liebach: Christian Zweng, *Die Dienststellen, Kommandobehörden und Truppenteile der Luftwaffe 1935-1945, Band 1 Nr. 1-10*, Osnabrück, Germany, Biblio Verlag, 1999, 77, 455.

[46] Sources, Bruno Loerzer: Matthew Cooper, *The German Air Force 1933-1945: An Anatomy of Failure*, London: Jane's, 1981, 27;

Karl Friedrich Hildebrand, *Die Generale der deutschen Luftwaffe 1935-1945, Band 2 Habermehl-Nuber*, Osnabrück, FRG, 1991, 309-310; Samuel Mitcham, Jr., *Men of the Luftwaffe*, Novato, CA: Presidio, 1988, 2-3.

[47] Sources, Günther von Lützow: Ernst Obermaier, *Die Ritterkreuzträger der Luftwaffe, Jagdflieger 1939-1945*, Mainz, FRG: Verlag Dieter Hoffmann, 1989, 29; Jochen Prien, Gerhard Stemmer, Peter Rodeike and Winfried Bock, *Die Jagdfliegerverbände der Deutschen Luftwaffe 1934 bis 1945, Teil 6/I: Unternehmen "Barbarossa" Einsatz im Osten 22.6. bis 5.12.1941*, Eutin, Germany: Struve, 2003, 216; Karl Ries and Hans Ring, *Legion Condor, 1936-1939: Eine illustrierte Dokumentation*, Mainz, Germany: Verlag Dieter Hoffmann, 1980, 251, 265-266.

[48] Sources, Manfred Mössinger: Kurt Mehner and Reinhard Teuber, *Die Deutsche Luftwaffe 1939-1945 Führung und Truppe*, Norderstedt, Germany; Militair-Verlag Klaus D. Patzwall, 1993, 55, 59; Willi Reschke, *Jagdgeschwader 301/302 "Wilde Sau,"* Stuttgart, Germany: Motorbuch Verlag, 1998, 17.

[49] Several sources postulate that he was shot down by First Lieutenant Edward "Buddy" Haydon of the 357th Fighter Group and Captain Ernest "Feeb" Fiebelkorn of the 20th Fighter Group, USAAF who was credited with a shared Me 262 victory at 12:45 that day over Achmer.

[50] Sources, Walter Nowotny: Ernst Obermaier, *Die Ritterkreuzträger der Luftwaffe, Jagdflieger 1939-1945*, Mainz, FRG: Verlag Dieter Hoffmann, 1989, 22.

[51] Sources, Hans von Obernitz: Kurt Mehner and Reinhard Teuber, *Die Deutsche Luftwaffe 1939-1945 Führung und Truppe*, Norderstedt, Germany; Militair-Verlag Klaus D. Patzwall, 1993, 48; Veit Scherzer, *Die Träger des Deutschen Kreuzes in Gold der Luftwaffe 1941-1945*, Bayreuth, FRG: Scherzer's Militair Verlag, 1992, 239.

[52] Sources, Walter Oesau: Ernst Obermaier, *Die Ritterkreuzträger der Luftwaffe, Jagdflieger 1939-1945*, Mainz, FRG: Verlag Dieter Hoffmann, 1989, 29; Jochen Prien, Gerhard Stemmer, Peter Rodeike and Winfried Bock, *Die Jagdfliegerverbände der Deutschen Luftwaffe 1934 bis 1945, Teil 5: Heimatverteidigung 10. Mai 1940 bis 31. Dezember 1941, Einsatz im Mittelmeerraum Oktober 1940 bis November 1941, Einsatz im Westen 22. Juni bis 31. Dezember 1941, Die Ergänzungsjagdgruppen Einsatz 1941 bis zur Auflösung Anfang 1942*, Eutin, Germany: Struve, 2003, 405; Jochen Prien, Gerhard Stemmer, Peter Rodeike and Winfried Bock, *Die Jagdfliegerverbände der Deutschen Luftwaffe 1934 bis 1945, Teil 6/I: Unternehmen "Barbarossa" Einsatz im Osten 22.6. bis 5.12.1941*, Eutin, Germany: Struve, 2003, 135; Jochen Prien, Gerhard Stemmer, Peter Rodeike and Winfried Bock, *Die Jagdfliegerverbände der Deutschen Luftwaffe 1934 bis 1945, Teil 7: Heimatsverteidigung 1. Januar bis 31. Dezember 1942, Einsatz im Westen 1. Januar bis 31. Dezember 1942*, Eutin, Germany: Struve, 2003, 213; Karl Ries and Hans Ring, *Legion Condor, 1936-1939: Eine illustrierte Dokumentation*, Mainz, Germany: Verlag Dieter Hoffmann, 1980, 265-266.

[53] Sources, Theodor Osterkamp: Karl Friedrich Hildebrand, *Die Generale der deutschen Luftwaffe 1935-1945, Band 3, Odebrecht-Zoch*, Osnabrück, FRG, 1992, 12-13; Ernst Obermaier, *Die Ritterkreuzträger der Luftwaffe, Jagdflieger 1939-1945*, Mainz, FRG: Verlag Dieter Hoffmann, 1989, 177.

[54] Sources, Kurd Peters: Ernst Obermaier, *Die Ritterkreuzträger der Luftwaffe, Jagdflieger 1939-1945*, Mainz, FRG: Verlag Dieter Hoffmann, 1989, 178.

[55] Sources, Josef Priller: Ernst Obermaier, *Die Ritterkreuzträger der Luftwaffe, Jagdflieger 1939-1945*, Mainz, FRG: Verlag Dieter Hoffmann, 1989, 36; Jochen Prien, Gerhard Stemmer, Peter Rodeike and Winfried Bock, *Die Jagdfliegerverbände der Deutschen Luftwaffe 1934 bis 1945, Teil 7: Heimatsverteidigung 1. Januar bis 31. Dezember 1942, Einsatz im Westen 1. Januar bis 31. Dezember 1942*, Eutin, Germany: Struve, 2003, 400, 402.

[56] Sources, Klaus Quaet-Faslem: Ernst Obermaier, *Die Ritterkreuzträger der Luftwaffe, Jagdflieger 1939-1945*, Mainz, FRG: Verlag Dieter Hoffmann, 1989, 182.

[57] Sources, Günther Rall: Ernst Obermaier, *Die Ritterkreuzträger der Luftwaffe, Jagdflieger 1939-1945*, Mainz, FRG: Verlag Dieter Hoffmann, 1989, 33; Hans Schreier, *JG 52: Das erfolgreichste Jagdgeschwader des II. Weltkrieges*, Berg am See, FRG: Kurt Vowinckel Verlag, 2002, 191.

[58] Sources, Bernhard Ramcke: Karl Friedrich Hildebrand, *Die Generale der deutschen Luftwaffe 1935-1945, Band 3, Odebrecht-Zoch*, Osnabrück, FRG, 1992, 76-78.

[59] Sources, Ernst Reusch: Ernst Obermaier, *Die Ritterkreuzträger der Luftwaffe, Stuka und Schlachtflieger 1939-1945*, Mainz, FRG: Verlag Dieter Hoffmann, 1976, 131; Veit Scherzer, *Die Ritterkreuzträger: Die Inhaber des Ritterkreuzes des Eisernen Kreuzes 1939-1945*, Jena, Germany: Scherzers Militairs-Verlag, 2005, 598.

[60] Sources, Heinrich Sannemann: Jochen Prien, Gerhard Stemmer, Peter Rodeike and Winfried Bock, *Die Jagdfliegerverbände der Deutschen Luftwaffe 1934 bis 1945, Teil 4/I: Einsatz am Kanal und über England, 26.6.1940 bis 21.6.1941*, Eutin, Germany: Struve, 214; Jochen Prien, Gerhard Stemmer, Peter Rodeike and Winfried Bock, *Die Jagdfliegerverbände der Deutschen Luftwaffe 1934 bis 1945, Teil 8/I: Einsatz im Mittelmeerraum November 1941 bis Dezember 1942*, Eutin, Germany: Struve, 2004, 83; Horst Scheibert, *Die Träger der Ehrenblattspange des Heeres und der Waffen-SS, Die Träger der Ehrentafelspange der Kriegsmarine, Die Inhaber des Ehrenpokals für besondere Leistung im Luftkrieg*, Friedberg, FRG: Podzun-Pallas-Verlag, 1986, 261.

[61] Sources: Roman Schneider: Kurt Mehner and Reinhard Teuber, *Die Deutsche Luftwaffe 1939-1945 Führung und Truppe*, Norderstedt, Germany; Militair-Verlag Klaus D. Patzwall, 1993, 47, 48; Veit Scherzer, *Die Träger des Deutschen Kreuzes in Gold der Luftwaffe 1941-1945*, Bayreuth, FRG: Scherzer's Militair Verlag, 1992, 298.

[62] Sources: Ernst-Albrecht Schultz: Jochen Prien, Gerhard Stemmer, Peter Rodeike and Winfried Bock, *Die Jagdfliegerverbände der Deutschen Luftwaffe 1934 bis 1945, Teil 5: Heimatverteidigung 10. Mai 1940 bis 31. Dezember 1941, Einsatz im Mittelmeerraum Oktober 1940 bis November 1941, Einsatz im Westen 22. Juni bis 31. Dezember 1941, Die Ergänzungsjagdgruppen Einsatz 1941 bis zur Auflösung Anfang 1942*, Eutin, Germany: Struve, 2003, 614.

[63] Sources, Herbert Sonnenburg: Karl Friedrich Hildebrand, *Die Generale der deutschen Luftwaffe 1935-1945, Band 3, Odebrecht-Zoch*, Osnabrück, FRG, 1992, 315-316.

[64] Sources, Hugo Sperrle: Karl Friedrich Hildebrand, *Die Generale der deutschen Luftwaffe 1935-1945, Band 3, Odebrecht-Zoch*, Osnabrück, FRG, 1992, 325-326; Samuel Mitcham, Jr., *Men of the Luftwaffe*, Novato, CA: Presidio, 1988, 35, 43, 254; Karl Ries and Hans Ring, *Legion Condor, 1936-1939: Eine illustrierte Dokumentation*, Mainz, Germany: Verlag Dieter Hoffmann, 1980, 265-266.

[65] Obermeitingen is 30 minutes south of Augsburg.

[66] Sources, Kurt Student: Karl Friedrich Hildebrand, *Die Generale der deutschen Luftwaffe 1935-1945, Band 3, Odebrecht-Zoch*, Osnabrück, FRG, 1992, 363-365; Franz Thomas and Günter Wegmann, *Die Ritterkreuzträger der Deutschen Wehrmacht 1939-1945, Teil II: Fallschirmjäger*, Osnabrück, FRG: Biblio-Verlag, 1986, 301-304.

[67] Sources, Hans-Jürgen Stumpff: Karl Friedrich Hildebrand, *Die Generale der deutschen Luftwaffe 1935-1945, Band 3, Odebrecht-Zoch*, Osnabrück, FRG, 1992, 369-370.

[68] Sources, Alfred Sturm: Karl Friedrich Hildebrand, *Die Generale der deutschen Luftwaffe 1935-1945, Band 3, Odebrecht-Zoch*, Osnabrück, FRG, 1992, 371-372.

[69] Sources, Wolfgang Tonne: Ernst Obermaier, *Die Ritterkreuzträger der Luftwaffe, Jagdflieger 1939-1945*, Mainz, FRG: Verlag Dieter Hoffmann, 1989, 54; Jochen Prien, Gerhard Stemmer, Peter Rodeike and Winfried Bock, *Die Jagdfliegerverbände der Deutschen Luftwaffe 1934 bis 1945, Teil 6/II: Unternehmen "Barbarossa" Einsatz im Osten 22.6. bis 5.12.1941*, Eutin, Germany: Struve, 2003, 115; Jochen Prien, Gerhard Stemmer, Peter Rodeike and Winfried Bock, *Die Jagdfliegerverbände der Deutschen Luftwaffe 1934 bis 1945, Teil8/II: Einsatz im Mittelmeerraum November 1941 bis Dezember 1942*, Eutin, Germany: Struve, 2004, 60.

[70] Sources, Hannes Trautloft: Ernst Obermaier, *Die Ritterkreuzträger der Luftwaffe, Jagdflieger 1939-1945*, Mainz, FRG: Verlag Dieter Hoffmann, 1989, 216; Jochen Prien, Gerhard Stemmer, Peter Rodeike and Winfried Bock, *Die Jagdfliegerverbände der Deutschen Luftwaffe 1934 bis 1945, Teil 5: Heimatverteidigung 10. Mai 1940 bis 31. Dezember 1941, Einsatz im Mittelmeerraum Oktober 1940 bis November 1941, Einsatz im Westen 22. Juni bis 31. Dezember 1941, Die Ergänzungsjagdgruppen Einsatz 1941 bis zur Auflösung Anfang 1942*, Eutin, Germany: Struve, 2003, 240; Jochen Prien, Gerhard Stemmer, Peter Rodeike and Winfried Bock, *Die Jagdfliegerverbände der Deutschen Luftwaffe 1934 bis 1945, Teil 6/II: Unternehmen "Barbarossa" Einsatz im Osten 22.6. bis 5.12.1941*, Eutin, Germany: Struve, 2003, 181; Karl Ries and Hans Ring, *Legion Condor, 1936-1939: Eine illustrierte Dokumentation*, Mainz, Germany: Verlag Dieter Hoffmann, 1980, 265-266.

[71] Sources, Friedrich Vollbracht: Ernst Obermaier, *Die Ritterkreuzträger der Luftwaffe, Jagdflieger 1939-1945*, Mainz, FRG: Verlag Dieter Hoffmann, 1989, 218.

[72] Sources, Gerhard Weyert: Karl Ries and Hans Ring, *Legion Condor, 1936-1939: Eine illustrierte Dokumentation*, Mainz, Germany: Verlag Dieter Hoffmann, 1980, 265-266; Peter Taghorn, *Die Geschichte des Lehrgeschwaders 1, Band 2 (1942-1945)*, Zweibrücken, Germany: 2004, 490.

[73] Sources, Wolf-Dietrich Wilcke: Ernst Obermaier, *Die Ritterkreuzträger der Luftwaffe, Jagdflieger 1939-1945*, Mainz, FRG: Verlag Dieter Hoffmann, 1989, 33; Jochen Prien, Gerhard Stemmer, Peter Rodeike and Winfried Bock, *Die Jagdfliegerverbände der Deutschen Luftwaffe 1934 bis 1945, Teil 8/II: Einsatz im Mittelmeerraum November 1941 bis Dezember 1942*, Eutin, Germany: Struve, 2004, 213.

[74] Sources, Gustav Wilke: Karl Friedrich Hildebrand, *Die Generale der deutschen Luftwaffe 1935-1945, Band 3, Odebrecht-Zoch*, Osnabrück, FRG, 1992, 520-521.

[75] Sources, Eugen-Ludwig Zweigart: Ernst Obermaier, *Die Ritterkreuzträger der Luftwaffe, Jagdflieger 1939-1945*, Mainz, FRG: Verlag Dieter Hoffmann, 1989, 228; Jochen Prien, Gerhard Stemmer, Peter Rodeike and Winfried Bock, *Die Jagdfliegerverbände der Deutschen Luftwaffe 1934 bis 1945, Teil 6/II: Unternehmen "Barbarossa" Einsatz im Osten 22.6. bis 5.12.1941*, Eutin, Germany: Struve, 2003, 262, 268, 272; John Weal, *Jagdgeschwader 54 "Grünherz,"* Osprey Aviation Elite 6, Oxford, England: Osprey Publishing, 2001, 62, 88, 92.

GLOSSARY

Abitur – qualification examination to enter a university
A Schule – primary flying training school
A/B Schule – primary/advanced flying training school
Ab – from
Abschuss – aerial victory
Abteilung – detachment (roughly equivalent to a battalion)
Abteilungsführer – acting detachment commander
Abteilungskommandeur – detachment commander
Abwehrkämpfe – defensive battles
Adjutant – adjutant (often with executive officer authority)
Ärmelband "Kreta" – Crete cufftitle
Aktiver Wehrdienst – active duty
Angriff – attack
Anlage – enclosure
April – April
Armee – army
Artillerie – artillery
Aufklärer – reconnaissance pilot
Aufklärungsabteilung – ground reconnaissance detachment/battalion
August – August
Ausbildung – training
ausgefüllt – fulfilled
Auszeichnungen – awards

Bataillon – battalion
Bataillonsführer – acting battalion commander
Bataillons-Kommandeur – battalion commander
Batterie – artillery battery
Batteriechef – battery commander
Batterieführer – acting battery commander
Bauchlanden – belly-landing
Beförderung – promotion
befürwortet – seconded (in agreement with)
Begründung – reason for consideration
Beobachter – observer
Beobachterabzeichen – observer's badge
Beruf – profession (normally associated with civilian profession before entering the service)
Bestrafung -- punishment
Beurteilung – judgment, estimation, evaluation
bevorzugten Beförderung – preferred, preferential (accelerated) promotion

Bordfunker – radio operator
Bordmechaniker – flight engineer

Chef des Generalstab(e)s – chief of staff

Deutsches Kreuz in Gold – German Cross in Gold
Dezember – December
Dienstantritt – date entered military service
Dienstgrad – grade/rank
Dienstellung – duty position
Division – division
Divisionskommandeur – division commander
Divisions Stabsquartier (Div.St.Qu.) – division headquarters
Draufgänger – daredevil
dunkle Nachtjagd (Dunaja) – dark night fighting (radar directed, not using searchlights)
Durchschnitt – average

Ehrenpokal für besondere Leistungen – Honor Goblet for Outstanding Achievement
Ehrenschale für hervorragende Kampfleistung – Honor Salver for Distinguished Achievement
Eichenlaub – oak leaves
Einheit – unit
einverstanden – in agreement
Eisernes Kreuz I. Klasse (E.K. I) – Iron Cross 1st Class
Eisernes Kreuz II. Klasse (E.K. II) – Iron Cross 2nd Class
Entlassung – discharge
Ergänzungs – Supplemental
Ergänzungsgeschwader – supplemental wing (an operational training unit)
Ergänzungsgruppe – supplemental group (an operational training unit)
Erprobungsgruppe – operational test group
Erprobungsstaffel – operational test squadron
erweiterter Luftwaffen-Flugzeugführerschein (ELF) – *Luftwaffe* Advanced Pilot's Certificate

Fallschirm – parachute
Fallschirmabsprung – parachute jump
Fallschirm-Fla-MG-Bataillon – anti-aircraft machine-gun battalion
Fallschirmjäger – paratrooper
Fallschirmschützenabzeichen – paratrooper's badge

Familienname – family, or last, name
Februar – February
Feind – enemy
Feindflug – flight against the enemy
Feldwebel – technical sergeant
Fernaufklärung – long-distance reconnaissance
Fernaufklärungsgruppe – long-distance reconnaissance group
Fernnachtjagd – long-range night fighting (usually over Britain)
Flak – anti-aircraft
Fliegerdivision – flying division (first associated with airborne, later with flying elements)
Fliegerführer – aircraft command/control headquarters, or its commander
Fliegerkorps – air corps
Fliegerschütze – aerial gunner
Fliegerschützenabzeichen – air gunner's badge
Fliegertruppe – flying troops
Fluglehrer – flight instructor
Flugzeug – aircraft
Flugzeugführer – pilot
Flugzeugführer-Abzeichen – pilot's badge
Frieden – peacetime
Friedhof – cemetery
Frontflugspange – operational flying clasp
Führungs- oder Bedienungsfehler – pilot or crew error (often associated with a fatal crash)

Geburtsdatum/Geburtstag – birth date
Geburtsort – place of birth
gefallen – killed in action
Gefangener – prisoner
Gefecht – battle, action, combat
Gefechtsstand – field headquarters, command post
geheim – secret
geeignet – suitable
Gemeinsames Flugzeugführer und Beobachterabzeichen – combined pilot's and observer's badge
General der Fallschirmtruupe (General of Parachute Troops) – lieutenant general (3-stars)
General der Flieger (General of Flying Troops) – lieutenant general (3-stars)
Generalfeldmarschall – field marshal (5-stars)
Generalleutnant – major general (2-stars)
Generalmajor – brigadier general (1-star)
Generaloberst – colonel general (4-stars)
geschieden – divorced
Geschwader – wing; air force operational unit of between 3 to 5 groups
Geschwaderkommodore – wing commodore/commander
Gruppe – air force operational flying unit of about 27 aircraft
Gruppenführer – acting commander
Gruppenkommandeur – group commander
gut ausgefüllt – well fulfilled

Hauptfeldwebel – first sergeant
Hauptmann – captain
Hauptquartier – headquarters
Heimatanschrift – home mailing address
helle Nachtjagd – bright night fighting; in conjunction with searchlights
Heer – the Army
Herausschuss – damaging an enemy aircraft so that it is forced to fall out of formation
heute – today

im Felde – in the field
Improvisationstalent – talent for improvisation
in Vertretung (i.V.) – acting as, representing
Infanterie – infantry
Inspekteur – inspector

Jagdbomber (Jabo) – fighter-bomber
Jäger – rifleman
Jagdabschnittsführer – fighter district commander
Jagdflieger – fighter pilot
Jagdfliegerführer – fighter command/control headquarters, or its commander
Jagdflugzeug – fighter aircraft
Jagdgeschwader (JG) – fighter wing
Jagdgruppe – fighter group
Jagdkorps – fighter corps
Jagdstaffel – fighter squadron
Jagdverband – fighter formation
Jahrgang – year group (Jahrgang 1922 equates to all military personnel born that year)
Januar – January
Juli – July
Juni – June

Kamerad – comrade
Kampfflieger – bomber pilot
Kampffliegergruppe – bomb group
Kampfgeschwader (KG) – bomb wing
Kampfgeschwader z.b.V. – special purpose transport wing
Kampfgruppe – bomb group (also battle group)
Katschmarek – slang term for wingman
Kette – 3 aircraft element
Kettenführer – leader of a 3-aircraft element
Kinder – children
Kompanie – company
Kompaniechef – company commander
Kompanieführer – temporary company commander
Konfession – religious affiliation
Korps – corps
krank – sick, ill
Krieg – war
Kriegsakademie – war college
Kriegsmarine – the Navy
Kriegsoffizier-Anwärter (KOA) – candidate for wartime commission
Kriegsoffizier-Bewerber (KOB) – applicant for wartime commission
Kriegsverdienstkreuz – War Service Cross
Küstenflieger – unit operating in cooperation with the Navy

Landung – landing
ledig – single/bachelor
Lehrgang – course of instruction
Lehrgeschwader – demonstration wing (which was also a combat unit)
leichtverwundet – slightly wounded
Leistung – achievement
Leutnant – second lieutenant
Lichtbild – photo
Luftflotte – air fleet (corresponded to a US Army Air Corps numbered air force)
Luftflottenchef – air fleet commander
Luftgau – air force administrative command
Lufthansa – the German national airline

Luftkampf – air battle
Luftkreis – air force service area
Luftlandgeschwader – air transport glider wing
Luftsieg – aerial victory
Luftwaffe – the Air Force
Luftwaffenkommando – a small Luftflotte
Luftwaffenpersonalamt – air force personnel office

März – March
Mai – May
Major – major
mit der Führung beauftragt (m.d.F.b.) – in temporary command
mit Wahrnehmung der Geschäfte beauftragt (m.W.d.G.b.) – tasked with attending to the duties of; acting commander, subject to confirmation

Nachrichten – signal
Nachtabschüssen – nighttime shootdowns
Nachtjagd – night fighting
Nachtjagdgeschwader – night fighter wing
Nachtjagdgruppen – night fighter group
Nachwuchs – new pilot, rookie
nächsthöheren – next higher
Nahaufklärung – close/local reconnaissance
Nahaufklärungsgruppe – close reconnaissance group
Nationalsozialist – National Socialist
Neuaufstellung – reorganization, new organization
nicht ausgefüllt – not fulfilled
nichts hinzufügen – nothing to be added
notlanden – emergency landing, forced landing
November – November

Oberbefehlshaber – commander of an army or higher formation
Oberfähnrich – master sergeant officer candidate
Oberfeldwebel – master sergeant
Oberleutnant – first lieutenant
Oberst – colonel
Oberstleutnant – lieutenant colonel
Offizier – officer
Offiziersanwärter – officer candidate
Offizierbewerber – officer applicant
Oktober – October
Ordonnanzoffizier – special missions staff officer
Ortsunterkunft (O.U.) – billets

Pak – anti-tank gun
Panzerabteilung – tank detachment/battalion
Panzerabwehrabteilung – anti-tank detachment/battalion
Panzerjägerabteilung – anti-tank detachment/battalion
Panzerjägerkompanie – anti-tank company
Pionier – engineer
Pionierbataillon – engineer battalion

Quartiermeister (Ib) – supply officer of a division or corps

Rangliste – rank list
Rangdienstalter – official date of rank
Regiment – regiment
Reichsarbeitsdienst – Reich Labor Service
Reichsluftfahrtministerium – German Air Ministry
Reserveoffizier – reserve officer
Reservelazerette – general hospital
Ritterkreuz des Eisernen Kreuz – Knight's Cross of the Iron Cross
Ritterkreuzträger – Knight's Cross winner
Rotte – two aircraft element

Rottenflieger – wingman in a two-aircraft formation
Rottenführer – leader of a two-aircraft formation

Sacharbeiter – technical staff officer with a special skill such as architect
Schlacht – battle
Schlachtflieger – ground-attack pilot
Schlachtgeschwader (SG) – ground-attack wing
Schlachtgruppe – ground-attack group
Schnellkampfgeschwader – fast bomber wing
Schule – school
schwache Seiten – weak traits
Schwarm – flight; flying formation of 4 aircraft (two *Rotten*)
Schwarmführer – leader of a formation of 4 aircraft
Schwerter – swords
schwerverwundet – seriously wounded
Seeaufklärungs – sea reconnaissance
Seeflieger – naval aviator
Seenotdienst – Air-sea rescue
Segelflugzeug – glider
sehr gut ausgefüllt – very well fulfilled
September – September
Sonder – special
Spähtrupp – patrol, reconnaissance patrol
Spange – clasp
Spanienkreuz – Spanish Cross
Spitzenzug – advance platoon
Splitter – fragment, shrapnel
sportlich – athletic
Stab – staff
Stabschwarm – staff flight
Stabsquartier – headquarters
Staffel – squadron
Staffelführer – acting, temporary squadron commander
Staffelkapitän – squadron commander
Standort – post, garrison
starke Seiten – strong traits
Start – take-off
Stellungswechsel – change of position
stellvertretend – acting, deputy
stellvertretender Führer – second-in-command
Stellvertreter – deputy, substitute
Sturzkampfflugzeug (Stuka) – dive bomber
Sturzkampfgeschwader (StG) – Stuka wing

Tapferkeit – bravery
Technischer Offizier – technical officer
Tiefflugangriff – low-level aerial attack
Torpedo – torpedo
Transportflugzeug – transport aircraft
Transportgeschwader – transport wing
Transportgruppe – transport group
Truppenteil – troop organization

über Durchschnitt – above average
Umgangformen – manners
unbesiegt vom Feind – unconquered by the foe; pilot who died in an accident, not by enemy action
unermüdlich – untiring
unter Durchschnitt – below average
Unternehmen – operation, undertaking
Unteroffizier – sergeant

Verbindungsoffizier – liaison officer
verheiratet – married

Verwaltung – administration
verwitwet – widowed
verwundet – wounded
Verwundetenabzeichen in Gold – wound badge in gold (5 wounds)
Verwundetenabzeichen in Schwarz – wound badge in black (1-2 wounds)
Verwundetenabzeichen in Silber – wound badge in silver (3 wounds)
vorbildlicher – exemplary
Vorschlag – proposal, nomination
Verwaltung – administration

Waffengattung – branch within a service: such as paratroops, flying troops, etc.
Wehrkreis – military service area
Wehrmacht – Armed Forces
Wehrmachtbericht – Armed Forces Bulletin (similar to Mentioned in Dispatches)
Wehrmachtteil – Service. Army, Navy, Air Force
Wilde Sau – wild boar; freelance night fighting over the bombers' target

Zahme Sau – tame boar; freelance night fighting within the bomber approach stream
Zerstörer – twin-engine long-range fighter (also navy destroyer)
Zerstörer-Ergänzungsgruppe – Destroyer Supplemental Group
Zerstörerflugzeug – twin-engine long-range aircraft
Zerstörergeschwader (ZG) – twin-engine long-range wing
Zerstörergruppe – twin-engine long-range group
zivil – civilian
Zug – platoon

German presentation of calendar dates

For all German military documents from World War II, dates are presented in the following order: day, month, and year. Thus, 12. 10. 1943 represents October 12, 1943, not December 10, 1943. Some additional examples follow:

1. 9. 1939 = September 1, 1939
8. 7. 1940 = July 8, 1940
7. 8. 1941 = August 7, 1941
10. 4. 1942 = April 10, 1942
11. 12. 1943 = December 11, 1943
1. 5. 1944 = May 1, 1944
8. 3. 1945 = March 8, 1945

BIBLIOGRAPHY

Books

Achkasov, V.I. and N.B. Pavlovich, *Soviet Naval Operations in the Great Patriotic War 1941-1945*, Annapolis, Maryland: Naval Institute Press, 1981.

Aders, Gebhard. *History of the German Night Fighter Force 1917-1945*, London: Jane's, 1979.

Aders, Gebhard and Werner Held. *Jagdgeschwader 51 "Mölders,"* Stuttgart, FRG: Motorbuch Verlag, 1985.

Amadio, Jill. *Günther Rall: A Memoir – Luftwaffe Ace and NATO General*, Santa Ana, CA: Tangmere Productions, 2002.

Angolia, John R. *For Führer and Fatherland: Military Awards of the Third Reich*, San Jose, CA: Bender Publishing, 1976.

Angolia, John R. *On The Field Of Honor: A History of the Knight's Cross Bearers*, Volume 2, San Jose, CA: Bender Publishing, 1980.

Antill, Peter D. *Crete 1941: Germany's Lightning Airborne Assault*, Osprey Campaign 147, Oxford, England: Osprey Publishing, 2005.

Balke, Ulf. *Der Luft-Krieg in Europa, Die Operativen Einsätze des Kampf-Geschwaders 2 im Zweiten Weltkrieg*, Teil 2, Koblenz, FRG: Bernhard & Graefe Verlag, 1990.

Baumbach, Werner. *The Life and Death of the Luftwaffe*, translated by Frederick Holt, New York: Coward-McCann, Inc., 1960.

Bekker, Cajus. *The Luftwaffe War Diaries*, London: MacDonald & Co., 1967.

Bishop, Chris. *Luftwaffe Squadrons 1939-45*, Stapelhurst, England: Spellmont, 2006.

Blumenson, Martin. *Anzio: The Gambit That Failed*, Philadelphia: J.B. Lippincott, 1963.

Blumenson, Martin. *Breakout and Pursuit*, U.S. Army in World War II, The European Theater of Operations, Washington, D.C: Department of the Army, Office of the Chief of Military History, 1961.

Boehme, Manfred. *Jagdgeschwader 7: Die Chronik eines Me 262-Geschwaders 1944/45*, Stuttgart, FRG: Motorbuch Verlag, 1984.

Brehde, Dietrich. *Der Blaue Komet: Geschichte des IV. Bataillons des Luftlande-Sturmregiments 1940-1945*, Munich, FRG: Schild Verlag, 1988.

Brütting, Georg. *Das waren die deutschen Kampfflieger-Asse, 1939-1945*, Stuttgart, FRG: Motorbuch Verlag, 1983.

Brütting, Georg. *Das waren die deutschen Stuka-Asse, 1939-1945*, Stuttgart, FRG: Motorbuch Verlag, 1976.

Busch, Erich. *Die Fallschirmjäger-Chronik 1935-1945*, Friedberg, FRG: Podzun-Palls-Verlag, 1983.

Caldwell, Donald L. *JG 26: Top Guns of the Luftwaffe*, New York: Orion Books, 1991.

Cooper, Matthew. *The German Air Force 1933-1945: An Anatomy of Failure*, London: Jane's, 1981.

Dierach, Wolfgang. *Kampfgeschwader 51 "Edelweiss": Eine Chronik aus Dokumenten und Berichten 1937-1945*, Stuttgart, FRG: Motorbuch Verlag, 1973.

Edwards, Roger. *German Airborne Troops 1936-1945*, Garden City, NJ: Doubleday & Company, 1974.

Ellis, Chris. *7th Flieger Division: Student's Fallschirmjäger Elite*, Surrey, England: Ian Allan Publishing, 2002.

Ellis, John. *Cassino: The Hollow Victory*, London: André Deutsch Limited, 1984.

Ethell, Jeffrey, and Alfred Price. *Target Berlin*, London: Jane's, 1981.

Feuerstein, Erwin. *Mit und ohne Ritterkreuz*, Stuttgart, FRG: Motorbuch Verlag, 1974.

Ford, Ken. *Cassino 1944: Breaking the Gustav Line*, Osprey Campaign 134, Oxford, England: Osprey Publishing, 2004.

Freeman, Roger A. *Mighty Eighth War Diary*, London: Jane's, 1981.

Galland, Adolf. *The First And The Last: The Rise and Fall of the German Fighter Forces, 1938-1945*, translated by Mervyn Savill, New York: Henry Holt and Company, 1954.

Girbig, Werner. *Jagdgeschwader 5 "Eismeerjäger": Eine Chronik aus Dokumenten und Berichten 1941-1945*, Stuttgart, FRG: Motorbuch Verlag, 1976.

Hildebrand, Karl Friedrich. *Die Generale der deutschen Luftwaffe 1935-1945, Band 1 Abernetty-v. Gyldenfeldt*, Osnabrück, FRG, 1990.

Hildebrand, Karl Friedrich. *Die Generale der deutschen Luftwaffe 1935-1945, Band 2 Habermehl-Nuber*, Osnabrück, FRG, 1991.

Hildebrand, Karl Friedrich. *Die Generale der deutschen Luftwaffe 1935-1945, Band 3, Odebrecht-Zoch*, Osnabrück, FRG, 1992.

Hinchliffe, Peter. *The Lent Papers: Helmut Lent*, Bristol, England: Cerberus Publishing, 2003.

Jurado, Carlos Caballero. *The Condor Legion: German Troops in the Spanish Civil War*, Osprey Elite 131, Oxford, England: Osprey Publishing, 2006.

Kiriakopoulos, G.C. *Ten Days to Destiny: The Battle for Crete 1941*, New York: Franklin Watts, 1985.

Kurowski, Franz. *Luftwaffe Aces: German Combat Pilots of WWII*, translated by David Johnston, Mechanicsburg, PA: Stackpole, 2004.

Lenfeld, Erwin and Franz Thomas. *Die Eichenlaubträger 1940-1945*, Wiener-Neustedt, Austria: Weilburg Verlag, 1983.

Lucas, James. *Storming Eagles: German Airborne Forces in World War Two*, London: Arms and Armour Press, 1988.

MacLean, French. *The Cruel Hunters: SS-Sonderkommando Dirlewanger, Hitler's Most Notorious Anti-partisan Unit*. Atglen, PA: Schiffer Publishing Co., 1998.

MacLean, French L. *Quiet Flows the Rhine: German General Officer Casualties of World War II*, Winnipeg, Canada: J.J. Fedorowicz, 1996.

Manrho, John, and Ron Pütz. *Bodenplatte: The Luftwaffe's Last Hope*, Browborough, England: Hikoki Publication, 2004.

Mehner, Kurt and Reinhard Teuber. *Die Deutsche Luftwaffe 1939-1945 Führung und Truppe*, Norderstedt, Germany: Militair-Verlag Klaus D. Patzwall, 1993.

Meimberg, Julius. *Feindberührung: Erinnerungen 1939-1945*, Moosburg, Germany, NeunundzwanzigSechs Verlag, 2002.

Middlebrook, Martin. *The Battle of Hamburg: Allied Bomber Forces Against a German City*, New York: Charles Scribner's Sons, 1980.

Middlebrook, Martin. *The Nuremberg Raid: The Worst Night of the War, March 30-31, 1944*, New York: William Morrow & Company, 1974.

Middlebrook, Martin and Chris Everitt. *The Bomber Command War Diaries*, New York: Viking Penguin, 1987.

Mitcham, Samuel Jr. *Men of the Luftwaffe*, Novato, CA: Presidio, 1988.

Mombeek, Eric. *Defending the Reich: The History of Jagdgeschwader 1 "Oesau,"* Norwich, England: JAC Publications, 1992.

Morgan, Hugh and John Weal. *German Jet Aces of World War 2*, Osprey Aircraft of the Aces 17, Oxford, England: Osprey Publishing, 1998.

Obermaier, Ernst. *Die Ritterkreuzträger der Luftwaffe, Jagdflieger 1939-1945*, Mainz, FRG: Verlag Dieter Hoffmann, 1989.

Obermaier, Ernst. *Die Ritterkreuzträger der Luftwaffe, Stuka und Schlachtflieger 1939-1945*, Mainz, FRG: Verlag Dieter Hoffmann, 1976.

O'Donnell, James P. *The Bunker: The History of the Reich Chancellery Group*, Boston: Houghton Mifflin Company, 1978.

Parry, Simon W. *Intruders Over Britain: The Story of the Luftwaffe's Night Intruder Force*, Surbiton/Surrey, England: Air Research Publications, 1987.

Potter, John Deane. *Fiasco: The Break-out of the German Battleships*, New York: Stein & Day, 1970.

Previtera, Stephen Thomas. *The Iron Time: A History of the Knight's Cross*, Richmond, VA: Winidore Press, 1999.

Prien, Jochen. *Pik-As: Geschichte des Jagdgeschwaders 53*, Hamburg, Germany: Self-published, 1991.

Prien, Jochen. *Geschichte des Jagdgeschwaders 77*, Teil 1, Hamburg, Germany: Self-published, 1992.

Prien, Jochen, Gerhard Stemmer, Peter Rodeike and Winfried Bock. *Die Jagdfliegerverbände der Deutschen Luftwaffe 1934 bis 1945, Teil 1: Vorkriegszeit und Einsatz über Polen - 1934 bis 1939*, Eutin, Germany: Struve, 2000.

Prien, Jochen, Gerhard Stemmer, Peter Rodeike and Winfried Bock. *Die Jagdfliegerverbände der Deutschen Luftwaffe 1934 bis 1945, Teil 2: Der "Sitzkrieg", 1.9.39 bis 9.5.1940*, Eutin, Germany: Struve.

Prien, Jochen, Gerhard Stemmer, Peter Rodeike and Winfried Bock. *Die Jagdfliegerverbände der Deutschen Luftwaffe 1934 bis 1945, Teil 3: Einsatz in Dänemark und Norwegen, 9.4. bis 30.11.40, Der Feldzug im Westen, 10.5. bis 25.6.1940*, Eutin, Germany: Struve.

Prien, Jochen, Gerhard Stemmer, Peter Rodeike and Winfried Bock. *Die Jagdfliegerverbände der Deutschen Luftwaffe 1934 bis 1945, Teil 4/I: Einsatz am Kanal und über England, 26.6.1940 bis 21.6.1941*, Eutin, Germany: Struve.

Prien, Jochen, Gerhard Stemmer, Peter Rodeike and Winfried Bock. *Die Jagdfliegerverbände der Deutschen Luftwaffe 1934 bis 1945, Teil 4/II: Einsatz am Kanal und über England, 26.6.1940 bis 21.6.1941*, Eutin, Germany: Struve.

Prien, Jochen, Gerhard Stemmer, Peter Rodeike and Winfried Bock. *Die Jagdfliegerverbände der Deutschen Luftwaffe 1934 bis 1945, Teil 5: Heimatverteidigung 10. Mai 1940 bis 31. Dezember 1941, Einsatz im Mittelmeerraum Oktober 1940 bis November 1941, Einsatz im Westen 22. Juni bis 31. Dezember 1941, Die Ergänzungsjagdgruppen Einsatz 1941 bis zur Auflösung Anfang 1942*, Eutin, Germany: Struve, 2003.

Prien, Jochen, Gerhard Stemmer, Peter Rodeike and Winfried Bock. *Die Jagdfliegerverbände der Deutschen Luftwaffe 1934 bis 1945, Teil 6/I: Unternehmen "Barbarossa" Einsatz im Osten 22.6. bis 5.12.1941*, Eutin, Germany: Struve, 2003.

Prien, Jochen, Gerhard Stemmer, Peter Rodeike and Winfried Bock. *Die Jagdfliegerverbände der Deutschen Luftwaffe 1934 bis 1945, Teil 6/II: Unternehmen "Barbarossa" Einsatz im Osten 22.6. bis 5.12.1941*, Eutin, Germany: Struve, 2003.

Prien, Jochen, Gerhard Stemmer, Peter Rodeike and Winfried Bock. *Die Jagdfliegerverbände der Deutschen Luftwaffe 1934 bis 1945, Teil 7: Heimatsverteidigung 1. Januar bis 31. Dezember 1942, Einsatz im Westen 1. Januar bis 31. Dezember 1942*, Eutin, Germany: Struve, 2003.

Prien, Jochen, Gerhard Stemmer, Peter Rodeike and Winfried Bock. *Die Jagdfliegerverbände der Deutschen Luftwaffe 1934 bis 1945, Teil 8/I: Einsatz im Mittelmeerraum November 1941 bis Dezember 1942*, Eutin, Germany: Struve, 2004.

Prien, Jochen, Gerhard Stemmer, Peter Rodeike and Winfried Bock. *Die Jagdfliegerverbände der Deutschen Luftwaffe 1934 bis 1945, Teil 8/II: Einsatz im Mittelmeerraum November 1941 bis Dezember 1942*, Eutin, Germany: Struve, 2004.

Prien, Jochen, Gerhard Stemmer, Peter Rodeike and Winfried Bock. *Die Jagdfliegerverbände der Deutschen Luftwaffe 1934 bis 1945, Teil 9/I: Winterkampf im Osten 6.12.1941 bis 30.4.1942*, Eutin, Germany: Struve.

Prien, Jochen, Gerhard Stemmer, Peter Rodeike and Winfried Bock. *Die Jagdfliegerverbände der Deutschen Luftwaffe 1934 bis 1945, Teil 9/II: Vom Sommerfeldzug 1942 bis zur Niederlage von Stalingrad 1.5.1942 bis 3.2.1943*, Eutin, Germany: Struve.

Priller, Josef. *J.G. 26: Geschichte eines Jagdgeschwaders*, Stuttgart, FRG: Motorbuch Verlag, 1980.

Quarrie, Bruce. *German Airborne Divisions: Blitzkrieg 1940-41*, Osprey Battle Orders 4, Oxford, England: Osprey Publishing, 2004.

Quarrie, Bruce. *German Airborne Divisions: Mediterranean Theater 1942-45*, Osprey Battle Orders 15, Oxford, England: Osprey Publishing, 2005.

Radtke, Siegfried. *Kampfgeschwader 54, von der Ju 52 zur Me 262*, Munich, Germany: Schild Verlag, 1990.

Reschke, Willi. *Jagdgeschwader 301/302 "Wilde Sau,"* Stuttgart, Germany: Motorbuch Verlag, 1998.

Ries, Karl and Hans Ring. *Legion Condor, 1936-1939: Eine illustrierte Dokumentation*, Mainz, Germany: Verlag Dieter Hoffmann, 1980.

Rosch, Barry C. *Luftwaffe Codes, Markings and Units, 1939-1945*, Atglen, PA: Schiffer Publishing, 1995.

Scheibert, Horst. *Die Träger der Ehrenblattspange des Heeres und der Waffen-SS, Die Träger der Ehrentafelspange der Kriegsmarine, Die Inhaber des Ehrenpokals für besondere Leistung im Luftkrieg*, Friedberg, FRG: Podzun-Pallas-Verlag, 1986.

Scherzer, Veit. *Die Träger des Deutschen Kreuzes in Gold der Luftwaffe 1941-1945*, Bayreuth, FRG: Scherzer's Militair Verlag, 1992.

Scherzer, Veit. *Die Ritterkreuzträger: Die Inhaber des Ritterkreuzes des Eisernen Kreuzes 1939-1945*, Jena, Germany: Scherzers Militairs-Verlag, 2005.

Schlang, Georg. *Die deutschen Lastensegler-Verbände 1937-1945*, Stuttgart, FRG: Motorbuch Verlag, 1985.

Schliephake, Hanfried. *The Birth of the Luftwaffe*, Chicago: Henry Regnery Company, 1971.

Schmidt, Rudi. *Achtung – Torpedos Los!* Koblenz, Germany: Bernhard & Graefe Verlag, 1991.

Schreier, Hans. *JG 52: Das erfolgreichste Jagdgeschwader des II. Weltkrieges*, Berg am See, FRG: Kurt Vowinckel Verlag, 2002.

Sharp, C. Martin and Michael J. F. Bowyer. *Mosquito*, London: Faber and Faber Limited, 1967.

Shores, Christopher and Brian Cull. *Air War for Yugoslavia, Greece and Crete*, Carrollton, TX: Squadron Signal Publications, 1987.

Shores, Christopher, Hans Ring and William Hess. *Fighters Over Tunisia*, London: Neville Spearman, 1975.

Smith, Peter C. *Stuka Squadron*, Wellingborough, England: Patrick Stephens, 1990.

Spick, Mike. *Luftwaffe Fighter Aces: The Jagdflieger and Their Combat Tactics and Techniques*, Mechanicsburg, PA: Stackpole Books, 2003.

Taghorn, Peter. *Die Geschichte des Lehrgeschwaders 1*, Band 1 (1936-1942), Zweibrücken, Germany: 2004.

Taghorn, Peter. *Die Geschichte des Lehrgeschwaders 1*, Band 2 (1942-1945), Zweibrücken, Germany: 2004.

Tessin, Georg. *Verbände und Truppen der deutschen Wehrmacht und Waffen-SS im Zweiten Weltkrieg 1939-1945, Vierzehnter Band: Die Landstreitkräfte: Namensverbände/Die Luftstreitkräfte (Fliegende Verbände)/Flakeinsatz im Reich 1943-1945*, Osnabrück, FRG: Biblio Verlag, 1980.

Thomas, Franz. *Die Eichenlaubträger 1940-1945, Band 1: A-K, Band 2: L-Z*, Osnabrück, Germany: Biblio-Verlag, 1998.

Thomas, Franz and Günter Wegmann. *Die Ritterkreuzträger der Deutschen Wehrmacht 1939-1945, Teil II: Fallschirmjäger*, Osnabrück, FRG: Biblio-Verlag, 1986.

Toliver, Raymond F. and Trevor J. Constable. *Das waren die Deutschen Jagdflieger-Asse 1939-1945*, Stuttgart, FRG: Motorbuch Verlag, 1981.

Trautloft, Hannes, Werner Held and Ekkehard Bob. *Die Grünherzjäger*, Friedberg, FRG: Podzun-Pallas-Verlag, 1985.

Trevor-Roper, H.R., *Blitzkrieg to Defeat: Hitler's War Directives, 1939-1945*, New York: Holt, Rinehart and Winston, 1964.

Weal, John. *Focke-Wulf Fw 190 Aces of the Russian Front*, Osprey Aircraft of the Aces 6, Oxford, England: Osprey Publishing, 1995.

Weal, John. *Jagdgeschwader 2 'Richthofen,'* Osprey Aviation Elite 1, Oxford, England: Osprey Publishing, 2000.

Weal, John. *Jagdgeschwader 27 'Afrika,'* Osprey Aviation Elite 12, Oxford, England: Osprey Publishing, 2000.

Weal, John. *Jagdgeschwader 52: The Experten*, Aviation Elite Units 15, Oxford, England: Osprey Publishing, 2004.

Weal, John. *Jagdgeschwader 54 "Grünherz,"* Osprey Aviation Elite 6, Oxford, England: Osprey Publishing, 2001.

Weal, John. *Luftwaffe Schlachtgruppen*, Aviation Elite Units 13, Oxford, England: Osprey Publishing, 2003.

Zweng, Christian. *Die Dienststellen, Kommandobehörden und Truppenteile der Luftwaffe 1935-1945, Band 1 Nr. 1-10*, Osnabrück, Germany: Biblio Verlag, 1999.

Government Publications

Hofmann, Rudolf. *German Efficiency Report System*, MS# P-134, Königstein, Germany: U.S. Army Europe Historical Division, 1952.

Unpublished Manuscripts

In addition to the actual promotion, recommendation and other personnel reports, generously made available by private sources (mostly in Germany), other unpublished manuscripts appear in this work.

Spires, David Nelson. "The Career of the *Reichswehr* Officer," PhD Dissertation, University of Washington, 1979.

Internet Sites

Tomasz Gronczewski, "Camouflage & Markings: Early Focke-Wulf Fw 190s," http://www.ipmsstockholm.org/magazine/2004/08/stuff_eng_profile_fw190a4.htm.

Volksbund Deutsche Kriegsgräberfürsorge Website, http://www.volksbund.de.

Interviews

Interview with former Private First Class Myron MacLean, who was assigned to the U.S. 1st Battalion, 39th Infantry Regiment, 9th Infantry Division, Decatur, Illinois, April 28, 2006.